IN THE
FOOTSTEPS
OF The University of Tennessee Lady Volunteers, the First Three Decades
CHAMPIONS

IN THE FOOTSTEPS OF CHAMPIONS

The University of Tennessee Lady Volunteers, the First Three Decades

Debby Schriver
With a Foreword by Mia Hamm

The University of Tennessee Press / Knoxville

All royalties generated by sales of this book support The University of Tennessee Lady Volunteer Scholarship Fund.

Library of Congress Cataloging-in-Publication Data

Schriver, Debby.

In the footsteps of champions: the University of Tennessee Lady Volunteers, the first three decades / Debby Schriver. — 1st ed.

       p. cm.

Includes bibliographical references.

ISBN-13: 978-1-57233-639-1 (hardcover : alk. paper)

ISBN-10: 1-57233-639-0

  1. University of Tennessee, Knoxville—Sports—History.

  2. College sports for women—United States—History.

  3. Sports for women—United States—History.

  I. Title.

GV691.U58S34 2008

796.04'30976885—dc22

2008008156

CONTENTS

When I went to my first Lady Vol game about twenty years ago, I actually cried. I am sixty-two years old, and women's sports were literally nothing when I was growing up. We played intramural volleyball for high school, ran track, and could try out as cheerleaders for the men's sports. Therefore, to see an arena filled with thousands of fans—men and women, cheering for women!—gave me a genuine thrill. We now tend to take it for granted, but we really need to remember that women were just on the sidelines until very recently. We need to continue to protect Title IX, which made women's sports possible.

Rosalind Andrews, Lady Vols basketball fan

FOREWORD

In 1951 the Craig Club Girls Soccer League of North St. Louis stepped away from their traditional gym classes to become the first organized women's soccer league in the United States. The league consisted of four teams and played full schedules for two seasons. While their history was short, it remains a milestone in the annals of women's soccer—even though a decade would pass before this sport would have a firm start at the college level.

Castleton State College in Vermont established the first US college varsity women's soccer team in the mid-1960s. Increasing popularity of the game in high schools and Title IX legislation fueled the steady growth that continues today. At once soccer found roots all over the country, and champions stepped forth.

Looking at these early years, I think of Coach Anson Dorrance at the University of North Carolina, who led the UNC soccer team to win sixteen of the first twenty NCAA championships. And there were relatively unknown champions—Stacey Enos, Ann Orrison, Denise Bender, and Kim Wyant—who were among the first women to play on the 1985 US National Team. These women had little practice time, no equipment to speak of, and minimal travel support. But their spirit and determination to play laid the groundwork for a surge of talented players—Michelle Akers of the University of Central Florida (who made the first goal scored by the US Team), Hall-of-Famer April Heinrichs, NCAA All-America Debbie Belkin, Joy (Fawcett) Biefield, Kristine Lilly, Carin Jennings, Julie Foudy, and Shannon Higgins. And the list goes on.

My name is among these early champions of soccer, and the thrills of achieving our dreams—in college, at World Cup competitions, and at the Olympics—are points of tremendous pride for me. The championships, medals, and record-setting performances provide wonderful memories. Recalling the spirited dedication and work of those who came before us, I am especially grateful for the opportunities we have to follow our passions. Today's possibilities are the great legacy of preceding generations. Playing soccer helped me to develop into the person that I am. My career as an athlete has given me self-confidence, abilities to be a part of a dynamic team, mental and physical fitness, and exhilarating opportunities to see

Mia Hamm. Courtesy, Dan Levy, Wasserman Media Group, LLC.

the world and make lifelong friends. I feel extremely grateful to have gotten to do what I did. I had help—from family, coaches, and friends—who taught me the value of hard work and respect.

Because of the early efforts of advocates who came before us, so much more is possible. At every level—whether it is a World Cup competition or a community league match—young girls and women can achieve

Mia Hamm
Career Highlights

- Youngest woman (at age fifteen) ever to play with the USA National Team
- University of North Carolina, NCAA Champion, 1989–90, 1992–93
- US National Team, 1987–2004
- World Cup Champion, 1991, 1999
- Named US Soccer's Chevrolet Female Athlete of the Year five years in a row, 1994–98
- Olympic gold medalist, 1996, 2004
- Women's Sports Foundation Athlete of the Year, 1997
- ESPY Award for Outstanding Female Athlete, 1998
- Broke all-time international scoring record for men and women on May 16, 1999, against Brazil in Orlando, Florida, with her 108th career goal
- Ended 1999 as the world's all-time leading scorer with 114 goals and 93 career assists
- Olympic silver medalist, 2000
- Inducted into the National Soccer Hall of Fame, 2007 Class
- Named to the All-Women's World Cup Team
- Started the Mia Hamm Foundation to benefit Bone Marrow Research
- Author of *Go for the Goal: A Champion's Guide to Winning in Soccer and Life*

Forward/midfielder Devon Swaim celebrates a Lady Vol score.

a sense of greatness and personal value. The athletic experience is a classroom that teaches values of commitment, working through defeat, communication, focusing on strengths, self-discipline, and goal achievement.

The University of Tennessee has set the standard for women's athletics programs. In the early years, the Lady Volunteers were among the first at the starting block, and three de-cades later, the program continues to move forward, eleven sports strong and dazzling us all with champions. Tennessee Lady Vols find fans, respect, and enthusiasm everywhere they go.

The teachers, coaches, friends, and fans in my life inspired me to be the best I could be. I know the strength of history and tradition. I too followed footsteps of champions. The Tennessee Lady Volunteer story stirs my sense of pride in our collective history and my belief in a positive future for all young women who strive to find their passions.

PREFACE

In the Footsteps of Champions is the story of people whose enthusiasm, determination, and vision created the foundations for one of the nation's leading women's athletic programs. The spirit of the Lady Volunteers begins as early as 1893, when the first female students entered the University of Tennessee.

Photographs and personal accounts provide a guided journey, beginning with this early history to the present day. Voices of fans, university faculty and staff, coaches, and student-athletes speak at a unique moment in time to share firsthand their memories of a program from its early development to the undeniable presence it has today.

The book follows the chronology of departmental growth over three decades, 1976-2006. The main sections, each dedicated to one decade, begin with a timeline providing an overview of events and coaches. Descriptions of departmental functions, sports additions, and community involvement and impact define the tenor of every decade. Characteristics of each decade find expression through first-person narrtives by student-athletes of the period. The appendixes provide season summaries, All-America honors of student-athletes, the Lady Volunteer Hall of Fame, and a roster of all Lady Volunteers known to date. As in all intercollegiate athletic departments, action is never still. Readers can find details not included in this book and accomplishments following its publication by consulting the University of Tennessee Women's Athletics Web site (http://www.utladyvols.com) for additional resources. Historical records are incomplete, and readers may send corrections and additions to the following address: UT Women's Athletics, 117 Stokely Athletics Center, 1720 Volunteer Boulevard, Knoxville, TN 37996.

This book has not attempted to recount all the record-breaking accomplishments throughout the years. The extraordinary women of the Lady Volunteers have achieved countless "firsts," and each has left a special mark on Tennessee history. For each story told there are countless others that make up the fabric of the UT women's athletics program. The women featured here are symbols of every Lady Vol whose determination, undeniable enthusiasm, strength, and courage stretched further than anyone ever thought possible.

Lady Volunteers use whistles; carry clipboards; manage ticket orders; coach; teach; discipline; counsel; mediate; motivate; restore; comfort; keep records; write media releases; prepare facilities; manage calendars; entertain fans; promote events; develop budgets; plan travel itineraries; lead; listen; learn; keep rules; make calls; develop Web sites; create new products; strategize; organize; analyze; train; strengthen; rehabilitate; encourage; build teams; recruit; sacrifice; make choices; practice; graduate; support; communicate; wear uniforms, suits, and sweats; do laundry; carry equipment; pour water; and celebrate and cheer. And that is just the beginning. Perhaps what Lady Vols most fundamentally do is create a community. The Lady Volunteers are a family of generations bonded by passion, pride, character, and integrity. "Once a Lady Vol—always a Lady Vol."

As we travel the pathways of our Lady Volunteers, the people we meet have varying uniforms, resources, facilities, and sports; but while the depth and breadth of the Lady Volunteers continue to grow and become stronger, the voices are remarkably the same. Their stories share laughter, determination, courage, and accomplishment that extend far beyond the win/loss column. Follow their journeys and walk in the footsteps of champions.

Opposite Page and Left: On March 22, 2005, the University of Tennessee named its basketball court at the Thompson-Boling Arena "The Summitt" to commemorate Coach Pat Summitt's 880th career victory, making her the all-time "winningest coach" in NCAA history.

Top Right: In 2005, after just nine seasons, the Lady Vol softball team brought fans to their feet when they earned Tennessee its first trip to the Women's College World Series.

Bottom Right: Lady Vol golf was the first sport added to the Tennessee women's program in 1992.

ACKNOWLEDGMENTS

Every student-athlete who wears the Lady Volunteer uniform brings honor to the University of Tennessee. To you we all are indebted. You take our breath away with close finishes and give us unforgettable images of strength; you show us the meaning of commitment. Thank you, each one, for defining the true champion.

To all the members of the University of Tennessee Women's Intercollegiate Athletics Department—you teach us the meaning of dedication to a mission and vision. You live the quality message as you teach and guide our growing young women. I have seen you comforting the injured, showing deep-hearted, unwavering belief to those chasing their goals, and teaching the meaning of pride when the best is always enough. The measure of your success is evident every day and throughout the generations of student-athletes who have graduated and become healthy, contributing women of society. You make our world better. I am in awe of your unwavering dedication.

I am especially indebted to Joan Cronan, who graciously embraced this project and opened the doors of women's athletics. Every coach welcomed my questions and took me in to experience their sports from vantage points of the student-athlete and the coach. Secretaries found rooms for me, answered endless questions, scheduled meetings, and made me feel welcome in the midst of their busy days. Staff members, interns, and graduate assistants greeted my requests with competence and willingness, even though my needs translated into more work for them and many hours of their time.

Jimmy Delaney, I will never know how you manage to be superhuman. You are the multitasking master, unwavering in the midst of major forces competing for your sole attention. Somehow you do it all. Lucky are your interns, luckier still are we all. I will never forget what you have taught me. You made this book happen.

Donna Thomas, your dedication to the Lady Volunteer tradition is stunning. Your standards are inspiring, and I am grateful for your close attention and reading (many times over) of this manuscript. I will always remember your words, "Let me tell you what hasn't changed."

Debby Jennings, the Women's Athletics Department finds its archives in your mind. You gave me time and invaluable guidance and shared your staff when I know you couldn't spare them. Somehow we need to find a way to retrieve all the memories from your vast experience with the Lady Volunteers. That will be volumes. Every staff member in Media Relations gave time they really didn't have to gather photographs, statistical records, rosters, and histories. Eric Trainer, Brian Davis, Cameron Harris, Casey Self, Courtney Tysinger, and Kelly Hayes—your positive attitudes, professionalism, and tireless enthusiasm are amazing. If errors exist in this book, they are certainly mine. Perfection belongs to you.

Angie Boyd Keck, as one of my first interviewees, you laid the groundwork. Your perspective as one of our first golf student-athletes and now as an administrator gave me a great jump start. Your character set the standard when you told me what you most like about golf: "It is a game of integrity."

Jenny Moshak, you opened my eyes to the lives and experiences of student-athletes when they are away from the game. You and your staff gave me a behind-the-scenes perspective. Your knowledge, experience, and heartfelt dedication touch every Lady Volunteer and me.

Dara Worrell provided the connection to the community supporters, the Boost-Her Club, and the events that strengthen the Lady Volunteer family. You gave me a better understanding of Lady Vol fan history. In spite of the many demands on your schedule, you always made room for one more question.

I give special thanks to Elizabeth Olivier, photographer on staff, who allowed us to

The Honorable Birch Bayh gave hours of his time, allowing me to learn from his experiences as the US senator from Indiana who chaired the Constitutional Amendment Subcommittee for Title IX. His enthusiasm and dedication are at once humbling and inspiring.

The support of Elizabeth Dunham of Special Collections, the University of Tennessee Libraries, has been invaluable. She

women's team to represent Tennessee at the National Championships. Her dream was to be a physician, and after two years as a student-athlete, she gave full-time focus to academics. She graduated from the University of Tennessee Medical School at Memphis in 1984 and later completed her residency in Houston, Texas. Making her home in Lebanon, Tennessee, Dr. Bondurant served her community as an orthopedic surgeon until her untimely death.

On December 26, 2002, the Lady Volunteer family suffered another tragic loss when former track and field standout Ilrey Oliver Sparks, aged forty, was killed in a car accident. A native of St. Thomas, Jamaica, Ilrey Oliver came to the University of Tennessee in 1983 on a track and field scholarship and forged a stellar career that included fifteen All-America citations and seventeen All-Southeastern Conference awards. In that number were four NCAA championships, including an individual crown in the 500 meter in 1986 and eight SEC titles. She also represented her country in 1984 at the Olympic Games in Los Angeles. Oliver held two degrees from the University of Tennessee—a B.A. in human services (1987) and a master's in sport management (1989)—and was named to the Lady Volunteer Hall of Fame. She joined the women's athletic department at Texas in January 1997. Until her passing, she had worked in the Longhorn academic support and student services department, influencing the lives of male and female athletes in numerous sports.

The measure of your success is evident every day and throughout the generations of student-athletes who have graduated and become healthy, contributing women of society.

pull her in even more directions to assure a quality visual record of our exciting Lady Volunteers.

I also want to thank Gloria Ray, Terry Crawford, Pat Summitt, Dr. Ed Boling, Dr. Joe Johnson, and all the early pioneers of the University of Tennessee whose leadership and willingness to stand firm set the groundwork for the program in place today.

Many people gave endless hours to interviews for this project. I am indebted to their generosity. Without their time, expertise, and vivid memories, this book would not have been possible. Their contributions are the rich heritage of the Lady Volunteers. I offer special thanks to Denise Wood and Susan Thornton, who searched their attics, basements, and memories to bring the early track and field years back to life.

has responded patiently to my seemingly endless requests, enthusiastically joined in my search for early photographs, and prepared them for inclusion in this book.

In the midst of thanking various people, I must take a moment, too, to remember two members of the Lady Volunteer family who are no longer with us. Their lives provide lasting inspiration to us all, and I hope their spirit is reflected in these pages.

In the summer of 1994, Dr. Fonda Bondurant died in a boating accident. She was the first Lady Volunteer to pass away. A member of the basketball team from 1975 to 1977, she was a guard her freshman and sophomore years, averaging two points and one rebound per game in thirty contests, and in 1977, she was a member of the first

Many individuals at the University of Tennessee Press deserve heartfelt thanks. They initiated this project. Jennifer Siler, director of UT Press, has been the advocate, providing professional guidance, support, and enthusiasm as a Lady Volunteer fan. I am especially grateful to Tom Post for his confidence in suggesting that I author this project. I suspect that my friend Brooke Bradley was an additional support for my involvement. Copyeditor Gene Adair, design and production manager Barbara Karwhite, designer Chad Pelton, Cheryl Carson, Scot Danforth, and others have contributed their expertise and dedication to assure that this work reflects the high qualities of Tennessee tradition. I also would like to thank the manuscript readers for their careful review and insightful suggestions.

My family, Rob and Kate, gave me personal support throughout this project. Their enthusiasm, love, and faith kept my confidence high. The duration of the work has taken much of my time away from them, and I treasure the many ways they take on my endeavors as their own. Rob, the journalist of our family, provided guidance for interviews and writing about sports, a new venture for me. Kate, my precious daughter and favorite UT Volunteer, gave me strength and made me laugh when I most needed a lift. Her persistent research through the *UT Daily Beacon* issues and microfilm provided significant documentation. My parents, LeRoy and Marie Moberly, opened a world of possibilities and introduced me to the excitement of sports in our hometown of Chicago.

Finally, my gratitude turns to the fans. Your cheers, unwavering loyalty, and love for the Lady Volunteers make this all worthwhile. What a Lady Volunteer family!

MESSAGES FROM THE UNIVERSITY LEADERSHIP

This is a "must read" for all who have followed the last thirty years of the Lady Vols.

—Dr. Edward J. Boling, President Emeritus

The Lady Vol athletics program and its outstanding administrators, coaches, and student-athletes are extraordinary examples of dedication, character, academic, and athletic success. They bring well-deserved acclaim to the University of Tennessee locally, statewide, regionally, and nationally. All of us associated with the Lady Vols have reason to be proud and grateful.

—Dr. Joseph E. Johnson, President Emeritus

In my former role as chancellor and provost at the University of Connecticut and now as president of the University of Tennessee, I have enjoyed a unique perspective on the highest levels of women's intercollegiate sports. Few eras or entities have been impacted as dramatically and powerfully as has the game of basketball by Pat Summitt and the Lady Vols over the past three decades. An account of the march of all eleven current University of Tennessee sports through history is a rewarding read.

—Dr. John David Petersen, President

INTRODUCTION
"We've Come A Long Way, Baby!"

Looking back, one should not be surprised that 1976 would be a monumental year. The United States of America was celebrating its two hundredth birthday, and declarations of "firsts" claimed the headlines:

- Tennis star Chris Evert, aged twenty-one, was heralded by the Associated Press as the "Female Athlete of the Year."

- The XII Winter Olympic Games officially opened in Innsbruck, Austria, with 900 athletes and a record 228 women from thirty-seven nations competing.

- American Sheila Young won a gold medal in the 500-meter speed-skating event in a new Olympic record time of 42.76.

- American Dorothy Hamill captured the gold medal in women's figure skating, and young girls everywhere began to fashion their hair in the stylish "Hamill" cut.

- Choynowska Liskiewicz of Poland sailed from Los Palmas in the Canary Islands, heading west in her thirty-three-foot fiberglass sloop. Two years later she became the first woman to complete a solo sail around the world.

- The first women enrolled as students in the service academies for the US Army, Navy, and Air Force.

- Nadia Comaneci, aged fourteen, of Romania became the first gymnast to score a perfect 10 on the uneven bars.

- The US Women's Basketball Team made its debut in the Olympic Games and, led by star players Pat Head (Summitt) and Nancy Lieberman (Cline), won the silver medal, finishing second to the Soviet team.

- Judy Rankin was the leading woman on the LPGA Tour with a record $150,734 in purse winnings.

The stage was set for something spectacular to happen. And so the dynasty of the University of Tennessee Lady Volunteers began.

Dynasties have their roots, and like many great successes, the Lady Volunteers find their roots in humble beginnings. The University of Tennessee first opened as Blount College in 1794. In the early years the name of the institution changed from Blount College (1794–1807) to East Tennessee College (1807–40), East Tennessee University (1840–79), and finally to the University of Tennessee (1879–present). Admission was open only to men until 1892, when women were first admitted on a trial basis. In 1893 women were admitted regularly, and in 1899 the creation of a dean of women position signified that women were there to stay.

The curriculum in 1899, according to Milton Klein's book *Volunteer Moments*, included physical education training for women with an aim "to strengthen weak ankles and increase their lung capacity;" the goal for both men and women was "the establishment and development of the physical foundation of students for a vigorous, useful life." Socially acceptable physical activities for women included croquet, archery, and tennis clubs. By the early 1900s, bicycling, boating, swimming, and golf were popular. Team sports, particularly field hockey and basketball, also added to women's enjoyment.

A women's athletic program, housed in the College of Education, emerged on a competitive level in the early 1900s, with basketball as the first women's varsity sport. There was no direct institutional funding for women's programs, so administrative responsibility, coaching, and other needs were chiefly met through the good will of the staff, faculty, and graduate students in the College of Education. The University of Tennessee women played against area schools, including Maryville College, the University of Chattanooga, Carson-Newman College, and Martha Washington College. With collegiate competition came a growing desire by women to participate with the same benefits as men, and on March 16, 1920, women asked the university for a single athletic association to include men and women and for the presentation of varsity letters to female student-athletes. These requests were granted, and varsity competition expanded to teams in track, swimming, and tennis. The basketball team gained new levels of play, with games against powerhouses like the University of Cincinnati. The team completed the 1924 season with five victories and only two losses.

In the late 1920s, educators at the University of Tennessee became concerned with the direction of women's athletics and denounced intercollegiate sports as elitist. They declared that the developing model of intercollegiate competition was exclusionary and undermined their belief that every female student should have the opportunity to participate in sports. Women's varsity basketball was eliminated after the 1926 season, and other intercollegiate sports followed. Women's sports were exclusively available on the intramural level, with opportunities for competition only in classes, sororities, and dormitories.

Throughout the decades of the 1920s, '30s, '40s, and '50s, women's sports competition was limited to intramural programs. Traditional team sports included volleyball, basketball, and softball. Individual sports such as badminton, golf, tennis, and swimming offered additional variety. The University of Tennessee, like other institutions, occasionally sponsored play days and sports days for women. Play days typically gathered individuals from several schools to participate in a multisport competition. Sports days followed a similar design but focused on teams of players with organized tournament competition. Both events emphasized playing rather than winning, socialization, and the ideals of good sportsmanship. In 1959 East Tennessee State University sponsored an invitational volleyball tournament. Female students in the UT Department of Physical Education asked their instructor, Jean Wells, to take them to the tournament. For the first time since 1926, Tennessee women entered intercollegiate competition. Breaking tradition, the host institution awarded a trophy to the winning team. Even though the University of Tennessee brought home the first-place trophy, fear that women's sports were moving to an unacceptable professional level and exclusivity brought an end to play days and sports days.

The 1959 volleyball tournament reignited the desire for intercollegiate competition, and in the spring of 1960 Nancy Lay, a graduate student from the University of Richmond, reestablished the basketball program. Tennis returned in 1963, and from that point until 1968, with no additional compensation, Lay and physical education instructor Jo Hobson shared coaching responsibilities for all three sports. The teams competed with neighbor institutions, including Carson-Newman College, Maryville College, and East Tennessee State

Basketball team with Coach Mary Douglas Ayres, 1920. Courtesy, the Special Collections Library of the University of Tennessee, Knoxville.

GIRL'S BASKET BALL

Josephine Reddish.

Yell

Hippity-hus! Hippity-hus!
What in the Thunder's the matter with us?
Nothing at all! Nothing at all!
We are the girls who play basket ball!

Motto-:-"Twas not so much dishonor to be beaten as 'tis an honor to have struggled."

'Varsity

Margaret Perkins (Manager) .... *Center*
Mabel Gildersleeve .... *Right Forward*
Grace Hood .... *Left Forward*
Daisy Wade .... *Right Guard*
Essie Polk (Captain) .... *Left Guard*

Substitutes

Bertha Rose Miller   Anna Weyland
Nannie Todd   Mary Cooper

Opposite Page, Top: Page from 1906 University of Tennessee yearbook. Opposite Page, Bottom Left to Right: 1905 basketball team with Coach L. T. Bellmont. 1924 basketball team with Coach Fay Morgan. 1926 basketball team with Coach Ann Huddle. 1908 basketball team with Coach W. C. Burnley.

Above: 1906 basketball team with Coach Essie Polk.
Bottom Left to Right: 1922 basketball team with Coach Mabel Miller. 1909 basketball team with Coach Andrew Weisenberg. 1903 basketball team with Coach Katherine Williams.

University and were composed primarily of physical education majors. The single mission was to provide fun for the participants. Deb Dyer (Handy) remembers her experiences as a member of the 1967–68 volleyball teams:

Above: Synchronized swimming. Courtesy, the Special Collections Library of the University of Tennessee, Knoxville. At Right: Bowling, 1961. Courtesy, the Special Collections Library of the University of Tennessee, Knoxville.

I came from a great small-town athletic program in Manassas, Virginia, where we were the state champions. At UT the volleyball program was just a small step up from intramurals. There was an interest sign-up sheet, and anyone could try out. We practiced and played in Alumni Gym. I remember our road trips. We all chipped in to pay whoever drove—six or eight cars would go. I remember playing at East Tennessee State University in a seven-state regional tournament. We all stayed in dorms. I think that was the farthest we traveled. We always had to scrape money together to go. I remember that we had a flat tire on one trip. We got together for the fun of it—for the camaraderie—just to play. There were no scholarships, of course. It was all about fun.

There were no athletic scholarships for women, but one extraordinary student found exception. In 1964 and 1965 Ann Baker (Furrow) joined the men's golf team as the first woman to receive a full men's athletic scholarship at the University of Tennessee.

Above: Swim Club. Courtesy, the Special Collections Library of the University of Tennessee, Knoxville. At Left: Ann Baker Furrow, first woman awarded golf scholarship (on the men's team).

This talented native of Maryville, Tennessee, also defied tradition as the first recipient of the prestigious Robert R. Neyland Academic Scholarship, named for the University of Tennessee's famed football coach. Furrow's commitment and community leadership roles, including eighteen years of service as the first woman appointed to the UT Board of Trustees, would later prove significant to the growth of the women's athletic program.

In the late 1960s a national movement to boost recreation opportunities for all collegiate students caught the attention of UT student affairs administrators. Sports clubs became a central programming focus, and many more new intramural club team opportunities opened to all students. Additionally, as student interests demanded, intercollegiate club competition became available for sports unavailable on a varsity level. In 1968 administration of the women's basketball, tennis, and volleyball teams moved to sports clubs in the Division of Student Affairs. The women's physical education staff continued to coach and tend to the operational needs of the teams. Inclusion in sports clubs, operated through the Student Aquatic Center and funded by student activity fees, offered women's sports an opportunity for more widespread competition and possibilities of increased funding.

Nationally, opportunities for women's competition were growing. In 1966 the Division of Girls' and Women's Sports (DGWS) of the American Association for Health, Physical Education, and Recreation (AAHPR) created the Commission on Intercollegiate Athletics for Women (CIAW) "to provide the framework and organizational pattern for conducting intercollegiate athletic opportunities for women," according to a February 1968 article in the *Journal of Health–Physical Education–Recreation*. As that article noted, Katherine Ley, chair of the CIAW, announced the establishment of national competitions for college women at a December 7, 1967, press conference. Ley stated that "young people need heroines as well as heroes. We'd like to see more young school girls emulating Pauline Betz [championship tennis player], Bobby Jo Gabrielson [intercollegiate golf medalist], Peggy Fleming [who would earn a gold

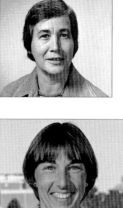

Clockwise from Top Left: A photographer captures a pose of a tennis club enthusiast. Nancy Lay, women's basketball coach, 1960–68, and faculty member, Physical Education Department. Terry Hull Crawford, student-athlete and head women's track and field/cross country coach, 1974–84.

medal in ice skating at 1968 Olympics], and other fine women athletes." Adding to the existing national championship competitions of golf and tennis were gymnastics and track and field in the spring of 1969 and swimming, badminton, and volleyball in the winter of 1969–70. At the state level Tennessee initiated a tennis championship tournament in 1968, and in the fall of that same year educators organized the Tennessee College Women's Sports Federation (TCWSF) to serve as a governing body to promote the cause of women's intercollegiate sports throughout the state. On July 1, 1972, the CUAW reorganized to become the Association for Intercollegiate Athletics for Women (AIAW), and the University of Tennessee joined as one of 260 charter member institutions. As Nancy Lay told reporter Janet Hunley of the *UT Daily Beacon* (July 14, 1972):

The AIAW was formed to prevent discrimination against women athletes. Women ought to run women's athletics, not men. Anyway, most men don't want to run women's competitions.

The organization fosters athletics for women at the national level, which includes swimming, tennis, golf, volleyball, and basketball. . . . In varsity competition, we want women who are dedicated and women who will practice. . . . We let each person develop to her own potential, but our program is not happenstance. We want the team that will represent UT well.

Women who would become icons for Tennessee women's athletic success entered the UT scene. In 1969 Terry Hull (Crawford), a junior from Greeneville, Tennessee, stepped up to compete in the National Intercollegiate Women's Track and Field Championship. A member of the Knoxville Track Club, Hull was representing the University of Tennessee for the first time. As the sole member of the UT women's track team, she claimed Tennessee's first individual titles by winning the national championships in the 220-yard and 440-yard dashes. Her achievements continued with a third national title in the 880-yard event the next year. In 1973 Terry Hull Crawford became coach of the UT women's track and field team and built a program that rose to national dominance in 1981 by bringing home the first national championship since the women's athletic department had officially formed.

Another notable addition to Tennessee was Joan Cronan, a recent master's degree graduate from Louisiana State University. In 1968, hired to a position in the School of Health, Physical Education, and Recreation, Cronan expressed interest in coaching basketball. Even this early in her career, Cronan had a vision of the strong future for women's intercollegiate athletics, and her leadership took the 1969 team to a competitive level just short of the first National Women's College Basketball Championship at West Chester University in Pennsylvania. Unofficially called the "Volettes," the team achieved some visibility because of a winning record and a change in playing rules that enabled a team to have two of the six starters to play as rovers anywhere on the court. Allowing two rovers was a new approach from the three-on-three half-court style of women's play. Cronan praised the new method, saying "the new style of playing has made the girls' basketball much more interesting and that the players themselves liked it better," according to a February 1969 article in the *UT Daily Beacon*. Lynne Greek (Fain), a member of that 1969 basketball team, recalls Cronan's commitment to the team:

Joan was my instructor in physical fundamentals [exercise class required for all freshman women]. Many players were physical education majors. Mary Dell [Hibler] asked me to play with them one day, so I just went over there and started playing. There were no tryouts. Anyone who wanted to play just went over and joined practice. Joan made it

a good experience for all of us. We played because it was fun and good exercise. I remember her later in the season telling us not to lie out in the sun—that the sun would take our energy. I remember road trips more than the home games in Alumni Gym. We traveled in a station wagon, with Joan driving. I remember playing at Western Carolina University. They beat us. They had some players who were six feet tall. That was huge for back then.

Joan Cronan, women's basketball coach, 1969–70, and instructor, Physical Education Department.

Cronan left Tennessee to pursue career opportunities at the College of Charleston in South Carolina where she advanced to athletics director before returning to Tennessee in 1983 to become the director of women's intercollegiate athletics. From 1971 to 1974 Margaret Hutson assumed coaching responsibilities for the University of Tennessee.

On the national scene, civil rights issues were taking center stage. Early political initiatives provided a context for later legislation that would eventually signify monumental changes for women's athletics. In 1923, three years after women won the right to vote, the Equal Rights Amendment (ERA) was introduced in Congress. From

1923 until 1970 Alice Paul, author of the ERA, saw that the amendment was introduced into each session of Congress. Despite Paul's efforts, the ERA remained buried in committees. In 1964 Congress passed the Civil Rights Act. Hoping to build on the momentum of that legislation, Senator Birch Bayh (D-Indiana) reintroduced the Equal Rights Amendment. Congress denied passage of the ERA, and in 1972, in an effort to assure some measure of gender equity, Senator Bayh and Representative Edith Green attached Title IX to the educational amendments of the 1964 Civil Rights Act. The senator's purpose was to decrease the amount of discrimination females encountered in the educational field:

I can remember as a young boy having breakfast with my parents one morning, and Dad said, "I am going to testify before Congress." I asked him what he was going to say. He said, "Well, I am going to tell them that they need to appropriate money for girls to have physical education in the school system just as well as boys. And if they ask why, I'm going to say, well, little girls need to have strong bodies to carry their minds around just like little boys."

One grievance that concerned me more than anything else was the second-class education. We not only had a number of colleges and universities that wouldn't let women in—others had quotas—but we had half the number of scholarships given to women—the amount was half. Now, we're talking about across the board, not [only] athletics—across the board—and to me that had such a profound impact on a generation of women. . . . So Title IX became a part of the higher education bill. We passed it wanting Title IX to apply to education across the board.

Title IX prohibits gender discrimination in schools and colleges receiving federal funds and includes specific guidelines for physical education and athletics. Conflicting interpretations of the applicability of Title IX to athletics stalled implementation. The financial implications were daunting, and in May 1974 Senator John Tower (R-Texas) introduced an amendment to exempt revenue-producing sports from being tabulated when determining Title IX compliance. The Tower amendment was rejected, and two

revenues from one sport to offset the costs of other sports. Other proposals suggested excluding revenue-producing sports from Title IX coverage. None of these proposals gained support for passage, and in 1975 President Gerald Ford, a Republican, signed the final Title IX regulations into law. The regulations included provisions prohibiting gender discrimination in athletics and established a three-year window for educational institutions to comply. Full compliance was required by 1978 and would be measured by the so-called 3-Prong Test: "(1) Does the institution provide participation opportunities proportionate to undergraduate enroll-

of Title IX regulations. In 1992 the NCAA completed a landmark gender-equity study of its member institutions. In 1994 Congress passed the Equity in Athletics Disclosure Act (EADA), requiring any coeducational institution of higher education that participates in any federal student financial aid program and has an intercollegiate athletics program to disclose certain information concerning that intercollegiate athletics program. Annual reports were required, calling for the first disclosure report to be available no later than October 1, 1996. These Congressional actions resulted in definition of equity expectations, standards for measurement, monitoring for compliance assurance, and public access to specific information regarding gender equity in intercollegiate athletic programs.

Title IX prohibits gender discrimination in schools and colleges receiving federal funds and includes specific guidelines for physical education and athletics.

months later Congress approved an amendment by Senator Jacob Javits (R-New York) stating that the US Department of Health, Education, and Welfare (HEW) must issue Title IX regulations, including the stipulation "with respect to intercollegiate athletic activities, reasonable provisions considering the nature of particular sports." Passage of the Javits amendment left no doubt that Title IX would apply to intercollegiate athletics. Motivated to protect the security of revenue-generating men's sports, Congress continued to consider amendments that would modify the financial impact of Title IX. Some proposals sought to use sports

ment; (2) Does the institution show a continuing practice of expanding opportunities for underrepresented gender; (3) Does the institution show that interests and abilities of underrepresented gender are being fully and effectively met?"

Implementation and applicability still remained on the discussion table. Finally, the Civil Rights Restoration Act became law on March 22, 1988, and held that all educational institutions that receive any type of federal financial assistance, whether it be direct or indirect, were bound by Title IX legislation. Numerous test cases and court rulings further clarified the implementation

The University of Tennessee, already nationally known for a strong, successful tradition in men's athletic programs, now faced the challenges of compliance with Title IX. The leaders of the university were not caught unaware. Human rights issues coming to the national forefront in the 1960s had captured their attention. Students, faculty, staff, and community leaders began to examine policies and procedures. Individual champions for civil rights and gender equity in education raised questions. Over a relatively brief course of time, a series of fortuitous and seemingly unrelated events occurred to create a strong foundation for what would come. In the fall of 1969, Dr. Sharon Lord arrived on campus to serve a joint appointment in the UT College of Education as the first female professor in the Departments of Educational and Counseling Psychology and Curriculum and Instruction. Coincidentally, Lord had been in Senator Birch Bayh's home state at Indiana University from 1966 to 1969 and was now joining a department chaired by Dr. Earl Ramer, a long-standing faculty representative on the UT Athletics Board and vice president of the NCAA (1963–68) who would later serve as president of the NCAA (1971–72). Dr. Lord focused her teaching and research interests on female development, known currently as the empowerment of women, gender integration, and leading a diverse workforce. Her exciting teaching style energized students to be actively involved in their learning. She was an inspiring voice, and people throughout the community sought her for speaking engagements and workshops. One speech in particular, "The Changing Roles of Women in Society," challenged the seemingly invisibility of women. Looking to participate in new opportunities, Lord enrolled in some physical education classes. She experienced first-hand the lack of adequate facilities for female students and learned that funding for sports teams depended upon bake sales and car washes. "I became acquainted with the PE faculty," she says, "walked in Stokely Athletic Center, saw the lack of locker space and facilities for women, and asked the question: What about women students? Up to now there had been a total lack of awareness."

In 1971 a new chancellor, Dr. Archie Dykes, arrived. In his fall address to the faculty senate, he stressed his strong commitment to include all constituencies of the university community in problem-solving processes. When encountering issues and problems on campus, he would seek solutions through task forces composed of students, faculty, and staff. By this time students

Charm presented to 1969 women's basketball team members following a Tennessee state tournament. Courtesy, Lynne Greek Fain.

and staff, becoming more aware of inequities, were regularly calling on Professor Lord for advice. Lord suggested that they share their concerns with Chancellor Dykes. Three weeks after Dr. Dykes's arrival, Lord herself requested a meeting with him. Although she was untenured and still new in her department, Lord was compelled to voice her concerns: "There I was—a young professor—but I had already been a 'grandmother' [first generation of women to open the doors to gender equity issues]. I shared my observations. The chancellor really listened and said, 'Well, there really are not many tenured women. What do you think I should do?' I said, 'Well, Dr. Dykes, you said that you would appoint task forces to address problems.' He then asked if I would chair it, and I declined, knowing that I needed to be dedicating my time to my academic goals. I did

agree to serve on the task force as a member to examine and revise curriculum."

Chancellor Dykes appointed the Chancellor's Task Force on Women to identify and address gender inequity at the university. Chaired by Dr. Lida Barrett, tenured professor in the Department of Mathematics, members included Lord; Martha E. Begalla, coordinator of Women's Programs; Patricia Ball, assistant coordinator of Women's Programs and Special Services; Ralph Boston, Olympic athlete and coordinator of Minority Affairs and Special Services; Barbara Wickersham, a secretary, representing non-exempt staff; Dr. Isabel Tipton, tenured professor in the Department of Physics; Dr. Helen Watson, chair of the Department of Physical Education; and a number of other students, faculty and staff. The task force subdivided into three committees: (1) Women in Curriculum, chaired by Lord; (2) Women in Physical Education and Sports, chaired by Dr. Nancy Lay; and (3) Office of Women's Affairs, chaired by Begalla. The task force submitted a summary report in the spring of 1972. In response to the task force's findings, Chancellor Dykes appointed a permanent Commission for Women that would report directly to his office. He asked Dr. Lord to share the findings with the UT Athletics Board.

From 1972 to 1973 Lord chaired the Committee on Women's Sports and the Committee on Curriculum, which later became Women's Studies. Mindful of the legislation of the 1960s and '70s, Lord spoke of the significance of Title IX and the regulations that were going to affect gender equity issues in all areas, including sports issues. She had the attention of Chancellor

Dykes, Dr. Earl Ramer, and other leaders of the university and the community at large. Increasingly more individuals added their concerns regarding inequities. One was volleyball coach Jo Hobson, who explained the dilemmas facing the women's athletic programs to the *UT Daily Beacon* (September 18, 1972):

Take my volleyball team for example. We went to the national competition in Miami earlier this year. Now, in order to go we had to sell concessions, wash cars and all sorts of stuff like that.

None of our coaches [in the women's program] are paid. We don't have the personnel to develop good teams. All our coaches are teachers too. Football coaches just coach. Basketball coaches [men's] just coach. Women's coaches can't do that.

. . . if I had a girl who wanted to try out for the Olympic Team, we don't have the personnel, the facilities, or anything to help that girl. Why, I don't know that much about volleyball. I don't have time to.

Basketball Coach Margaret Hutson voiced the same concerns to a Beacon reporter in March 1973: "This year the team has sold 500 dozen doughnuts to raise enough funds to eat and pay for motel rooms when we play away. We only have enough money to give each girl one dollar for a meal. They have to pay the balance."

Looking back at that time in an April 2007 interview, Dr. Archie Dykes remembered the commitment and challenges of addressing equity issues: "Sharon Lord was a key player. It was difficult to say 'no' to Sharon. We wanted to find the money to fund women's

athletics. The university leadership was sympathetic and helpful. President Dr. Edward Boling; vice chancellor for Academic Affairs, Dr. Walter Herndon; vice chancellor for Student Affairs, Dr. Howard Aldmon; vice chancellor for Administration, Dr. Luke Ebersole—these individuals and others were committed to doing what was right."

Dr. Helen Watson, chair of the physical education department, underscored concerns for funding and advocated a new administrative home for women's athletics in an October 1972 letter to Dr. Walter Herndon:

There are 8 sports clubs funded by the aquatic center that are in actuality varsity teams for women. . . . The coaches of these teams do not consider them to be sports clubs and find it impossible to operate within the current organizational structure. The money available for sports clubs is totally inadequate to operate a varsity program. . . . The coaches are therefore recommending that intercollegiate teams for women be identified as such and that money be made available to conduct a reasonable program. The need for such programs is apparent and the Women's Physical Education Staff would like to have an opportunity to administer intercollegiate athletics for women at the University of Tennessee, Knoxville.

From 1968 until 1973 the Department of Physical Education administered women's sports clubs and intercollegiate teams. The placement was consistent with the educational purpose of providing fun and assuring accessibility for all participants. The 1970–71 season saw the addition of field hockey to

women's sports offerings. Volleyball won its first state title, and the basketball team advanced to its first postseason tournament after hosting and winning the East District Tournament. Tennis, track and field, gymnastics, and swimming and diving also scored in competition during this season, but without significant institutional support or notice. The struggle for equal opportunities for women was continuing to gather momentum with students and faculty raising their voices of concern. In a September 1972 letter to Dr. Earl Ramer, chair of the UT Athletics Board, Professor of Education A. Montgomery Johnston expressed his concern for equity in women's sports:

I have become convinced that women are being discriminated against here at UT (and elsewhere) by not being offered the opportunity to participate in intercollegiate varsity athletic programs involving highly competent paid coaches, athletic scholarships, and challenging schedules. . . . I am not suggesting that women compete with men— but that they have the chance to compete with other women.

My inquiries suggest that there are many young ladies who are athletically talented who would like to come to UT but do not do so because scholarships and varsity athletic programs are not available to them. . . .

If athletic programs are defensible for men, they are also defensible for women— and for the same reasons.

Lady Vol Linda Evers, 1976–80.

The Student Senate proposed establishment of a student recreation board "to report to the Senate upon the possibility of raising women's sports to levels closely paralleling that already attained by athletics for males," according to the *Knoxville News Sentinel* (February 9, 1972). Administrative leaders held a commitment to equity but faced a challenge for funding. "The decision to go full-scale ahead with a women's program really happened in the late 1960s," said Dr. Joe Johnson, UT President Emeritus, in a 2006 interview. "We saw what benefits would come: favorable attention to the University of Tennessee; fine students; opportunities for female student-athletes to be great role models; opportunity to generate pride in the University of Tennessee. We wanted the women's program to be fiscally independent."

During the summer of 1973, leadership of the Knoxville campus changed from Dr. Archie Dykes to Dr. Jack Reese. Chancellor Reese continued the efforts to address gender equity concerns. In fall 1973, Dr. Nancy Lay, now designated coordinator of women's intercollegiate athletics, received $20,000 for the funding of women's sports. These dollars enabled the addition of a $400 graduate assistant position to coach the tennis team, and Gloria Ray responded to the call. Ray would later make history as the first director of women's intercollegiate athletics as a freestanding department for the university. The remaining $19,600 was spent for travel, meals, and equipment needs. Continued funding in 1974 brought yet another significant player into the UT fold. Patricia Head (Summitt), a graduating senior and volleyball and basketball player at the University

of Tennessee at Martin, accepted a graduate assistantship position in the Department of Physical Education. Her responsibilities would include teaching and serving as assistant coach to the women's basketball

Top: Margaret Hutson, women's basketball coach, 1971–74, and faculty member, Physical Education Department. Bottom: Pat Head (Summitt), women's head basketball coach, 1974–present.

team. Plans were revised, however, when Margaret Hutson decided to leave her UT basketball coaching post for an educational sabbatical. On April 30, 1974, Dr. Helen Watson wrote a letter requesting that Head consider serving as the coach for the women's basketball team, and in the fall 1974 she began her initial season as the Tennessee head coach.

Coach Terry Crawford remembers the positive impact of even small funding in the early days: "We were so excited back then. I remember several of us—including Gloria, Pat, and me—sitting in a booth at

the Old College Inn, a restaurant on the Strip [Cumberland Avenue]. We were thinking of what we could have printed on T-shirts for our teams. That's when we came up with T-shirts with orange printing: 'We've Come a Long Way, Baby.'"

Women's athletics had, indeed, come a long way. In spring 1974 Ann Furrow made a $25,000 deferred gift in the form of a life insurance policy to women's athletics, marking the first major financial donation to women's athletics at Tennessee. The 1974–75 and 1975–76 academic years saw funding boosts to $32,000 and $45,000, respectively. The cross country team joined the other sports, field hockey, tennis, volleyball, track and field, swimming and diving, basketball, and gymnastics. Two new coaches, Janie Barkman Tyler (a 1972 Olympian) in swimming and Sandra Standing in tennis, came onto the staff. The daily campus newspaper reflected the growing support for women's athletics in articles, letters, and editorials. As writer Ike Adams noted in early 1974:

For the past two years I have heard how the women's physical education department has been asking for money to equip teams for various sports. I read over and over again of how the various women participating in these sports put in long hours selling doughnuts and what-have-you, trying to raise money in order to buy uniforms and pay for expenses on road games.

In these two years I never attended these games or any sports that these women engaged in. Yet I laughed at the idea of girls playing basketball, field hockey, or even swimming in competition with other schools. Now, after attending several

Volleyball, 1962. Courtesy, the Special Collections Library of the University of Tennessee, Knoxville.

Original Lady Vol T-Shirt designed by Gloria Ray, Pat Head (Summitt), and Terry Crawford. Courtesy, Terry Crawford.

different events of Women's Athletics this quarter, I have found these girls to be some of the most spirited, competitive and dedicated people on campus. . . . These girls, believe it or not boys, are really good at what they do. They perform with a zeal that many of our "scholarship jocks" are lacking. If you don't believe me, go to one of the girls' basketball games this week. There is no admission charge, although their play merits one. I'll see you there.

Increasing need for support of women's athletic programs was apparent nationwide. Given that other institutions administratively housed men's and women's programs under one department, budget comparisons of the

University of Tennessee with other institutions were misleading. Writing in the *Daily Beacon* (August 16, 1974), Rob Schriver observed:

All over the country, financial assistance is coming to women's sports programs. Sharp changes in women's athletic budgets from last year to this year are evident at the University of Washington (from $18,000 last year to $200,000 this year), at UCLA (from $60,000 to $180,000) and Penn State (from $40,000 to $80,000).

These athletic departments, however, have both men and women under one large program; whereas UT's men's and women's athletic departments are run separately.

Implications of Title IX legislation generated public forums to discuss new directions for women's athletics that included issues of scholarships, funding, and administrative responsibilities. Two schools of thought regarding a future course were apparent: to continue within the current educational model, or to follow the men's model, advocating selective recruiting and scholarships for female athletes. Recognizing the need for decisive action to meet the 1978 Title IX compliance requirement, in May 1975 Chancellor Reese appointed a Task Force on Women's Athletics to be chaired by Martha E. Begalla, coordinator of Women's Programs. Members of the task force were Dr. Howard Aldmon, vice chancellor for Student Affairs; Nancy Montgomery, alumni representative; Dr. Earl Ramer, professor, Department of Continuing and Higher Education; Lynn Sheffield, member, field hockey and track and field teams; Dr. Helen Watson, chair, Division of Physical Education; Sharon Woodman, vice president, Student Government Council; Bob Woodruff, director, Intercollegiate Athletics; and Zsa Zsa Yow (Young), member, track and field Team. Chancellor Reese charged the group with the following questions:

1. What legal requirements will be imposed by the new Title IX guidelines, assuming that they will be approved by President Ford and the Congress?

2. Quite apart from these legal requirements, what kind of program would we like to see developed for women's intercollegiate athletics on campus?

3. How well has our current program functioned? What deficiencies can be identified?

4. The present program is administered by the women of the Physical Education division reporting (fiscally) to Vice Chancellor Aldmon. Is this the most suitable administrative structure?

5. Assuming that athletic scholarships for women will eventually be awarded, how many scholarships should be awarded, what kind, and in what sports?

6. How will these scholarships and other increased costs be funded?

7. Again assuming that athletic scholarships will be provided, what regulations will be followed in the awarding of the grants?

To complete its charge, the task force conducted a number of studies. They explored components of the history of women's intercollegiate athletics at the University of Tennessee: (1) sports offered, (2) student participation, (3) competition results, (4) administration and staffing, and (5) funding. The task force identified alternative models for intercollegiate athletics programs and considered their effectiveness. The Office of Institutional Research conducted a study of women's programs at other institutions. A series of open hearings with students, coaching staff, and any interested persons helped to define current problems, concerns, and future needs. The task force also studied the guidelines for Title IX of the Educational Amendments of 1972 as they apply to intercollegiate athletics. Task force members believed that "the development of an intercollegiate program for women should occur not merely to comply with Title IX, but as an appropriate and needed program for women students." They foresaw rapid changes in national trends for athletic pro-

Smokey, the University of Tennessee mascot since 1953, leads the crowd in cheers.

grams and designed their recommendations to move the University of Tennessee program forward and retain options for future development.

The final report of the task force began with a statement describing the current women's program:

The current program can be characterized as providing a wide range of athletic opportunities through the number of teams offered, involving a substantial number of athletes, operating with a minimal amount of fiscal support and being understaffed. While the investment of monies in the past may be viewed as substantial to some, many reasonable provisions remain unmet—clerical and

administrative support are inadequate, team expenses barely meet minimal standards and coaching arrangements limit the development of teams. The relationship between the men's and women's intercollegiate programs has been one of sharing some facilities and equipment; however, the administration, committee structure, coaching and budgets for the two programs are separate.

The task force based recommendations on three principles:

1. The opportunity to participate in intercollegiate athletics is a desirable part of the student's total educational experience.

2. Esteemed values sought and achieved through men's athletic programs can also be sought and achieved through programs for women.

3. Intercollegiate athletics should be consistent with the educational commitments of this institution. If campus choices in athletics have not always been so compatible, this fact should not alter the determination that they now should be.

Seventeen specific recommendations completed the work of the task force. The final report, presented to Chancellor Jack Reese on April 1, 1976 (see Appendix), provided data for the administration to act on their commitment to expand and upgrade women's athletics to a stature equitable to the men's programs. The chancellor's staff and President Edward Boling's staff established the Department of Women's Intercollegiate Athletics as a single, freestanding unit, separate from the men's program and reporting to the vice chancellor for Student Affairs.

Coaches, Scholarships, and a Little Red Wagon, 1976–1986

Putting a New Program in Place

"Surprise! Surprise!" wrote Mitch Parkinson in the *UT Daily Beacon* on July 9, 1976. "UT does, indeed, have an up and coming intercollegiate sports program for women!"

The Women's Intercollegiate Athletics Department was front and center, and the news created quite a stir. The campus newspaper ran a four-part series surveying the history of women's intercollegiate sports at the University of Tennessee. The challenges of funding and support immediately raised attention, and endorsement of the move was clear:

Women's intercollegiate athletic programs are making great strides, but the hurdles have been high and the progress slow. . . . funding is "minimal" according to the chancellor's task force report and needs to be beefed up if there is to be further improvement and expansion. . . . University funds constitute the bulk of the women's athletic budget. However, the UT [men's] Athletic Department . . . is contributing $20,000 to the women's budget for 1977. . . . women

athletes are receiving scholarships for the first time this fall. The money is only approximately one tenth of what is available to the men because, proportionately, there are fewer women athletes. These scholarships are a step in the right direction, but many more are needed to make up for the lack of them in the past. . . . The fight goes on. The fight for comparable training and housing facilities, medical care and scholarships is far from won. . . . Despite the obstacles, things are looking up for female athletes at UT and around the country. . . . Women's athletic programs need university funding if they are to exist at all. After the years of discrimination, they deserve it (UT Daily Beacon, July 9, 1976).

The decision to move women's athletics from the College of Education to a business model fashioned after the men's program compelled Dr. Nancy Lay to relinquish her administrative duties of directing the women's sports programs. Lay expressed concern that the educational component of collegiate sports would be lost to the pressures of winning. "From my vantage point," she said, "the program has been a success.

We've had those educational values that I've tried to maintain. But, I suppose, everyone else would rate it a failure in terms of big money expenditures and our won-loss record. Very few people seem to understand what we've been trying to do" (quoted in Mitch Parkinson, "Money Called the Problem," *UT Daily Beacon*, 13 July 1976). Dr. Lay continued to teach in the College of Education and remained a strong supporter of women's athletic programs at Tennessee.

In a statement to the *Beacon* (July 16, 1976), Bob Woodruff, director of men's athletics, expressed support for the women's program and also raised funding concerns:

The future of the women's program here depends on the financial support that can be mustered. Since women's sports are all of the non-revenue type, we'll have to raise all the money we can from every source we have to insure the program's initial success. . . . I think the women's program here is headed in the right direction; women should be allowed to compete if that's what they want. But you have to operate within the limits of available funds. I'm willing to work together with anyone who wants to make

the program better. . . . When the women's program gets leadership, they'll be off and running. We're not very far away from having a good, winning program.

Dr. Earl Ramer, then chair of UT's Athletics Board and faculty member in the College of Education, concurred with Woodruff regarding funding issues. Ramer added his support for the women's department to maintain a structure separate from the men's. Parkinson reported in the *Beacon* (July 16, 1976): "While most women's programs elsewhere have been closely identified with respective men's programs, UT has managed to keep its women's program altogether separate from the men's. Ramer said he is convinced this is what most UT sports women have desired from the beginning, and he also thinks this is the best course to pursue."

Students polled by the campus newspaper in July 1976 expressed support for the new commitment to women's athletics:

"It's important for women, just like me, to know that they have the opportunity to fulfill their potential in athletics. I think there are plenty of great women athletes who never get the chance to show their talent just because of their sex, and that's not right," said Ann Kellighan, a senior in microbiology. . . .

Dawn Durham, a recent UT graduate, said there's always been a big social hang-up about women being active in sports. "People have always thought women didn't belong in sports because their participation would cause them to lose their femininity." . . .

Bernard King, UT Volunteer basketball star from New York, said they have seen excellent women basketball players. King said physical make-up is the only thing that keeps women from competing evenly on the same court with men. He also said he particularly enjoys women's sports during the basketball off-season when he has enough time to take them in.

Hiring a Full-Time Director

The news hit the headlines! Effective August 9, 1976, Gloria Sue Ray was appointed as the first full-time director of women's athletics at the University of Tennessee. As Mitch Parkinson in the *Beacon* would declare on August 6, shortly before Ray assumed her duties, "Gloria Sue Ray is in the starting gate ready and raring to go with post time just around the corner. She's clad in Big Orange silks and racing on home turf. Bet against her if you dare."

Ray was selected from more than fifty applicants and recommended by a search committee of students, faculty, and staff. Dr. Howard Aldmon, vice chancellor for Student Affairs, announced the news: "We are very pleased that Ray has agreed to direct the growing women's athletics program on our campus. She brings to this position knowledge obtained from both previous experi-

Gloria Ray, first director of UT women's intercollegiate athletics, 1976–82.

ence with UT sports programs and a valuable perspective gained as an administrator at other institutions" (quoted in the *UT Daily Beacon*, August 3 1976).

A native of Knoxville, Ray earned her undergraduate degree at East Tennessee University and taught and coached at Stonewall Jackson Junior High School in Orlando, Florida. While completing her master's de-

gree at the University of Tennessee, Ray coached the UT women's tennis team to the state intercollegiate title in 1974. She then left UT to serve as assistant director to women's athletics at Mississippi University for Women (MUW) in Columbus. During her time in Mississippi, Ray saw significant growth in women's sports programs, with $32,000 in athletic scholarships going to women at MUW. She witnessed booming basketball popularity when Delta State, a small school in nearby Cleveland, Mississippi, won the National Championship after only two years in existence.

Gloria Ray brought enthusiasm and determination to the new women's department at Tennessee. Having seen women's athletic ventures move quickly upward in a relatively short time period, Ray knew that Tennessee had the potential to build a strong program. "I consider myself as a promoter," she told the *Beacon's* Mitch Parkinson. "If I believe in something, then I want to pass it along to people with all the excitement and enthusiasm I can muster. I want to tell UT sports fans what our women's sports program is all about, what it can be, and how important it is."

The 1976 Women's Intercollegiate Athletics Department was now a separate

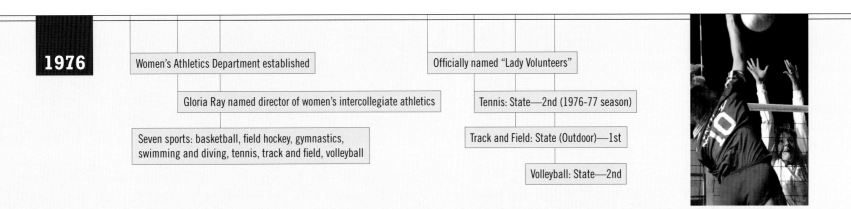

1976

Women's Athletics Department established

Gloria Ray named director of women's intercollegiate athletics

Seven sports: basketball, field hockey, gymnastics, swimming and diving, tennis, track and field, volleyball

Officially named "Lady Volunteers"

Tennis: State—2nd (1976-77 season)

Track and Field: State (Outdoor)—1st

Volleyball: State—2nd

HISTORY MAKER

Jane Haist
Track and Field, 1977–79
Home: Canada

Sport Stats

- Canadian Olympic Team, 1976
- Finished fourth in shot put, AIAW Outdoor Championships, 1977
- AIAW Outdoor champion in the discus throw, 1977
- AIAW Outdoor runner-up in the discus throw, 1978
- Helped UT finish fourth at AIAW Outdoor Championships
- School record-holder in the discus throw
- Ranks sixth on UT's all-time outdoor performers list in the shot put
- Stands at seventh on UT's all-time indoor performers list in the shot put

entity with direct reporting lines to the vice chancellor for student affairs, Dr. Howard F. Aldmon. With no real office, staff, or even team name, Ray was quick to address immediate needs and articulate goals. One of her first priorities was to select an official team name that would be distinctive for the women and still communicate the Tennessee tradition. The University of Tennessee's female student-athletes were named the Lady Volunteers. Budget planning and fund development were front-running issues. At their January 1976 meeting, the UT Board of Trustees had for the first time approved $25,000 in scholarships for female student-athletes. By drawing upon multiple sources, including student activities fees and a donation from the men's athletic department, the women's athletic department began 1977 with an approved budget of $126,000. Ray's goals were to budget what was needed to assure logical, strategically planned growth. Priorities were (1) to fund full-time coaching positions, (2) to fund scholarships for student-athletes, and (3) to create a highly competitive playing schedule. Basic needs drove expenditures. Student-athletes needed shoes, supplies, uniforms. Coaches were still carrying dual responsibilities of teaching in the College of Education and coaching intercollegiate sports. Strong fiscal commitment to coaches would attract more competitive student-athletes.

Fall 1976 began with seven sports and seven coaches: (1) basketball, Pat Head (Summitt); (2) field hockey, Barbara Mullinix; (3) gymnastics, Donna Donnelly; (4) swimming, Janie Tyler; (5) tennis, Mary Jane Ramsey; (6) track and field, Terry Crawford; and (7) volleyball, Jody Lambert. The

coaches were of high caliber and optimistic about the potential of their programs.

Pat Head had just returned from playing in the 1976 Olympics with a silver medal finish. Official tryouts for the team were conducted on October 5, and the starting lineup was Lisa McGill, Sue Thomas, Patricia Roberts, Suzanne Barbre, and Holly Warlick. Other team members were Fonda Bondurant, Sherri Fancher, Susie Davis, Jackie Watson, Kathy O'Neil, and Emily Roberts. The team was to play sixteen games, two tournaments, and four doubleheaders with the Tennessee men's team.

Field hockey was not a popular sport in the South, and the twenty-two team members were mostly from the North. Barbara Mullinix would coach her team against regional competitors that included the University of the South, Furman, Berea, and Vanderbilt. No scholarships were offered, and 1976–77 would be the final season for the intervarsity sport at Tennessee.

Gymnastics also would see its final year at Tennessee with meets including Morehead State and Appalachia State Universities. Coach Donna Donnelly said that the low number of student gymnasts was due to lack of high school gymnastic programs.

Swimming and tennis also were eager to begin competition. Two-time Olympian Janie Tyler was preparing the Lady Vol swimmers for their season with a conditioning program. Tennis provided four scholarships to freshmen Beth Ford, Sally Isabell, and Linda Evers and junior Cathy Green. A total of nine student-athletes would work out and compete for team positions before spring competition. The 1976–77 season included the Florida State Invitational, Mary

Gymnastics saw its final Lady Vol season in 1976–77. Courtesy, the Special Collections Library, University of Tennessee, Knoxville.

petitive playing schedules. Her strategy was always to budget for what was really needed and remain guided by one priority at a time. She believed that logical, strategically planned growth would create a strong foundation for steady expansion. Ray spent much of her time educating administrators, the campus, and the Knoxville community about women's athletics. She was committed to fostering an educational rather than adversarial relationship.

Women's athletics were not revenue-generating and needed institutional support. Women's athletics would add significant benefits to the university, including favorable public attention, a new source of pride, outstanding students, and the addition of significant role models for young women. President Emeritus Edward J. Boling remembers the building years and said, "We wanted to establish a women's department that is equal and independent of the men's program. We did not want the women to take a backseat to the men. It was just the right thing to do."

As her first priority, Ray appointed Pat Head (Summitt) and Terry Crawford to full-time coaching positions. Ray was convinced that once her coaches had full-time responsibility, the program would be ready to attract student-athletes. Her second goal, to grow scholarship money, would take time, and these early years found student-athletes in transition with partial scholarships at best. The walk-on student-athlete was still the heart of the program.

Ray and her coaches were ambassadors of women's athletics and made great efforts to develop relationships with university administration, the campus, and the Knoxville community. A small fan base had already

Baldwin College, the University of Kentucky, Ohio State, and the University of Tennessee at Chattanooga.

Terry Crawford's track and field team had already won two cross country meets. She was optimistic, anticipating the Tony Wilson Invitational and Tennessee Women's Invitational meets at home in October.

Volleyball awarded two partial scholarships and boasted a young team of five freshmen, two sophomores and one junior. Coach Jody Lambert's team was preparing

to face Eastern Kentucky University in the UT-Knoxville Invitational on October 15. Lambert predicted that the Lady Volunteers would win the state tournament.

The University of Tennessee Lady Volunteers were ready for their inaugural season.

First Steps

Athletics Director Gloria Ray identified three priorities: (1) funding for full-time coaches, (2) scholarships for athletes, and (3) com-

HISTORY MAKER

Patricia Roberts
Basketball, 1976–77
Hometown: Monroe, Georgia

Sport Stats

- Olympic silver medalist, 1976
- USA National Team, 1976–78
- Kodak All-America, 1977
- Set a new UT single-season record for field goals (428), points scored (987), scoring average (29.9), rebounds (467), and rebound average (14.2)
- Also set UT single-game records for field goals made (24 vs. Kentucky, Nov. 13, 1976), field goals attempted (31 vs. Kentucky, Nov. 13, 1976), points (51 vs. Anderson Junior College, Feb. 19, 1977)

Academic stats

- B.S. Education, University of Tennessee

Postcollegiate Career Highlights

- WBL player, 1978–80
- Assistant coach, Central Michigan University (1982–84), University of Illinois (1984–85), University of Wisconsin (1985–86), University of North Carolina (1986–88)
- International coaching experience: athlete liaison for US Olympic Committee at World University Games (1988–96); US Olympic Festival West Team (silver medal, 1990); USA Junior National Team (1992); member of the US Basketball Selection Committee
- Head coach, University of Maine, 1989–1992, four straight winning seasons with a combined 82–32 record (.719); won two North Atlantic Conference titles (1990, 1991) and a Seaboard Conference title (1989); runner-up in 1992 North Atlantic Conference Tournament; earned bid to the Women's National Invitational Tournament, 1989–90; her teams compiled highest GPA of all men's and women's athletic programs at the university
- Head coach, University of Michigan, two players earned All–Big Ten honors and spot on SportsChannel Chicago All-Freshman team; in 1994–95 one of her players named SportsChannel Chicago Freshman of the Year; seven players earned Academic All–Big Ten honors
- ABL head coach of the Atlanta Glory, 1996–97; 18–22 mark in inaugural season
- Head coach at Stony Brook, 1999–2004, where fifty victories in first three seasons equaled Dec McMullen's mark for fastest start for a new coach in school history; posted 66–76 record in five seasons
- Women's Basketball Hall of Fame
- Lady Volunteer Hall of Fame

been in place, sports enjoyed strong support in the area, and Ray knew that the future looked great.

The third goal, to develop competitive playing schedules, was important to draw fan excitement, player commitment, and talented coaches. "Early on," Ray said, "we traveled where we needed to go to find competition. As we grew better, we went further." Given that the department was in its infancy, funding was limited. Early road trips were made in cars, and when distances called for overnight accommodations, teammates piled into one or two rooms to keep expenses at a minimum. Student-athletes brought their own money for food and many times raised money by selling doughnuts and cookies, or hosting car washes so that they could go on the trips.

The staff of the department was limited. Debby Jennings, a journalism student, provided assistance with media responsibilities. Graduate assistants helped as team managers; worked with athletic training, strength, and conditioning; and performed many other functions to support the student-athletes. Some teams shared uniforms, and others even created their own. Track and field team member Susan Thornton (1977–80) still has the team jacket that she sewed. She remembers equipment being scarce, and as a thrower, she had heavy tools for her trade. Known for pulling her equipment in a little red wagon, Susan was a familiar sight on campus.

Student-athletes of the inaugural years had many personal reasons to choose athletics. All of them shared one common bond: the love of the game. They played hard, worked hard, and felt pride in their achievements. Many had responded to posters announcing tryouts. Others had come along

Lady Vol track and field team jacket, 1977–80. Courtesy, Susan Thornton.

with a friend. All thrived on the benefits of competition and sports.

After gymnastics and field hockey programs closed, five sports continued to build. Track and field consistently placed first in state outdoor competition and began to be more competitively nationally at the AIAW outdoor meets. The Lady Vols were a familiar presence at the AIAW Final Four tournaments, with tennis, volleyball, swimming, and diving reaching the upper levels of competition.

Here Come the Fans
Volunteer Parents

Active involvement of the community was a key to growing a fan base for women's athletics. The Lady Volunteers already had a core of faithful supporters. Gloria Ray and her staff thought about how to involve them even more. Many student-athletes came from other states and countries to the University of Tennessee. Thinking of the family-like atmosphere that the small department already enjoyed, Gloria, Ann Furrow, and other friends discovered a new idea. They could create "families" for the Lady Volunteers who couldn't go home often and whose families couldn't always see them compete due to distance.

The Volunteer Parent program was an immediate hit. Upon admission to UT, the student-athlete was assigned to a Knoxville family who provided her with a "home away from home." Lady Vols still treasure their memories. Tanya Haave (1980–84) from Evergreen, Colorado, remembers how great it was to get away from campus to her volunteer parents, and she still communicates regularly with them. Tanya's volunteer parents, Scott and Donna Trimble, were thrilled to serve as her "home-away-from-home" family. Donna remembers, "We met Tanya right when she arrived, and she was a little homesick. We gave her dinner, and she would nap on our couch. It was fun for our family, and I think it was good for Tanya to be with people who saw her as a person first and athlete second. The Volunteer Parents program cemented our commitment to the Lady Vols and gave us the opportunity to have great new friendships."

Pam Passera (1981–84), a Lady Vol track and field team member, fondly remembers her Volunteer Parents, Mr. and Mrs. Jim Claxton:

What a wonderful program that was! In the summer before I arrived, I received an information sheet to complete about favorite foods, hobbies, etc. I will never forget my first interaction with Mr. and Mrs. C. It was Sunday, and I was working out in the weight room in Stokely Athletic Center. They were dressed up from going to church, walked right up to me, and handed me a box of homemade chocolate chip cookies. We hugged and from that point on I was basically their daughter. They had me over to the house, cooked steaks because they were my favorite; we went to Gatlinburg. They were the greatest people. When we went away for our first track meet, they came to the airport with a bushel-full of apples— one for each team member, and they had a bow tied on my apple with an "I love you" note.

Volunteer parents helped Pam and other Lady Vols to cope with loneliness and apprehensions that first-year college students typically experience. These student-athletes found comfort and support in their community families. The program was mutually beneficial, growing support for the Lady Vol program and enhancing the retention and success of the student-athletes. The Volunteer Parents program concluded in 1981 in anticipation of upcoming 1982 NCAA regulations.

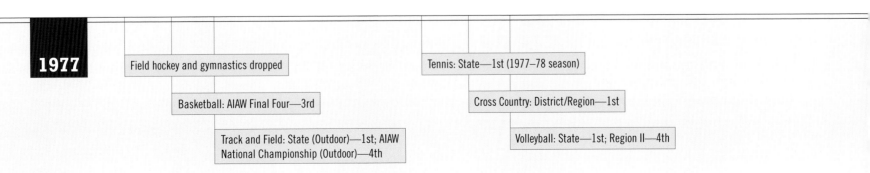

1977

Field hockey and gymnastics dropped

Basketball: AIAW Final Four—3rd

Track and Field: State (Outdoor)—1st; AIAW National Championship (Outdoor)—4th

Tennis: State—1st (1977–78 season)

Cross Country: District/Region—1st

Volleyball: State—1st; Region II—4th

Boost-Her Club pin designed by club members in early 1980s. Courtesy, Tom and Peg Haynes.

Lady Vol Boost-Her Club

All five sports had loyal fan followings, but basketball drew the largest numbers. It made sense to consider strategies to build on that fan base. Before 1977 women's basketball teams played games at Alumni Gym, with tickets available at the door. A change would take the Lady Vols a great step forward. Gloria Ray announced that for the 1977–78 season all home basketball games would be played at Stokely Athletic Center, with only a small number of doubleheaders with the men's team. Season tickets were available for sale to individuals and corporations. This marketing approach led to improved attendance and support.

In 1979 Sue Miller, a Knoxville realtor, chartered two buses to drive fans to support the Lady Vol basketball team in the AIWA Final Four Tournament, held in Greensboro, North Carolina. The enthusiasm generated among this group inspired Athletics Director Gloria Ray to encourage a booster group to grow fan support for Lady Vol sports. After several organizational meetings, the Lady Vol Boost-Her Club became a reality.

Founding members included Charlie and Barbara Goan, David and Jane Stroud, Gerry Campbell, Louise Josephson, Anna Ryburn, Becky Smith, Emily Tyson, Jean Wycoff, Doris Lewis, Lee and Susie Shugart, Virginia Sutton, Mel and Dorothy Stulberg, Sue Miller, Peg and Tom Haynes, and Ron Leadbetter. University participants included Doris Carter, Claudia Woody, Debby Jennings, Gloria Ray, various coaches, and Jack Williams. Since that time the list of dedicated volunteers has multiplied.

The contributions of the Boost-Her Club are invaluable. The group generated new awareness for the support needs of the women's athletic department. Club committees answered needs and provided services that would eventually become integral functions of the department. The hospitality committee created opportunities for all Lady Vol fans to become better acquainted, building camaraderie and long-term commitment. The ways and means committee generated income sources for the operating expenses of the club, produced Lady Vol T-shirts and other items for fans, and donated proceeds to the Lady Vol Scholarship Fund each year. The special events committee coordinated group travel options to away games for fans and supported the club's sponsorship of community fund-raising activities for the Lady Vol Scholarship Fund. Communication was the focus of the publicity committee with the writing and distribution of a newsletter called the "Bulletin." The development committee worked in concert with university staff to grow a community base of financial contributors.

The Boost-Her Club provides a strong central core of individuals who support all Lady Volunteer sports. Activities of the group

change to meet the needs of the program, and the mission of support continues to be strong. These Volunteers are valued and essential members of the Lady Volunteer family. The small group that organized in 1979 today numbers more than 2,600 and is growing steadily each year.

1982: A Giant Step Forward

When the NCAA began in 1906, football was the focus of the organization, and as other sports joined the list, membership was exclusive to men's athletics. While the NCAA did consider women's participation as early as 1922, the Association for Intercollegiate Athletics for Women (AIAW) formed in 1971 to oversee women's intercollegiate athletics. The AIAW had close ties to physical education departments and a variety of rules differing from those of the NCAA.

Passage of Title IX in 1972 renewed the interest in including women's sports in the NCAA. At their 1975 convention, the NCAA adopted a resolution requiring collaboration with AIAW. When the NCAA started offering women's championships, the AIAW lost grounding; institutions dropped their memberships and joined the NCAA. In 1982 the NCAA became the governing body for men's and women's intercollegiate athletics. Intercollegiate athletics for men and women gained more equal opportunities for National competition.

Against the backdrop of national change, leaders for UT women's athletics had built a foundation for a progressive women's athletic department. The fiber of success finds its story in the remarkable Lady Volunteer student-athletes and coaches.

Running the First Steps
Terry Hull Crawford

Legendary Terry Hull (Crawford) began her stellar career running track at the University of Tennessee before the days of a women's team. And she remembers every step.

Terry in Her Own Words

I grew up in Greeneville, Tennesse. When I was in high school, I did not have an opportunity to play any organized women's sports, but I did find a niche in running through my physical education classes. I came to the University of Tennessee as a freshman, majoring in physical education. At that time sports opportunities for women consisted only of a few club teams, and these were housed in the physical education department. I remember meeting Joan Cronan, an instructor, and her husband Tom, a PhD student in the department. Joan was the coach of the women's basketball team.

A friend, UT graduate, and runner himself, Kent Mulley, encouraged me to pursue track. He introduced me to a group of people who were connected with the UT men's track program. This group decided to start a community track club and to include women. So, I found my start as a freshman running in a track club. By my junior year I was running in meets throughout the country with the support of the Knoxville Track Club. I trained every afternoon with the UT men's track team and had a coach, Roger Gum, Knoxville-area business person. There was really no organized track program in the state other than the Ten-

Terry Crawford, first Lady Volunteer student-athlete to compete nationally in track and field and first Lady Volunteer coach to win a National Championship (1981).

nessee Tiger Bells in Nashville. I was very fortunate.

I was really the only female on the Knoxville campus who was participating in any kind of organized track. I have to say at that time, the male athletes and the male coaches around me were all very supportive. If I had not been accepted and encouraged by them, I don't know that my career would have taken off at all. UT men's track coach Chuck Roe, people on the team, and others in the men's

athletic department were all very supportive of the success I was having.

A breakthrough in institutional awareness began when the newly formed AIAW announced National Championships in seven sports: badminton, basketball, golf, gymnastics, swimming and diving, track and field, and volleyball for the 1972–73 season. Helen Watson and Nancy Lay really were excited about this and thought UT should be involved. They started talking to administrators. Faculty from the physical education department, including Dr. Ben Plotnicki, Dr. Andy Kozar, and others rallied and said they would find the money to send me to the AIAW Nationals.

I borrowed a men's warm-up suit, sort of came up with my own uniform, and took off for Denton, Texas, and represented UT at the first AIAW championship. I ran three events and came away in the top five, in-

of myself as a pioneer. At the time I wasn't thinking of myself as a pioneer; I was just enjoying the experience. But really if I had not had the people behind me to pave the way for me and introduce me to what was out there, I don't know that I would have accomplished what I did. There were some great people in the UT community who were willing to reach out and help me, and when the time came, they were also ready to sup-

all the women's teams. The physical education department decided the teams that they were going to support: basketball, track, volleyball, swimming, tennis, field hockey, and gymnastics. At that time the decision to support gymnastics was very controversial. Even in those early days there were the same kind of issues concerning where to spend the money and how to form an athletics department.

In 1972 I pretty much retired from running because of injuries. I was completing my graduate work and serving as an instructor in the physical education department when Nancy Stubbs left the university. I was asked to become the full-time track coach. That is another example of being in the right place at the right time, because I did not have any credentials to coach. Those of us who were hired at the beginning are really appreciative. People trusted us and recognized our passion and our commitment to UT.

I know as an athlete myself I would sneak into the men's athletic training room a few times to get some treatments.

dividually placing higher than some teams did in total scoring. That was the beginning of UT's involvement in the national collegiate athletic scene for women. I went to the AIAW championships the next year in Urbana, Illinois, and won two championships there.

I was really fortunate to be in the right place at the right time. I guess I do think

port women's athletics. We were ready for women's athletics to emerge because of some key people like Nancy Lay, Helen Watson, and people in the administration who were ready to accept that women did have a place in college athletics.

With the official decision to start women's athletics, Nancy Stubbs, who was a graduate student, posted flyers to advertise for

There were ongoing struggles to achieve equality. Women's athletics wasn't on the same level financially as men's athletics, and there definitely were stalls and struggles to find the funds to start to move women's athletics up the ladder.

Gloria Ray was a great crusader and fighter for women's athletics. In 1976 she was named director, and the department be-

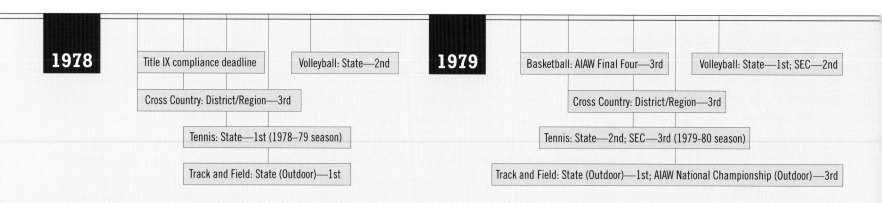

1978

Title IX compliance deadline

Volleyball: State—2nd

Cross Country: District/Region—3rd

Tennis: State—1st (1978–79 season)

Track and Field: State (Outdoor)—1st

1979

Basketball: AIAW Final Four—3rd

Volleyball: State—1st; SEC—2nd

Cross Country: District/Region—3rd

Tennis: State—2nd; SEC—3rd (1979-80 season)

Track and Field: State (Outdoor)—1st; AIAW National Championship (Outdoor)—3rd

came freestanding—a great step forward. It wasn't easy back then. It was just a very slow start. Even though we had started, it was challenging to find the money to be able to go out and recruit student-athletes.

The people that were in the mix from the get-go really have to be commended for their staying power and for their effort and tireless work. It was really a position of passion and of working together as opposed to great financial rewards or having the adequate resources to do some of the things that were being accomplished.

Gloria Ray was out there urging people, state legislators, and school administrators to understand the value women's athletics could bring to UT. And that was really before Title IX come to be a mandate. Title IX was out there and UT immediately jumped on it.

Gloria was battling for money, for space, for everything essential—an athletic training room, a weight room. Those were male facilities and quarters, and there were emotional decisions and concerns about giving up space. And I know as one of the first coaches that we didn't go out and resource anything. We did everything in-house. We started out using the offices in the physical education department because we were all connected to that department. One of the first things we realized was that we needed a weight room and an athletic training room because at that time there was no understanding of how men and women could be in the same athletic training room. I know as an athlete myself I would sneak into the men's athletic training room a few times to get some treatments. After hours they would sneak me in there.

When the student health center was going to be rebuilt, Gloria arranged for us to go over and pick out some of their old equipment that could serve as supplies and equipment for an athletic training room. We converted one of the old men's locker rooms in the physical education building into a women's athletic training room. I remember we tried to figure out how we would cover up the urinals. We put that athletic training room together before we ever had an athletic trainer. The physical education department gave us certain hours when our women could use the weight room, but time was limited because the room was really for physical education classes. Those were difficult times.

In some ways it was hard not to draw a line in the sand and say, "Pick a side." People were being challenged to give up ownership. That is always difficult, because once you have something, it is yours. To have to share it can stir up fears of losing a strong position or support. That was a lot of what was going on at that time. It was hard. The men's athletics department wanted to embrace women's athletics as long as the women's programs didn't interfere with anything that they did. I think that is just sort of natural. It is human nature.

We began experiencing significant results of our efforts in fall 1980. That 1980–81 track and field team set the tradition for women's track and field at Tennessee.

After winning the 1981 AIAW National Championship, the first National Championship in UT women's athletics, we faced a dilemma to pick one athlete of the year. We struggled because we had these great athletes like Delisa Walton, who had won a National Championship, and Benita Fitzgerald, and the relay had won. How do you say any one person made that happen over another one? To name one person would slight others. We were very fortunate because everyone bought into the decision to select all ten as a group with the power of one, even though it sort of went against the concept of picking a most valuable athlete. But as I look back on it, I think everyone was very pleased. It was very appropriate.

During my years at UT, I ate, slept, and breathed track and field. It was a passion

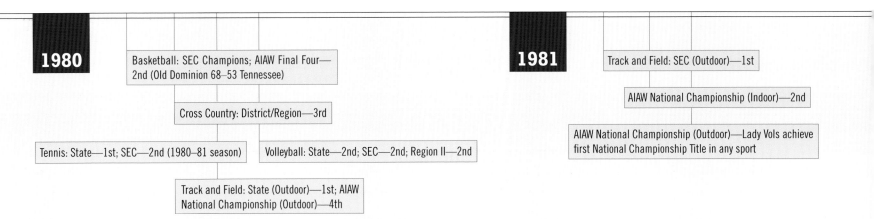

1980

Basketball: SEC Champions; AIAW Final Four—2nd (Old Dominion 68–53 Tennessee)

Cross Country: District/Region—3rd

Tennis: State—1st; SEC—2nd (1980–81 season)

Volleyball: State—2nd; SEC—2nd; Region II—2nd

Track and Field: State (Outdoor)—1st; AIAW National Championship (Outdoor)—4th

1981

Track and Field: SEC (Outdoor)—1st

AIAW National Championship (Indoor)—2nd

AIAW National Championship (Outdoor)—Lady Vols achieve first National Championship Title in any sport

Terry Hull Crawford
Career Highlights

- Three-time All-America at Tennessee
- University of Tennessee, women's head track and field coach, 1972–84
- Coached Lady Vol track and field student-athletes to 120 All-America certificates
- Trained numerous Lady Vol student-athletes to World, American, and Collegiate records
- Produced nineteen individual AIAW and NCAA National Champions
- Notched NCAA National runner-up finishes outdoors in 1982 and 1984
- Tallied NCAA National runner-up results indoors in 1983 and 1984
- Posted a pair of second-place finishes in AIAW indoor competition in 1981 and 1982
- Her Lady Vol track and field squad won the 1981 AIAW Outdoor Championship, the first National team title for any women's sport at Tennessee
- Led UT to the first four SEC Outdoor Championships (1981–84) and inaugural SEC Indoor Championships in 1984
- University of Texas, women's head track and field coach, 1984–1992
- US Olympic track and field head coach, 1988
- California Polytechnic State University, director of track and field/cross country, 1992–present
- Lady Volunteer Hall of Fame
- Lady Longhorn Hall of Fame

that I discovered. I feel very blessed that I had the right people around me to help discover this passion and give me ongoing support throughout my career. Three people at UT especially influenced my coaching career. Ben Plotnicki, who was a great lover of track and field, really inspired me and helped to create this huge appetite I have for track and field. Also, I was fortunate while I was at UT to know two coaches of the men's track team, Chuck Roe and Stan Huntsman. I tried to watch everything they did. I really modeled my coaching after them. They supported me, and I learned a lot from them.

I loved being an athlete, and after being injured I felt that my career was cut short, so I took that disappointment and dumped all that energy into my student-athletes and into my coaching. It was very rewarding. I never thought once about the hours it took and the time commitment. It was my life.

Everybody around me, whether it was my parents, my friends, or my spouse, just had to accept that, because that is who I was. The story at the Hall of Fame banquet will tell you a little bit about my passion for UT athletics and how imbedded I was in my job. When I first started coaching, my mantra was to say that I was the luckiest person in the world to be paid for going out and playing. Gloria had a meeting for us to review our salaries. We were all working for minimal salaries at that time. We each were given a life insurance policy. I think it was valued at $25,000. In my youthful wisdom, I chirped up to say that I was going to name women's athletics as beneficiary to my life insurance policy, and I thought everyone should do that. We were obviously struggling to get our scholarship dollars up. To me, this

seemed like an obvious start. My first thought was to make UT women's athletics my beneficiary. I think most people were thinking about making a member of their family the beneficiary.

That is just who I was pretty much my entire coaching career; I have been driven like that. And now after thirty years I feel very fortunate to be coaching still. The job has changed tremendously. I have had some great opportunities in the places I have worked. I feel very fortunate to be in my current position (director of track and field/cross country, California Polytechnic State University). But even still my favorite time is 2:00 p.m. when I go out to track practice. To be on the track, to be in the midst of the sport is really the love of my life. That is still really the fun part for me. Seeing the student-athletes respond is just a great thrill.

I think there are still some struggles for female athletes regarding who they are as people and how they perceive themselves as athletes. It is a difficult trail women go down, no matter what profession they pursue. The glass ceiling has gone up, but it is still there. Women go through major transitions about the time they go through puberty, of how their peers perceive them and how they perceive themselves. What do they think that society expects of them? Women who become athletes take on the double whammy. There are just more social mores that we have to overcome.

That has not changed. But certainly today's female athletes have no idea what women athletes went through when they started back in the 1970s and even prior to that. I remember my freshman and sophomore years. I lived in a residence hall. I went

Terry Crawford, Lady Volunteer head track and field/cross country coach.

to practice every day about 4:30 p.m. I would get to the track just as the men's track team was leaving. My coach came after he got off work. At the time the most popular fashion on campus were London Fog raincoats and penny loafers. So every day, I would put on my cotton sweat pants, pull them up above my knees, put on my loafers, put my track shoes in a bag, put on my London Fog coat, and head across campus to the track. You just didn't see girls walking across campus in athletic gear in the 1970s.

So, as opposed to sticking out like a sore thumb and being embarrassed about that, I was not projecting who I really wanted to be. I was afraid I would be labeled. I think other women had similar stories like that in terms of the struggles they went through internally sorting out who they wanted to be and what they thought was acceptable. Young women today don't have the same degree of that. There may still be some issues but certainly not to the extent that there were back in those days.

I do remember a couple of times in those early years something that we talked about on our team—Tennessee pride. We did use the men's team as a model because they were very successful. We worked hard and talked about taking on that Tennessee pride

in terms of how we competed and how we looked and how we wanted to be the most fashionable athletes on the track. We wanted to have the demeanor of winners, and we didn't show disappointment or defeat. It was an attitude that we cultivated.

I can remember having some stern conversations and how people responded to see how they could turn around some lackadaisical performances. I think I was an example showing that young women were ready to be challenged and were ready to make a mark in that whole area of being able to attach themselves to a goal, whether it was to a team or an organization.

We were fortunate to have some community people that rallied around the team. They really made those young women feel good about themselves in representing Tennessee. One of the programs that Gloria Ray started was the Volunteer family program. It was really effective in connecting community and our women athletes. I will always hold that program near and dear to my heart in terms of how it affected athletes. There are some great stories from that program.

Winning that first National Championship was just like a dream come true. I can't tell you the sense of accomplishment and satis-

faction that I had as a coach. It will always be very special to me.

But sitting in the stands at the Los Angeles Olympics and seeing Benita Fitzgerald (Mosley) win a gold medal was also a great sense of accomplishment.

And there are people like Mitzi James, who walked onto the team and had never run a step of track in high school. Her mother had told her she needed to get involved in something when she came to UT. She walked on to the track team, and she was totally committed. We became great friends as coach/student-athlete. And then to see her make an Olympic team was the kind of story that makes coaching so rewarding. That was as rewarding of a success as any accomplishment I had as an athlete myself.

I think that one of the fun qualities about track and field is that there is something for everybody. It doesn't matter whether you are short, tall, thick, or thin. You can find an event to suit your energy and talent. Women's athletics is holding its own now in terms of getting the recognition it deserves. Track and field is continuing across the country to establish itself as a fan-supported sport in all areas. It is making great headway in terms of advancing the

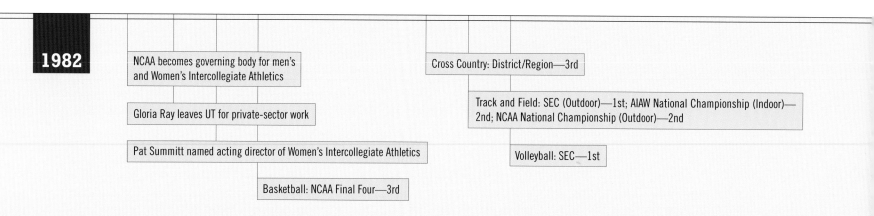

1982

NCAA becomes governing body for men's and Women's Intercollegiate Athletics

Gloria Ray leaves UT for private-sector work

Pat Summitt named acting director of Women's Intercollegiate Athletics

Basketball: NCAA Final Four—3rd

Cross Country: District/Region—3rd

Track and Field: SEC (Outdoor)—1st; AIAW National Championship (Indoor)—2nd; NCAA National Championship (Outdoor)—2nd

Volleyball: SEC—1st

cause of women's athletics. I think the future is very bright. Probably if you go throughout the country, you still find struggles in various women's athletics departments. The glass ceiling for career opportunities beyond college has lifted. Women are making a living playing sports as professional athletes. Everything that was hoped for in the early 1970s has been accomplished and is still growing.

If there is a downside in what has happened in women's athletics, it pertains to the early opportunities there are for young women to participate and get involved in athletics. The urgency and intensity that now surround a lot of the activities in women's sports are dangerously close to being extreme. There is still a lack of understanding about what sports are and how they relate to play as opposed to competition. If there is anything bad about women having these great opportunities, it is what the extremes have brought to female athletes in terms of pressure. As we have evolved over the last thirty years, we were not able to avoid some of the pitfalls that we saw in men's athletics. That really speaks to our society and the kind of value that we put on things in our fast-paced, upwardly mobile society today. That is a challenge for both genders.

The ticket office generates thousands of tickets for Lady Vol fans each year. Pictured is Brionna Bell, student employee.

The Work Behind the Play
Lady Vol Tix

The good news is that the Lady Volunteers are growing a large base of fans. That phenomenon is no surprise to the small group of women's athletics staff members whose work is solely dedicated to ticket sales. A typical day registers four hundred to six hundred telephone calls, high usage of online services, and a steady flow of walk-in traffic. The University of Tennessee athletics ticket office processes more tickets than any other ticket office in the country. The large venues, facilities expansion, and popularity of traveling to away games keep staff on their toes.

Front-line employees, often students, are continuously challenged to stay on top of policy changes and events. Customers with questions and requests require personal attention and care. Sometimes meeting their

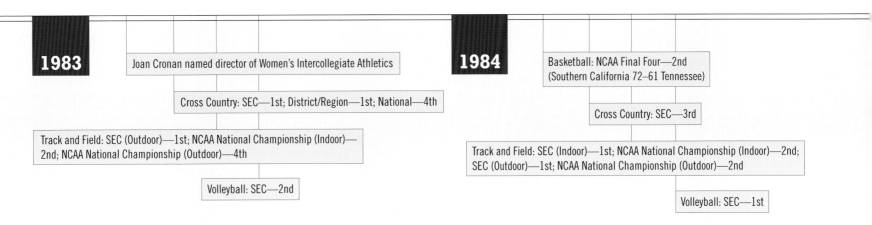

1983
Joan Cronan named director of Women's Intercollegiate Athletics

Cross Country: SEC—1st; District/Region—1st; National—4th

Track and Field: SEC (Outdoor)—1st; NCAA National Championship (Indoor)—2nd; NCAA National Championship (Outdoor)—4th

Volleyball: SEC—2nd

1984
Basketball: NCAA Final Four—2nd (Southern California 72–61 Tennessee)

Cross Country: SEC—3rd

Track and Field: SEC (Indoor)—1st; NCAA National Championship (Indoor)—2nd; SEC (Outdoor)—1st; NCAA National Championship (Outdoor)—2nd

Volleyball: SEC—1st

Tara Brooks works with team managers to prepare equipment for the 2007 Mercedes-Benz Collegiate Golf Championships.

needs takes effort, as in the instance related by a ticket office staff member who said, "The customer came to the office and wanted tickets to a game that had already occurred the previous week. It took some convincing, but finally he believed me. The fan left happy with tickets to the next home game."

Technology has transformed processes from the early days of ticket production. Some things don't change, though. Dedicated staff members are still stuffing envelopes, stamping addresses, and certifying mail. They are still taking care of every fan, one fan at a time.

The Magic of Unsung Heroes

Quiz question: Who is essential to the performance of every athletic team?

A number of responses are correct—certainly the student-athletes and the coaches are integral to the program. In fact, every job in the department ties to a basic connection

with sports performance. One particular individual who is often overlooked and almost invisible is the team manager.

When student-athletes practice, work out, and compete, they have a prepared bench, water, equipment, towels, and all the other trappings needed for them to play. Almost magically everything they need is within an arm's reach, thanks to the manager.

Managers are volunteers or scholarship recipients, and their functions are clearly specified. NCAA guidelines apply to both scholarship and non-scholarship managers. These guidelines specify roles and prohibit managers from serving as practice players with a team. Managers typically are supervised by an assistant coach and ultimately answer to the head coach.

Managers all agree that the unending task they face daily is "laundry, laundry, and more laundry," as one of their number, Brian Rice, puts it. But there is a little bit more to it. A typical day in the life of manager is anything

but dull. Game-day schedules vary among sports, but basic functions and needs apply to all. Rice offers a glimpse behind the scenes of a volleyball match:

Early morning—set up gym with balls, equipment, and locker room for visiting team.

Mid-morning—meet visiting team in the gym, talk with their manager, coach, show them facilities, locker room.

Early afternoon—return to gym, set up equipment, check balls, clipboards for coaches, be sure all is ready for game.

Later in afternoon—eat pre-game meal with the team.

After meal—go to gym, set up balls, equipment, t-shirts, flags for officials, meet with ball kids to be sure they know how to do their jobs, gather all materials needed, towels (at same time marketing, media and other staff are preparing venue with banners, sound equipment, lights, inflatable mascots, etc.).

Pre-game practice—help in warm-ups, hand players balls, assist as directed by coaches.

During game—stand behind bench, hand players towels, wipe chairs when they get up, provide water; attend to needs as directed by coaches.

After game—gather all equipment, count balls, put all equipment into storage; gather shirts, team jerseys, towels, do laundry. After jerseys are laundered, hang them on the teams' lockers for the next morning's practice.

Day usually ends at 11:00 p.m.—midnight.

Managers are in the thick of the action and can recall many stories when they had to think quickly to resolve problems from unexpected occurrences and last-minute changes. One year, just days before picture day, team uniforms had not arrived. Persistent work of the manager with the dedicated suppliers found white uniforms with embroidery that would work for the season start. Less daunting but still demanding are the searches for food after late-night road game finishes and taking cases of equipment through airport security. Tara Brooks, director of student-athlete services and veteran manager for the women's basketball team, recalls her first year working with the team:

We didn't get the balls out quickly enough when the team was practicing free throws. Pat [Summitt] was upset because everyone should have a ball to make best use of the time. Pat said that she was going to make the managers run. I didn't think that she was serious about making us run, so after practice, I immediately began to clear and clean the supplies. Pat was true to her word, though, and she told all the managers to line up on the base line. Everyone—players, coaches, athletic trainers and the maintenance crew—came out to watch the managers run. I couldn't believe it. One of the managers asked to shoot a free throw. Whenever the players were told to run at the end of their practice, this was the one way they could all earn a pass on the run: if a player successfully made a free throw, everyone was free to go. If she missed, they would have to double run. We all agreed to let our co-worker attempt the free throw. Thankfully, she made the shot and we didn't have to run. We never forgot the balls again.

Managers work as a team, communicating and taking initiative to do whatever it takes to get the job done. A member of the 2006–07 National Championship basketball team in her senior year, and team manager for her sophomore and junior years, Elizabeth Curry, a graduate assistant in the women's athletic department, has seen the manager's job from different perspectives:

I am around the game in all areas: seeing the x's and o's in practice [diagrams of play plans]; coordinating visiting team practice times; handling facilities for sports camps. When we do our jobs well, that allows the coaches and players to do their jobs effectively. Managers are masterful at multitasking. We like being in the background, and we all know the impact of our job on the front line. We definitely have tired nights, but I am getting tenfold of what I am putting into it. I want to be a coach to help maturing young women grow. Pat [Summitt] has taught me that while the game is a focus, there is a whole other output that has significance on our lives beyond the game.

What motivates an individual to serve as a team manager? Tara Brooks is drawn to the rewards of seeing fans having fun and knowing the ways managers contribute to the program's success. Craig Fain, veteran softball team manager, did it because he loves the sport: "I love sports and did it for the student-athletes. It is really rewarding to see the respect given to the Lady Vols." Brian Rice, a team manager from his early high school years, agrees that it is all about pride and says that managers cherish pinnacle moments just as much as every other team member. Rice recalls a favorite moment when the Lady Volunteer volleyball team surprised opponents by winning the regional tournament in Pennsylvania and claiming a berth at the 2006 NCAA Final Four. "I knew that I had contributed to that moment," he says. "I knew that what I do makes a difference. To be a

1985　Basketball: SEC Champions; SEC Tournament Champions

Cross Country: SEC—3rd

Track and Field: SEC (Indoor)—3rd; SEC (Outdoor)—2nd

1986　Basketball: NCAA Final Four—3rd

Track and Field: SEC (Indoor)—3rd; NCAA National Championship (Indoor)—2nd; SEC (Outdoor)—2nd; NCAA National Championship (Outdoor)—4th

good manager you have to have a passion for the sport and for the school. It has to mean something to you. Women's athletics programs are a priority at Tennessee. We care about every sport and every person as a member of the Lady Vol family."

For every student-athlete there is a manager who is providing support before, after, and during competition. These members of the Lady Volunteer team are truly unsung heroes.

On the Front Line

They are the gatekeepers. They are the faces and voices of women's athletics. And we may not even know their names. Administrative professionals, accounting personnel, and program assistants are the points of service for the department. These individuals touch every customer, every incoming and outgoing communication. They manage schedules, calendars, correspondence, questions, and concerns. They assure that speaking engagements are kept, that meetings occur and records are maintained. They manage work groups, respond to problems and treat every individual as a significant member of the community—even when requests might be unusual, even when work demands exceed the hours in a day, even when they might not be the ones who are cheered by wild and crazy fans.

The Women's Intercollegiate Athletics Department functions with the support of competent staff members who collectively bring 221 years of service to the department. Every day brings something new to the work front. Fans request special attention from coaches such as hospital visits, autographed articles, and letters. Fan mail from throughout the

Lady Vol administrative professional staff: (front row, left to right) Donna Muir, Judy Porterfield, Cindy Connaster, Velma Allen, (back row left to right) Katie Wynn, Linda Lewis, Suzy Sutton, Alberta Randles, and Beverly Dunkin. On Right: Dara Worrell, assistant athletics director for development.

world calls for personal responses. The recruiting process needs to follow correct NCAA protocol. The steady pressure and nature of work that greet these individuals on a daily basis make their work challenging and rewarding. The Lady Vol family atmosphere generates a supportive and cooperative work team.

Developing Community

As long as there have been Lady Volunteers, there have been fans. The first director of women's intercollegiate athletics, Gloria Ray, recognized the importance of community support and spent much of her time speaking to civic groups and educating the community at large about women's athletics. Fans showed their early buy-in through the Volunteer Parents program (until 1981) and the Lady Volunteer Boost-Her Club (1979–present).

Development of alumni support and a community donor base has been growing with the department. Shannon Mulkey, Susan Richardson Williams, and Betsy Roberts established a foundation of grassroots support and community visibility. Joan Cronan, the current director of women's intercollegiate athletics, spends a major portion of her time meeting with community corporate sponsors, individual donors, and community partners. Dara Worrell, assistant athletics director for development, describes the process as a relationship-building venture: "We host a number of events to reach out to the community. An annual event, 'Salute to Excellence,' is very popular and successful. A silent auction, dinner, and dancing provide a fun evening for people in the community to be with coaches, some players, and women's athletics staff."

Other events throughout the year also generate support. There are many ways that

Press Row, reporters preparing on-the-spot news releases at a basketball game.

donors can be more closely involved with a sport. For example, each home Lady Volunteer basketball game has a limited number of "guest coach" slots for fans to observe pregame and halftime in the locker room with Coach Pat Summitt and the Lady Volunteers. Guest coaches sit directly behind the team's bench, attend the press conference following the game, and experience a rare perspective as an "insider." Guest coaches Marc and Susie Carter from Morristown, Tennessee, comment, "Pat is so inspiring. Being in the locker room to see and hear the players as they analyze the game is really fun. Our respect for the Lady Vols just continues to grow."

Basketball season-ticket holders have options to join courtside clubs and participate in special programs throughout the year. As fans become more involved in Lady Volunteer activities, energy and momentum grow. The addition of sports and the expansion of facilities open more opportunities for fans

to participate. In a sense, everyone in the department performs a development function through their contacts with the public. Worrell says, "Development is the work of a lot of people building relationships." Thirty years of student-athletes and fans translate to a sizable number of family members. Efforts to organize and record the history of the donor base are strengthening possibilities for the future. Growing technology enables the department to keep touch with donors and the Lady Volunteer family. The people in development ensure that each touch has the personal assurance of the Lady Vol spirit.

Never Too Much Information

"Everyone needs to know something," it's often said, "but not everyone needs to know everything." The staff members of media relations are the ones who know everything and know who needs to know it. Confused?

The information generated by an athletics department is mind-boggling. One sport alone is a year-round generator of scores, people, events, and headline-making news. Eleven intercollegiate sports multiply media demands by thousands. Debby Jennings, the associate athletics director for media relations, has provided leadership for this area throughout the department's existence. Media relations is a clearinghouse for all community members of the media and coordinates publications, interviews, news releases, and information pertaining to athletic events, results, and schedules. All internal and external communications are handled through this unit. The student interns, staff, and assistants assure quality, accuracy, integrity, consistency, and professionalism in all forms of media communications, including the Web, written materials, and television and radio coverage.

Media relations staff members are the face and voices of the UT Women's Intercollegiate

Spotlight
Missy Alston
(Kane Bemiller)
Track and Field and
Cross Country, 1974–77

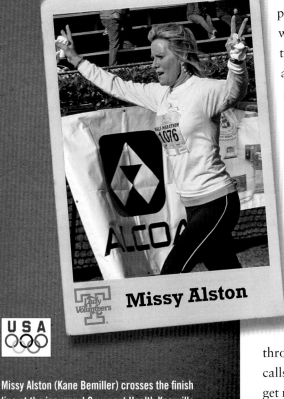

Missy Alston (Kane Bemiller) crosses the finish line at the inaugural Covenant Health Knoxville Marathon, 2005. Courtesy, Covenant Health.

Athletics Department. Their work creates a solid, two-way connection between local, national, and even international communities and the Lady Volunteers.

On the Starting Block

When Missy Alston (Kane Bemiller)'s mother told her to run around outside and play, she didn't know how prophetic those words would be. A few years later, when that same mother prayed for her teenaged daughter to keep her life on track, she had no way of knowing how literally that prayer would have an answer.

Virginia Millicent Alston loved to play outside, was dubbed a "tomboy" by those who knew her, and pushed boundary limits as most teenaged daughters do. So, in the fall of 1973, when Missy left Nashville to become a freshman at the University of Tennessee, her parents were hopeful that her life would find a healthy direction. "My Mom and Dad had become devout Christians through their own life challenges," she recalls. "They regularly prayed that I would get my life on track. My Mom wanted me to become involved in something at UT, and she suggested that I try sports. One day I was walking by the track with a sorority sister, and she invited me to try out for track with her the next day. I thought that maybe I would."

And she did. What Missy lacked in experience she overcame with her determined, positive willingness to work hard. She liked running and challenging herself to get better. "Running hooked me," she says. "It was

my first real challenge. I liked being tired after practice and getting better. Running gave me focus. Even my grades improved. I was in awe of just being on a sports team for the first time."

In 1974 women's track and field was administered by the Department of Health, Physical Education, and Recreation (HPER) in the College of Education. Coach Terry Crawford was an instructor as well as the coach, and budgetary support was very small. Missy says:

Terry was a great coach. We didn't have an athletic training room. We would run up to Terry's office in the HPER building, and she would tape our feet. We shared our warm-up clothes with the swim team. I remember washing our warm-ups and then running them over to the Aquatic Center so the swim team would have them too. There was no such thing as free shoes. I remember that Ron Addison, a member of the men's track team, was selling old Nikes. I was so excited—I thought they were "Mikes" (with an "M") and went around telling everyone that I had Mikes.

The UT men's track and field team won the 1974 National Championship, and Missy remembers that the women's team felt a little intimidated by them at first: "We stayed out of their way—stretched on different sides of the track. They did accept us, but we were definitely on a second tier. Over time we became great friends, and many of us are still close today."

Undisturbed by the funding disparities, Missy and her teammates enjoyed the opportunities to compete and see others who were great in their sport. "We weren't upset that we had to spend our own money—just excited that we had our opportunities," she says. "Lean times made us appreciate what we did have. We competed at AIAW meets that were for women only. We also went to big meets like the Florida Relays, Dogwood (now Sea Ray) Relays, and Gatorade Classic where men and women competed. It was fun to see competitors like George Watts [UT distance runner and current UT men's cross country coach] and Reggie Jones, a great sprinter from Michigan."

Missy recalls the road trips as especially fun and bonding for the team: "We saved our own money to get a UT van for trips to meets and stayed at people's houses along the way. One year we drove to Florida on spring break, stayed at Seagrove Beach with Terry's in-laws, then stayed with a teammate's family in Naples, and went to the Florida Relays. We trained on the beach. I remember trying to keep Terry awake—she was driving all the way to Florida. She did it all."

The small size of the women's team presented challenges, and at times they barely had enough members to run cross country. Coach Crawford placed her runners wherever they needed personnel to get the job done. Stressed by the pressure to compete in the cross country event, Missy briefly left the team in her sophomore year but soon realized the strength of her commitment. "I saw myself as a sprinter," she remembers. "Terry had me running cross country—one and a half miles back then. I thought that was so far to run—she was having me run four miles in practice. (Women race about four miles today!) I quit the team for two weeks midway through the season. I kept running

around campus and missed it. I thought that maybe God was telling me something, so I called Terry and got back on the team."

In 1976, when offered one of the first women's scholarships, Missy accepted money only for books. Already supported by her family, she was concerned that she might feel added pressure if she had a scholarship.

The women's track and field team continued to grow and improve, and the team began to realize their progress. "One of my favorite memories is a tri-meet when Ohio State and Michigan came to Knoxville," Missy recalls. "I won the mile and the 800-yard. Our team did really well. It was great—just that feeling from being a walk-on to doing pretty well, seeing that our team was getting better, that these other schools had older programs and we could beat them."

Missy praises her coach for providing a motivating learning environment and instilling the confidence that guides her career today:

I knew that I might not be genetically as gifted or have the high school experience that others had, so I needed to work on form and things that I could do—develop a mental edge, determination. With Terry it was intense. I was a "nervous Nellie." With Terry's coaching and the Fellowship of Christian Athletes, I tried to learn to trust in what God has given me and not to worry so much about how I would look in front of people. I learned that God can use our weakness as strength. I wrote down Bible verses, put them in my warm-up bag, in my shoes, and dropped them on my spikes to remind me of what to focus on. That reminded me to give my all and not to focus so much on

Missy Alston (Kane Bemiller)

Sport Stats
- Team captain, 1976, 1977
- Fourth-place team finish, 1977 AIAW Outdoor Championship

Academic Stats
- B.S., Education, University of Tennessee, 1977
- M.S., Education, University of Tennessee, 1984

Postcollegiate Career Highlights
- Bronze Medalist, 1983 Pan American Games (1500m)
- Bronze Medalist, 1983 National Sports Festival (1500m)
- Third-place finish, 1983 TAC Outdoor Nationals (1500m)
- Sixth-place finish, 1983 World University Games (1500m)
- Ranked third in the United States in the 1500 meter in 1983
- US Olympian, 1984
- NBC Sports track and field commentator, 1987 Indoor and Outdoor World Championships
- FOX Sports Net commentator, 1987–present
- SEC cross country Coach of the Year, 1990
- Guided 1990 Lady Vol cross country team to SEC championship
- Knoxville Sports Hall of Fame inductee, 1996
- Health Promotions Coordinator, Covenant Health Care
- Lady Volunteer Hall of Fame

the outcome. I had to have those talks with myself to counter the negative fears of failure and to strengthen my faith in knowing that "yes . . . I can do this." We learned to focus with Terry. On mornings of the meet—those first hours before the event—dread, fear would creep in, and then the gun went off, and I would just zoom in on what I was doing. It was great to know that I didn't give up on myself.

I know that helped me to prepare for a live sports journalism career—going from that extreme low—"Oh no, I have to do this"—and then to the extreme high—"I did it!" I was a little too nervous, too worried—"What if . . . what if I don't have enough energy to go on?"—but something about it hooked me in; the team was fun. I had never been on a team. It was so fun being part of a group of women competing, laughing, helping each other, holding her blocks.

Terry was a great coach and a great teacher. She motivated me to want to be a teacher and coach. So many wonderful professors in the College of Education—Dr. Ed Howley [professor of exercise, sports and leisure studies] and others—taught me so much about training. They made me want to teach and help others.

Along with lessons of skill-building, confidence, and discipline, Coach Crawford knew the value of expanding horizons and took advantage of competitions to open the world to her team. "I remember going to AIAW Nationals my senior year," Missy says. "Holly Warlick ("Hollywood," we called her) was on our team. The meet was at UCLA, and Terry made the trip fun. She scheduled our flight to go through San Fran-

Health advocate Missy Alston (Kane Bemiller) leads hiking expeditions in the Great Smoky Mountains National Park.

cisco with enough time to shop and see the sights. Gloria [Ray] came with us. We went out for a special dinner. It was so fun to travel."

The world kept opening to Missy, and eleven years later this walk-on student-athlete would be representing the United States in the opening ceremonies of the 1984 Summer Olympics in Los Angeles. Missy recalls her genuine excitement and thrill to be a member of the Olympic Team: "I remember thinking, 'Wow—eleven years ago I was just a walk-on at UT!' I was so excited to be along with so many amazing athletes. I snapped pictures and wrote Michael Jordan's name on his photo just so I wouldn't forget who he is. It was so great to see Benita [Fitzgerald Mosley] win the gold. It was amazing that God brought me that far—the excitement, the American feeling. We hadn't been in the Olympics for eight years because of the boycott in 1980. To be on our soil—it

was a very patriotic moment to walk in with the US flag."

Missy continues to live her life with a spirit that calls to the champion in us all. Her commitment to healthy living stands on foundations of strong faith. Following the early prayers of her parents "to stay on track," Missy strives each day to "fight the good fight, keep the faith, finish the race." A visible role model for the community, now Missy is the teacher and coach, and she has a profound impact on those around her. What is her advice to young women today?

God has given everybody a different gift. Find your passion and pursue it. Today we want everything so immediately. We want to go through the drive-thru window and get it fast. The best rewards don't come that way. Stick to your goals even when you don't get immediate success. Be consistent. Realize that if you face your fears, when you look back on the good times in college, you're probably not going to be upset that you missed a party—but you will remember that National Championship or going to San Francisco with your team. You'll remember working hard, overcoming odds, and winning the SEC. You will remember digging really deep and your team winning. Collegiate athletics provide the training field for life—for handling stress, adversity. I look back and am very grateful for the Lady Vol program. I am very proud of how far it has come. I am always proud to be a Lady Vol. Being a Lady Vol opened doors and changed my whole life.

This Lady Vol is one of the first. Missy describes her collegiate experiences with humility and gratitude. One might almost for-

Spotlight
Susan Thornton
Volleyball, 1976
Track and Field, 1976–80

Susan Thornton

Susan Thornton shows Lady Vol strength and determination throwing shot put.
Courtesy, Susan Thornton.

get that she was fast, that she set standards, and that her dedication, endurance, and faith established examples that future Lady Vols would strive to reach. Indeed, when she walked through the Tennessee doors, she opened the way for others and changed many lives.

The Lady Vol with the Little Red Wagon

When Susan Thornton enters a room, she fills it with confidence, spirit, and strength. This Tennessee Lady Vol is thoroughly orange. Owner of a thriving construction business in her hometown, Nashville, Tennessee, Susan tells her stories with quick wit that is sure to draw some smiles:

When I was growing up—athletically as a girl—if you were going to be a shot putter, you'd better be a good one. There were not many of us then. You don't really decide to be a thrower; "it" decides you. In high school I made varsity volleyball team as a freshman. There was an hour break between the end of classes and volleyball practice when the intramural track team practiced. Our school had a shot put. No one knew why we had a shot put, and no one knew how to use it, but we had one. So, to pass the time until volleyball practice, I taught myself the shot put in the grass using two socks to outline the circle and throwing into a sand pit. I don't remember learning—I just did it.

Susan's first coach was Brian Oldfield. She never met the world champion thrower, but she watched him on ABC's *Wide World of Sports* and learned. She began throwing in competitions and quickly rose to the top as a daunting force. Terry Crawford, UT's head track coach, talked to Susan about throwing for UT, but she hadn't decided between UT and North Carolina State. At the state track meet in May of her high school senior year, Coach Crawford was in the stands. Susan had a discus with an orange dot on one side and a red dot on the other. After the competition was over, she went behind the stands, flung the disc in the air to decide where to attend college. It landed with the orange dot up.

"I went over to Terry Crawford and asked if she still needed a thrower," Susan remembers. "UT was serious and professional about women's sports, and they were committed to success. I literally fell into the best by the flip of a discus! I threw for track and field and played volleyball my first year. I met Pat Head (Summitt) then and remember getting $300 at first and then $200 more in scholarship money."

Susan recalls the creativity it took to find facilities and equipment:

I had so much stuff to carry to practice each day—jump ropes, shot puts, discus, towels, medicine balls, shoes. We didn't have managers for throwers and were responsible for our own gear, so I got a little red wagon. It worked great. I went back and forth, every day, from Andy Holt apartments, across the Aquatic Center, and down the sidewalk to the track. Traveling to meets presented further challenges. The equipment was so heavy and difficult to carry through the airports. I ruined two suitcases carrying equipment. Finally, I went to a junk store and found an

Susan Thornton

old metal suitcase. I made foam forms to put around the equipment. The suitcase weighed about 400 pounds, but it worked.

At that time UT did not have a women's weight room. Susan and other team members made their way into the men's wrestling room for conditioning and strength training. "We were welcome there because we were serious about what we were doing," she says. "We didn't disrupt the 'mojo' of the place and were accepted by the men as athletes. They recognized that we could train together. Some of them even admitted to respecting us for the work we were doing. Many other people were looking for ways to discount what we were doing. Even women didn't support us at first. When I would train in health clubs away from UT, I would draw attention and comments such as, 'You'll never be cute doing that.'"

Any barriers and doubts Susan encountered served to strengthen her determination to succeed. Looking back, she says, "People who had the experience of sports have become better people because of these challenges. We learned to put ourselves at risk— to prepare and compete with all we had— until the whistle blew, then to assess and move on. Many of us would not have gone to college without the athletics."

The student-athletes of these early years developed special bonds as teammates. "We were a whole team," Susan says. "Even though we had individual events, we all practiced together and rooted for each other at meets. Terry [Crawford] built a closely-knit group. I have great memories of our trips together. One time we went to Naples, Florida, for the Florida Relays during spring

break and stayed with the family of a teammate. Another time we rode a bus to an indoor track meet that was held in a cow barn. The UT women's basketball team had a game there on the same weekend, so we traveled together. After that trip we all got the measles, one after another, and went to Terry's house to be quarantined."

The student-athletes were mainstream students. Like everyone else, they lived in residence halls, ate at the campus cafeterias, and pursued academic programs. Juggling schedules could be challenging, and Susan changed her major from civil engineering to engineering science and mechanics to accommodate class schedules with track practice.

These first years the women's athletic department was working to develop visibility and identity. Susan remembers Athletic Director Gloria Ray's efforts to raise support: "One of the slogans was 'Support Women's Athletic Teams' [SWAT]. I liked the idea of being involved in building a program. We went to so many meets. I remember the Becky Boone Relays in Kentucky. The trophy was a bonnet, a frontier-woman's bonnet. The first years those were the kinds of competitions we did. I also remember going to the Canadian National Team training camp. Terry opened incredible opportunities for us. These early people in the department —Debby Jennings and others—took UT women's athletics to the next level."

Susan believes that young women today have benefited from the work of the previous generations. "Now parents are supportive of young women and involved in their sports," she comments. "It never occurred to the men that they might not be accepted, but women have had a learning curve. Today Lady Vols

The dollar bill Susan Thornton split on a friendly wager with Gloria Ray over whether the Lady Vol track and field team would qualify for the Nationals. Courtesy, Susan Thornton.

Susan Thornton and Women's Athletics Director Gloria Ray. Courtesy, Susan Thornton.

don't have to sell doughnuts to raise money for travel; they have uniforms, equipment, and championship rings."

Uniforms were not standard issue in the early years. Armed with creativity, Susan and her teammates were not discouraged. They purchased orange jackets during a shopping trip to a local sporting goods store. A javelin thrower was a fashion major, and she designed a logo to silk-screen onto the jackets. The resulting creation became their version of the first Lady Vol letter jacket.

At the end of the season, Lady Vol student-athletes received certificates of appreciation for participating in women's athletics. Even though the tangible symbols of accomplishment were not well established, the Lady Vols had as much pride in their achievements as student-athletes have today.

"We never got jackets, rings, or regular media coverage," she says, "but we knew that the university was backing us. Pat [Summitt] and Terry [Crawford] were the two premier coaches and world-class athletes. We were headed for the national scene, and we knew it. One time at the Tennessee state track meet, Gloria Ray bet us a dollar that we would be at Nationals. Lynn Lashley, a distance runner, and I took Gloria's dollar and tore it in half. We each still have our halves, and we each did make it to Nationals."

Susan injects energy and conviction in her advice to students aspiring to be athletes:

Go for your own goals for yourself—not for your parents, friends or school. If you aren't doing it for yourself, you will cut corners. Every workout matters. You need to have intention about what you are doing every time you practice. No one expected me to do anything. I never had in my mind that I would qualify for or go to Olympic Trials or end up almost making the team (I was sixth). If you are going to participate in a sport, do it completely. Know why you are doing it; enjoy it. If it's not fun and feeding you, don't do it. Set expectations that you are going to participate to the fullest—you never know what you will achieve.

One day Susan Thornton bought a little red wagon. That was just one of many examples of how she confronted a barrier and overcame it. Her determination, perseverance, and genuine joy for the sport remain the cornerstone of Lady Volunteer athletics today.

The 1979–80 track and field team: (seated, left to right) Benita Fitzgerald, Donna Lake, Susan Thornton, Vata Allen, Vanessa Robinson; (kneeling, left to right) Jane Cobb, Shannon Cline, Lynn Emery, Melissa Foster, Joanne Soldano, Lynn Lashley, Barb Tieperman, Miriam Boyd, Ellen McCallister, Sally Thomas; (standing, left to right) Assistant Coach Andy Roberts, Kelly Austin, Cathy Kirchner, Delisa Walton, Missy Rutherford, Susan Manning, Penny Towers, Alma Cobb, Rosemarie Hauch, Linda Portasik, Sandy Smith, Ramona Melvin, Lisa Sherrill, Coach Terry Crawford. Courtesy, Susan Thornton.

From Rocky Hill to Rocky Top

As far back as she can remember, Holly Warlick has treasured family, sports, and being outdoors. She has also enjoyed the kind of support that comes from the hearts and cheers of hometown fans.

Born in Anderson, South Carolina, Holly and her family moved to Knoxville, Tennessee, when she was six years old. Settling in the Rocky Hill area, just ten miles west of downtown, Holly smiles as she recalls how far from Knoxville Rocky Hill seemed: "We were way out from Knoxville. The business coming west wasn't at all developed. We used to swim at Concord Park pool, and that seemed so far away. Now I live even further out west and don't think anything of it."

Everyone in Holly's family participated in sports. Keeping pace with the seasons, Holly, along with her brother and sister, could be found on the softball and baseball fields, basketball court, and track. Holly's father coached "at least half the guys in Knoxville," and the entire family pitched in to build the ball park in Rocky Hill. "We were all athletic," she says. "With Dad involved, we all were involved and pretty entrenched sportswise. As the youngest, I looked up to my brother and sister. They were always around, and we did so much together."

This hard work, dedication, and family togetherness instilled Holly's strong work ethic. "Mother has always been in the hotel business," she says. "She always saw the importance of good, hard work. When I became ten, we all went to work—keeping score at the softball field and at basketball games—we would have to be working. My mother is retired and still works two days each week. To this day, when I tell her I am going to work, she says, 'That's good.'"

A pivotal event occurred in the fifth grade when Holly's teacher at Rocky Hill Elementary School encouraged her to run track. "I still have a good relationship with my fifth-grade teacher, Katherine Shook. I try to talk with her every two weeks and go to her house on Christmas Eve when I can. She still follows my career."

Holly's career proved to be exciting to follow. At Bearden High School she rose as a track star, winning the state tournament twice. She competed in the 400, 100, 200, high jump, and long jump. Known for her quickness, Holly also applied her skills to the basketball court. At that time the girls' game was half court with three players on each side. While her team regularly won the city tournament, powerhouses from other regions took the competition at the state level. Holly loved basketball. She had three different coaches in high school, the last one, Bud Fisher, also serving as the football coach. Her dream was to earn a basketball scholarship to the University of Tennessee. "Pat Head (Summitt) came to one of our games to see me play," she recalls. "I had just sprained my ankle and didn't play very well. She didn't come back. I didn't make a very good impression."

Holly's track prowess didn't go unnoticed, however. Terry Crawford, UT head coach for track and field, offered her a partial scholarship with the understanding that she could try out for the basketball team once she enrolled. "I was at the right place at the right time," she says. "When I first came here, there was already someone on the basketball team as point guard, wearing number 22. That was the number I had always wanted. Right before I tried out, that player quit, and not only did I get on the team, but I got that number."

In Holly's freshman year the Tennessee basketball team for the first time went to the AIAW National Tournament. Held in Minneapolis, Minnesota, sixteen teams met at one site. Holly remembers that exciting time: "It was great because we could play and then watch everyone else play. With so many more fans and teams, we couldn't do that today. Williams Arena had two floors with games playing simultaneously. It was so much fun to be totally immersed in basketball when you love the game so much. We lost to Delta State in the semifinals [Tennessee–58, Delta State–62], and then won the consolation game against Immaculata [Tennessee–91, Immaculata–71], coming in third overall."

That tournament marked a turning point for Holly's athletic career. "That was a long basketball season," she remembers. "We went well past February when I should have been in track. I didn't give track much of a chance. I ran the 400 relay at the AIAW Nationals that year. It was a great experience for me, being new on the scene. I couldn't give the time required to develop my track skills and play basketball, so I chose basketball for my sole focus. I was blessed with quickness, and kind of wish I could have done both. But basketball was my love."

The student-athletes of the 1970s have memories unique to the times when basketball programs were first growing foundations of support. As Holly says:

I have so many memories. We used to travel with all of us piled into a van and Pat [Summitt] drove. Pat did everything back then. A team assistant would drive a station wagon with the luggage. Mississippi College for Women used to host a large tournament. We always hoped we wouldn't lose. Every time we lost, Pat would pile us in the car and wouldn't stop until we reached Knoxville. That was a long drive. I remember Pat driving and hanging her head out the window to stay awake. For one thing, we didn't have money to stop, and then, she was so mad at us for losing that she didn't want to spend any more time with us than she had to.

With tongue-in-cheek humor, Holly recalls the early basketball home venue, Alumni Gymnasium, and then the team's first game in Stokely Athletic Center:

Tennessee women first played in Alumni Gym. In the early days [before Holly's era] the uniform required skirts. About twenty people were in attendance, and ten of them were ushers.

I remember my first game in Stokely Athletic Center [1976]. We were playing Kentucky. I remember the first two points I made there—I was at the top of the press, guarding the player out of bounds, and the ball tipped my hand, and I just laid it back in. I shot at least eight lay-ups that hit the iron and bounced back to the free throw line and every time Trish Roberts trailed me and put the ball in. She broke the Stokely Field house record with 51 points.

The reputation of Pat Head (Summitt) was becoming well-established, and Holly credits Pat as her coaching mentor:

She taught me a lot. I already had the work ethic, but she shot me into the right direction. She gave me a stage. Pat was pretty tough on me. That's how you coached back then. If she had done something different, I don't know if I would have had that drive. I didn't have a basketball background really. I was pretty raw.

My sister and her friend Margaret Cox went to the games to watch me. They sat right over the tunnel where the team ran in from the locker room and always wanted to know what Pat said to me. They tried to convince me to take a tape recorder into the locker room at half time. In those days we didn't have guest coaches and press in the locker room.

If Pat didn't get on you, then you worried. Back when I was playing, we didn't have all that much talent, but we did have lots of overachievers. We were kids who would run into the wall for our coach and teammates. Most of us were from Tennessee, and we loved Pat. We always knew she cared about us.

Holly recalls one unforgettable road trip:

We were playing in South Carolina and were up by 20 at half time. We came out the second half, didn't score until the last nine minutes of the game, and lost the game. The next day in silence we bused back, and as we pulled into Knoxville, Pat told us to put on our uniforms. She made us wear those sweaty, nasty uniforms, and we were going to practice the twenty minutes we didn't play.

Holly Warlick

Sports Stats

- US Olympic Basketball Team, 1980 (boycott)
- Kodak All-America, 1980
- US Junior National Team, 1977
- US National Team, 1978–80
- SEC All-Tournament Team 1980
- 400m track student-athlete
- Walk-on basketball student-athlete
- First Tennessee basketball player (male or female) to have her jersey retired (number 22), 1980
- Member of Basketball Final Four Team, 1977, 1979, 1980
- From 1976 to 1980 held UT records for most assists in a game (14), most steals in a game (9), most assists in a season (225) and most games in a career (142)
- Participated in Jones Cup, Pan American Games, World Championship Competition

Academic Stats

- B.S., Business Administration, University of Tennessee 1981
- M.S., Athletic Administration, Virginia Polytechnic Institute and State University, 1983

Holly Warlick, associate head coach, Lady Vol Basketball.

We even had to put on our smelly socks. We were in Stokely—Jill Rankin, Kathy O'Neil, and I were coming out through the tunnel— acting like we were in a game, announced our names, came running out, holding up our hands, making crowd noises. I went out; Jill came out; and then Kathy came to the edge of the court. About that time Pat came up behind her. Kathy said, "Come on, y'all— aren't you going to introduce me? Well, I'll just introduce myself." We were trying to signal with our eyes that she needed to stop, but she ran out, called out her name, and cheered loudly. Seeing that we weren't excited, Kathy said, "What's the matter?" Pat came out and said, "You all think this is funny? I'll show you what is funny."

Being a Lady Vol meant hard work, discipline, and staying the course. But even student-athletes are still learning and capable of falling prey to unwise decisions. She

says, "We were college students—we would do stuff. Pat would hear about it, and Pat would make us run. In one of her books Pat tells about a time when a team ignored a Saturday-night curfew and partied well into the early morning hours. That was my team. Arriving at Sunday practice, we felt terrible. There was a trash can positioned in each corner of the court. Pat ran us—we would get sick—we got back on the line and ran some more. We all finished, and the point was made."

The discipline and strong work ethic of Pat Summitt's Tennessee program paid off in countless ways. "I was in my best physical shape in the summer of my freshman year," she says. "I made the US. Junior National Team, and we trained in Squaw Valley [California]. Some people were affected by the high altitude. It didn't faze me because Pat ran everybody, and we had to be in great shape."

Now coaching the Lady Vols alongside her mentor, Pat Summitt, Holly is still amazed by the opportunities she has had because of basketball:

Before I came to UT, the farthest west I had been was Nashville; the farthest north was Knoxville; the farthest east was Charleston; and the farthest south was Florida. Now I have been everywhere—to Mexico, Poland, Bulgaria, Russia, Czechoslovakia, Japan, Korea, Taiwan, and all over Europe—it's unbelievable. I went to those places when they were still behind the Iron Curtain—we got off the plane and walked through people with machine guns. Fences were around the courts so people wouldn't throw things at us. I played in Seoul, Korea, for the World

Championship before an audience of 22,000 people, whose tradition is to whistle instead of booing. The education I have received is amazing. I played every summer until the Olympics and the boycott. I have kept journals of all my travels. Just think—this is all because of basketball!

Holly participated in the transformation of women's basketball as a student-athlete. She continues to be a key influence on women's collegiate athletics, and her pride is evident as she talks about her coaching role:

I am doing exactly what I want to do. I get to work with young women—help them grow up. I love it when they come back and recognize the tradition that they are a part of. It is so fun to watch them grow—they come in as freshmen; their bodies are still strengthening; their game skills are still developing. They learn to speak in public, to carry themselves with pride, to make hard decisions—it is incredible to watch these young women transform in four years.

Our Lady Vol program is distinctive. It didn't happen overnight, and challenge is always there. Winning hasn't changed us and it won't, because that is who we are . . . we are going to continue to be there. We developed a great base and worked extremely hard to get where we are. At the top of the flagpole you are constantly swirling—people are gunning for you. Everywhere on the road we draw people—opponents and supporters—and that is a huge compliment.

And what advice does Holly have for the aspiring Lady Vol?

You have to enjoy what you do, love the sport, and have your whole heart in it. You have to be disciplined, to say "no" to friends, to make hard decisions to do something when maybe you don't want to do it. The work ethic here is huge. You have to have a little bit of enthusiasm about you—you have to get excited about other people. This is a team sport, and you need to have a way to bond your team together. Not everyone has that, and I know that. I guess that is part of my game, of me growing up. I got excited about others, and I made it known. If somebody makes a mistake, that's OK; you will get it back, so try to keep everything positive. It is amazing how positive we have to be these days—student-athletes get down on themselves. Even the most successful, best players in the country can feel insecure.

On February 18, 1980, Holly Warlick became the first Tennessee student-athlete, male or female, to have her jersey retired. Number 22 will forever be a reminder of the agility, dedication, and pride that Holly gave to the Tennessee tradition. Over the years the game has changed, her roles have changed, but Holly Warlick still captures the spirit of her fans. The hometown has just gotten a little bit bigger, the cheers just a little bit louder, and the hearts just a little bit deeper.

Holly Warlick

Postcollegiate Career Highlights

- Player representative on the USA Basketball Council
- Member of the USOC Advisory Council for Basketball WPBL All-Star as she led the Nebraska Wranglers to the championship of the Women's Professional Basketball League, 1981
- Associate head coach, University of Tennessee, 2003–present
- Tennessee Sports Hall of Fame
- Lady Volunteer Hall of Fame
- Women's Basketball Hall of Fame
- Knoxville Sports Hall of Fame
- Basketball Final Four coach, 1986, 1987, 1988, 1989, 1991, 1995, 1996, 1997, 1998, 2000, 2002, 2003, 2004, 2005
- Named "Top Assistant Coach" in Division I Women's Basketball by the WBCA, 2007
- Assistant coach, Virginia Tech, 1981–83
- Assistant coach, University of Nebraska, 1983–85
- Assistant coach, University of Tennessee, 1985–2003
- Ranked one of nation's top assistant basketball coaches in the Women's Basketball Journal, 1998
- Selected to the Converse/Lady Volunteer Team of the Decade for the 1980s
- Ran Olympic Torch through Knoxville as it made its way to the 1996 Olympic Games in Atlanta, Georgia

The 1979–80 basketball team: SEC Champions, SEC Tournament Champions, and AIAW Championships 2nd place winners. Pictured here are (front row, left to right) Head Coach Pat Head, Debbie Groover (52), Jill Rankin (13), Cindy Noble (32), Cindy Ely (55), Kathy O'Neil (40), team manager Donna Thomas; (back row, left to right) Assistant Coach Nancy Darsch, Lea Henry (44), Becky Clark (24), Bev Curtis (51), Susan Foulds (42), Susan Clower (34), Holly Warlick (22), and graduate assistant Nanette Fisher.

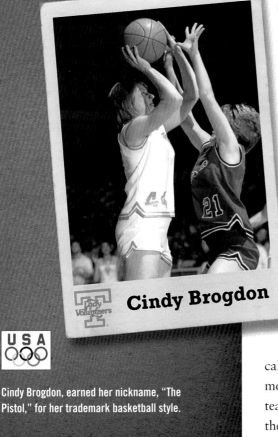

Spotlight
Cindy Brogdon
Basketball, 1977–79

Cindy Brogdon

Cindy Brogdon, earned her nickname, "The Pistol," for her trademark basketball style.

A Straight Shooter

In high school they called her "Pistol." She wore those floppy socks, and when she handled the ball, you could almost see Pistol Pete Maravich himself in her quick dribbling and sharp, crisp passes. Ironically, her professional play for the WNBA New Orleans Pride would match her with Pistol Pete's former coach, Butch Van Breda Koff. But we are getting ahead of the story.

Cindy Brogdon, one of three girls, was born in Buford, Georgia, and grew up in the Atlanta area. As a child she loved sports and played softball in a church league. As she became more competitive, she joined a travel club and played softball throughout the summers. She did play basketball, but it was her second sport and held a place among many other activities that she played day-to-day in the neighborhood.

The shift to basketball was accidental. When Cindy was in eighth grade, a teacher came into her physical education class and said that they needed more basketball players for the ninth-grade team. Cindy was one of the tallest students there, so she was their choice.

Fortune smiled on Cindy Brogdon that day. She put on her basketball shoes and never looked back. Her high school coach for her first three years, Dale Vickery, played a major role in developing Cindy's skills and her competitive edge. "I like the competition of basketball," she says. "I love working as a team. I like individual sports, but I am very team-oriented. I like working and communicating with people and working toward a specific common goal."

Her high school career filled the trophy cases with three state championships and one state runner-up. She was MVP of the state tournament all four years and set twelve new school records. Cindy was a top college pick and entered Mercer University as the first woman in the state of Georgia to receive a full athletic scholarship.

Cindy's college freshman year saw Olympic dreams become reality when she earned a place on the US team. At age eighteen, she joined her Olympic Team roommate, Pat Head (Summitt), and brought home the silver medal from the 1976 Summer Olympic Games in Montreal. She remembers:

When I made the Olympic Team, I was eighteen and I believe Pat was twenty-four. We had only a six-year age difference. I admired her at that time because she had such self-discipline. She had such a strong work ethic. She was just very goal-oriented, and I like that in a person.

But I think the main thing that drew me to Pat was her honesty. Both of us came from a small town, and I felt safe and comfortable with her. I knew she was a tremendous athlete from watching her and practicing with her, and I knew that she could push me to a level where I had never been athletically. I just looked at her as a coach and mentor. I felt that she was someone who was put in my life for a reason.

During her sophomore year at Mercer, Cindy realized that she was not likely to meet her goals as a student-athlete. Small colleges were not funding scholarships to attract the top athletes. Fueled by the desire to play on a National Championship team, Cindy considered transferring to another school. She visited the University of Tennessee, Tennessee Technological State University, and the University of Georgia. Cindy chose Tennessee and Pat Head to be her coach.

"I roomed with Pat in the Olympics," Cindy says. "She was a great friend but also a great influence on me. I just really wanted to be at Tennessee. It was in my heart and soul. My decision had a lot to do with Pat. She is the type of person I wanted to be around and that I trusted. So that was one reason that I selected Tennessee at the end of my sophomore year."

Cindy found her fit with Tennessee. She felt support through the student body and the community. "I was totally amazed by the people from the community that came to the games regularly," she comments. "And they are still regulars today. I had a volunteer family who would have me out to eat. I was so impressed with the professors—especially in physical education, my major. They were very supportive of Lady Vol athletics. And that was in 1977."

Like her teammates, Cindy practiced hard and followed a regimen to prepare for games. At the time the women's team did not eat at the university's "training table" for pregame meals. Cindy developed a regular habit of eating a steak, baked potato, and tossed salad before every game. Looking back on that, Cindy smiles and notes how such a meal would be inadvisable today. Cindy believed that preparation led to top performance. She did follow one routine that probably didn't fall into everyone's game plan: "I will tell you this. I had game underwear. I wore the same underwear every game. I don't care if they had holes in them. It was game underwear.

Cindy Brogdon, high school educator and administrator, 2007. Courtesy, Cindy Brogdon.

I had to wear the same ones. If they weren't clean, they got cleaned."

Lucky underwear aside, Cindy flourished as a Lady Volunteer and set the bar for competition. Coach Pat Head called her one of the "finest shooters in the country." In her two years playing at Tennessee, Cindy's career totals included 1,458 points scored (including her two years at Mercer, her overall total was 3,204), 20.8 points per game, and

261 assists. She shot 51 percent from field and 84 percent from the free throw line. She had 423 rebounds and played in a total of 70 games. She was featured in *Sports Illustrated* (1978) and *Newsweek* (1979) as one of the nation's top athletes. She was a Kodak All-America and named to the Hanes Underall and Street & Smith All-America teams. Cindy is quick to say that the tutelage of Coach Pat Head taught her about more than basketball:

One thing that I can say that UT gave me is a sense of discipline. They gave me a sense of focus on what is important in life. I learned great basketball skills. I improved my skills to a level that I would have never achieved without Pat's assistance. But I also learned life skills. And that is one of the most important things that I got from the University of Tennessee. Deep down, if I look back, that is why I went there.

Pat wanted me to score and she pounded defense into my head because I hated it. But she also wanted us to be the best that we can be in our life and carry that on in our life.

Pat has instilled discipline in me that I continue whether it is in my job or in my workouts. I thank God that she came into my life. She helped me get through a really tough time when I lost my mother at an early age, and then my dad passed away not too long after that. Living your life without parents is terrible. My mother and my dad were at every game. They were my supporters. So when you lose that in your life, you have to find some kind of internal strength. And I feel that through athletics, something has been instilled in me. Being around Pat helped me get through issues in my life. I don't think

she realizes how awesome she is—the impact that she has had on her Lady Vols from a long time ago.

After graduating from UT, Cindy played pro basketball for the WBL New Orleans Pride. Immediately she experienced a big change. She says:

I improved my skills to a level that I would have never achieved without Pat's assistance. But I also learned life skills.

I played for the New Orleans Pride, and practices were about an hour and a half. It was nothing like the intensity of the workouts that I had been through with Pat. I found myself after workouts trying to get myself in better shape. The money wasn't bad for doing that. I wasn't complaining. But I just wasn't used to it emotionally. That was a huge adjustment.

The pros were just trying to get off the ground. Our coach was Butch Van Breda Koff, who had coached the New Orleans Jazz when Pistol Pete Maravich played for them. They thought he would bring in a lot of spectators. But his first thought was women cannot play basketball. As the season progressed, he started changing his way of thinking.

In 1998 Cindy stepped into the career shoes of her mentor, Pat Summitt, and began coaching. She was at Centennial High

School in Roswell, Georgia, for two years and then completed her master's degree in health studies at the University of Alabama. She returned to the Atlanta area to help open Northview High School, where she serves as chairperson of the Health and Physical Education Department. Cindy went on to complete the education specialist's degree in administration. Just as she did as a student-athlete and professional player in basketball, Cindy seeks higher levels for personal challenge and continuing education. Her life philosophy, "to live as if you are dying tomorrow," clearly directs her choices and achievements.

As an educator, Cindy is concerned with current challenges facing youth:

Kids are pressured to succeed in everything they do. I find that kids cannot focus today. There are so many distractions. They can't focus on the important things in life because they are so stimulated by other things in their environment. When I was growing up, all we had to do was play ball. There was only one mall, and that was thirty miles from my hometown. There were no nearby movie theatres. Your mindset maybe was small, but you were able to stay focused on things and perfect those things.

Cindy Brogdon

Sports Stats

- Kodak All-America, 1976, 1978, 1979
- Street and Smith's All-America, 1976, 1977, 1978
- Montreal Olympic Games silver medalist (averaged 15.2 points in five games), 1976
- US National Team, 1976–78
- Led team in free-throw percentage, 1977–78
- Led team in scoring, 1977–78, 1978–79
- Wade Trophy runner-up, 1979
- Stayfree East-West All-America MVP
- Hanes Underall All-America, 1978
- WBL All-America

Academic Stats

- B.S., Education, University of Tennessee, 1980
- M.S., Health Studies, University of Alabama, 2002
- Educational Specialist, Administration and Supervision, Lincoln Memorial University, 2006

Postcollegiate Career Highlights

- WBL, St. Louis and New Orleans, 1979–81
- Head basketball coach, Centennial High School, Roswell, Georgia
- Facilities Coordinator, Northview High School, Duluth, Georgia
- Department chairperson, Health and Physical Education, Northview High School
- Lady Volunteer Hall of Fame
- Women's Basketball Hall of Fame
- Georgia Hall of Fame

Life is really competitive now. And I think the reason it is so competitive—more so than when we played—is because there are more talented athletes now. And everybody wants to be in the media. Everybody wants to have that fame. Why did we play? We played because we loved to play basketball. When I was little, all I wanted to do was play college basketball. There were no pros at the time. There were no Olympics. The only goal that I had at my age was to play college ball. So, I think we played because we loved the game.

Every sport is becoming a year-round sport. I see this in high school. Kids never take a break. I know that when I played, we played our season, went to camps in the summer, and then we were just kids for about a month. We don't allow kids to be kids and have fun. Part of developing mentally and emotionally is just being a kid. We need to have breaks from structured environments and being told what to do all of the time. I see a lot of burnout at the high school level.

Far from burnout, Cindy's energy continues to propel her as an athlete, educator, and community leader. On April 22, 2002, Cindy Brogdon was honored among the best when she was inducted into the Women's Basketball of Fame. When asked about her achievements, Cindy says that discipline, a strong work ethic, and associating with positive people have been instrumental to her success.

I would tell young women today to stay focused on your goals. Surround yourself with positive people that have the same lifestyle as you and are practicing discipline. And what I mean by that is you need to hang out with people who do not do drugs. You need to choose friends who share your interests. Don't hang out with people that could just care less about life. Anything you try, do it with excellence. Be honest. Always tell the truth. Don't just tell the half-truth. And even though you may have a bad day, you need to look and see how you have treated people today. You just never know when your last breath is. It is hard sometimes to overcome sadness. I think you just have to really look at it and say, "I know I have choices here." That takes a lot of mental strength.

Sometimes I ask myself why I do the things that I do. Why do I run at 5:30 in the morning? Why do I go to church? It's just what's inside me. I think, it is how I was created. And I think it is because of the people I have surrounded myself with since I was in high school. If you look back on your life, there are people in your life and they are there for a reason.

Why did I play basketball? I played for the team and for me, but I also played for the fans. I liked to entertain the fans. That brought a lot of joy to me.

Cindy Brogdon was an extraordinary student-athlete. However we know her—as a player, a coach, a teacher, administrator, or friend—she is at once a champion. And with all the choices she made and the challenges she faced, she built a foundation of fun and exciting memories that are the tradition of the Lady Volunteers. And that brings a lot of joy to us.

Spotlight
**Paula Kelly and
Peta Kelly (Slade)**
Tennis, 1978–82

Paula Kelly

Peta Kelly

Sisters Peta and Paula Kelly were a dominant doubles team during their four years at Tennessee, earning All-America status from 1980 through 1982.

Doubles of Wins for Tennessee

They hailed from Down Under, and the shots of this tennis duo turned heads and brought the University of Tennessee tennis program to new levels. Paula and Peta Kelly were born in Brisbane, Australia. Both grew up with sports, playing netball as children. Paula enjoyed track and field and softball, and Peta added swimming to the list. Both found their love in tennis.

In 1978 Paula and Peta enrolled in the University of Tennessee. The move to the United States introduced them to new adventures. One of Paula's most memorable moments is her first UT football game. "At seventeen years of age," she says, "I had never seen or experienced such fanaticism and so many people at once. It was very scary and intimidating but exciting all the same."

Even though English is the language of Australia, communication could still present some challenges. Laughingly Peta recalls an incident with her tennis coach, Mary Ellis Richardson:

Just a few days after our arrival to UT our coach took Paula and me somewhere in her car. Coach asked me to pass her pocketbook to her from the back seat. I was scratching around trying to find the "pocket-sized notebook" that she wanted. She kept repeating that it was on the seat right next to me, but I couldn't find it. As she continued to repeat that it was on the seat next to me, she began to get a little irate and probably a little concerned about whether or not I was completely "stupid." I became quite frustrated at my inability to locate this notebook, so

I grabbed the handbag that was on the seat next to me and blurted out, "Are you sure it's not in this handbag?" Coach joyfully exclaimed, "That's it!" Think about it: pocketbook has nothing to do with your pockets and looks nothing like a book!

Australia is on the other side of the world from Tennessee, and there were times when Paula and Peta were acutely aware of the distance. Peta recalls their homesickness during the first year at UT:

I especially found my first winter term very hard as I come from a very sunny, warm climate; so to be under grey, cold, and snowy skies for three months or so was very depressing. It was good to have my twin sister with me, as we supported each other through these times. It was also hard to see our college friends go home for the weekend knowing there was no way we could just pop home. The high telephone cost to Australia limited our calls. Dad wrote to us every week, and it was such a joy and pure excitement to receive his letter. Mum was still working at that time because our younger brother and sister were still at school. Dad had retired.

Despite their difficult adjustment to Tennessee winters, December brought smiles to the twins' faces with their first white Christmas. The summer season in Australia usually finds families celebrating the holiday at the beach.

Paula and Peta's close connection as twins buoyed their spirits when they were low. As Peta says, "Paula and I have always been close, so it was a comfort to have each other as roommates and teammates.

Paula Kelly and Peta Kelly Slade at home in Australia, 2007.
Courtesy, Peta Kelly Slade.

We knew exactly what the other one was experiencing, and when we did argue, we knew it would be all over in no time. We have always had the same friends throughout school, and university was no different. Our academic interests differed but not our commitment to excellence."

Paula and Peta's commitments to excellence certainly extended to the tennis courts. Their tough competitive spirits and disciplined hard work lifted the team to first-time SEC and regional achievements and earned both women the title of Lady Volunteer Athlete of the Year in 1982. Looking back on their collegiate days, Paula and Peta loved playing tennis but particularly value the friendships they made through their sport:

The camaraderie with all the extraordinary people that I had the opportunity to meet as well as play with or against is what I truly treasure from my Lady Volunteer experience. Being a Lady Vol taught me that being a part of a team is much more fun than playing individually, as you can share all the highs and lows of competing. The Lady Vol team is like an extension of your own family (Paula).

So many people had an impact on my life in those four short years at Tennessee. Being a Lady Vol reinforced the ideals of commitment, dedication, and perseverance. The UT women's athletic department gave us great opportunities as student-athletes to achieve not only in our chosen sport but also in our academic pursuits. The spirit among the teammates was fabulous. I remember many funny incidents on road trips and loved spring break trips to Florida.

We were able to experience college life as students and athletes. I also have special memories of my studies. I recall many late nights in the computer science lab typing a programming assignment that was due or trying to get ahead of schedule because of a tennis road trip. I thank the teacher of my first computer science class for making it as interesting as he did. This class made me decide to major in computer science, and I have been hooked ever since (Peta).

Here are a few fun facts about the twins:

Game Superstition

Paula: I have always been a little superstitious about stepping on the lines of a tennis court when walking around it before a match.

Peta: I always like to play with exactly the same racquet.

Motto

Paula: "Virtue non Verbus," Latin for "Actions not Words" (from high school days).

Peta: Nobody is Perfect. Practice makes one a little less perfect (her father's words).

Hobby

Paula: Beach walks, reading, movies, spending time with her son.

Peta: Gardening, traveling, and spending time with her husband, daughter, and son.

Current Sports

Paula: Indoor cricket, tennis.

Peta: Tennis, aerobic workouts, yoga.

Both advise young women today to grasp opportunities with determination. "Make the most of your opportunities," says Peta. "They may not come around again. Determine what makes you happy and be sure your goals reflect this. I also believe that balance is the key to a happy and successful life." And Paula advises, "Work hard; stay focused on your goals. Above all—have fun and enjoy what you are doing. Life is too short!"

At the young age of seventeen, Paula Kelly and Peta Kelly Slade traveled far from home because they wanted the opportunity to study abroad and continue to play tennis. In a few short years, they changed the momentum of Lady Vol tennis and moved the program to new competitive levels. The spirited, energetic twins won Tennessee hearts and inspired others to embrace challenge. In 1978 Paula and Peta were a long way from home. Today Australia is just around the corner.

Paula Kelly

Sports Stats

- UT Career (1978–82) Records: singles, 133–30 (second all-time); doubles, 156–8 (first all-time) NCAA or AIAW Highs: singles, AIAW Consolation Finals, 1980; doubles, AIAW Second Round, 1980; Doubles All-America, 1980, 1981, 1982; All-SEC Doubles Team, 1980, 1981; All-Region II Doubles Team, 1979, 1980, 1981, 1982; All-SEC Singles, 1981, 1982; All-Region II Singles, 1980, 1981, 1982
- Lady Volunteer Athlete of the Year 1982

Academic Stats

- B.S., Business Administration, University of Tennessee 1982
- M.S., accountancy, Charles Sturt University, Australia 2001

Postcollegiate Career Highlights

- Career in hospitality, 1983–present
- Played professional tennis in United States and Australia for twelve months
- Lady Volunteer Hall of Fame, Inaugural Class, 2001

Peta Kelly (Slade)

Sports Stats

- Career Records: singles, 104–47 (sixth all-time); doubles: 156–8 (first all-time)
- NCAA or AIAW Highs: doubles, AIAW 2nd Round, 1980; Doubles All-America, 1980, 1981, 1982; All-SEC Doubles Team, 1980, 1981; All-Region II Doubles Team, 1979, 1980, 1981, 1982
- Lady Volunteer Athlete of the Year, 1982

Academic Stats

- B.S., Business Administration, University of Tennessee, 1982
- Chancellor's Citation for Extraordinary Academic Achievement, 1982

Postcollegiate Career Highlights

- Systems programmer, computer software engineer for twenty-four years
- Lady Volunteer Hall of Fame, Inaugural Class, 2001

The 1979-80 Lady Vol tennis team: (front row, left to right) Debbie Southern, Paula Kelly, Heidi Frensz, Linda Evers, (back row, left to right) Coach Mary Ellis Richardson, Peta Kelly, Beth Yeager, Terri Kirk, Karen Stewart, and team manager Kim Hughes.

Spotlight
Mary Ostrowski
Basketball, 1980–84

Mary Ostrowski

Mary Ostrowski moves to the inside.

Hooked on Mo

A colleague poked her head in the door to Mary Ostrowski's office and said, "Hey, want to play on our office basketball team? It's OK if you're not any good." Little did that colleague know that under the familiar UPS brown of their company color she would find the color orange. Mary Ostrowski acknowledges this incident with a smile and admits that it would have been kind of fun to see her coworkers' faces registering shock if she were to drop the ball in the basket with her famous hook shot.

OK, maybe her colleague was new to Knoxville. Maybe she never watched basketball. Maybe she was never in the UT women's athletic department halls to see all the pictures documenting past glories. Maybe she never read a newspaper. While it seems nearly impossible to miss that Mary Ostrowski must have played basketball somewhere and sometime in her life, seeing her today as an accomplished executive, one can almost forgive the momentary lapse.

With a quiet and humble exterior, on first impression Mary Ostrowski's determination and focus might be missed. But this Lady Vol speaks volumes through her actions. Growing up with two brothers and a sister in Parkersburg, West Virginia, Mary remembers playing sports right along with her brothers. She was on a basketball team in elementary and junior high school, and when high school play entered state-wide competition, her basketball talents became evident. "Title IX was just coming into play,"

she remembers. "Parkersburg Catholic was known during that era for its talented basketball players. We went to state tournaments, won two out of three years, and during my time there we had a career record of about ninety-three wins and three losses. We had a great coach and great players."

Mary attributes her athletic development to her father and high school coaches: "My dad allowed and encouraged me to play in a time when some parents wouldn't permit daughters this opportunity. He worked on skills with me. My high school coaches for the girls' and boys' teams gave me lots of help and support."

In fact, it was the hook shot taught by her father that especially captured the attention of Pat Head (Summitt). Traveling to visit family in Texas one summer, Mary (or "Mo," as she was often called) remained there with her uncle to attend a basketball camp. Pat Head (Summitt)'s fame from the 1976 Olympics was high on Mary's mind, so when basketball camp gave her the opportunity to meet Pat, she was thrilled, and her college future was sealed. As she says:

All those memories are so vivid. I knew that I wanted to play for Pat. I remember my scholarship papers. She sent the paperwork and kept calling. "Who are you going to sign with, Mo?" Pat asked. "I don't know," I responded. Pat kept after me. We are both stubborn. I couldn't commit even on the day of signing. The scholarship papers are null and void at midnight on signing day. I called Pat at 11:59 that night—that's the time I signed them. Whatever is going on with an eighteen-year-old trying to make a decision like that? I remember it as such an excit-

Mary Ostrowski shares memories as a Lady Volunteer Hall of Fame inductee, 2006.

ing time. I can see us right now: we were all around the kitchen table—my family, coach. It was a big decision.

Mo played international ball between high school and college, and the exposure to high-caliber players prepared her well for the college level of play and discipline. She was ready to face the intensity of Lady Vol basketball: "You have to know that the intensity Pat brings out is challenging. I was a young woman focused on playing basketball. I played because I liked to play, wanted to play—not because of what anyone was going to give me. Pat demands excellence, and if you can survive a practice with Pat, you have done something. You are prepared for life afterwards."

Mary's first step into life after college was to become assistant coach to former Lady Vol assistant coach Nancy Darsch's women's basketball team at Ohio State University. Five years later Mo elected to accept a position with United Parcel Service, transferring her skills to the business arena. The same drive, determination, and desire displayed on the basketball court became trademarks of Mary's business competence. While working full-time, she earned a graduate degree in organizational management. In 2006, in celebration of their one hundredth anniversary, UPS presented Mary as one of five outstanding employees worldwide. In keeping with her character, Mary's comments on her accomplishments are quiet and appreciative. "It's humbling," she says. "I am not one to talk about past accomplishments. I tend to keep that behind me and go forward."

While she goes forward, Mary takes with her the great memories and lessons from her Lady Vol college years: "I especially remember my senior year [1984] at a regional tournament. No one thought Tennessee would make it to the Final Four. Winning that game [Tennessee 73–Georgia 61] by coming from behind—wow—getting to go to Los Angeles—it was so unexpected—a great time." That memory brings to Mo's mind an earlier Final Four experience. She recalls:

It was my freshman year—in Oregon playing Old Dominion, I think, in the semifinals. Pat called timeout and designed our play. I always took the ball out. I was supposed to throw it to Pat Hatmaker. As we got out of the huddle, Pat came up to me and, with a face of panic, whispered, 'I don't want the ball—don't throw it to me.' I don't

Mary Ostrowski

Sports Stats

- US Olympic Festival, 1978–79
- US Junior National Team, 1978, 1979, 1980
- US National Team, 1981, 1982, 1983
- NCAA Final Four appearance, 1981, 1982, 1984
- Led team in scoring, 1981–82, 1983–84
- Led team in rebounding, 1981–82, 1982–83, 1983–84
- SEC All-Tournament Team, 1982
- Kodak All-America, 1982
- All-SEC, 1982, 1984
- World University Games Gold Medalist, 1983
- NCAA Regional Tournament Most Outstanding Player (Mideast), 1984
- NCAA All-Regional Tournament Teams (Mideast), 1984
- NCAA All–Final Four Team, 1984 (leading scorer, leading rebounder)
- Member of Tennessee 1,000 Point Club with 1,729 career points
- Member of Tennessee 1,000 Rebound Club with 1,001 career rebounds
- Tied for fifth place in UT record books for blocked shots in a single game with six rebounds (as of 2006)

Academic Stats

- B.S., Business Administration, University of Tennessee, 1985
- M.S., organizational management, Tusculum College, 2001

Postcollegiate Career Highlights

- Executive business coach
- United Parcel Service, service excellence manager
- Assistant coach, Ohio State University, 1984–89
- Lady Volunteer Hall of Fame

remember who I threw it to, but it wasn't to Pat Hatmaker. Out of the corner of my eye I could see Coach coming out of her chair, and I avoided all eye contact. We won the game [Tennessee 68–Old Dominion University 65], and since it all turned out OK, Coach was OK—I think.

Changing roles from being a student-athlete to a coach and then to a business professional suggests a number of transitions. Mo acknowledges that after college one of the greatest challenges facing student-athletes can be described by the question, "What do you do after the ball stops bouncing?" From her earliest memories basketball filled Mary's life, framed her relationships with family and friends, and even guided her college choice. Following graduation Mary felt challenged by the pathways her life would take. What did she do when the ball stopped bouncing?

I persevered, determined my goals, and kept going forward. What do I leave behind? It appears easy for some—harder for others to move on. Follow your heart—do it because you want to do it—not because someone is telling you to do it. If you truly believe in your dream, it can come true.

And what about that hook shot? With a slow, sly smile, Mo says, "It's still fun to watch and still fun to do."

Mary Ostrowski eludes opposing defenders with her signature hook shot.

Spotlight:
Tanya Haave
Volleyball, 1980, 1984
Basketball, 1980–84

Tanya Haave

Tanya Haave was a competitive force on volleyball and basketball courts.

La Machine

They called her La Machine. She could shoot with relentless accuracy. She led the Lady Vol volleyball team with 756 kills. She bore weapons of strength, precision, and intelligence. She was a fierce competitor. She came from the mountains of the West. She is Tanya Haave.

When just a young girl growing up in Evergreen, Colorado, Tanya knew that she loved sports. Her younger brother asked for a basketball hoop on the garage door, but she was the one who ended up playing with it. They lived high in the Rocky Mountains, and many a day she shoveled snow and then spent hours shooting. "I started playing basketball when I was in the fourth or fifth grade—ten or eleven years old," she recalls. "I didn't start playing volleyball until the eighth grade when they had it in junior high for us. I would play basketball year round but I would only play volleyball when it was in season. I liked basketball a lot better. I mean, I liked volleyball, but basketball was my passion. I remember watching it on TV with my dad, and the defending and the shooting—all the different skills—it was just fun for me. It was a way to compete, and I'm competitive."

Tanya grew up playing a variety of sports throughout the year, and she really liked the pace and flexibility that came with the changing seasons. She ran track and played volleyball and basketball in high school. Drawn to her favorite pastime, basketball consumed all her free hours, and she played throughout the summer. "I was so lucky because I got to run track and play volleyball in addition to basketball," she says. "The variety helped avoid burnout and I was able to train other muscles through the other sports I played."

When her senior year approached, Tanya began looking at colleges with the goal to play both basketball and volleyball. She remembers:

Back then there was not even an early signing period. I was making my visits in December of my senior year. Things have changed a lot since then. It was back in the AIAW days before the NCAA was the governing body of women's basketball. And there were not paid visits. So anyone who was going anywhere had to pay for their own visits. I got a letter from Tennessee, and my high school coach said that she thought it could be a good place for me. So I called them. Recruiting then was not what it is today. They made phone calls but not as early on as today. I called Pat [Summitt], and she said to come on out for a visit. So I went to Tennessee, Georgia, and North Carolina State on my first round of recruiting visits.

Even though I went to Tennessee to visit basketball, I met the volleyball coach [Bob Bertucci] too. It worked out great because I was able to do that. And Pat said I could play both sports my freshman year and we would see how it worked out. On my visit to Tennessee, the basketball team played Louisiana Tech at home. I knew after my visit I wanted to go to Tennessee. That was in December of my senior year. By February I knew for sure. I had kept talking to Pat. We talked about what I wanted and what they were looking for. It just seemed like a great fit for me.

Tanya Haave

Sports Stats

- US Junior National Team, 1981
- US Olympic Festival, 1981
- Second-place team, AIAW Championships, 1981
- Team leader in free-throw percentage for three consecutive seasons, 1981–82, 1982–83, 1983–84
- Third-place team, NCAA Championships, 1982
- US National Team, 1982
- SEC All-Tournament Team, 1982
- Team leader in scoring with 18.6 points per game, 1982–83
- Kodak All-America, 1983
- All-SEC Team, 1983, 1984
- NCAA All-Regional Tournament Teams (Mideast), 1983, 1984
- Academic All-America Team, 1983 (Third Team), 1984 (First Team)
- Academic All-America, 1983, 1984
- Academic All-SEC, 1983, 1984
- NCAA Postgraduate Scholarship Winner, 1984
- Second-place team, NCAA Championships, 1984
- Member of Tennessee 1,000 Point Club with 1,771 Points
- Volleyball: 1980 school record holder: 756 kills; 1,631 attacks; 92 aces; 164 blocks; 1980 All-State, All-SEC, All-Region II

Academic Stats

- B.S., Communications, University of Tennessee, 1985

So, the 1980 UT freshman class included a new dazzling and eager Lady Vol. Living on her own in a different region of the country and facing a different level of academic intensity presented challenges typical to freshmen in transition. Adding the rigors of two intercollegiate sports introduced even more factors. Tanya found comfort in the volunteer family provided for Lady Vol student-athletes.

"I went through probably a five-to-six-month adjustment period," Tanya says. "The Boost-Her Club provided each freshman with a family. I tell you, my family was a godsend for me. They were great, and I still keep in touch with them—Donna and Scott Trimble. They were awesome people and helped me get through typical freshman transition issues. Because of NCAA regulations, schools can't provide that anymore, but it really helped me adapt."

That adjustment period did not detract from Tanya's performance. On the court and in the classroom, she excelled, earning high honors and accolades. She was voted All-SEC in both volleyball and basketball, the only Lady Vol to hold that distinction. It was her basketball prowess that earned her a notable nickname. "My freshman year we were playing Southern California at home," she recalls. "It was in mid-February, and we were in the middle of a slump. I came off the bench and had a good shooting game, making 21 points. The newspaper said something about my being a shooting machine, and my teammates started calling me 'La Machine.'"

After her freshman year, Tanya decided to concentrate on one sport, basketball. The team flourished during her tenure. Some of Tanya's best memories are of the close, nail-biter games. "We were playing Southern Cal in the Elite Eight in Knoxville," she says. "The game went to overtime, and I remember Shelia Collins having just a phenomenal game, especially a couple of steals for lay-ups that put the game away for us. To be able to win a game like that at home was extremely special."

Tanya especially recalls the thrill of playing against Southern California for the National Championship in her 1983–84 senior season:

Well, I was pretty lucky because at my last game—our seniors' last game—we played against Southern California in Pauley Pavilion for the National Championship. We were ranked fifteenth, and no one expected us to go to the Final Four and to play Southern Cal with the McGee twins [Pamela and Paula], Cheryl Miller, and Cynthia Cooper. They said we didn't have a chance. We just came together at that point of the season, and it was a game where we controlled the tempo most of the game. Then they had about two minutes of their game and ended up winning. But it was the kind of game that even though we lost, Pat said we gave it our all and had nothing to be ashamed of. Even though we ended up losing and wished we could have won that championship, it was still a good feeling. So that's a game that I will always remember.

When Tanya's basketball eligibility ended, she returned to volleyball and treated fans to one more year of competition as a Lady Vol.

Following graduation, Tanya's professional career took her around the globe.

Head Coach Tanya Haave in the huddle with her University of San Francisco women's basketball team. Courtesy, Tanya Haave.

She played in France, Italy, Sweden, and Australia. After fourteen years, Tanya decided to pursue basketball from a different direction. "All through college," she says, "I admired Pat Summitt so much; I thought I would like to do what she does. And I looked at how she was able to help people and help people develop. After graduation I wasn't completely sure whether to keep playing or start coaching. I ended up going overseas and playing for fourteen years. But I always had in the back of my mind that I wanted to coach. I just wanted to be involved in the game."

Now head coach for women's basketball at the University of San Francisco, Tanya has found a way to stay involved from a significant vantage point: "What I like most about coaching is seeing how your players come in as freshmen and how much they change and grow by the time they leave as seniors. It's so satisfying to see individuals and teams achieve their goals and dreams!"

Reflecting on her own career so far, Tanya acknowledges that the transitional times in life can be the most difficult and exciting. She attributes her success to the support she always had from parents, coaches, teammates, and community friends. She carries her lessons from these experiences to her coaching role today.

"Transitions can be difficult," she observes. "And now with my first senior class here, there may be some ways I can help them. This first class of seniors at USF is going to have an easy transition to the 'real' world. They are great people and they have balance. They are ready to move on to the next chapter of their lives. Now they may come back to me in six months and say, 'I don't know what I am going to do without basketball.'

Tanya Haave

But I do think that is part of our jobs—to help our students with that change."

Tanya looks to her Lady Vol playing days as a significant learning ground where she developed confidence and resilience. "You go through some ups and downs during your college career, and I learned that I have the mentality to do whatever it takes to succeed," she comments. "I think that is the biggest thing. Commitment and discipline are what I took away from the UT program. And working with a team—if you work as a team, all that individual stuff will take care of itself. Just when you are dealing with a little adversity, to say, 'We are going to get through this.' Everyone is going to have a little adversity every now and then; the key is what you are going to do with that adversity. Are you going to quit or try your best to get through it?"

Thinking of young women meeting their own life challenges, Tanya conveys her advice: "Never give up on your dreams. And dream big. I was a little girl from Evergreen, Colorado, and I got to see the world and play basketball for one of the elite basketball programs in the country. Live your dreams, find whatever it is you are passionate about, and go for it! If you are passionate about something and love it, everything will fall into place. Follow your dreams and know there are no limitations on what you can do with your life!"

Tanya Haave lives by the motto "whatever it takes." La Machine is still a sharp shooter. She has shifted from ball handling to something more far-reaching as she coaches others to shoot for their own dreams and find their own victories.

Left to right: Debbie Groover (52; 1977-81), Paula Towns (51; 1980–84), Cindy Noble (32; 1978–81), and Karla Horton (55; 1984–87).

Spotlight
Ten National
Champions
Track and Field, 1981

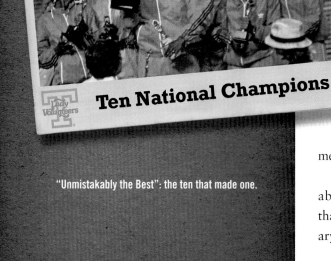

Ten National Champions

"Unmistakably the Best": the ten that made one.

The "Ten That Made One"

Fall 1980 began like every other fall term at the University of Tennessee. Cars crowded the campus as students unloaded their belongings, waved goodbye to their families, and greeted new and old friends. Approximately 3,500 freshmen enrolled on that September day—each one carrying a special set of hopes and dreams.

As the students arrived, some of them might have glanced over at the track and marveled that some students were already running laps. Had they looked a little more closely, they might have seen that these students were working hard and wore faces of determination and focus. An even closer examination might have revealed that these student-athletes also felt excitement and anticipation.

But probably no one really thought much about it. How could they have known that it was the beginning of an extraordinary year?

A few weeks earlier, Coach Terry Crawford had prepared for the arrival of her University of Tennessee women's track team. Her assistant coach, Andy Roberts, and graduate assistant, Denise Wood, joined her as they anticipated the young women who would be arriving on campus. Among the numbers, ten particular young women were on their way.

From Harriman, Tennessee, Sharrieffa Barksdale was eager to begin her freshman year as a Lady Volunteer. Especially inspired by the incomparable Wilma Rudolph, Sharrieffa's eyes were set on Olympic gold.

Freshman Kathy Bryant was attracted to the warmer Tennessee climate after growing up in Columbus, Ohio. Kathy loved running and would earn the nickname "Pac Man" because of the way she would "eat up" her competition as she passed them in the distance races.

Myrtle Chester (Ferguson) joined her freshman teammates from Laurel, Maryland. Already an accomplished international performer, Myrtle represented her native Guyana at the 1979 Junior Pan Am Games in Canada and in the 1980 Caribbean Games.

Also experienced in international competition, Joetta Clark (Diggs) arrived from South Orange, New Jersey. This number-one high school recruit came to Tennessee because of the commitment she saw in Coach Terry Crawford. She not only shared Crawford's goal for a National title but also set her sights on Olympic gold.

Throughout her high school career, Benita Fitzgerald (Mosley)'s coach took her team to visit the University of Tennessee. When the time came to select her college, there was no contest. Benita already knew she had a fit with the Lady Volunteers. As a sophomore, this decorated hurdler was returning from Dale City, Virginia, and would see Olympic gold in her future.

Hailing from Chesterfield, Ontario, Canadian Rosemarie Hauch was looking forward to her junior year at Tennessee. Rosemarie consistently earned big points for the Lady Vols as a shot put and discus thrower. She would provide team leadership as the captain this year.

Another thrower, Pam Passera, arrived from Peters Township, Pennsylvania. In her high school career she earned eleven varsity letters in volleyball, basketball, softball, and track and field. It was the javelin that would become the tool of choice for this freshman. On her recruiting visit, she instantly connected to the enthusiastic and friendly Tennessee campus.

Linda Portasik from Alexandria, Virginia, was returning to the team as a sophomore. The mid-distance runner not only excelled in sports but was also a top academic scholar. Active throughout the campus community, Linda thrived on the diverse opportunities available to University of Tennessee students.

A freshman from Kingston, Jamaica, Cathy Rattray (Williams) especially liked the friendly atmosphere of the UT community. She was motivated by Coach Crawford's enthusiasm and commitment to track and field. When she met Benita Fitzgerald (Mosley) on her campus visit, she knew that Tennessee would be her college home. International and Olympic competition would be in her future.

Returning from Detroit, Michigan, Delisa Walton was ready for her sophomore year as a Lady Vol. The mid-distance runner already was motivated by the strong dedication of Coach Crawford. She would prove to be a key to the success of the Lady Vols and would become an international performer.

They were ten student-athletes. They had ten championship dreams. Coach Terry Crawford remembers that fall and the development of the team:

That was just a really special team that came together. And wow—when I look back on that, I don't think we realized how good we were. What a blessing when athletes like

Benita Fitzgerald and Delisa Walton chose to come to Tennessee. They were Olympic caliber when they walked in the door.

A nucleus of a team like that and some great opportunities to get some great athletes—what fun it was to go across the country and make a name for ourselves! They were just driven athletes. They were great competitors. And they really bonded together as a group.

That fall in 1980, these ten student-athletes came with their own reasons to win and their own life experiences, but they all found common ground through shared values of respect for best effort, strength in community, and pride in the school they represented.

Sharrieffa Barksdale came with a ready-made goal. With five sisters and a brother, she grew up knowing the importance of hard work and responsibility. Her father died when Sharrieffa was nine, and her mother, Carrie Barksdale, worked as many jobs as needed to support her family. Her mother's strong dedication to her children and grounding in her faith taught Sharrieffa the values and priorities of faith, family, and work. When her brother, Val Barksdale, entered the University of Tennessee as a member of football Coach Johnny Majors's first class in 1977, there was no doubt that Sharrieffa would be motivated to become a Lady Volunteer. She had the discipline and drive to work hard and the desire to be at the University of Tennessee. She just needed one more element to prepare her for the next step.

When she was a freshman in high school, Sharrieffa asked the librarian to help her

Sharrieffa Barksdale, 1980–84

Sports Stats

- Helped Tennessee win 1981 AIAW Outdoor National Championship
- Claimed SEC Outdoor long jump titles, 1981, 1983
- Aided UT's first-place 4x100-meter relay unit, 1982
- Ran on victorious league outdoor 4x400-meter relay teams, 1981, 1982, 1983
- Two-time All-America in 400-meter hurdles, finishing second in 1983
- Roared to SEC Outdoor 100-meter title, 1982, and 400-meter hurdles crowns, 1983, 1984
- Won 440-yard dash and anchored 4x440-yard relay to victory as UT won inaugural SEC Indoor Championship meet in 1984
- US Olympian in 400-meter hurdles, 1984
- Twelve-time All-America
- Five-time National Champion on Lady Vol relays
- Assisted on six other runner-up national team finishes
- Ranks second in Lady Vol annals with eleven total SEC titles (six indoors/five outdoors)
- SEC Indoor Championships record holder in the 440-yard dash
- School record-holder for 400-meter hurdles and with 800-meter medley relay

Postcollegiate Career Highlights

- Employment specialist, Goodwill Industries of Kentucky
- Assistant coach, track and field, Henry Clay High School, Lexington, Kentucky
- Founder and director, Kentucky Diamonds/KD Boys, a dance team of inner-city children who perform community service through performance
- President (with partner, four-time Olympian Johnny Gray), JS & Associates Innovation in Motivation (speak at prisons throughout the United States)
- Owner, Savebucks Travel Agency

From Left to Right: Delisa Walton, topping the marks in 800-meter runs, 800-meter relays, and 4x400 meter relays, won nine National Championships and was a twelve-time All-America. Benita Fitzgerald, five-time National Champion and fourteen-time All-America, claimed gold in the 100-meter hurdles at the 1984 Olympics. Sharrieffa Barksdale, twelve-time All America, brought legendary speed to the Lady Vols' 1981 championship team. Kathy Bryant, four-time All-America, hailed as one of the fastest distance runners in the country. Joetta Clark, record setter in the 880-yard indoor run and outdoor 800-meter run, was a fifteen-time All-America and on four US Olympic teams.

From Left to Right: Myrtle Chester, three-time All-America, set UT records in the heptathlon. Rosemarie Hauch, six-time All-America, was captain of the 1981 AIAW National Championship team and record-setter in shot put. Linda Portasik, two-time All-America, stands among the Lady Volunteer top-ten all-time outdoor performers in the 1500-meter, mile, and 300-meter events. Cathy Rattray, collected seventeen All-America citations and represented Jamaica in four Olympiads. Pam Passera was one of UT's all-time outdoor performers in javelin and captured All-America honors.

Sharrieffa Barksdale

Postcollegiate Career Highlights (continued)

- Vice president, USA Track and Field Alumni Association
- Assistant coach for USA World Junior Track and Field Team in Italy, 2004
- Liaison for Junior USA Pan American Track and Field Team, 2005
- Pool manager for the World Junior Championship in Beijing, China, 2006
- Pool manager for the World Championships in Osaka, Japan, 2007

Kathy Bryant, 1980–83, 1985

Sports Stats

- Placed eighth in 1980 at the AIAW Championships and ninth in 1981 at the NCAA Championships
- Helped UT win 1981 AIAW Outdoor National Championship
- Three-time SEC Outdoor Champion, winning 5000 meter, 1981 and 1982, and taking 3000-meter crown, 1981
- Won NCAA Outdoor 5000-meter run, 1982
- Runner-up at NCAA District III cross-country meet, 1982
- Was AIAW Indoor runner-up in both the two-mile and three-mile runs, 1982
- Posted three top-ten national finishes in cross country with a best of seventh in 1982
- School record holder in outdoor 5000 meter
- UT indoor record holder for three miles
- Second on UT indoor performers list for two miles
- Four-time track and field All-America
- Three-time All-America in cross country

Postcollegiate Career Highlights

- Outside Sales Representative since 1991

find a book about Wilma Rudolph. When asked why she would want that book, Sharrieffa responded that she was going to be in the Olympics someday. The librarian said, "Silly child, you will never be in the Olympics." Left on her own, Sharrieffa found that book and read it cover to cover. Determined to reach her goals, Sharrieffa ran track and single-handedly won every event at the state meet her senior year. The University of Tennessee offered her a partial scholarship. Sharrieffa knew that she could work hard enough to earn a full scholarship.

Before she graduated from high school, a telephone call provided her with the last ingredient to motivate her success. When she answered the phone, Sharrieffa heard a voice say, "This is Wilma Rudolph." Believing that her friend was playing a trick on her, Sharrieffa said, "Get out of here," and hung up the phone. When the phone rang again, Ralph Boston [Olympic athlete and UT administrator] was on the line and said, "Sharreiffa, do you know who you hung up on?" Sharreiffa said tentatively, "Was it my friend playing jokes on me?" Ralph said, "No, it was Wilma Rudolph."

"I couldn't believe it!" she says. "Then Wilma Rudolph came to the phone and gave me some very encouraging words that I heed to this day: 'Sharrieffa, follow your dreams; be all that you can be, because you can do anything.'"

Armed with the work ethic of her mother, the Tennessee spirit of her brother, and the belief that she can achieve her dreams from the example of Wilma Rudolph, Sharrieffa Barksdale came to win.

Kathy Bryant also knew the power of family support. The youngest of five chil-

dren, Kathy used to play under the bleachers while her brother Tom ran track. It was Tom who encouraged her to try running, and Kathy fell in love with the sport. Providing support without pressure, her parents, Ernie and Pat Bryant, enabled Kathy to keep the fun in running while still striving to be her best. "I am so lucky for the support I had growing up and to have such great coaching," she says. "Terry was a genius. She could have told me to eat spaghetti for breakfast, and I would have done it. We learned to conduct ourselves with class—win or lose."

One of the fastest distance runners in the country, Kathy would set new records to enable many Tennessee wins. Kathy brought to the team her competitive desire to win and willingness to work hard. She also valued the support generated through her extended Volunteer Family at Tennessee. "We were matched with UT fans who were willing to be volunteer 'parents' to us," she recalls. "My parents were the Sullivans [Dr. and Mrs. William]. Being more than six hours from home, it was great for someone like me. I remember it was nice to spend a Sunday afternoon with them and then enjoy a home-cooked meal. It was great to know that we were valued as much as the other student-athletes at a school that is known for its football program."

Academic success is a prerequisite to athletic competition for Lady Vols, and Kathy remembers that part of her UT experience as well: "Joetta Clark (Diggs) and I had an accounting class together our freshman year. We just weren't 'getting it' at first. I thought Joetta was overly worked up about our first test results, proclaiming over and over, 'My dad is going to kill me!' I mean, she was

Myrtle Chester (Ferguson), 1980–84

Sports Stats

- SEC Outdoor runner-up in heptathlon, 1981
- 1981 AIAW Outdoor National Championship
- Three-time track and field All-America
- SEC Outdoor champion in heptathlon, 1982, 1984
- NCAA Outdoor heptathlon runner-up, 1984
- UT record-holder for highest heptathlon score
- SEC Outdoor runner-up in high jump, 1983
- National Sports Festival heptathlon runner-up, 1983
- SEC Outdoor runner-up in high jump and long jump and third in 100-meter hurdles, 1984
- Inaugural SEC Commissioner's Trophy winner at 1984 outdoor meet as the top-scoring female
- All-SEC performer all four seasons

Academic Stats

- B.S., Business Administration, University of Tennessee 1984

Postcollegiate Career Highlights

- TAC National Indoor pentathlon champion, 1985
- 1985 TAC National Indoor pentathlon champion, 1985
- Head track and field coach, University of Tennessee, 1998–2002

Joetta Clark (Diggs), 1980–84

Sports Stats

- Member of US National Team (800 meter), 1979–2000
- Two-time Olympic Festival Champion 1979, 1980
- Pan-American Juniors Champion and US Junior Champion, 1980
- 1981 AIAW Outdoor National Championship
- On three SEC victorious outdoor 4x400-meter relay teams, 1981–1983
- Outdoor 800-meter SEC champion, 1981, 1983, 1984
- Outdoor 1500-meter SEC champion, 1982, 1983

Joetta Clark (Diggs)

Sports Stats (continued)

- Outdoor 800-meter national champion, 1983, 1984 (second in 1982, third in 1981)
- Indoor 880-yard SEC winner and 4x880-yard relay champ, 1984
- Fifteen-time All-America
- Nine-time national champion (five individual, four relays)
- Eleven-time All-Southeastern Conference selection
- Ten-time SEC champion (six individual, four relays)
- Holds SEC records (standing as of 2006) in the 880-yard run (2:08.29, 1984) and outdoors in the 800-meter run (2:01.15, 1984)

Academic Stats

- B.S., Communications, University of Tennessee
- M.S., Education, University of Tennessee

Postcollegiate Career Highlights

- Lady Volunteer track and field volunteer assistant coach, 1985–1987
- Four-time US Olympian (800m), 1988, 1992, 1996, 2000
- Top finish was seventh in 1992 Olympics
- Two-time bronze medalist at World Indoor Championships, 1993, 1997
- Six-time US Indoor Champion, 1988, 1989, 1990, 1996, 1997, 1998
- Five-time US Outdoor Champion, 1988, 1989, 1992, 1993, 1994
- Captain of Women's Olympic Team, 2000
- Member of Clark family US 800-meter trio to qualify for Sydney Olympiad in 2000, with sister-in-law Jearl Miles-Clark and sister Hazel Clark
- New Jersey's Athlete of the Century, 2000
- Lady Volunteer Hall of Fame, Inaugural 2001 Class
- Distinguished Honoree Award for Somerset County Commission on the Status of Women, 2001
- New Jersey Scholastic Coaches Association Distinguished Award, 2001

hammering that issue. I thought, 'Wow—my dad is going to be ticked too, but chill out.' Then, I came to find out that Joetta's father is Joe Clark, the tough high school principal whose life was chronicled in the movie *Lean on Me*. Gulp!"

Joetta's father was a significant role model. He and Joetta's mother, Jetta, provided direction and focus. They challenged her to be prepared and to believe that "the sky was the limit." She says, "I responded well to my parents' discipline. I always trained hard and knew I was ready to compete. Preparation makes the difference. I sacrificed and was committed. I live by the motto that 'Failure is not an option—it is just a nagging reality to keep you focused.' One must have the capacity to be made focused and disciplined in order to be successful."

Jo, as she was called by her teammates, was inspired by the women leading Tennessee athletics. For the first time she saw women in power and began to realize the possibilities for her future. "I gained much from being a Lady Vol," she comments. "Seeing women in power—Gloria [Ray], Pat [Summitt], Debby Jennings, and Terry—that was the first time I had seen women working in the sports world, outside of my mother. The athletic directors and coaches I had known were all men. Now I could envision the different careers you could have in the sport."

Benita Fitzgerald (Mosley) agrees that the leadership of the women's athletic department created a strong support base and inspired her career advocating women's advancement:

The women's athletic department being a separate entity from the men's played a huge key to my growth as an athlete and put a different timbre on the process. Our coaches had the autonomy to send us to meets that we needed for competition to be positioned at the top. I knew that people cared about me and still care about me. My academic and athletic successes were equally important. I want to help other women have the same gold medal experiences in their own lives— to find their niche, to apply their passion and exceed beyond their dreams. I want to help them have the courage to take a risk when they could very easily maintain. We used to do an exercise on the track that would force us out of our comfort zone. Terry would put the hurdles closer together, and we would run against the wind. This would create a different experience and sometimes we had a fear of falling. With practice and mental courage we could extend ourselves to a new comfort zone. This is what we need to do to move forward in our lives.

Eager to move forward in her life, Rosemarie Hauch brought to Tennessee her eagerness to see the world and expand her horizons. Her parents emigrated from Germany to Ontario, Canada, where they kept a dairy farm. Hard work was a given in Rosemarie's life. When she discovered her talents at shot put and discus, she knew this would be a means to realize her dreams. Called "Imp" by her teammates, Rosemarie's strength was legendary and also the center of memorable stories. Javelin thrower Pam Passera recalls one such experience: "Our throwing unit couldn't practice if the weather was bad. One day we had a heavy snow, so Rosemarie, throwers' coach Denise [Wood], Susan [Thornton], and I went to a pizza restaurant near campus. A Volkswagen Beetle had gotten stuck in a snow bank. Rosemarie literally picked up this man's car and put it in the middle of the street."

Rosemarie smiles at that memory and adds, "We had fun. I guess our goals were a lot similar—to compete, to have fun and to do the best we could. And go for broke. I had a strong mind and a strong heart and I was stubborn. I will tell you that. There are times it worked for me and against me."

Love of sports and competition is also in the spirit that Pam Passera brought to the team. Distinguished as a javelin thrower, Pam embraced the entire Lady Vol program. "Looking back—wow it was a special time—at the time we didn't know it," she says. "We had all just come out of high school. We all excelled at something, and we all got together. It was the first thing we did before school started—all the teams had a meeting together at Stokely Athletic Center. We got to meet everybody. There was no one on campus—just us. The coaches and staff told us that we are the Lady Vols and would always have someone to go to. That kick-started us for a good year. I would see other Lady Vols coming to watch us. We just gelled as a group and saw each other constantly. We would hang out in the TV room in Stokely every afternoon."

Pam's personal motto is: "Everything you do is a reflection upon yourself." This commitment to giving her best underscores the values that Coach Terry Crawford instilled in the team. "We worked hard and talked about taking on that Tennessee pride in terms of how we competed and how we looked and how we wanted to be the most fashionable athletes on the track," Crawford recalls. "We

wanted to have this demeanor of winners and we didn't show disappointment or defeat. It was an attitude that we cultivated."

Benita Fitzgerald (Mosley) echoes the words of her coach and teammates when she points to their Tennessee pride: "When we walked into a stadium, people took notice. So we felt pride rise up in us when we wore that Tennessee uniform. We were the ones to beat—they were looking out for us—to beat us individually and as a team."

Benita's talents and energy combined with Terry Crawford's dedication to the Lady Vols drew Cathy Rattray (Williams) into the fold. Like her teammates, Cathy found that her Volunteer family helped to cultivate a close and welcoming community for the freshmen. "I always tell people who are going away to school that I had a ready-made family," she says. "We got to know our athletic director, coaches, other Lady Vols, and fans. It turned out that my volunteer family even knew people from my home town in Jamaica."

Thriving on competition, Cathy was motivated by the thrill of competition. She too experienced the pride that is generated from being a Lady Vol and developing team unity. "I did track because I was successful at it," she comments. "I ran track to go to college and enjoyed it. We had good relationships with teammates and coaches. Every year was fun. We traveled—flew almost everywhere. When we did take a bus, it was an adventure. We were successful, so we were invited to meets and got to travel many places and meet so many people. You worked out for your teammates—for the entire Lady Vol program. We were friends with other sports teams. On top of that, a lot of team members went on to international teams. Every year good things happened."

Joetta Clark (Diggs)

Postcollegiate Career Highlights (continued)

- Received the New Jersey Pioneer Woman of the 90s Award
- Inducted into Millrose Games Hall of Fame at Madison Square Garden, 2002
- Received the Visa Humanitarian Award, Distinguished Honoree
- President, Joetta Sports & Beyond, LLC
- Producer and host of Fitkidz, NJ, a cable fitness show
- Appointed by the governor as a commissioner, New Jersey Sports and Exposition Authority
- Chosen as *Sports Illustrated* hometown hero

Benita Fitzgerald (Mosley), 1980–84

Sport Stats

- US Olympic Trials runner-up (100-meter hurdles), 1980
- Made Olympic Team in 1980 but unable to compete due to US boycott
- Two-time US Olympic qualifier in the 100-meter hurdles, 1980, 1984
- Helped Tennessee win 1981 AIAW Outdoor National Championship
- Part of UT's victorious 4x800-meter relay, 1981
- US Indoor Champion (60-yard hurdles), 1981
- Ran second leg of National Champion 800-meter medley relay, 1981
- Won SEC 200-meter titles, 1981, 1982
- Claimed first three SEC 100-meter hurdles titles, 1981, 1982, 1983
- Captured SEC 100-meter crowns, 1981, 1983
- Claimed 100-meter hurdles titles in 1981, 1982, 1983 (third, 1980)
- Member of Tennessee's victorious 4x100-meter relay, 1982, and runner-up squad, 1981
- Won 60-yard hurdles, 1982 AIAW Indoor Championships, IAAF World Championships, eighth-place finisher (100-meter hurdles), 1983

Benita Fitzgerald (Mosley)

Sports Stats (continued)

- Gold medalist, Pan American Games, 1983
- US Outdoor Champion (100-meter hurdles), 1983, 1986
- Won gold medal in Los Angeles at the 1984 Games (100-meter hurdles)
- Alternate, 1988 US Olympic Team
- Member of US National Teams (60-yard/meter hurdles, 100-meter hurdles)
- Fifteen-time All-America
- Five-time National Champion (four individual, one relay)
- Ten-time All-Southeastern Conference selection
- Nine-time SEC outdoor champion (seven individual, two relays)

Academic Stats

- B.S., Engineering, University of Tennessee, 1984

Postcollegiate Career Highlights

- Named "Hurdler of the Decade" for the 1980s by Track and Field News
- United States Olympic Committee, varying roles, 1995–2001
- Lady Volunteer Hall of Fame, Inaugural 2001 Class
- One of eight US Olympians to carry the Olympic Flag into the stadium during the opening ceremonies of the Centennial Olympic Games in Atlanta
- Named 1996 Distinguished Service Award winner by the US Sports Academy
- Honored with a street named Benita Fitzgerald Drive in her hometown, Dale City, VA
- Named "Sportswoman of the Century" by The Potomac News
- Named "Top Female Sports Figure of the Century from Virginia" by Sports Illustrated
- Virginia Sports Hall of Fame
- Virginia High School Hall of Fame

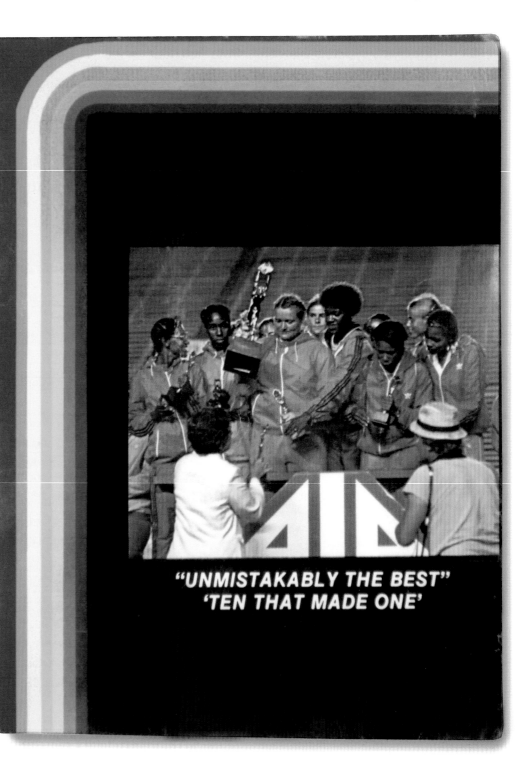

"UNMISTAKABLY THE BEST"
'TEN THAT MADE ONE'

Because Cathy is central to a story that several of her teammates recall with laughter, Cathy has earned the right to tell it: "We were competing in the mile relay at a dual meet in California. I forgot to pass the baton. I will never forget. I had something else on my mind, and I was thinking about those things instead of thinking about the race. So, they told us to take our sweats off, and so, I went into the infield with the baton, took off my sweats, and went to the parking lot. And Sharrieffa was the second leg, and she was right there and said, 'Where did she go?' I was the third leg. I took off running and didn't have the baton in my hand. They blew the whistle, but the Stanford coach said to keep going. It wasn't funny at the time."

Laughing together and working hard together are indications of a solid team. Delisa Walton treasures the unity they shared. From bringing determination and stamina to the team, they learned how to work together and experienced the power that results. She worked hard because she loved her team and had a deep respect for her coach.

Terry Crawford did hold fast to the standards set for the team. "I can remember having some stern conversations about how people responded when there were some lackadaisical performances and how they could turn that around," she says. "I think our team was an example that young women were ready to be challenged and were ready to make a mark in that whole arena of being able to attach themselves to a goal, whether it was to a team or an organization."

And so the fall of 1980 came to a close, and a new year unfolded. Ready to meet the challenges of the remaining season, the Lady Volunteer track and field team returned to campus. Ten individuals stepped up in the competition—each one with outstanding talent, each one with a reason to compete, and each one with a will to win.

The schedule was demanding and punctuated with successes. The Lady Vols came in first place at the Houston Dual Meet, were voted "Most Outstanding Team" at the Texas Relays, and placed first at the Four Way at Tennessee. Conference competition reached another high point when the Lady Vols won the Southeastern Conference Championship.

May arrived, and ten team members headed for Austin, Texas, to compete in the AIAW National Track and Field Championships. The day of the meet was stormy, and the occasion would be remembered as extending into the night due to severe rain delays. Upon arrival, team members probably prepared much as they had throughout the season.

Sharrieffa ("Ruby Red Lips") was perhaps experiencing her usual prerace jitters, breaking out in hives, arms shaking, and maybe eating a bit of toast and tea.

After an evening of Italian food the night before, Kathy Bryant ("Pac Man") was possibly sizing up the competition and thinking to herself, "We all put on our pants the same way—one leg at a time. We are all human."

Joetta ("Jo") was focused and ready to compete, knowing that she had prepared at her best.

Benita ("Fitz") was most likely warming up on a flight of eight or ten hurdles and rubbing her pressure points to get the adrenalin going.

Benita Fitzgerald (Mosley)

Postcollegiate Career Highlights (continued)

- Penn Relays Hall of Fame
- President and CEO for Women in Cable Telecommunications

Rosemarie Hauch, 1979–82

Sports Stats

- SEC Outdoor Champion in discus, 1981
- Helped Tennessee win 1981 AIAW Outdoor National Championship
- SEC Outdoor Champion in shot put, 1981, 1982
- Won AIAW Indoor title in shot put, 1982
- UT Indoor record-holder in shot put, 1982
- UT Outdoor record-holder in shot put, 1982
- Six-time All-America
- Four-time shot put runner-up at national outdoor meet

Academic Stats

- B.S., Education, University of Tennessee, 1982

Postcollegiate Career Highlights

- Qualified for 1986 Commonwealth Games in England
- Medical transcriptionist, Ottawa Hospital, General Campus
- Member of numerous Canadian National Teams that toured Europe
- Competed in Pan American Games, Caracas, Venezuela
- Competed at the World Championships in power lifting in Switzerland

Pam Passera, 1980–84

Sport Stats

- Helped Tennessee win 1981 AIAW Outdoor National Championship
- SEC Outdoor runner-up in javelin, 1981, 1984
- SEC Outdoor champion in javelin, 1982
- All-America in javelin, 1984
- Finished fourth in javelin at 1984 NCAA Outdoor Championships
- Second on UT's all-time outdoor performers list in javelin

Academic Stats

- B.S., Education, University of Tennessee, 1984

Postcollegiate Career Highlights

- Recreation supervisor, Chanute, Kansas, 1984–87
- Recreation director, Indiana Parks and Recreation Programs, 1987–97
- Maintenance Division, Indiana Parks and Recreation Programs, 1997–present
- Volunteers with Special Olympics
- Volunteer track and field coach for children

Linda Portasik, 1980–83

Sport Stats

- Member of victorious 1981 SEC Outdoor 4x800-meter relay team
- Finished fourth in 1500 meter at 1981 AIAW Indoor Championships
- Helped Tennessee win 1981 AIAW Outdoor National Championship
- SEC Outdoor 1500-meter champion, 1981, 1982
- Academic All-America, 1982
- Placed third in mile at 1982 AIAW Indoor Championships
- Took third in 800 meter at 1982 SEC Outdoor Championships
- Two-time All-America

Rosemarie ("Imp") was mentally centering her strong, determined spirit on the challenge ahead.

Pam could be seen warming up and catching the excitement of all the competition around her.

Cathy Rattray ("Fido") was steadying her nerves by focusing during her warm-up and visualizing her race, wearing mental blinders to look past the competitors.

Delisa ("Dee") was eating a grilled cheese sandwich and French fries.

Whatever those ten Lady Vols really did that day, whatever dreams and experiences they brought to the track that day, only they know.

That day in May, the 1981 Tennessee track and field team finished the meet as National Champions. Team members will tell you that as the meet ended, the sky began to clear, and a double rainbow appeared. They were bringing home the first National Championship trophy of all Lady Vol sports.

That year each team member was so significant to the whole that they found it impossible to single out one as the "Most Valuable Player." In unprecedented fashion for an unprecedented achievement, all members of the University of Tennessee Women's track and field team were honored with the distinction as the "Ten That Made One."

Returning to cheering fans at the Knoxville airport, Rosemarie Hauch remembers being speechless when asked to comment on the win as captain.

Terry Crawford says, "Winning that first National Championship was just like a dream come true. I can't tell you the sense of accomplishment and satisfaction that I had as a coach. It will always be very special to me."

The team came home, and life went on. There would be many personal and team achievements after that day in May. Individual team members would continue to set records and step into international fame. Each would leave Tennessee for other pursuits. But never would they forget that special team and that special year.

Today Sharrieffa Barksdale works with the prison system to help offenders learn job skills, become employed, and create the support systems for successful lives. She dedicates her life to creating better communities for our children and the future. Of the "Ten That Made One" Sharrieffa says, "We were all in tune—we were a family. They are my best friends. It is rare when you can still call your college team your best friends."

Kathy Bryant enjoys her home base in Arizona while working as a sales representative for a national marketing firm and loves the opportunities she has to travel and meet new people. Looking back, she treasures the many great trips she experienced because of her sport, especially her first European trip, which took her to Norway. When asked if she knew how special that 1981 team was, Kathy responds, "We knew it was a huge, awesome, great accomplishment, but we didn't know that we were making history. We were close as a team. It was so cool to have sprinters or throwers cheering for distance runners. In Texas I was supposed to run the 5000 meter at the beginning of the meet. My event had to race at the end due to storms, so I scored the last points. We had already won, but it was great—icing on the cake!"

Myrtle Chester Ferguson, the champion Lady Vol heptathlete, says that "it was a great experience—being a part of UT's rich tradition, and if I had it to do again, I would sign with Tennessee."

Joetta Clark Diggs, president of Joetta Sports & Beyond, LLC, now provides motivational seminars to athletic programs, businesses, and other organizations throughout the country. She has established her own nonprofit foundation to provide mentoring and internships for young people in the sports industry. Joetta also produces a cable fitness show for kids called Fitkidz, NJ. A top-ranking athlete with history-making achievements and a stellar business woman in the sports industry, Joetta has taken women's athletics to new levels and continues opening the doors of possibility for others to come. Joetta remembers that "all of my teammates and each of their attitudes helped me to be a better person—through laughter and heartache."

Benita Fitzgerald Mosley currently serves as president and CEO for Women in Cable Telecommunications. She directs the mission to develop women leaders who transform the cable industry. Benita is extraordinary in her profession, with honors that include being named "Greatest Female Sports Figure of the 20th Century from Virginia" by *Sports Illustrated* in December 1999 and the "Most Powerful Women in Cable" by Cable World Magazine in 2005 and 2006. She has served on the United States Olympic Committee. Of her 1981 Lady Vol team, Benita says:

Star players on a team can go one way or the other. We gelled together as a team. We didn't necessarily love each other—we were individually goal-driven and understood that if we did that, collectively we could win. We cheered on individuals because we knew that would help the team. I knew that my relays had to bring it in. Momentum built around the competition, and one person's accomplishment spurred on your accomplishment. There was no jealousy. As a team we brought home the National Championship. It was even more thrilling because we were a team. I remember the opposite experience my senior year. I was the only person—just me—it was kind of a lonely feeling because we didn't have the team spirit or chance to bring home the title. It was an empty feeling. [Benita won an individual National Title at the NCAA National Championships in 1983. She was the only senior to compete that year.]

Rosemarie Hauch "has been around the world and back." After graduating from Tennessee, Rosemarie continued athletic competition for Canada. She loved to travel and treasures the opportunities she had to see the world. She remembers being in Paris: "I stood on top of the Eiffel Tower at midnight, and the whole city was lit up. And when you are looking out from the tower, the streets of Paris were like a pie. I was in the center of the pie. I get goose bumps talking about it. And I got very emotional. I remember thinking this is so worth it."

Rosemarie returned to her childhood home in Canada where she cares for her father and does medical transcriptions in a hospital. A lifelong learner, Rosemarie is studying as a Reiki practitioner and has reached the seventh of twenty-one levels of mastery. Reiki is a holistic approach to

Linda Portasik

Sports Stats (continued)
- Ranks among top ten on UT's all-time outdoor performers lists in 1500 meter, mile, and 3000 meter
- Ranks among top 10 on UT's all-time indoor performers lists in 1500 meter and mile

Academic Stats
- B.S., Communications, University of Tennessee, 1983
- J.D., University of Virginia

Cathy Rattray (Williams), 1980–84

Sport Stats
- Four-time member of Jamaican Olympic Teams, competing in 1980, 1984, 1988, and 1992 Olympic Games in the 400 meter and 4x400-meter relay
- Was part of four National Champion relays (800-meter medley, 4x400 meter, mile), including two during the Lady Vols' AIAW National Outdoor Team Championship victory in 1981
- Her UT outdoor record in the 400 meter stood from 1982 until 2003, and the 4x400-meter relay she ran with posted a collegiate record in 1982 and still stands as the best Lady Vol unit ever assembled
- Claimed nine SEC titles during her tenure, including back-to-back 400-meter crowns in 1982 and 1983
- Won 600-yard run at the very first SEC Indoor Championship in 1984, and her mark has never been beaten
- Member of 1984 Southeastern Conference Academic Honor Roll
- Claimed five collegiate National Championships as a Lady Vol, including the Indoor 500-meter crown in 1984
- Placed fifth on 4x400-meter relay with Team Jamaica at 1984, 1988. and 1992 Olympiads
- Collected seventeen All-America citations during her career

Cathy Rattray (Williams)

Sports Stats (continued)

- Was also on Tennessee's finest quartets in the 4x800-meter and 800-meter medley relays and is atop the school's indoor 500-meter best-times list

Academic Stats

- B.S., Education, University of Tennessee, 1984

Postcollegiate Career Highlights

- Placed fifth on 4x400-meter relay with Team Jamaica at 1984, 1988, and 1992 Olympiads
- Principal, St. Hugh's Preparatory School
- Lady Volunteer Hall of Fame
- Author of Spanish workbooks and musical compact discs (for which she played the music) used in elementary schools throughout Jamaica

Delisa Walton, 1980–84

Sports Stats

- AIAW Outdoor champion, 1980, and NCAA Outdoor Champion, 1982, in 800-meter run
- Ran on runner-up 800-meter medley relay at 1980 AIAW Outdoor Championships
- SEC Outdoor 400-meter champion, 1981
- Anchored 4x800-meter and 800-meter medley relay to victory at 1981 SEC Outdoor Championships
- AIAW Outdoor runner-up in 800-meter run, 1981
- Set world record in winning 600-meter run at 1981 AIAW Indoor Championships
- Anchored 800-meter medley and 4x400-meter relays to victory at 1981 AIAW Outdoor Championships
- Helped Tennessee win 1981 AIAW Outdoor National Championship
- SEC Outdoor 800-meter champion, 1982
- Anchored 4x400-meter relay to victory at 1982 SEC Outdoor Championships

healthy living and can have beneficial results for people with illness when used in conjunction with traditional medical treatments. Rosemarie is working to teach Reiki to doctors and nurses. Of 1981, Rosemarie says, "That year I will never forget. I was captain of the team, and we were in Austin, Texas. And just before the final relay there was a downpour of rain. They had to squeegee off the track. Then we ran the relay, and we won it. That won the championship. But as the final leg of the relay was running, a double rainbow came over the stadium. I will never forget that. It was just awesome. I wouldn't trade the experiences I had for anything."

Linda Portasik continued adding to her athletic achievements and then, after graduating from the University of Tennessee with top honors, she enrolled in law school at the University of Virginia. Today she practices law.

Pam Passera is working with parks and recreation programs in Indiana. The "Rails to Trails" program, one of the first in the country to create trails on abandoned railroad tracks, is just one example of the areas where Pam puts her efforts. She still finds satisfaction in sports as a coach for children and giving her time to Special Olympics. Her appreciation for her family and the opportunities she has had come through clearly in her positive spirit. What does she say is special about the 1981 team? "I think it's that we were so young—mostly freshmen and sophomores," she notes. "We all came from winning teams and had individual success in our sports. We always thought that we would win. We weren't cocky—maybe more naïve and down to earth. We did everything together—always practiced together, always

ate together at our meets. We did everything as a team. At the time I didn't know it was special to do that, and now I see that it made a difference in the dynamic of our team. I enjoyed the company of everyone. I feel quite privileged to have had those people as teammates."

Cathy Rattray Williams is currently a principal at a preparatory school in Kingston, Jamaica. She has written Spanish workbooks accompanied with instructional compact discs that have been used in elementary schools throughout Jamaica. Her many interests include dancing, athletics, and music. Cathy and her family enjoy a menagerie of pets including birds flying among outdoor trees within large netting. Cathy laughingly remembers singing and moving her hands when running long distances and that she "used to drive other people on the team up the wall." Finding her passion and working hard led to rewards that return to her even years later. "I was going to buy a new car the other day," she says. "I went to test drive the car, and the sales person said, 'Oh my goodness, I am actually being driven by Cathy Rattray! You don't know how many years I used to watch you compete.' You don't realize how many people that you inspire. He had no aspirations to be an athlete or anything, but it is amazing how many people you can inspire and motivate just by seeing you do something that you love."

Delisa Walton today works with Fox Sports. Her motto underscores the way she has found success: "The road to victory comes with many obstacles, challenges, and adversities, but through hard work, dedication, and a positive attitude, the impossible dream becomes a reality." Delisa vividly describes her more memorable UT moment: "We were at Austin. It came down to the final event, the 4x400-meter relay. Sherri Howard from UCLA and I were fighting the last one hundred meters and whoever won would win the meet. It was amazing to hear both of our teams screaming on the sideline as we approached the finish line. I edged her out the last ten meters of the race to capture the win and the team title."

They were "ten that made one." Each an extraordinary woman. Each with the power of ten.

Delisa Walton

Sports Stats (continued)

• Won 600-yard run at 1982 AIAW Indoor Championships and 1983 NCAA Indoor Championships, setting world record in that event at NCAA meet

• Ran on victorious mile relay at 1983 NCAA Indoor Championships

• Twelve-time All-America

• Nine-time National Champion

• Two-time 800-meter National Champion

• Three-time 600-yard/600-meter National Champion

• Four-time relay National Champion

• School record-holder indoors at 600 yard and 600 meter (standing as of 2006)

• School outdoor record-holder with 800-meter medley relay (standing as of 2006)

• On UT's all-time indoor performers list at 800 meter

Postcollegiate Career Highlights

• Pan American Games, second place (800-meter run), 1987

• US Olympian, finishing fifth (800-meter run), 1988

• Employed by Fox Sports

• Training for masters 4x400-meter relay, 2008 Olympics

Spotlight
Liz Brown (Jarvis)
Swimming and Diving, 1981–84

Liz Brown, freestyle and butterfly champion.

Step Up and Fly!

When she closes her eyes and remembers her Lady Vol college days, Liz Brown (Jarvis) smiles and describes going to the nearby Great Smoky Mountain National Park and running up and down the trail to the Chimneys. That might sound more like a track star's memory than a swimmer's, but when Liz dove into the pool, her aquatic prowess left no question that she was a championship swimmer. Her swim coach, Terry Carlisle, periodically took the team to the mountains for a different kind of physical workout. Liz treasures those times because of the team spirit that resulted. "We all would gripe," she remembers, "but it really was fun, different, and bonding. Those were great times."

Liz spent her elementary school years in Huntington, West Virginia. She played basketball and tennis, and at the age of ten, she began swimming on a team at the YMCA. When her family moved to Richmond, Virginia, doors opened for greater competition, and even though she continued playing tennis and basketball, Liz realized that her passion was for swimming. By the time she had to pick one sport as a junior in high school, Liz had already set a state record and was a standout in the freestyle, butterfly, and backstroke.

Liz cites her mother as her mentor and role model, especially during her high school years. "My parents divorced when I was a sophomore in high school," she says. "My mom worked so hard to be sure that all three of her daughters had everything we needed to be successful. She was always at events when she could be there and was so supportive of us all. She didn't push and said that I didn't have to swim if I didn't want to—even though it would pay for schooling."

The University of Tennessee came into Liz's vision through her high school swim coach, whose parents lived in Knoxville. Her coach brought her to Knoxville for a campus visit, and Liz was instantly drawn to Joe Gentry, then the UT women's swim coach. She recalls, "UT was impressive—the entire women's department. Being separate from men was really neat—being their own entity. I couldn't afford to visit all the schools I talked to, but I was really impressed with Tennessee. UT was well ahead of other schools and the times."

Coach Gentry left UT that summer, but Liz found a home in a cohesive, supportive program:

I was very fortunate to come into sports when I did—scholarships were just growing. The women's athletic department was such a close group of people. I had friends on the basketball team, track team—all the Lady Vols did things together. My roommate, Libby Hill, and I were polar opposites. Today we are still great friends.

I had a volunteer family—Bo and Mary Shafer. They were so sweet. It was so great to have home-cooked meals and to have a home off campus when my home and family were so far away. I know they are not allowed to do much of this today. [The Volunteer Parent Program ended in 1981 to comply with upcoming 1982 NCAA regulations.]

The Student Aquatic Center, home to the Lady Vols until the opening of the Jones Aquatic Center in 2008.

Some student-athletes attribute their wins to preparation beyond regular practice. Even though Liz believed in regular, consistent practice, she doesn't completely discount the value of a little superstition: "In high school I had a lucky hat that I always had to wear. I was a little superstitious year to year. We visualized our races before we swam. But if something worked right when I did well, I would continue with the same format. For example, my goggles had a little arrow that pointed "up." I always made sure that the arrow pointed the same way. A lot of swimmers are kind of particular about wearing their goggles the same way or the same swim cap."

Even if she might attribute some of her success to luck, there is no question that talent, discipline, and hard work were the main factors in Liz's championship achievements. As a freshman, Liz was genuinely surprised when her 50-yard butterfly won first at the SEC Championships. "One of my favorite memories is when I won the SEC in 50 fly my freshman year," she says. "I wish I could relive it and enjoy the moment more—at the time it was so surprising."

Lady Vol swimmers are always some of the first students to be awake and practicing every day. Even in the winter on dark, cold mornings the swim team could be found practicing their strokes. Liz recalls one such memory: "There was a really bad ice storm. Knoxville was paralyzed, and no one could get to campus. Classes were called off, I think. But our coach was iced in on campus,

Liz Brown Jarvis, still at the pool, volunteers at community swim meets. Photo by Sarah Shute; courtesy, Liz Brown Jarvis.

and so all of us living on campus had to go to practice. It was so impossible to walk on the ice that we had to sit down and slide down the hills. There were huge icicles over the side door of the aquatic center. A teammate threw a snowball just as the coach opened the door. The ice didn't fall on him, but we all stood quietly for a minute, not knowing how he would respond. Then we all laughed, and that really lightened the mood—we had been griping because we had to be there."

The team practiced every day with Sundays being optional. The coach allowed the student-athletes to substitute Sunday practices for another regularly scheduled practice when they might want to take a break during exam periods or when they needed the time. They called these hours "money in the bank." She says:

Our coach was a laid-back guy—not about winning totally. I remember when we were swimming against Georgia—my senior year. It came down to the last event—the free relay. I had done well. The coach had me going second—that's not where you usually put your faster swimmers. I always had a quick start. When I dove in, I noticed that my competition in the next lane was way ahead of me. Our coach was jumping up and down. I thought he was mad at me—he was throwing flip boards—he was so mad. I felt awful. Then I realized that he wasn't mad at me. He was mad at the judges because she had false started—he was just sticking up for us. That was the only time I saw him show emotion like that.

Liz loves the Tennessee spirit for sports and treasures the traditions that grow with conference rivalries. "It was such an honor to swim for Tennessee," she comments. "The tradition is magical. Joan Cronan is there; Smokey [the mascot] comes; the band plays 'Rocky Top.' Alabama used to send funeral wreathes to our locker rooms. Our coach's glasses would fog up, he would get so mad. He had a safety pin to hold his glasses together—his glasses would wiggle."

Today, Liz sees her collegiate years with the additional perspectives that come from the passage of time, having a career, and raising her family of three children (Lauren, Kathleen, and Tom) with her husband, Howard. She observes:

Being a Lady Vol is very rewarding: you can be a good example; you meet lifetime friends, share a common bond that nobody else can experience. It's hard work—it's a struggle. I think it's only now when I look back, that I can really appreciate everything that everybody did for me—what I got to experience because of the sport. I would never have had the opportunities to go to the places I went and to meet such incredible people. We had Irish and South African women who trained with the team—we learned a lot about the world, got to meet people from all over the world.

The most important advice that I would give young women today is to enjoy what you do: don't stress about it, enjoy it, experience it, don't put your self-worth on your performance times. I was too nervous—I wish I could have had that ease. I put too much self-worth on what I did. I have always had a strong faith, but I didn't really think about it much back then. It might have taken the pressure off—to know that my worth

is not all about swimming performance. The most important thing is to enjoy the experience.

Liz points to those who use their accomplishments to impact others. She admires those who see beyond self-importance to do greater good. Her strong values show through as she considers people she admires:

I really admire people who have means and do good things with it for the community and those in need. It touches my heart—to work on causes that are very important, to use their public visibility to give notice to a cause. It can be very rewarding to be an example and have someone say that because of you they did the right thing. It would be wonderful to make that kind of difference in people's lives.

Peyton Manning is the epitome of a great athlete who is humble, grounded. Peyton has really impressed me all along because it is not all about him. He gives back so much to the community. I would love to give back to the Lady Vols.

Because of the choices she makes, the care she gives to so many, and the standards she lives by, with quiet humility Liz Brown Jarvis already gives back to the Lady Vols. Every day.

Liz Brown (Jarvis)

Sports Stats

- CSCA Academic All-America, 1984
- Career Highs: 50-yard freestyle, 23.49; 100-yard freestyle, 50.86; 200-yard freestyle 1:50.29; 100-yard butterfly, 56.33; 200-yard butterfly, 2:14.80; 50-yard butterfly, 25.68
- SEC Highs: 50-yard freestyle, 23.49; 100-yard freestyle, 50.86; 100-yard butterfly, 56.79
- NCAA or AIAW Highs: 200-yard freestyle, 1:50.29; 100-yard butterfly, 56.33; 50-yard butterfly, 25.68
- Sixteen All-America certificates
- First-Team Knoxville News Sentinel All-SEC

Academic Stats

- B.S., Business Administration, University of Tennessee, 1984

Postcollegiate Career Highlights

- Budget analyst, auditor
- Community volunteer with children's soccer and swimming
- Board member, Greater Knoxville Area Interclub Swimming Association
- Lady Volunteer Hall of Fame

Spotlight
Beverly Robinson (Buffini)
Volleyball, 1981–83

Beverly Robinson

Beverly Robinson's record-setting play motivated the volleyball team to achieve stunning wins.

Point! Beverly Robinson!

Volleyball is a game of strength, strategy and precision. It is a game that requires focus, readiness, and a will to win. Add to these qualities the talents and determined spirit of Beverly Robinson (Buffini), and no doubt a champion will be born. Sumter, South Carolina, is where it all began. Beverly says:

I am from Sumter, South Carolina. My mom, Julia, is from there. My father, James, is from Pittsburgh, Pennsylvania, and met my mother when he was stationed at Shaw Air Force Base. Not long after they met, my father worked a little bit for my grandfather to help him with his business. When my grandfather brought him by the house, my mother said, "What a handsome young man!" [They were eventually married.]

I lived in Sumter for about four or five years until my father transferred to Scott Air Force Base in Illinois. We lived in Illinois for six years. Being a military brat is a good experience because you learn that when things change, you go with the flow. I learned that pretty quickly, because even in Sumter my father was gone for two years overseas to Thailand back in the 1970s.

The family's move to Illinois triggered Beverly's interests in sports and history. She loved to explore Springfield, Illinois, the home of Abraham Lincoln. Beverly also spent exciting times as a fan of the St. Louis Cardinals. As she remembers:

I think that going to baseball games was the first bit of inspiration that I got related to high-level sport competition. It is really amazing to see these great athletes in person—being in great shape and excellent at what they do. So that was my first inclination to try to play. I started playing sports at field days at my school and began realizing that there was some potential here as I would race and win and get ribbons. It was fun. The long jump, the broad jump, all those little field day races—I would just get energized doing that. It was my favorite time of the year when they had those athletic events going on. I loved it, and I think that is when my confidence started to grow.

Beverly loved field days at school and treasured the family outings to professional ball games. Her father loved sports and also loved the military. Clearly, Beverly cites her father as a source for her passion and strong work ethic. "My dad loved the military, and that is a huge part of who I am," she says. "It is a lot of discipline. Seeing him come home everyday in his blue air force uniform, that helped also. He was gone at a certain time, home at a certain time, and he was consistent. He never called in to say, 'Oh, I am sick today.' I never remember my dad missing a day of work. When duty called, he was there. That instilled a lot of who I am. I know it did."

Beverly began playing softball in about fifth grade and remembers her joy at just being in motion. She loved running, playing "chase," and hide-and-seek. She was a natural athlete and blessed with ability. She was also blessed by the support of her family. This strong, loving family taught Beverly about unconditional love, dedication, and even death.

Beverly Robinson Buffini, motivational speaker, 2007. Courtesy, Buffini & Company.

"I have an older sister and a younger sister who was adopted," Beverly explains. "She was the daughter of my mom's sister. My mom's sister died, and so she came to live with us. When I think back, I realize what a loving thing my mom did, to take her little baby in. To think about what they did, to say, 'Yeah, I'll take her in.' And she was just like our sister from birth. She was only about six months old then. I also had a brother. One of the toughest things that I experienced was that my brother died in 1997. That was a tough life challenge."

When Beverly was eleven years old, her father transferred to Maxwell Air Force Base in Alabama. While changes accompanying a move require new adjustments, Beverly was still in the familiar "town" of a military base. She became more involved in organized sports activities. She played speedball, which combined the skills of soccer, basketball, and football. When seasons changed, so did the sports, and volleyball, basketball, and track added to her schedule. And Beverly excelled.

"I started getting more exposure my junior year in high school," she says. "There are a couple of camps in Auburn, Alabama. And I started meeting coaches from around the country at those camps. And I won some honors at those camps—MVPs and things like that. And so a lot of those coaches were encouraging me and suggesting that I had a future in one of these sports, whatever I wanted to do."

Beverly attended many camps with multiple sports and seriously considered basketball or track as her focus. Then she went to a volleyball camp, where volleyball was the sole sport. Coaches from California were there, and they saw her, approached her, and told her that she was very good. Just simple words like that made the difference:

They believed in me. I enjoyed the sport so much. And I love the aspects of it—the jumping, the passing, everything. And I said, "You know, I probably have the best chance at this. This is what I want to pursue." I felt that if I'm going to college, and I'm going to do a sport, why not volleyball? I did have a better chance at excelling at volleyball. And I really enjoy this sport. So, that is why I chose volleyball.

The encouragement from those coaches made me say, "Maybe I can do this." I sent letters to colleges. No one was knocking down my door in Montgomery, Alabama, even though I did well. I actually set a state record for the 110 low hurdles, but I still wasn't out there with the main colleges. I did get a sole offer from a few of them, but the University of Alabama was the main offer at that time. Of course, I said, "Absolutely," and went there and played there for two years.

At the end of her second year at Alabama, the coach gathered the team and announced that the volleyball program was going to end. It was an administrative decision, and the sad news could have meant the end of college and volleyball for Beverly. Her faith and spirit kept her sights ahead, though, and she started thinking about the University of Tennessee:

Whenever we played against Tennessee or saw them at tournaments, I always thought,

"Wow, that team has got it together." Their bright orange bags were always lined up outside the benches. And you could see that the team was very regimented, and because of the military side of me, I am attracted to that. So when I thought of Tennessee lined up and in their warm-ups, I knew that was what I wanted.

Alabama did drop the volleyball program, and then I did get the offer from Tennessee. I was giving everyone high fives—YES—because I knew that it would be a great opportunity for me to get to the next levels where I wanted to be.

Beverly's expectations were met. She learned to give her best effort every time she was on the court. There were no dress rehearsals. She says:

I remember Alumni Gym like it was yesterday—being in there practicing, walking down those steps to the gym, getting dressed out. One thing that I loved doing as a team a lot was visualizing. We would all go outside the gym into this little room and turn the lights off and visualize as a team.

And I used that preparation technique when I was on the US team, too. I would just quiet down and visualize going into plays. We always got the scouting reports before the games. So I would go over those, think of each person. A lot of times I would just listen to soft music to be focused on the game and the upcoming match. I would see myself performing well and being successful.

Beverly sought ways to keep her motivation high and to be positive. Even as a

Beverly Robinson was the volleyball program's first player to earn All-America honors.

young girl she would decorate her walls with inspirational quotations, mottos, and scriptures. She carried this same habit to college, where her dorm room was covered with motivational messages. Her friends would tease her and compare her decorating scheme to theirs, which were typically posters more popular with young college women. Beverly found that books, movies, and positive-minded people built her up and enriched her spirit:

One of my favorite movies is Chariots of Fire. *In this movie Eric Little says that when he is running, he "feels God's pleasure." And when I am working out in the gym or I am running and diving after a volleyball, it is just as enjoyable to me. I just feel pleasure in doing that.*

I also just loved practices at UT. They were very, very hard. But that is what I wanted. I loved sweating in Alumni Gym. It was hot there and practices were hard, but I loved being there and experiencing that with my teammates. I was growing, and at that time the sport was just pure for me.

Hard practice and discipline reaped results. Beverly was a powerful catalyst for the team and set incredible new records for the Lady Volunteers. But it was the benefit to the team that truly stirred Beverly's sense of pride. "I believe one of the best moments, because it was a team moment, was when we were playing Northwestern [Dec. 4, 1982]," she recalls. "I was just so focused. You have heard people say that they were in the zone. I served eleven aces in a game. It was incredible. I was in the zone. The team was winning. We were all just fired up. Everyone was together and it helped us as a team to get to the next level—which was our goal anyway. To have that much impact and to feel that excellence, it was just phenomenal."

Being a Lady Volunteer remains a treasured part of Beverly today. "Coming to UT after my sophomore year could have been a difficult transition," she says. "I didn't know anyone, and it was in the middle of my college years. But I felt such a strong sense of community. The Boost Her Club and my volunteer family were wonderful. Every time I see the Lady Vols and Big Orange, I feel a part of them. I identify with it and feel the loyalty and connection. Being a Lady Vol taught me to have high expectations to perform whenever I go out—even at practice."

Today Beverly's motivational examples might easily adorn the dorm room walls of a new, aspiring student-athlete. As she continues to embrace life with her husband, Brian, and their six children, Beverly doesn't hesitate when she considers her message to young women today:

Believe in the values that you represent. Even Olympic athletes depend on their strong sense of values. No matter where you are or how successful you are in business, a lot of your success or how you handle business depends on what you think of yourself and how you believe you can contribute to whatever you are doing.

You are an important person. You are valuable and you make a difference—no matter where you are, no matter what your past is. So often we dwell on our weaknesses instead of our strengths. So the word that I would put in a neon sign around me is "Believe." Believe in yourself; believe in your dreams. Believe in the values you represent. Believe that you can achieve your dreams. It may take a lot of work, but you can do it. It has to start with believing. If you don't believe, how can you get to the next steps? If an obstacle comes and you don't believe you can do it, then you are going to give in to that obstacle and think that you aren't good enough. There were many times along my way when I could have said, "OK, I'm not good enough." I remember a sports festival in Alabama when I didn't perform as well as I had hoped. I could have quit then. Look at what I would have missed.

And look what we all would have missed. Beverly Robinson Buffini is a powerhouse of positive energy. She embraces the challenges of life and injects confidence into everyone around her. This Lady Vol has a spirit that invites us all to step forward and believe in a new day.

Beverly Robinson (Buffini)

Sports Stats
- All-SEC, 1981, 1982, 1983
- AVCA First-Team All-America, 1982
- SEC Tournament MVP, 1982
- Career Highs: Kills, 29 vs. Penn State (Oct. 7, 1983); attacks: 65 vs. Penn State (Oct. 7, 1983); Aces: 11 vs. Northwestern (Dec. 4, 1982), a school record
- Career Records: hitting percentage, .359 (first all-time in Lady Vol history)

Academic Stats
- B.S., Liberal Arts, Human Services and Criminal Justice, University of Tennessee, 1983

Postcollegiate Career Highlights
- National Sports Festival IV, 1982
- World University Games, 1983
- US National Training Team, 1984–89
- Pan-Am Games, 1987
- US Olympic Team, 1988
- Author, I Can, I Will, I Believe (Providence Systems, Inc., 2003)
- Lady Volunteer Hall of Fame

LaVonna Martin marked her Lady Vol career with record-breaking times, securing NCAA titles in the 55-meter and 100-meter hurdles and later winning a silver medal at the 1988 Olympics.

Taking the Hurdles One by One . . . and Fast!

They call her "Vonnie," and when she was little, she always wanted to be an Olympian and a teacher. LaVonna Martin (Floreal) accomplished these goals and more.

Born in Dayton, Ohio, Vonnie grew up in the nearby suburb, Trotwood. She is quick to say that her father and mother were her most significant role models. Both of her parents grew up during the times of segregation, and both were track and field enthusiasts. Her mother, Brenda Martin, was an outstanding track athlete, but the temper of the times led her family to decide to keep her close to home rather than allow her to accept an opportunity to run track at Tennessee State University. Her father, Harold "Lefty" Martin, graduated from Central State University in Ohio and is a track and field fixture in that state. When Vonnie was about ten years old, her father discovered her natural talent, and she recalls his excitement: "I remember his noticing that I was interested in track and taking my brother Duane and me to a recreational park. And at that time he was shocked by what he saw. That just got the ball rolling. He got excited and started taking us around the country to various track meets and letting us use our skills. About two years later he founded the youth program called the Northwest Track Club."

While her father mentored Vonnie in the athletic realm, her mother influenced character development. "My mother is, and was at that time, so bent on who I was going to become as a person—my character, how I treated others, how I saw myself, where I placed the significance of God in my life," she observes. "And that is probably the one single factor that kept me from being burned out in my life. There were times when I found it difficult to practice and stay focused on track. That was normal for a kid. But Mom would always bring me back with a reminder that talent is a gift that God had given me, and I needed to be responsible with the gift and give all I could while I could—at the age I could do it."

Vonnie had other interests as well. She loved dancing, gymnastics, and soccer. Soccer provided a great way to stay in shape and strengthen her running skills through middle and high school. In high school Vonnie earned All-State honors in soccer. And no one could outrun her.

Track and field held her passion. Her mother and father guided Vonnie to stay focused but balanced. Her father was her coach and closest advisor. As college commitment time approached, Vonnie received contact from over a hundred schools. She learned of this only recently. To free her from the stress caused by the inundation of so much information, Vonnie's father sorted through the materials and gave her only the communications from schools in which she had expressed interest. One of those schools was the University of Tennessee. She remembers:

When I was growing up, my idol was a woman named Benita Fitzgerald [Mosley]. We used to have stats books around the house. And I loved poring over them and particularly looking at my event, which started off as the quarter-mile and later became the hurdles. *I remember looking in this book and seeing this tall, beautiful black woman. She captured my attention. And from then on I was captivated by her career and just wanted to know more about her. I found out that she went to the University of Tennessee. And I remember I struck up a relationship with Terry Crawford, who was the coach at that time, and I had a chance to meet Benita. And Benita kind of took me under her wings even before I had made a decision to come to Tennessee. And I just wanted to be like her, so it was a natural draw for me.*

On a campus visit Vonnie met some members of the Lady Vol team, including Joetta Clark (Diggs) and Sharrieffa Barksdale, notable student-athletes. Tennessee also offered a location close enough to Ohio so that Vonnie's parents could see her compete.

When Vonnie arrived to begin her freshman year, she was disappointed to learn that Terry Crawford had accepted a coaching position at Texas and another coach, Loren Seagrave, had left to coach at LSU. Benita Fitzgerald (Mosley) had graduated. The class-room was also an unfamiliar territory. She says:

I had not had a lot of freedom at home because of my commitment level to athletics. And so I had a great time that first quarter. I was just partying and hanging out and shopping with my friend—you know, doing all the things that are important to a young girl. A teammate and I were in an African-American studies class together. I remember sitting in this particular class, and we could not figure out how to know what we were supposed to accomplish. How do people know about the

readings and the assignments? I didn't know what a syllabus was. It wasn't until midway through the quarter when I figured out that we were supposed to be looking at this paper that was called a "syllabus" to guide us through what we were to read through the quarter. And as you can imagine, I didn't do well in that class or any other class that first quarter. I don't know why I didn't know about that. Consequently, I had a pretty bad GPA that first quarter. My coach at that time was Beverly Kearney, who is at Texas now. She came down hard on me, and my parents came down hard on me. And that kind of changed the course of my focus.

Vonnie majored in elementary education at UT and found success in the classroom and on the track. When she was a junior, pledging Delta Sigma Theta sorority expanded her circle and helped her meet people on campus in other areas. Her accolades are many, collecting eighteen All-SEC certificates in her four years, including twelve for first place. She holds school records in four events and leads all Lady Vols with twelve SEC titles (eight individual, four relay) won during her career. She was inducted into the Lady Volunteer Hall of Fame in 2002.

Vonnie made the cut for the US Olympic Teams in 1988 and trained for that year with the coach who had recruited her to Tennessee, Terry Crawford. She participated for a second time on the US Olympic Team in 1992 and returned home with the silver medal in the 100-meter hurdles. Of that experience, she says:

If you were to ask me any aspects of my Olympic race, I couldn't tell you because I

LaVonna Martin (Floreal)

Sports Stats

- Gold medalist in the 10-meter hurdles at the 1987 Pan Am Games
- Won NCAA indoor titles for 55-meter hurdles in 1987 and 1988 and was the runner-up in 1985
- Captured NCAA 100-meter hurdle crown outdoors in 1987 and took second in 1986 and 1988
- Decorated fourteen times as an All-America at Tennessee
- Six-time SEC indoor champion, including twice in the 55-meter hurdles, twice with the 4x440-yard relay and once each in the 60-yard hurdles and 300-yard hurdles
- Four-time SEC outdoor 100-meter hurdle victor and two-time 4x400-meter relay champion
- Collected eighteen All-SEC certificates in her four years at UT, including twelve for first place
- Holds school records in four events and is the all-time Lady Vols leader with twelve SEC titles (eight individual and four relay)

Academic Stats

- B.S., Education, University of Tennessee, 1989

Postcollegiate Career Highlights

- US Olympic Teams in the 100-meter hurdles, 1988, 1992, 1996
- Claimed the Olympic silver medal in the 100-meter hurdles in 1992
- Lady Volunteer Hall of Fame

was in such a zone. I don't remember any of the specifics of my Olympic final. I had gone to two Olympic Games—'88 in Seoul and '92 in Barcelona. They both were totally different. In '88 I was so young and what was important to me was shopping and more shopping. I had a boyfriend at the time, and I was thinking how much I missed him. I just really wasn't focused. But then in '92 my focus was that I wanted to do well and possibly get a medal. And so going into that race, I had enjoyed the entire Olympic experience—from going to the training camps, to walking into the stadium for the opening ceremonies, to all of my rounds of running (I had to do four), the Olympic Village, the whole experience. I soaked it all in and was able to come out victorious. It was an incredible high but it was a low as well because in life I think the training part is what gives you that rush. And oftentimes, you accomplish

LaVonna Martin Floreal and family: Edrick, E.J. (Edrick Jr.), and Mimi (Mikaielle), 2007. Courtesy, LaVonna Martin Floreal.

would have anticipated the most difficult one of all:

In 1991, I had a positive drug test. I was working with a Russian coach. She gave me a pill and didn't tell me what it was. I had grown up where you just trust your coaches. In a lot of ways, I was naïve. I didn't question. Why would a coach give me something that

I guess she thought she was helping me. I don't know. I was facing a possible twenty-four-month suspension. That was pretty difficult, and if you do the math, there was no way I was going to be able to compete and make the Olympic Team in 1992. But I believe in the power of God, and I believe the Lord found a way for me to be reinstated. The coach admitted that she lied to me. I took the substance. I admitted that I should have been responsible for what was going into my system. During this time, there was a small clause within our governing bodies that state if you as an athlete help in the prosecuting of a coach, then that would allow for special circumstances. And they had the ability to cut the length of my suspension from a possible twenty-four months to fourteen months. That enabled me to regain eligibility in January of 1992.

Vonnie made quite a journey. From Ohio to Tennessee and Seoul to Barcelona, she gathered friends, medals, and character-building experiences. Married to Edrick Floreal, Stanford University's director of track and field and two-time Canadian Olympian, Vonnie reflects on the significance of Lady Vol values on her unwavering family strength:

I realize now that I needed to be let loose just a little bit and enjoy the life "Rocky Top" Tennessee had to offer.

that goal and then what else is there. I was a little disappointed in how I felt. The fun part was getting to that point. Sometimes the best part of reaching a goal is the journey you have getting there.

Vonnie was a dedicated student, a gifted athlete, and a person of solid character. Of all the hurdles that she jumped, she never

would be on the banned list? And as a result I had a positive test for a diuretic. Diuretics are on the banned list because they can help you expel water, and some people use them to take out steroids.

I was having the best year of my career. And I was suspended. The coach had been concerned that I was struggling with weight, which has always been my life struggle.

Being a Lady Vol allowed me to reach for a goal, not just athletically but in being a young woman—a goal of excellence, a goal of commitment, and being a person of integrity—all of these things that were instilled in me by my mother and my father. Family was a theme throughout my life. I was able to choose mentors who supported my goal, like Joan Cronan, who always supported

and encouraged me through my years there at Tennessee. Coaches I could trust looked after me. There was a great church community that I could rely on. When you are young, it is easy to gravitate towards your friends or peers, but the wisest of young people know that they need some strong, older mentors.

Because track is such an individual sport, I think it is important to know that I was a part of a team. I relied on my teammates. I gained my fortitude through encouraging my teammates. I had a great coach while I was a Tennessee, Beverly Kearney. She actually helped me get to the medal stand. She took me under her wings and was one of the good people to whom I couldn't say "thank you" enough. Also, Terry Crawford always encouraged me to do my best. She took me under her wings when I needed some guidance and direction and that too made a difference in my career.

I wouldn't say that during that time period that I was the best athlete or the most talented. But I had a drive and a commitment. I had some goals that I wanted to accomplish. My parents helped me to stay focused on what my commitments were. I look back now and I am thankful. I realize now that I needed to be let loose just a little bit and enjoy the life "Rocky Top" Tennessee had to offer.

LaVonna Martin Floreal competed in the Olympics twice. She is a wife, mother, and a teacher. Imagine that.

Through the years, Lady Volunteer track and field student-athletes have brought national and international honors to the University of Tennessee.

A Tennessee Original
Debby Jennings

Debby Jennings

Debby Jennings, Associate Athletics Director for Media Relations

Just Ask Debby

If you want to know which Lady Vol played in the last five seconds of the basketball game featuring Tennessee and Louisiana Tech in 1979, don't go to the record books or the library. Just call Debby Jennings. She is associate athletic director for media relations. She is the archivist. She is the historian. And she has it all in her head.

This remarkable individual dropped right into her profession during her undergraduate days at the University of Tennessee. A journalism student, Debby worked on the student newspaper, the *Daily Beacon*, as a staff writer and sports editor when the university was addressing the implications of Title IX and determining the future organization for women's athletics. She could not have been in a more ideal position to witness firsthand the early beginnings of the Lady Volunteers. Debby graduated in 1977 and holds the distinction of being the first and only director of media relations for the University of Tennessee Lady Vols. Her value cannot be overstated, as evidenced by the comments of Joan Cronan, director of women's intercollegiate athletics: "There is nobody who knows more about the history of the Lady Vols than Debby Jennings. She has a vast knowledge of everything that goes on. I depend on her a lot."

As a staff member in the early days of the Women's Intercollegiate Athletics Department, Debby has a unique vantage point. She has the objectivity of a journalist, saw UT women's athletics from a student perspective, and was on the ground floor with the first staff that organized in 1976. She is a creator and a reporter whose job early on was to communicate the program's values, purposes, mission, and accomplishments to the public. Debby's words captured the Lady Vol spirit, and she established the strong media relationships essential to draw fan support and develop regular communication throughout the campus, state, and nation. In the early years Debby did it all: she recorded and maintained player statistics, coordinated needs for external media representatives covering events, served as point person for player and coach interviews, developed brochures, handled press conferences, prepared news releases, planned promotional drives, and performed any other duties as needed. Debby still does it all, but now she has a staff of permanent professionals and a dedicated group of student-interns to meet the ever-growing demands of media relations.

Debby has grown from a relatively unknown professional doing the work of a department in its infancy to being one of the most respected professionals in the nation. In 2002 she became just the third woman to be inducted into the College Sports Information Directors of America (CoSIDA) Hall of Fame, and the next year she became a member of the CoSIDA Quarter Century Club. Debby has received more than two hundred national publications awards, more than half distinguished as the best in the nation.

Head Basketball Coach Pat Summitt emphatically proclaims that "Debby Jennings is the dean of media relations—not just on the University of Tennessee campus but in the world of women's sports. No one in the field is more respected, talented, and admired."

Sports media staff are always a significant presence at athletic events. These individuals serve as the communication links between the event and everyone else. Debby was quickly spotted for her extraordinary abilities. She has been selected by the US Olympic Committee to serve as a media relations coordinator at international events, including the 1984 and 1996 Summer Olympics, the 1987 Pan American Games, and the 1983 and 1989 World University Games. Nationally she works in similar roles for NCAA events and has also given her service as president of the Southeastern Conference Sports Information Directors Association.

Danielle Donehew, former UT director of basketball operations and Executive Vice President for the WNBA Atlanta Dream, reflects the sentiments of many when she notes the admiration and respect that Debby has earned: "Debby Jennings is certainly an asset! She is a walking statistical dictionary not only for our program, but also for the history of women's basketball. Debby's media guides have won national recognition, and she is widely respected in the industry."

Debby has coauthored two books: *Basketball*, with Pat Summitt (W. C. Brown, Company), and *Lady Magic: The Nancy Lieberman-Cline Story*, with Nancy Lieberman-Cline (Sagamore Publishing). She takes her skills to the classroom as an adjunct professor and is the first-ever sports information director to receive the Mel Greenberg Award in 1995 for lifelong contributions to women's basketball. In 2008 Debby was named the Arch Ward Award winner by the College Sports Information Directors of America, honoring outstanding contribution to the field of college sports informa-

Joan Cronan declared November 26, 2002, "Debby Jennings Day" to commemorate Jennings's twenty-fifth year on the Lady Vol staff. Debby's parents joined the festivities at the basketball halftime presentation.

tion. She is only the second woman to receive the award, which was initiated in 1958.

Debby's longevity with the department testifies to a perfect fit for the department and for her. Angela Kelly, head soccer coach, supports this claim: "Debby is the stat buster and has been at the side of Coach Summitt and her program from almost the inception. She and her staff are both professional and passionate about what they do and who they are representing. The awards just keep coming!"

Debby knows every Lady Vol and serves as their representative to the media. She also involves the student-athletes in the creative sessions to develop media guides for their sports. The Lady Vol family concept is put into action with shared ownership. Lady Vol and WNBA player Tamika Catchings recalls times with Debby: "What can I say about DJ? I loved going to her

office and just talking about different things that were going on in the world and on campus. DJ always had great jokes, and she could come up with ideas at the snap of a finger. We would go over different themes for our media guide, and it never failed for her to come up with something super creative and different. Amazing!"

Judi Pavon, head golf coach, shares Tamika's admiration for Debby's consistent high-quality work. "Debby has great talent and creativity," says Pavon, "and does an awesome job making all the coaches and Lady Vol teams look good. We have a very strong media relations department, and I am proud of the way Debby and her staff communicate our program to the community."

Writer, organizer, communicator, ultimate professional, colleague, and friend, Debby Jennings is truly a Tennessee Original.

02

Seriously Fun, 1987–1996

Gathering Momentum, Expanding the Program

The 1987–96 period continued to gather momentum of fan support, media attention, and a serious commitment to sport expansion. Athletics Director Joan Cronan saw the addition of golf in 1992, rowing and softball in 1995, and soccer in 1996. Her efforts joined with university and community support to generate increased funding for student-athletic scholarships and coaches for the additional sports.

Fans of all ages—children, parents, grandparents, UT students, faculty, and staff—cheered Lady Volunteer student-athletes in eleven sport offerings. Their Lady Vols brought home four NCAA national championship titles in basketball and regional titles in volleyball, swimming, and track and field. In 1983 the volleyball team broke through to the NCAA regional rounds, and the infant golf program achieved NCAA regional competition. The Lady Volunteers promised serious fun.

Lady Volunteer Golf (Est. 1992): Beginning at the End of the Rainbow

When Ann Furrow entered the University of Tennessee in 1961, she was determined to play golf as a student-athlete. Well before athletic scholarships opportunities for women, Furrow earned a full scholarship to play on the UT men's golf team. The opportunity worked for her, but from that point on she was determined that the University of Tennessee would one day support a women's golf program.

In 1991 Ann Furrow called Joan Cronan and offered to help start the intercollegiate golf program for women. The time was right, and Cronan agreed to move forward. Their first goal was to obtain the funding to endow the golf program fully with scholarships. Furrow and Cronan enlisted the help of Pat Summitt and Susan Williams and proceeded to meet with donors, identify the best recruits, and hire a top golf coach. In a short time, the energetic group raised an impressive sum and moved their attention to finding a coach. Furrow and Cronan identified a number of individuals to consider more closely. They made interview trips,

talked with possible candidates, and still had not found the perfect match. They were in Tampa Bay, Florida, when Furrow spotted Linda Franz (Sower) working at a shoot for an advertising agency. A coach with marketing skills as well as knowledge of the sport was appealing. A quick call to Cronan, who was at the hotel, resulted in a meeting that sealed the deal. Good fortune smiled on the group with a rainbow breaking through the sky as they were sharing their excitement of the inaugural golf program.

Lady Vol golf was the first sport added to the Tennessee women's program in 1992.

With a coach on board, the next goal was to recruit five top golfers. With no golf presence on campus, the strategy needed to be creative. They decided that football weekends would be great times to bring recruits to campus and that current Lady Vol student-athletes could help as hosts. Furrow, Franz (Sower), and Cronan studied scouting reports in magazines and devoured every resource they could find to identify the top talent ready for college. The first Lady Volunteer golf team was stellar: Angie Boyd (Keck) (first women's golf scholarship recipient), Abby Pearson, Katharina Larsson, Susan Conger, Shelley Kinder (Anderson), and Sofi Stromgren. Everyone was excited about being a part of the building year where the tradition begins.

Today Linda Sower remembers the first year as a really exciting time: "Other SEC schools immediately perceived us as a threat. It looked as if we had no budget limit because we had endowed scholarships, a nice travel van, and we were doing everything in first-class fashion. I learned so much from Joan about moving and touching people, about how to pull heartstrings with true stories. I also learned how to be tough. It was a most exciting time."

Ann Furrow, the Volunteer golf coach, says that the program teaches student-athletes about more than golf: "Student-athletes learn how to be gracious learners in golf, a true game of integrity. They learn that as women they can excel, compete, and be winners."

The first season of Lady Volunteer Golf, 1992–93, presented a program defined by respect and a shared vision to be winners. The Lady Vols had found the greens in Tennessee.

Joan Cronan, director of women's athletics, welcomes golf to the women's athletics program.

Ann Furrow, community leader and advocate for women's athletics, served as the volunteer golf coach.

Lady Volunteer Rowing (Est. 1995): Painting a River Orange

It is a dark early morning. A line of Lady Volunteers carrying boats on their shoulders can be seen quietly moving toward the river's edge. It is twenty-nine degrees, and a heavy mist covers the water like a shroud. Without a word the teams quietly put the three boats into the water, climb in, and move silently onto their course.

Each crew is synchronized, intent on their job. Following the calls of the coxswains, adjusting speed, direction, or technique, the team presses harder and harder to match the calls of command. The voice of the coach adds encouragement through the darkness, and her words create their own rhythm to meet the motions of the boats: "Get it—get it—get it—watch—let the rest come to you—easy now—harder—harder—build it—build it—that's it—that's it—we can do better—come on, Tennes-

see—crescendo—help the person in front of you—stern four—now bow four—tips up—square—trim down—you are the power—you are in control—feel your body at one with the boat."

The boats become an extension of the rowers and smoothly, seemingly without effort, skim over the dark, cold waters. Without notice the sun has appeared, and the light dances on the water as the boats continue to glide in single motion. Almost like a yoga instructor, the coach calls out for small body adjustments to guide the crew to reach a maximum force as one synchronized organism. Every detail counts.

The crew returns to the dock, put the boats on their shoulders, and carry them into the boat house, where they wash the boats before returning them to the racks. Every crew member knows her job, and the crew performs as one. After the water workout, the team begins exercise stretches and discusses each boat—what went well, what

Angie Boyd Keck, assistant athletics director for facilities and operations, was a member of the first Lady Volunteer golf team in 1992.

do. When a crew experiences that point of almost effortlessness—when there seems to be no separation between the crew and the boat, with all in perfect synchronization—the feeling is like none other."

Historically, rowing was the first intercollegiate sport in the United States. The crews used to sing while they rowed to maintain a steady rhythm to stay together. Early boating clubs at the University of Tennessee may well have added their voices to the gentle flow of the Tennessee River.

The rowing program has a varsity team of about thirty-five to forty student-athletes and a team of about fifty novices, who are students interested in learning to row. Each fall semester a general campus meeting is held to explain rowing and encourage interested students to try it. Individuals who have backgrounds in dancing, horseback riding, swimming, and other sports calling for strong endurance and repetition may find their skills especially transferable to the skills required of rowers.

Rowing, like many sports, provides a training ground for life. Coach Glenn says, "The rower needs to learn to serve the team before her own individual needs. The trust and accountability of team members helps you become better in everything you do."

got in the way, what to do next time. At the end of the session, the group circles and confirms with a joined hand grip the phrase for the day, "Start with it!"

Morning practice has ended for the rowers, and they scramble upstairs to the kitchen for a quick breakfast and then run off to classes. The afternoon will bring them together for land practice with the strength and conditioning coach. Other sessions will call for power workouts on rowing machines, circuit training, running, and two-person boat races.

Head Rowing Coach Lisa Glenn is an enthusiastic advocate for her sport: "Rowing requires endurance, and the sport calls for full involvement of the heart, mind, and body. There is no limit to what a rower can

1987

Basketball: NCAA National Champions (Tennessee 67–44 Louisiana Tech)

Track and Field: NCAA National Championship (Indoor)—2nd; NCAA National Championship (Outdoor)—4th

Volleyball: SEC—3rd

1988

Civil Rights Restoration Act of 1987 requires Title IX compliance of all educational institutions receiving federal funds for any program/activity

Basketball: SEC Tournament Champions; NCAA Final Four—3rd

Volleyball: SEC—2nd   Swimming and Diving: SEC —2nd

Track and Field: SEC (Indoor)—3rd; SEC (Outdoor)—3rd

A Rower's Testimonial

I have realized in retrospect that I went to Tennessee to be a member of the rowing team for a reason. As a freshman, I had no idea what I wanted to do with my life. I was welcomed as a part of the Lady Vol family, and rowing and classes became my life. One day I met a physician at a rowing event, and he invited me to shadow him in an operating room. I continued to shadow for my remaining four years at UT. I had found my calling in life.

Currently I am an anesthesiology resident at the University of Florida. Being a physician requires commitment, dedication, and passion. Those three words embody what it meant to be a part of the rowing team. We committed ourselves to our team members, doing whatever it took to succeed together. We were dedicated to our team's goals of moving forward and taking the team to a new level. When I started with the team, we were rowing out of a glove factory warehouse and not even close to breaking into the national scene. As I graduated, we were in a new boathouse and becoming a rowing threat to some of the best teams in the country. It takes passion to be able to wake up everyday and push yourself harder and further than you ever believed that you could. The traits that make me a good physician are the same traits that were cultivated when I was at Tennessee. I will forever be grateful for my time at UT as a Lady Volunteer. I know now that my experiences helped me to be better in my chosen profession, and more importantly, being a Lady Vol helped me to be a better person.

—Kacey Montgomery
Lady Vol Crew Member, 2000–03

Rowing joined the Lady Volunteer athletic department in 1995.

Glenn loves to challenge her student-athletes to think bigger and to move to their greater possibilities. Each year offers new opportunities. Glenn identifies one of the greatest rewards she experiences as a coach: "I love to turn the race over to the team. I have been right next to them throughout practice and preparation, but at races they are on their own. I am so proud of them and love to show what Tennessee can do. They always make us proud."

All Lady Volunteers work diligently and practice with relentless determination. The rowers are no exception. This group of women exemplifies the dedication and work ethic that define Lady Volunteers.

Head Rowing Coach Lisa Glenn tracking times.

Lady Volunteer Softball (Est. 1995): Welcome to the Ball Park!

Three back-to-back-to-back trips to the College Women's World Series, a new stadium, and high-profile student-athletes choosing to be Lady Volunteers don't sound like features of a young softball program. Further program achievements are equally stunning:

The Lady Volunteer softball team rose to the top three in the SEC four consecutive seasons (2003–04, 2004–05, 2005–06, 2006–07).

The team boasts a 100-percent graduation rate for those who complete their eligibility.

From 2003 to 2006, the Lady Volunteers had ten First-Team All-Americas and the most in the United States in 2006.

The Lady Volunteers rose from the bottom to being the top defensive team in the nation in 2004 and 2005.

The Lady Volunteers led the NCAA in hitting in 2006.

The Lady Volunteers went to the NCAA Women's World Series 2005, 2006, and 2007.

The Lady Volunteer softball team was born in 1995. The coaches and players in this

Young fans cheering their favorite Lady Vols.

program have achieved what many lifetimes fail to deliver. Softball popularity is obvious on any home game date when fans are standing in line for a ticket hours before the first pitch. Television audiences have fallen in love with women's fast-pitch softball with the bonus exposure in the 1996 Olympics.

The Tennessee Lady Volunteer program attracted extraordinary players from the very start with the lure of building a new program. The commitment of the University of Tennessee to women's athletics is well known through the successes of other sports, particularly the basketball teams coached by Pat Summitt. Longstanding sports have set a high bar of expectations, and the softball program has met the challenge. Co–Head Coaches Ralph and Karen Weekly agree that commitment and passion for women's athletics create a climate nothing short of excellent: "Tennessee's sole support of women's athletics sends a message to all that women's athletics are important enough to have sole dedication. We are part of a big family and

1989

Basketball: SEC Tournament Champions; NCAA National Champions (Tennessee 76–60 Auburn)

Volleyball: SEC Tournament—3rd (tie)   Tennis: SEC Championships—3rd

Swimming and Diving: SEC—2nd; NCAA—4th

Cross Country: SEC—2nd   Track and Field: SEC (Indoor)—2nd; SEC (Outdoor)—3rd

The marketing and promotions staff provides free pizza in response to cheering Lady Volunteer fans.

Co-head Coach Ralph Weekly with players.

1990

Basketball: SEC Champions

Cross Country: SEC—1st

Volleyball: SEC—3rd (tie)

Swimming and Diving: SEC—2nd

Track and Field: SEC (Indoor)—3rd; SEC (Outdoor)—3rd

the high expectations are an integral part of the Lady Vol Tradition. We want to live up to that standard. We want to take the program all the way."

The Lady Volunteer softball program teaches discipline and healthy competition. Student-athletes learn how to prepare to meet the best, to be even better and how to deal with defeat. Lady Volunteer softball teaches the lessons of life.

Lady Volunteer Soccer (Est. 1996): Building the Tradition

Make no mistake about it: Tennessee Head Soccer Coach Angela Kelly loves competition. Jerseys of three University of North Carolina teammates hang on her office wall, and Kelly is quick to note that she experienced four National Championships during her play at UNC. But she also made three friends, and that is the true reward. On another wall is a large map with pins to indicate the locations of all the football stadiums in the United States. Her goal is to run in every one. Kelly loves running, and football, particularly the Indianapolis Colts. She especially admires Peyton Manning. A friend challenged her to run no less than one mile every day for a year. On December 26

of that year, she was riding to Florida with her family. Nearing midnight, she pulled into a shopping center parking lot and drove in circles to measure one mile. Then she and her golden retriever, Jake, ran a mile so that she would keep on her goal.

Kelly grew up in Scotland and played all sports depending upon the season. Influenced by her father, she focused on soccer and played in Canada before landing in the United States. Kelly says that Coach Pat Summitt influenced her to go into coaching. "I was an assistant coach for the Lady Vols when Head Coach Charlie MacCabe left," she says. "Joan Cronan presented me the offer to serve as head coach for Tennessee. I walked into Pat's office, told her of the Tennessee coaching offer, and Pat said, 'So, what is it going to be for you—coaching or playing?' I said that my passion is playing. Pat looked up and said, 'You are a coach.'"

Soccer players agree. Angela Kelly's leadership has positioned Tennessee as a perennial participant in the race for the NCAA Women's College Cup. Coach Kelly cites many pinnacle moments: her first year achieving second finish in the East with an overall 12–8 record; a memorable 2001 victory over Florida; and the challenges of the 2005 season with a team of thirteen

Elated soccer teammates carry head soccer coach Angela Kelly at the 2002 SEC Championship victory celebration.

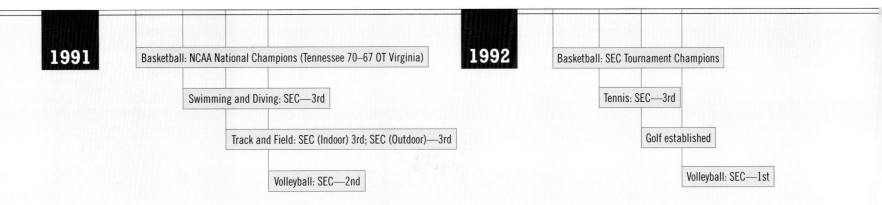

1991
- Basketball: NCAA National Champions (Tennessee 70–67 OT Virginia)
- Swimming and Diving: SEC—3rd
- Track and Field: SEC (Indoor) 3rd; SEC (Outdoor)—3rd
- Volleyball: SEC—2nd

1992
- Basketball: SEC Tournament Champions
- Tennis: SEC—3rd
- Golf established
- Volleyball: SEC—1st

Back: Kristen Doukakis; Left: Ali Christoph; Right: Haley Prendergast.

freshmen who, with a 0=4-1 record, faced Virginia on the road, won the game, and finished the season first in the SEC East. Kelly's Lady Volunteers are drawn to their coach, and she is a natural motivator. One Lady Vol said, "Coach Kelly really respects us and knows how to pull out the best in us." Kelly motivates with tangible results, has an open-door policy, and is willing to do whatever she asks of others.

At the conclusion of the stellar 2005 season, a newspaper reporter asked Kelly how she felt about her players' success. She responded, "Ask me that question in about thirteen years when we see these young women in successful lives. Then measure my success. Soccer is just a game; life skills are what count the most." Angela Kelly knows that hard work and enthusiasm for the game build success. Her care for student-athletes on and off the field generates loyalty and commitment.

Former Assistant Coach Jen Laughridge Grubb played on the Tennessee team and worked side by side with her college coach. As a player, Grubb listened to crazy loud music before the game. As a coach, she listened to calm music and resisted the urge to run out on the field. Grubb says, "The Tennessee program is about the pursuit of

excellence. I appreciate so much the opportunities I had as a student-athlete and as a coach to provide the same experiences for others."

Current Assistant Coach Keeley Dowling also returned to coach her collegiate team. The University of Tennessee women's soccer program is relatively young. Already Coach Angela Kelly has protégés. The tradition of Lady Volunteer soccer has begun.

Keeping Lady Vols Healthy

Athletic Training

When one steps into the athletic training facility, it takes only a moment to recognize that the Lady Vols athletic training department is about more than mending the injured. Posted front and center, the mission statement is clear: "In support of the University of Tennessee–Knoxville and women's athletic department Missions, the Lady Vols athletic training department creates a safe and healing environment for student-athletes through the professional skills of caring sports medicine personnel. The staff provides a solid program for the prevention of athletic injuries and illnesses and brings the knowledge and training needed to effect

1993

Basketball: SEC Champions

Golf: SEC Championships—2nd; NCAA East Regional—8th

Volleyball: NCAA Championships—17th (went to second round in tournament)

Basketball: NCAA Final Four—3rd

recovery and a return to sport performance and healthy living."

At the entrance, a bulletin board lists a staff of individuals whose lifestyles exemplify total healthy living. A wall display celebrates academic and goal accomplishments of student-athletes, and another honors individual fan support. An electronic sign scrolls reminders about hydration, nutrition, and exercise with helpful hints and Lady Vol facts. Posters celebrate sport greats, legendary moments, and values of the Lady Volunteer program. But it is not the visuals that really capture one's attention as much as the atmosphere. The athletic training area is a place that student-athletes call "home."

The staff is a group of highly trained sports-medicine personnel who provide comprehensive services. Jenny Moshak, assistant athletic director for sports medicine, demands top-quality excellence and total commitment in a professional environment. Jenny leads by example, and all staff members reflect the values of ethical behavior, hard work, respect, and continuing education. Athletic trainers are certified and dedicate their efforts to specific sport areas to provide coverage for all student-athletes.

Every student-athlete receives complete attention and care regardless of her year,

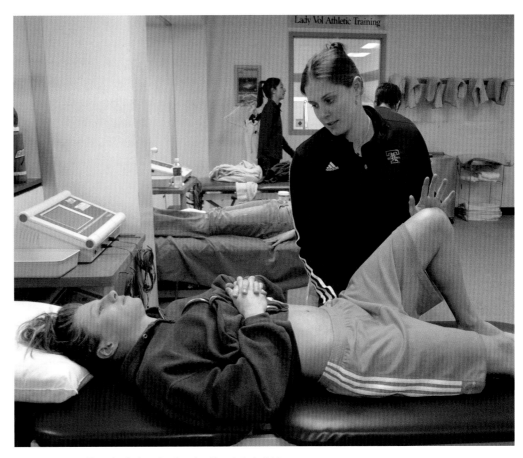

Athletic training staff member Bethany Strock works with a student-athlete.

sport, scholarship status, or talent. From opening day physicals until check-out at graduation, each Lady Vol has a personal athletic trainer who teaches her injury prevention and provides ongoing care for healing when injury or illness occur. State-of-the-art treatment and rehabilitation techniques aim to assure that the student-athlete will return safely and injury-free to her sport. Athletic trainers are always front and center during events, providing medical guidance and direction, and they are the first responders to

1994

Basketball: SEC champions; SEC Tournament Champions

Golf: SEC Championships—4th; NCAA East Regional—5th

Track and Field: (Outdoor) SEC—3rd

1995

Basketball: SEC Champions; NCAA Final Four—2nd (Conn 70–64 Tenn)

Swimming and Diving: SEC Championship—3rd

Tennis: SEC—3rd   Volleyball: SEC—1st

Rowing established   Softball established

distress. It is not uncommon for the athletic trainer to lose sight of the score or a team possession. The eyes of the athletic trainer are always on the student-athletes.

Dr. Rebecca Morgan, primary care physician for the Lady Vols, has a full-time office on campus and spends regular hours in the athletic training facility. She is present at most home athletic events and is on call for emergencies. Community physicians of specialty areas are also a part of the care team.

Over the course of time, Dr. Morgan has observed significant changes in the health-care needs of collegiate student-athletes:

Our society has seen changes in the ways we approach sports. Today's children tend to focus on one sport early rather than experiencing different sports with each season. The level of competition has risen considerably, and bigger payoffs increase pressures to perform. While overall athletic ability and achievement are higher, there are some costs. Specializing too soon can affect healthy growth. Cross-training helps bodies and muscles to develop better. Even when older athletes are ready to specialize in one sport, they benefit from the varying activities of cross-training. Pressures to perform can blind us to the importance of rest and restorative activties necessary for good health.

Dr. Morgan points out that some issues are particularly pertinent to female athletes and that the physical-psychological connection is different for each gender. Women who are strong with developed muscles, tall, large, and athletically competitive may feel that they stand out. Even though women's athletics have become much more commonplace, society is slow to change the definition of feminine beauty. Dr. Morgan notes that female student-athletes may struggle with body image and identity issues. Student-athletes experience the same developmental issues as other college students, but pressures to perform, increased time demands, and financial dependency on an athletic scholarship can cause additional stress. Pathological coping mechanisms may emerge to the detriment of good health.

Jenny Moshak proactively meets the ever-growing challenges of sports medicine. A recognized leader in her profession, Jenny sets a high priority on education. Ongoing staff development to sharpen skills, knowledge, and expertise is essential. Additionally, Jenny and others on her staff teach graduate students in the classroom and on-site. Student-athletes learn responsibility for every aspect of caring for their daily health and well-being. When a Lady Vol steps into the athletic training room, she is certain to leave with a strong dose of care that goes well beyond the surface.

Strength and Conditioning

The hallways of Stokely Athletic Center are silent and empty. An occasional student-athlete trots by, and footsteps quickly fade. Suddenly a door opens with a blast of heat and the sound of body-pounding music to reveal strong-willed competitors setting pace to the music with every mechanical muscle bender known to humankind. Circling the room with intensity is an alert, energetic commander calling out words of encouragement and direction.

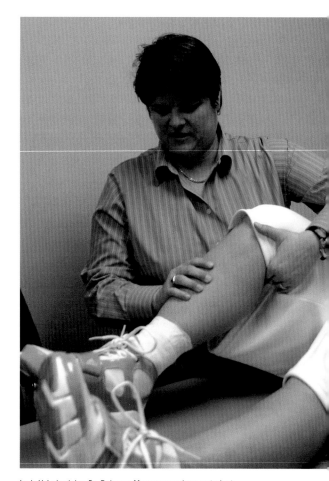

Lady Vol physician Dr. Rebecca Morgan examines a student-athlete's injury.

We have entered the world of strength and conditioning. Heather Mason, head strength and conditioning coach, has the uncanny ability to observe an entire room full of student-athletes and be so closely connected to each that she is at once a personal coach and commander of an "army." Working closely with the coaches, Mason develops personal plans for each student-athlete and monitors her progress. The goals are to "maximize strength and power to increase sport performance and decrease the likelihood and severity of injury," according to the UT Media Guide.

The weight room is an environment built on "camaraderie and competition at the highest levels" (UT Media Guide). Student-athletes have full responsibility for their workouts. Upon entry they pick up an instruction sheet and move through the equipment workout stations as a team. They focus on their tasks, work in partners for exercises that call for assistance, and encourage one another along the way. Rules include:

- **Mandatory ten push-ups for every yawn**
- **No chit-chat**
- **Courtesy at all times**
- **Faltering in an exercise means restarting the sequence from the beginning**
- **Do it right the first time**

Motivational posters line the walls, and student-athletes have full responsibility to wipe the equipment after use. The weight room belongs to the student-athletes, and they are accountable to each other.

Mason develops workout plans to include games that appeal to the competitive nature of the student-athletes. As student-athletes move through their workouts, Mason quizzes them on anatomy, muscles, and the impact of their work on their bodies. She creates a classroom of physiology in action where failure is not an option. Mason says that the student-athletes thrive and grow in their self-confidence and accountability, not to mention their strength.

"Our strength and conditioning facility provides a place where women can be strong and develop their bodies athletically," Mason explains. "They learn that the 'Tennessee effort' is a metaphor for life. Working hard produces results. They learn more about the mind-body connection and the power of focus. This is where each student-athlete really has her own 'face' time. She has emotional attachment here with the physical and mental preparation."

Student-athletes are on their own during the summer break, and many choose to remain on campus to work on their own individual goals. The strength and conditioning room and staff are always available for them. Mason and her staff offer creative events to keep the fun in the workout. One event, "Red, White, and Boom," is a summer competition of games. Mason creates teams of student-athletes from different sports so that they have the added experience of becoming better acquainted with other Lady Volunteers.

Just a brief time in the strength and conditioning area shows the dedication and hard work that student-athletes bring to their sports. What fans see on the court, in the pool, at the track, on a river or in the stadium is really just one part of the life of a student-athlete. It's behind the scenes where the action really counts.

Team ENHANCE

She was a long way from home, shy, and had never spent much time away from her family. She had always excelled in sports, and now here she was, with a full scholarship to college. It was a dream come true. Everyone in her hometown had celebrated, and people were already following the sports pages of their newspapers, eager to see their hometown girl become a star. She could still hear the cheers and words of encouragement as she had stepped onto the plane to fly to Knoxville, Tennessee.

What had happened to her? Where had things gone so wrong? The words of her coach still ringing in her head, Janie (a fictitious name) was beginning to believe that she had made a terrible mistake. How was she supposed to manage it all? She had lost ten pounds just since coming to school, but

1996

Basketball: SEC Tournament Champions; NCAA National Champions (Tennessee 83–65 Georgia)

Soccer established: SEC record—3–5; Eastern Division—5th

Softball: overall—54–14

Swimming and Diving: SEC—3rd; NCAA—9th

Heather Mason, strength and conditioning coach, encourages Lady Vol basketball player Alexis Hornbuckle.

Heather Mason challenges Lady Vol basketball players Alberta Auguste (in straps) and Shannon Bobbitt (foreground). Basketball team members in background are Sydney Smallbone (left) and Angie Bjorklund (right).

she really couldn't eat much. Her stomach hurt all the time except when she was at practice. So, she spent much of her time running—even when she didn't have to, just to keep her stomach from hurting and her thoughts from racing.

The other members of her team seemed nice enough, but they were so much better than she was. "I don't think I will ever get to play," she says to herself. "My parents keep talking about coming to see us compete. What will I do when I don't even get to compete? What will they think?"

Then there was school. Her classes seemed OK, but she just couldn't concentrate. She was already behind in her class work, and that too was troubling. She had always made high grades, so surely she would pull that out. But if she lost her athletic scholarship, what difference would her grades make anyway? There was just no hope.

This Lady Vol's story is not unique. All freshman students experience stress and self-doubts when they meet the challenges of transitions to college. The university provides services to help students, and most adjust and have successful, happy college experiences. Student-athletes face the same transitional adjustment challenges, but their challenges can become compounded. They are stepping into a highly competitive level of athletics, facing a daunting test at time management, building new relationships with teammates and coaches, finding new friends, and learning to live independently. Academic expectations are high, and college classes are different from those in high school. Self-identity and confidence are tested during these developmental years.

Dr. Kristen Martin (right), Team ENHANCE coordinator, consults with Jenny Moshak, assistant athletics director for sports medicine.

In 1990 Jenny Moshak, assistant athletic director for sports medicine, pioneered a program to help student-athletes with issues that affect performance, Team ENHANCE (Enhancing Nutrition, Health, Athletic Performance, Networking, Community, and Education). Committed to the project as "the next right thing to do," Moshak gathered a team of professionals from the community to pool their resources. Experts include the team physician, athletic trainers, eating disorder/addictions specialist, nutritionists, therapists/counselors, strength and conditioning coaches, exercise physiologist, coaches, athletic administrators, sport sociologist, and sport psychologist. This integrated team, according to the UT Media Guide, "provides education and early intervention for the student-athlete's emotional, mental and physical health, well-being and performance."

Kristen Martin, L.C.S.W. and Team ENHANCE coordinator, was a competitive swimmer in college and knows firsthand the struggles that student-athletes experience. "Every freshman goes through transition," she says. "Student-athletes have to adjust so quickly to school, practice schedules, media attention, and many other issues. They have no time for themselves—no ME time. Student-athletes live such different lives from other students. Problems coping can show up as eating disorders, irregular sleep patterns, depression, and other ways."

Injuries are another reality that can be emotionally difficult for the student-athlete. When activity in her sport stops even for a short time, she may find that her identity is lost, and she may struggle to find a way to bounce back.

Student-athletes may be especially hesitant to confide in coaches or teammates for

Softball "high-fives" tell the story: (left to right) Kristi Durant, Caitlin Ryan, Monica Abbott, Kenora Posey, and Tonya Callahan.

Performance can also take a toll on self-esteem. A Lady Vol shared her experiences with disappointment:

I am a senior now and realize that I am not going to be the best in my sport. I do really well, but for a long time in my life my only goal was to earn a gold medal. I have done my best, but that achievement is not realistic for me. I had a hard time dealing with this. I felt like such a failure. At a time when everyone is excited to graduate, I felt awful and as if my life was over. With my counselor I figured out that I can be successful in so many ways. I have been successful in athletics and can continue to do good work in athletics if I choose. Success and championships aren't just about the medals. It's about the people I can affect as an athlete and a person.

When you come to Tennessee, you are making a difference in people's lives. You have to make good choices—you are a leader whether you like it or not. It is OK to be scared. Team ENHANCE is here. We are so lucky; not every school offers this. We are like a family, and I am never just one person alone. Someone is always here, available 24/7.

fear of appearing weak or vulnerable. Team ENHANCE provides a confidential, safe place for student-athletes to find the support they need to take on life-changing experiences. One Lady Vol expressed her appreciation for the services: "In the push to be the best, you can lose sight of the personal. I have a professional relationship with my coach and am friends with my teammates. Team ENHANCE gave me a place to find an objective, outside perspective from a counselor who has been a student-athlete. I know she understands what life is like for me. I have learned how to balance my life so that I keep a priority on what is really important."

Another Lady Vol suggested the difficulties that women especially can face: "I had trouble being comfortable with an athletic body type. I need to train my body and have strong muscles. That isn't consistent with what people sometimes see as the ideal female body. I had to learn to be comfortable, proud to accept the differences. It can be difficult for women not to let others dictate what they should look like."

Team ENHANCE stays busy—so busy that one wonders how student-athletes existed without it. Sports present a wonderful venue for fun, satisfaction, and exercise. Team ENHANCE provides support to keep the fun in athletics and to help student-athletes remain centered on their own personal passion for their sports. With this essential ingredient, Lady Volunteers will treasure their collegiate athletic careers long after their days at Tennessee.

Spotlight
Alisa Harvey
Track and Field, 1984–87

Alisa Harvey

Alisa Harvey raced to an NCAA Outdoor victory in the 1500 meters in 1986 and collected nine All-America honors.

Her Way

It all started with President John F. Kennedy's physical fitness testing. In the days of Kennedy, schools throughout the nation incorporated a set of fitness benchmarks into their physical education curriculums. It was such a curriculum that tested a young girl in northern Virginia every year. Always the fastest girl, Alisa Harvey was second to only one boy in the 600-yard dash. Elementary school teachers were already identifying Alisa as the one to watch in high school track and field.

During her summers without training, Alisa would jump into some Hershey Hall of Fame track races just for fun. She didn't know why she excelled, but it thrilled her nonetheless. One day Alisa watched *Wilma*, a television movie about Tennessee native Wilma Rudolph, who overcame childhood handicaps to become a champion runner. "And I remember watching the whole thing," Alisa recalls. "And at the same time I think the Olympics were on. And Wilma was this amazing Olympic sprinter. She overcame polio. And she grew up very poor. I remember that I wanted to be a sprinter from that day on."

The instability of her parents' relationship handed Alisa the challenges of attending five different elementary schools in her first six years. As she explains:

My parents didn't get divorced until I went to college. I was actually kind of a loner. My parents moved around a lot, and so I never did associate with an old group of friends.

When we got to a new place, I was on my own. I would ride my bike or go to the playground. But I was on my own a lot.

I think that is why I gravitated toward individual sports like gymnastics and track. I would watch TV or teach myself gymnastic moves. And I watched the Olympic Games. I wanted to be an Olympic athlete. And it was gymnastics first and then sprinting. We couldn't afford gymnastics classes so I taught myself a lot from the playground bars, the back yard, and the living room floor on blankets.

By the time Alisa entered high school, she was good enough to compete in the regional events. With no formal training in gymnastics, she realized that her progress would be limited. After taking a bad spill on the uneven bars, Alisa decided to focus on track and field. That decision brought two significant individuals into her life: Betty Stegall, her high school coach, and Bill Kamenjar, her club coach. She says:

I consider myself to be very fortunate. My father was a postal worker. My mother worked as a bank teller. There was not any extra money for lessons and things like that. I was lucky because my high school coach became my mentor. She would drive me wherever I needed to go. She would even go into her own pocket sometimes for expenses for me. I was lucky to have someone other than my parents who could help me financially support what I had to do.

My club coach would take us up and down the eastern seaboard for competition with the state junior teams. I didn't have finances to pay for this. A lot of times I think they helped me with that. I was so lucky to have them as mentors. They were important in my youth—during my high school years.

Lady Volunteers of the University of Tennessee were gaining national attention, and Alisa eagerly added their names to her list of inspiring student-athletes. "Delisa Walton and Joetta Clark (Diggs) were in *Track and Field News,*" Alisa says. "Delisa was one of the big Olympic hopefuls and Joetta was right there with her. I cut out their photos and put them on my wall. I set myself on going to Tennessee. Plus the connection with Wilma Rudolph [who attended Tennessee State] always stuck out in my mind. We also had some locals here that went to Tennessee—Linda Portasik and also Benita Fitzgerald [Mosely]. So there were a lot of local women that went to Tennessee and found that it was an Olympic school for my day in women's track and field."

Alisa was headed for the University of Tennessee. Recruited by Loren Seagrave, Alisa had only one year with Terry Crawford before Coach Crawford moved to Texas. She was disappointed after her freshman year. "My freshman year I did overdo the hours," she remembers. "I took seventeen credit hours. And I nearly failed out. I think that there were some times when Terry was not convinced of my abilities. I didn't have much time to form a relationship with her. I had some great coaching and some great workouts during my freshman year. I gained fifteen pounds my freshman year. And we could have actually won the NCAA cross country championship that year, and I went from being first or second on cross coun-

try to dead last. And here I was a freshman. I thought I had just messed myself up completely."

Alisa decided that she would quit. Her Pell Grant had fallen through, Terry Crawford was leaving, and she simply wasn't happy. Learning of her situation, Gary Schwartz, the new track and field coach, flew to Alisa's home in Virginia and asked her to return to Tennessee with a full scholarship. "Gary Schwartz was a mentor to me as I look back on it," she says. "I didn't realize then how powerful he was for me. Sometimes you just need a good down-to-earth person. And that is who he was. And he was there for the workouts. And he was there for whatever I needed. He was a good friend and person."

When Alisa returned to Tennessee, she put all her commitment and energy into track and field. She also worked hard to excel in the classroom and left time for little else: "My sport was my life. I wasn't into the clothes and the guys. I just wanted to run and run well. I attribute my success to my desire and my focus. I kind of coached myself. For me I have always focused on one thing. And that is what I want to do with my running. And I have the desire to do it, the desire to get it done. It means going to bed early. It means eating the right things. It means running when I don't want to. I loved the team trips and I would have my fun there. The challenge was juggling three competitive seasons including travel with school work. There was just no room for anything social."

Alisa began to add her own records to the wall of Tennessee champions. Among her achievements, she was nine-time

All-America; thirteen-time All-SEC performer; 1986 NCAA Division I Outdoor 1500-meter champion; 1987 NCAA Division I Outdoor 800-meter and 1500-meter runner-up; a participant in the 1987 World University Games in Zagreb, Yugoslavia; and a Tennessee and SEC record-holder in both indoor and outdoor events. In 1984 Alisa set the world record at the time as the NCAA Indoor Champion, 4x800-meter relay. That event is still a special point of pride for Alisa.

"I've had a lot of really nice moments that I just treasure from being at Tennessee," she declares. "I think the one that stands out is the 4x800 Penn Relays championship race in 1984. It was I, Joetta Clark [Diggs], Cathy Rattray [Williams], and Karol Davidson. We set the meet record. That record held until 2007. We got a plaque recently for holding a twenty-year record. We didn't realize then how fast we all ran. Each split was so quick. It was two freshmen and two seniors. It was a 'who knew' moment because who knew the record would last twenty-three years!"

Alisa brought honor to Tennessee and felt pride as a Lady Volunteer: "Being at Tennessee made me more comfortable as a female athlete. Once I got to Tennessee, I realized how much pride and power and history is at the University with its own women's athletic program. It is such a strong image that I felt completely comfortable as a female athlete. And I think people were proud to see us perform. And that is one thing that I did take from the university—the pride of the women's athletics program. I am proud of that department for making me proud to be a female athlete."

Alisa Harvey

Sport Stats

- SEC Indoor champion, 4x880-yard relay, 1984
- NCAA Indoor champion, 4x800-meter relay (setting world record at the time: 8:40.17), 1984
- Shares UT record in the Outdoor distance medley relay, 1984
- Shares UT record in the Outdoor 4x800-meter relay, 1984
- SEC Team Champion, Indoor, 1984
- SEC Team Champion, Outdoor, 1984
- SEC Outdoor Champion, 1500 meter, 1984, 1985, 1987
- Holds UT record in the indoor 1500m, 1985
- SEC Indoor Champion, 1000 yard, 1986
- NCAA Outdoor Champion, 1500 meter, 1986
- Holds UT record in the indoor mile, 1986
- Holds UT record in the Outdoor 1500 meter, 1986
- Holds UT record in the Outdoor mile, 1986
- SEC Outdoor Champion, 800 meter, 1986, 1987
- SEC Indoor Champion, 1000 meter, 1987
- SEC Indoor Champion, 1500 meter, 1987
- SEC Indoor Meet record, 1000 meter, 1987
- SEC Indoor Meet record, 1500 meter, 1987
- NCAA Outdoor 800 meter and 1500 meter runner-up, 1987
- Holds UT record in the Indoor 1000m, 1987
- Shares collegiate record in the Outdoor 4x800-meter relay
- Nine-time All-America
- Three-time All-SEC in Cross country

Academic Stats

- B.A., Communications, University of Tennessee, 1988

Postcollegiate Career Highlights

- Sponsored athlete: Nike Corporation/Athletics West (1987–89), Kinney Corporation (1991–95), New Balance, Inc. (1997–98), FILA (1998–99)
- US Olympic Trials 1500-meter finalist, 1988
- World Indoor Track Championships, Budapest, Hungary, 1989

Alisa Harvey continues her competitive running career at the Masters Competition in Orono, Maine, 2007. Courtesy, John Irby.

Being recognized as a Lady Vol also created some funny moments. Alisa and her teammates remembered an encounter at a cross country meet away from home. "Gary Schwartz and the cross country team were traveling," she says, "and we stopped at the hotel where we were going to stay. A nice older man was coming down the hallway. We all came in with our bags. And he stopped us and said, 'Lady Vols.' And then he said, 'What's a Vol? Is it some kind of bird?' And that made us all laugh. And then he asked us if we were the basketball team. Now I am 5'2", and my roommate is 5'1". So that was pretty funny."

Alisa earned the nickname "Joyce" (after Dr. Joyce Brothers) because she always seemed to have an explanation for her ailments. Prone to allergies and colds, her coach and teammates enjoyed teasing her whenever she offered a self-diagnosis. Because of her allergies, Alisa especially likes to run near the water. One of her favorite locations is Havana, Cuba, where she ran in the Pan American Games. There the stadium sits just next to the ocean, which offers a warm, steady breeze.

"I have always loved running and the feeling you get with the wind blowing through your hair," Alisa says. "I love being on your own and hearing yourself breathe and the kind of high you get from the endorphins after you finish."

Alisa Harvey's talents and goals defy tradition. Her motto, "I did it my way," aptly describes her running career:

People over the years have questioned what I was doing. The 800 and 1500 meter are my specialties. I also run marathons. And I have run pretty close to my 1500 and 800 races. And it is not the thing to do. Usually you are a sprinter, or you are a distance runner. But I like doing both. So I got this running chain for my wrist that says, "I did it my way."

And I am very fortunate with my talent that I can do different distances. In 1998 I qualified for the Olympic trials in the marathon. I wanted to do a marathon. It was my first marathon in Richmond, and I went out there and nearly died it was so hard. I actually qualified for the Olympic trials.

I ran a trail marathon in Sparks, Maryland, about four years ago. It is an out-and-back race. It was hard. The footing is different. And it gets monotonous. There is nothing to see but the pretty trees. And I got cold because the sun was hidden behind the trees. But it was a great experience.

Every moment of life isn't necessarily happy or easy. But with each step comes an opportunity to build confidence and move forward. Alisa's independent spirit and willingness to learn from others are essential elements as she ponders advice to others. "Rely on your intuition when you pick a coach," she says. "Coaches are very important for a career in running. So be careful. Also, don't be afraid to stand alone. Be your own person. And it is tough socially. Be willing to go by yourself. The top athletes I have seen don't mind being individuals."

As a young girl, Alisa Harvey looked at the eyes in the pictures on her wall and saw her champions. And with a pair of shoes, a willing spirit, and some coaches along the way, she became one.

Alisa Harvey

Postcollegiate Career Highlights (continued)

- Pan American Games, Havana, Cuba, 1500-meter gold, 800-meter silver, 1991
- US Olympic Trials 800-meter and 1500-meter finalist, 1992
- World Outdoor Track Championships, Stuttgart, Germany, 1993
- US Olympic Trials, 800-meter and 1500-meter finalist, 1996
- Olympic Training Center athlete, 1996
- Goodwill Games Women's Mile, Long Island, New York (4:29.), 1998
- Army Ten-Miler champion, 1998
- Personal trainer, National Sports Professional Association Certified, 1998–2000
- World Indoor Championships, Maibashi, Japan, 1999
- Army Ten-Miler champion, 1999
- Richmond Marathon runner-up (2:49:28), 1999
- Motivational speaker/sponsored athlete: Avon Products, Inc., 1999–2001
- US Olympic Trials Marathon, 800 meter and 1500 meter, 2000
- Avon Women's Global 10K Championships, Milan, Italy, 2000
- Volunteer coach, George Mason University Women's Track, distance events, 2001–02
- Army Ten-Miler champion, 2003
- Assistant coach, George Mason University Women's Track and Cross country, 2003–05
- Marine Corps Marathon Senior Champion, 2005
- W40 800 meter, Indoor US record (2:07.), 2006
- W40 mile, Indoor US and world record (4:50.), 2006
- W40 Mile Outdoor US record (4:50.), 2006
- Army Ten-Miler Champion, Masters Champion and Masters record holder (59:00), 2006
- Selected "Masters Athlete of the Year" by USA Track and Field, June 2007
- Lady Volunteer Hall of Fame

Bridgette Gordon

USA

Bridgette Gordon was the driving force behind four consecutive trips to the Final Four (an NCAA-record) and two NCAA national championships (1987 and 1989).

If It's Gold and Glitters, It Must Be Gordon!

No basketball Lady Vol will ever wear Tennessee number 30 again. Bridgette Gordon played with the dedication and commitment that retired her jersey. In 2007 she was inducted into the Women's Basketball Hall of Fame. She earned a gold medal as a member of the 1988 US Olympic basketball team and made an NCAA record four consecutive trips to the Final Four at the University of Tennessee. She won two national championships (1987 and 1989), was named Women's Final Four Most Valuable Player in 1989 and Final Four All-Tournament team member in 1987 and 1989. And the accolades go on and on.

This remarkable woman was born third youngest of eight children and raised in DeLand, Florida. Growing up, she played all sports and especially liked softball. Her father, a native Jamaican, was Bridgette's softball coach. She and her best friend, Robin, played against boys to experience tougher competition. Until eleventh grade Bridgette played softball and volleyball and ran hurdles in track. In eleventh grade she focused solely on basketball.

Bridgette's choice of sport was motivated by her desire to earn a college scholarship. Basketball was the sport that would most likely take her further than softball or volleyball. Even though possibilities for professional basketball careers didn't yet exist for women, as a little girl Bridgette aspired to the highest conceivable accomplishment: to compete in the Olympics. She says:

I have to give a lot of credit to my father. He was always my mentor and my coach. He always told me to dream high and think high—and not only in sports but in the classroom, too. I was a straight-A student until I got to high school.

My mother and father separated when I was young. My mom worked so hard raising eight kids; that motivated me to go out and be successful on my own. And just to see my father go out and work hard—he worked three jobs then. I was able to see what he could accomplish from hard work. And it made me want to do the same.

Bridgette's athletic prowess was well-documented by the time she was a high school senior. She was Parade All-America, *USA Today* All-America, All-South, All-State, All-Star, and All-Conference. And she was recruited from all directions:

I was being recruited by everybody. I was getting a lot of pressure from people in the state of Florida to stay in the state. I verbally committed to the University of Florida. But an alum from Tennessee saw it in the newspaper and called Pat (Summitt). Pat was so upset. She said, "Don't you play games with me. I have other kids who want to come here—you need to let me know." Pat's friend and mentor, Billie Moore at UCLA, was the one who had told Pat about me. I guess Coach Moore figured I would not go to UCLA.

After that, I visited Tennessee. On my recruiting visit Pat came to pick me up at the airport, and she was driving a 300 ZX. And I forget where we were going, but she did doughnuts in the parking lot while I was in the car. I thought, "Wow!" She was trying to get my attention. She was telling me something.

I decided to go to Tennessee because it seemed that I could accomplish the things I wanted to do. My biggest goal was to become an Olympian. Pat had the credential of just winning the 1984 Olympics. And her graduation rate was perfect; she just had everything that a kid could want to do.

Bridgette's freshman year was a period of adjustment to the rigorous Tennessee workouts. At the minimum, Bridgette's daily schedule began at 6:30 a.m. with a run on the track. At 7:45 a.m. she had class and then returned after classes to the weight room and a three-hour practice.

Every day was challenging playing for Pat. A lot of people don't give athletes the credit that they deserve, because we have to perform in both the classroom and on the basketball court. If you were having a bad day in the classroom, you couldn't let that bother you on the basketball court. And because Pat was so demanding and so disciplined, it was difficult sometimes for an eighteen-year-old.

Pat knows which buttons to push. And I was so tough that my freshman year I got into so much trouble for doing things like rolling my eyes and putting my hands on my hips. She let me know that I was not in DeLand anymore. Even the littlest things were not going to be tolerated.

Bridgette earned the name "Flash Gordon" because of the way she used to get out on the fast break on the wing. She was also called "Miss T" because she loved to wear a lot of gold jewelry. One time Bridgette's fondness for gold caused her a bit of trouble with the coach. "In the summer of 1987," she says, "after we had won the national championship, we were working a basketball camp, and I told Pat that I needed to go to the dentist. I went and had a gold front tooth put in my mouth. Pat was so upset with me. She said, 'If I had known you were going to the dentist to get a gold tooth put in, I would have never let you go.' She said, 'What job interview will you be going on with a gold tooth in your mouth?' And I looked at her and thought, 'What have I done? What are the rest of my years here going to be like?' She got on me in front of everyone at camp. I was so embarrassed."

Bridgette and her teammates were especially close, with Pat as the center. She remembers:

My teammates and I cherish our friendships. The relationship that Pat has with each one of her players is different. They used to call me her pet. But I was not her pet. She used to get on me so hard. But I would never let her see me cry. I used to go back to my room at night and cry. And I would ask my mom if I could come back home. And my mom would say, "No, you are going to get yourself a good education." My mom had given Pat permission to take care of her daughter. And I knew she was something special for my mom to do that. Pat was my mom away from home. I was the member of the team who was furthest from home, but I was by no means Pat's pet.

Bridgette Gordon

Sport Stats

- NCAA Team of the Decade (1980s)
- Kodak All-America, 1988, 1989
- Olympian (gold), 1988 (one of two collegiate members of US Olympic women's basketball team)
- NCAA All-Regional Tournament Teams: Mideast, 1987; East, 1988; East, 1989
- NCAA Regional Tournament Most Outstanding Player: Mideast, 1987; East, 1989
- US Junior Olympic National Team, 1986
- US Olympic Festival, 1986
- SEC Freshman of the Year, 1986
- All-SEC Team, 1986, 1987, 1988, 1989
- NCAA All–Final Four Team, 1988, 1989
- US National Team, 1987–89
- Naismith All-America Team, 1988, 1989
- SEC Tournament Most Valuable Player, 1988, 1989
- SEC All-Tournament Team, 1988, 1989
- Honda Cup Winner, 1989
- NCAA Tournament Most Outstanding Player, 1989
- SEC Female Athlete of the Year, 1989
- Made an NCAA-record four consecutive trips to the Final Four
- Co-SEC Rookie of the Year, 1986
- Led SEC in scoring, 1988, 1989
- Holds record for most career steals (338) and is second all-time leading scorer in school history (2,450 points) after averaging 18 points and 6.7 rebounds in 137 games (as of 2007)
- Two-time National Champion, 1987, 1989

Bridgette Gordon

Sport Stats (continued)

- Member 900 Rebound Club with 917 career rebounds
- Member 2,000 Point Club with 2,460 career points

Academic Stats

- B.S., political science, University of Tennessee, 1989

Postcollegiate Career Highlights

- WNBA—Sacramento Monarchs, 1997–98
- Overseas Professional Play: Italy, 1989–97 (won seven Italian Championships as an All-Star performer); Turkey, 1999–2000
- Broadcaster, Fox Sports South
- Assistant women's basketball coach, Stetson University, 2001–06
- WNBA regional scout
- Assistant women's basketball coach, Georgia State University
- Second Lady Vol to have her jersey retired (number 30), 1990
- One of five players named to NCAA's 25th Silver Anniversary Team in 2006
- Lady Volunteer Hall of Fame, inaugural class, 2001
- Women's Basketball Hall of Fame inductee

Sometimes when we were in the airport, everybody would say, "You go ask Pat if we can get some ice cream. She's going to give it to you." But Pat knew that I was going to work hard. And whatever she asked of me, I would go out and give 100 percent.

The eyes and ears of the coach seemed to be everywhere. Bridgette recalls:

I got my ear pierced in the top of my ear, and Pat asked what that meant. Every little thing she wanted to know. There wasn't anything that she did not find out about. People would call and let her know what club they saw us in.

Once, I saw that it was snowing outside, and I thought I didn't have to go to class. But I didn't call and ask if classes were cancelled. I didn't go to class, and Pat asked me if I attended class. I looked at her and I said, "No, because it was snowing outside." Pat said, "Well, you can meet me in the morning at 5 a.m. in the training room, and we will do five miles on the bicycle." And I never missed class again.

Bridgette's four-year leadership on the team resulted in four consecutive trips to the Final Four and two NCAA and two SEC championships. Bridgette is quick to say that these accomplishments were achieved by the team, not by one individual:

I think we all came together collectively. Look at how long Pat had been there and everything that she accomplished as a player herself, plus everything she accomplished as a coach and where she was trying to take us. Before my class came in, she had been

to the Final Four. She never had won it. Just looking at where she had been and where she wanted to go, we had to buy into it. And I was already there. I mean, I hate losing. I was determined, too. I wanted to be a part of her first national championship. So, we just all came together as a team. Especially Melissa [McCray], Sheila [Frost], and I—we said we wanted to win. And we wanted to win a Final Four. Our first year, we got a taste of the Final Four. We said, "We want to do this again and again." And we did; we were the first female team to go to four Final Fours. It was such a great accomplishment. I look back at my résumé sometimes, and I'm amazed at the things I have been able to accomplish. I am a very humble person, and so sometimes I think, "Oh my gosh, I really did that!"

People look back at those years, and it is not about how many points each individual scored. It is about team. They say, "She was a part of the team that won the first National Title." We had mutual respect.

Bridgette and her teammates enjoyed popularity on campus and had friends outside of basketball. They were always aware of the extra responsibility they had as Lady Vols. Bridgette says:

Pat always talked to us about how we should behave and how we were representing our families and our school. And that was something that my father always taught me. "Your name is all that you have," he said. "No matter what comes and goes, you always have your name. Be proud of it." Being an athlete can be very tough—especially when you are a student-athlete. You are a role model. You are always in the public eye. You have to be careful because one thing you do wrong can be the determining factor as to how people see you for the rest of your life. I think about it now, the lessons Pat instilled in me and the way that I can live my life now. I watched myself go from a little girl to a woman. What Pat did for us is priceless. She prepared us for the real world. When they talk about Pat, I think they are talking about my mom.

In 2007 the Lady Volunteer Basketball team won the NCAA National Championship. The date marked twenty years since the first national championship of 1987. Bridgette and her teammates were present to cheer the 2007 team to victory. "It was so great to celebrate the twenty years of our first national championship," she comments. "And I think it was motivating to the 2007 Lady Vols to see how all thirteen players and a manager came back to celebrate. As the team saw and listened to what it means to us, I think they not only wanted to win the championship but to be part of the tradition."

The people who become a part of the Lady Vol tradition are what made Bridgette's Tennessee years so special. She says:

If I had to do it all over again, I would do it with flying colors—most definitely. It was so enjoyable—the memories. We went through a lot. They were my sisters. We shared clothes and ideas and talks about boys. I never came back home in the summer because I was competing internationally. In those four years I probably came back to DeLand four times.

It is not about the wins and the losses. It is about the friends and relationships that I established and the lives that I touched along the way. They are priceless. When we had our reunion, we just picked up like it was yesterday. It is the friendships that you build. And they are always there, and no one can take them away from you.

And when I speak to people, I tell them that you don't realize how precious your college years are. Those are the most memorable years of my life. I have done a lot, and I always want to go back to my college years. You are always a part of the tradition and the legacy.

Bridgette has played professional basketball in the WNBA and on two international teams, coached collegiate basketball, and served as a talent scout for the WNBA. Now an assistant coach at Georgia State University, Bridgette has joined the staff of another Lady Volunteer, Head Coach Lea Henry (1979–1983). She has learned that there is life after basketball but acknowledges the significant role basketball plays in her life.

"I am what I am because of basketball," she says. "Basketball has done things for me I never thought of. It took me places I never dreamed of going. Athletes are no better than anybody else. That is just our title. We have our faults. We are not perfect people. Sometimes we make bad decisions. I tell young people to choose their role models wisely. A role model is someone who is there on a day-to-day basis to inspire you. I have my faults, but I try to do things to the best of my ability. Use me to help you to get where you want to be, but

Bridgette Gordon, inducted into the inaugural class of the Lady Volunteer Hall of Fame, October 26, 2001.

don't strive to be the next me. Be better. Be the next you."

In 1985 a bit of gold stepped onto the Tennessee basketball court. As Bridgette Gordon led in scoring, grabbed those rebounds, and broke those records, her brilliance reflected in the eyes of every Tennessee fan. Dazzling the world with Olympic gold, Flash Gordon had arrived. And Tennessee orange turned a little bit gold.

Spotlight
Tonya Edwards
Basketball, 1986–90

Tonya Edwards

Tonya Edwards, a guard from Flint, Michigan, joined great Lady Vol scorers with 1,309 career points.

It Had to Be "T"

If you are one of six children, and all your names begin with "T," it might be prophetic that at least one of you would end up at the University of Tennessee. But the distance between Michigan and Tennessee is measured by more than miles.

Tonya LaRay Edwards and her five older siblings—Tamara, Terry, Todd, Teresa, and Timothy—grew up in Flint, Michigan. Their mother, Emily Edwards, a single parent, provided a home that defined the meaning of love, commitment, and hard work. Tonya says:

They say it takes a village to raise a kid. Well, back then I had an older sister who really sacrificed. She was going to attend the University of Michigan, and she came back home to help my mother raise us. So she as well as my mom contributed a lot to make sure we had everything that we needed. Mom held down two jobs. And what blows me away even more is that no matter what she was doing, she always managed to make it to our games. She never missed a game that I played. That lets you see the influence that she had on my life. Even then when I was so young, she made me feel that I could accomplish anything. I could become anybody that I wanted to become as long as I worked hard and persevered. I knew it wouldn't be easy.

Tonya's grandparents raised her mother, Emily, in Mississippi, where cotton was the chief crop. Seeking a life other than picking cotton, Tonya's grandparents moved to Michigan. "My grandmother worked at a bakery," she recalls, "and we would stay there with her sometimes while my mom was at work. We would go in there and play in the doughnut shop. We could help make doughnuts."

While Tonya might have been influenced by the work setting in her grandmother's bakery, she found another pastime that was even more compelling:

A guy in the neighborhood just up the street had a rim on his house, and we used to play basketball there. He was taller than I was then, and he used to say that there was no way I was going to get around him. So I would go in between his legs. I always used to go there when I was younger, and I would end up playing with the guys. Looking back, it is ironic that today's coaches are questioning where guys fit into women's basketball for practice. That is how I got started and that is how guys fit. I guess I would never be against having guys practice with women's teams since I grew up competing against guys. It gives you so much as far as strength and competitive spirit. You are able to compete at a higher level.

Tonya tagged along with her older brothers despite her sister's protests that she would become a "tomboy." One day when she was waiting for her sister Teresa after school, the community school director, Otis Spann, noticed Tonya in the hallway. Spann invited her to play basketball in the gym, and at age ten she joined the school team. Before long, because of her height, she was playing on the area summer team with girls who were older than she was. Tonya also played football in elementary school. Tonya

The 1987 NCAA National Championship basketball team: (front row, left to right) Gay Townson (14), Melissa McCray (35), Dawn Marsh (4), Lisa Webb (34), Shelley Sexton (23), Tonya Edwards (33), Sabrina Mott (40), (back row, left to right) Cheryl Littlejohn (44), Jennifer Tuggle (32), Karla Horton (55), Sheila Frost (12), Carla McGhee (24), Kathy Spinks (11), and Bridgette Gordon (30).

Tonya Edwards

Sports Stats

- US Junior National Team, 1986
- US Olympic Festival, 1986
- US National Team, 1987
- NCAA Tournament Most Outstanding Player, 1987
- NCAA All-Final Four Team, 1987
- All-SEC Freshman Team, 1987
- Two-Time National Champion, 1987, 1989
- SEC Tournament Champion, 1988, 1989
- Academic All-SEC, 1990
- *USA Today* Co–Comeback Player of the Year, 1990
- Member, ESPY Awards Co-Team of the Decade for the 1990s
- Member Tennessee 1,000 Point Club with 1,309 career points
- Tied for sixth on Tennessee list of free throws made in single game with 13 (as of 2006)
- Sixth on Tennessee career list of free throws made, 371 (as of 2006)

Academic Stats

- B.S., Education, University of Tennessee 1990

remembers the boy whose position she took as quarterback complaining because she was able to play and he had to sit on the bench and hold her jacket.

"Even then I remember my mom coming to the football games," she adds. "She would be there on the sidelines. And when it was over, she would go back to work. But my mother was the pro and my sister was the con. My sister was saying, 'Why does she get to play football? Boys play football. She's the only girl out there on the football field.' It was flag football back then, so not much could happen to me. Otis Spann would say, 'Don't you mess with her or you will have to deal with me.' And he was a big guy."

Nate Jones introduced Tonya to AAU basketball, and she continued to play through junior high and high school. She had not really considered a collegiate career, but recruiters began to call. Tonya narrowed her choices to Tennessee, Iowa, the University of Southern California, Georgia, and Texas. After a closer look, she chose Tennessee. Of that decision, she remembers:

I thought all the schools were pretty much equal. What separated them was the feeling I had when I was there with the team, with Pat [Summitt] and the staff. I just felt like that was the place I belonged. I am really thankful that my mom encouraged it to be my decision. They sat down and talked with me and were just really frank. And I appreciated that.

It was funny. I think I kind of brushed Pat the wrong way. I said that all during growing up, I had never been coached by a woman.

Tonya Edwards

Postcollegiate Career Highlights

- Women's basketball coach, Northwestern Community High School (Flint, Michigan), 1990–95: guided team to 1993 state championship with perfect 28–0 record; 1992 state champion runner-up finish and compiled a 78–23 overall record (.772)
- Overseas Professional Basketball: Spain, 1991–92; Turkey, 1994; Israel, 1995–96
- Named "High School Coach of the Year" in Michigan, 1993
- American Basketball League: Columbus Quest, 1996–98 (won two championship titles)
- Interim head coach, Columbus Quest, 1998
- Women's National Basketball Association: Minnesota Lynx, 1999–2000; Phoenix Mercury, 2000–01; Charlotte Sting, 2001–02
- Radio commentator for Phoenix Mercury games, 2004
- Assistant coach of women's basketball team, University of Detroit Mercy, 2006–present
- Assistant coach, National Women's Basketball League
- Lady Volunteer Hall of Fame
- Head women's basketball coach, Alcorn State, 2008–present

And she gave me a look that said, "I'm going to give you a run for your money."

Tonya joined the Lady Vol lineup in the fall of 1986. That's when she began to learn what it would be like to be coached by Pat Summitt:

People don't always understand when a coach is trying to get others to perform at their maximum potential. I guess it does not come off that way. You might be thinking that this mean lady just keeps riding me. So it is sometimes after you leave the program when you realize what that coach is doing for you.

I think the pressure under Pat probably brought our team together. She didn't care who she picked on. I used to be thankful when she was on someone else. Most people would call me "Ice." Pat was the only one who called me "T." When she was upset with me, my name was Tonya. Other days my name was "T." I found out the difference very quickly. And I would say, "Whew, I'm glad it's not my day today."

But it did bring us together because we were always trying to give a pat on the back to whoever's day it was. I once said in the media that you knew how bad a day it was going to be by how Pat came around the curve.

Pat Summitt had built a stunning program at the University of Tennessee, but the Lady Vols had not yet won the National Championship. Tonya was drawn to Tennessee to win that trophy. "I thought about Pat and all her other accolades," she says. "The one that eluded her was winning the National Championship. I said to myself

Tonya Edwards with Joan Cronan at her induction into the Lady Volunteer Hall of Fame, 2006. Photograph by Patrick Murphy-Racey.

that I am going to help her win a National Championship. So that kind of helped my decision to go there."

That year the Lady Vols were victorious over Louisiana Tech in Austin, Texas, to bring home the 1987 NCAA National Championship trophy. Tonya Edwards, netting 13 points and grabbing 7 rebounds, was named most outstanding player and joined teammate Bridgette Gordon on the All-Championship team. "At the time it was kind of a relief winning the championship," she remarks. "Even though it was my first year, there was a relief after all the hard work. The tournament was over, and we were the last ones standing. It was a great feeling and sense of accomplishment. And I felt like you can reach your goals. Your goals are attainable."

Sometimes unforeseen events bring added challenges, and such was the case when Tonya tore her anterior cruciate ligament. "I remember going in for surgery," she says. "And my

mom had not yet arrived from Flint. And I was sitting there with Pat. It was early in the morning, around 6 a.m. I was lying there waiting to go into surgery, and I guess Pat could tell I was nervous. I saw another side of Pat that I had not seen—the compassionate side. She said that it was going to be OK. And she said, 'I love you.' And by that time I was about ready to pass out. I was thinking, 'I don't need any anesthesia now.'"

Recovering from knee surgery, Tonya continued to focus on books and basketball. She maintained her priorities and competitive edge: "Carla McGhee and I were roommates. And I used to tell her, 'Whatever doesn't get done by 11 p.m. doesn't get done, because I am going to bed. I've got to get up to see Pat in the morning.' Those mornings came quickly, and we were up at 6:00 running on the track."

Hard work, dedicated practice, and even disappointments are all special memories.

Tonya recounts a memorable return trip to Knoxville after losing at Auburn:

My sophomore year at the beginning of the season the coaches implemented the "rebound, two points" rule. If you made a mistake, you would just say, "rebound" and head down the floor. Then if they gave you a compliment, you would say "two points." That was for a good thing.

So one day we were getting ready to come home from Auburn, and we had loaded up the bus. And we had lost the game. After a loss, we were supposed to have fifteen minutes to blow off steam and then "park it." Pat got on the bus and some of us were in the back laughing. And she said, "I don't see anything funny. We just got our butts whipped and you are back there laughing." So Carla McGhee and I looked at each other and said, "She needs to park it." Pat did not hear us. Carla was back there just laughing.

The most precious thing that I took from the program was the friendships that I developed when I was there—and the camaraderie with the young ladies. Everybody was on the same page. We discovered that we can achieve great things if we work together. Everybody has to make a sacrifice to be successful.

Tonya Edwards has given Tennessee fans joy, fun, and pride. Certainly, her love of competition always sparks her energy. But in reality, her motivation comes from a desire even more special. "I wanted to please my mother," she says. "I wanted to make her proud of me. I wanted to see her smile."

With no doubt Tonya Edwards has given her mother many occasions to smile. And make no mistake about it: she still plays a little basketball here and there when her "knees don't hurt." And she still plays with the guys.

Jasmin Jones

Jasmin Jones (Keller), twelve-time All America, captured the attention of Lady Vol fans with championship records including cross country, indoor 4x800-meter relay, outdoor 800-meter, and outdoor 4x1500-meter relay.

All That Jas

Jasmin Jones (Keller) has focused on goals her entire life. When she saw the obstacles that poverty presents a community, she wondered why a president couldn't help people who needed more. When she ran, she ran with the wind and felt a passion like no other. She knew she wanted to be a social worker. She knew she wanted to run. And she was only eight years old.

By eighth grade Jasmin was running a mile in under six minutes and captured the attention of Edward Church, track and field coach at her hometown high school in Hackensack, New Jersey. The next four years saw Jasmin develop as a remarkable athlete under Church's tutelage. Jas modestly describes herself as a "tall, skinny high school student" who simply loved to run. Behind her passion to run was a determined spirit to compete to be the best. "I love the anticipation, the nerves—when the gun goes off—the adrenalin before a race," she reflects. "Some people have that competitive drive. I have that drive to win or be the best that I can be. Even in high school I was a little bit better than the athletes around my county—but for me even if I was ten to fifteen seconds ahead of the second-place person, I was still competing with the clock. It was a race between the clock and me."

Recalling her college recruitment, Jas was first attracted to school in Houston. The students she met there seemed fun, while her visit to the University of Tennessee left her feeling a little out of place as a middle-distance runner. Her high school coach was a friend of Gary Schwartz, then head coach of the

Lady Volunteers, and Coach Church's advice to Jasmin had significant impact on her decision to attend the University of Tennessee. Jasmin recalls Church's counsel: "He said, 'You are going to make your own decision— but I know Gary as a person, and I know it will be about more than athletics at UT.' That was all I needed. I trusted my coach, and it was important to know that my college coach was a good person. Thank goodness for Mr. Church."

The Lady Vol program offered Jasmin the support she wanted to achieve academically as well as on the track. She says:

The Lady Vol athletic program is not just about athletics—for me that was important. I wasn't really motivated academically in high school. At UT it was important for me to graduate. I am proud of our 97-percent graduation rate and all the women who go on to get secondary degrees. I had wanted to pursue social work and running since I was eight years old. UT made both of these goals happen. I went on to get my graduate degree here—a master's of social work and my professional social work license. When I had one bad year academically, I thought, "You have to get it together here—what do you have to go back to?" Kerry [Howland], our academic counselor, would ride me—I can remember Kerry howling—and I thank her for keeping me on track academically. We were expected to graduate.

Missy Kane (Alston Bemiller) was Jasmin's coach her sophomore year, and Jas remembers especially remembers her as a motivator: "Missy really worked well with every person on the team—especially the ones who had to work really hard to develop their talents. She gave walk-ons the same attention as those whose achievements came more easily."

Jasmin's personal challenge was to keep an appropriate race pace. One of her most vivid Lady Vol memories describes her inner conflict between running fast and pacing to win:

In 1991 when we won indoor NCAA for the 4x8 [relay] is one of my best memories. To understand why I treasure this moment so much, we need to go back to the year before. We were running against Villanova, a powerhouse in track and field at the time. My relay team gave me a huge lead. My adrenalin was running so high—I went out in a fifty-six-second quarter—too fast for two laps. Missy was yelling to slow down—I was fatigued—at about fifty to seventy meters my legs buckled. I could have walked and still beaten Villanova—our team had given me that much of a lead. But I fell two or three steps prior to the finish line, crawled over the line—all in slow motion—grabbed the baton. They helped me up—I was so fatigued. I thought we had won, but we were disqualified because I didn't have the baton in my hand when I fell—I had picked it up when I crawled across the finish line. When I fell, the Villanova coach stood up and clapped because their team had won. I felt terrible. I really believed that I had let our seniors down—that I was the reason they didn't win their last year. It was on the front page of the newspaper the next day. After returning home from that meet, I received a letter from Coach Webb of the University of Kentucky. I still have it framed in my athletic

The Penn Relays, one of the oldest and most prestigious meets, remains a favorite of many Lady Vol competitors. In 2004, the Lady Vols were victorious in the distance medley, spring medley, and 4x800-meter relay. Pictured here (left to right) are Taleatha Diggs, Joetta Clark Diggs (inducted into the Penn Relays Wall of Fame, Class of 2004), Lindsay Hyatt, Brooke Novak, Leslie Treherne, Nicole Cook, Bill Cosby (a longtime Penn Relays supporter, a competitor in the master's men's 100 meter dash, and "court jester" at the meet), Kameisha Bennett, Dee Dee Trotter, and Tianna Madison. Relay team member Toyin Olupona is not pictured.

room. He wrote that the Lady Vols were far superior to anyone else and that the effort I gave—the determination and will that I showed for our team—reminded him of Sabrina [Robinson] and Patty-Sue Plummer at the 1988 Olympic Trials. I knew what he was talking about because I ran at the trials as well. That letter really helped at a difficult time. So, that following year, 1991, I was going to run smart and not let that happen again. This time I came from behind, ran smart, smooth, and beat Villanova. I am not a showboater, but that year it was really sweet. There had been so much emotion for that whole year, and everyone was so supportive. There were many more moments. That one stands out, though.

Competition inspired Jas to strive to be the best. She carried special energy with an edge on race days. As she remembers:

I just took it out from the gun and really liked to compete from the back. I loved to be in the back and come out—feel the elation of passing each person—what a great feeling— passing with conviction—it is a rush! If I didn't feel nerves, it wouldn't be a good day. I used those nerves to my benefit. My nerves would be stored. I would feel so tired before a race and then get pumped. Preparing for a race, I gave myself lots of time to warm up, to stretch, to do a two-mile run and still have time to put my feet up and listen to my Walkman—getting into a zone, thinking

Jasmin Jones (Keller)

Sport Stats

- SEC Indoor Champion, 4x800-meter relay, 1988, 1990,1991
- UT record holder, outdoor 4x1500-meter relay, 1989
- SEC Indoor Champion, 1000 meter, 1989
- SEC Outdoor Champion, 1500 meter, 1989, 1990, 1991
- SEC Indoor Champion, mile, 1990
- SEC Outdoor Champion, 800 meter, 1990
- UT record holder, indoor 4x800-meter Relay, 1990
- UT record holder, outdoor 800 meter, 1990
- NCAA Indoor Champion, 4x800-meter relay, 1991
- Three-time All-SEC in cross country
- Twelve-time All-America (eleven, track and field; one, cross country)

Academic Stats

- B.S., Social Work, University of Tennessee, 1991
- M.S.S.W., University of Tennessee, 1993

Postcollegiate Career Highlights

- World University Games bronze medalist 800 meter, 1991
- Competed in three Olympic Trials, 1988 (still in college), 1992, 1996

about what I am going to do—getting my mind away from the other competitors and getting into my own zone.

Poignant moments and hard work combined with friends inevitably recall laughter as well:

We had a person on our team—Lisa Richardson—a wonderful walk-on. Lisa was my friend. We called her "Little Jasmin," and she was my little buddy. We did things together—she was a free spirit—cool. One time on or just before the day of a race, Lisa and I got in a little car accident. It was OK, but I hit my head on the dashboard so I had a little bump on my head. Lisa was really stressed about this, especially because she was the driver. I said, "I am fine." In one of the pictures that they posted later I had this huge bandage on my head. Here I was— running with a big bandage on my head— still won the race—parents upset—Lisa scared. We laughed, but this is not what you want to happen the weekend of a race.

Jasmin also remembers times when she was the object of her teammates' laughter. "I couldn't swim, and we worked out in the pool" she says. "I would hold onto the wall—scared even with a life jacket on. My friends constantly teased me about clinging to that wall. After runs we would go to the cafeteria, and everyone would get healthy food. I was always so thirsty and would get twenty cups of fruit punch, line them up, and not eat a thing—just drink that punch. Then later on at night I would be starving and raid the vending machines. I didn't learn to drink water until later in life."

Like all Lady Vols, Jasmin faced the challenge of juggling the demands of being an athlete as well as a student. "Things didn't come easily," she explains. "I had to study hard—never went out. Others went to parties while I would be in there with the typewriter and studying. I was focused on keeping my scholarship. I was not going to jeopardize that. I stayed focused on goals. It was hard to come back from road trips to the school world of class work. We were in two different worlds. Being an athlete is a job. Self-discipline comes with perseverance. I did what I had to do. I don't regret anything."

Having competed all over the world, Jasmin is quick to identify the Penn Relays as her favorite place to compete: "I started there as a freshman in high school, competed there throughout college and after college. I was a nervous wreck at the Penn Relays. The setting is like miniature Olympics—stands are packed. The football stadium looks huge, and the track looks bigger because of so many lanes even though we ran the inside lanes. People in the stands screamed when someone caught you."

Relays and dedication to team are particularly special to Jasmin. She says:

I always got a rush from competing on a relay. On our level everyone was equally good and when put all together, we would just run our hearts out. One time when Villanova beat us, we didn't even care because we each had run so well. I started out, and Patty [Wiegand] was our anchor. Patty ran her guts out—a 4.36 minute mile—but she was all disappointed, crying. We all had run our fastest splits ever—we were so proud.

Jasmin Jones Keller with husband, Andy, and sons, Cameron and Kaden, 2007. Courtesy, Jasmin Jones Keller.

In track the team relies on you. I would run several events—sometimes not my particular event—because the team needed points. I might place fifth or sixth, but of course, I ran when asked because that helped the team. It's not about Jasmine winning—it's about team. Vince Anderson [UT women's and later men's sprint coach] would always say, "Jas, you give your all. You ran the 3000 after running three other events—not to mention the trials. Thanks for being a team player." I scored maybe three points, but he knew that I put everything I had out there. If I won my event, I was happy, but watching my teammates and then coming together as a team to celebrate—that is what it is all about. With our middle-distance team there were no ego issues. We were such close friends. We were competing against each other, but it was to

help each other be better. Nobody was the big dog—everyone had equal talent and gave 100 percent. When you surround yourself with great people and your team comes all together, that is when you really know the power of individuals and team. All of us—sprinters, distance runners, etc.—had respect for each other. For example, I would work out with sprinters to work on speed. We all supported each other to excel.

When posed with the question of why she enjoys running, Jasmin responds enthusiastically:

What do I love about running? So many things—just running. I always love to compete—now I don't run at that level. You hear about the runner's high. It feels good to do something healthy for myself. Running is so strenuous. I don't feel complete if I don't do a run every morning. I am blessed that God has given me this particular talent. Running makes me feel good and stay in good physical shape. I am fortunate enough that I can do this. I think when I run. I am always thinking. I run every morning with Val [Bertrand], another Lady Vol, who is now a teacher. We talk about our lives, scrapbooking, our families, and our jobs. We talk about how we miss our teammate, Patty Weigand Pitcher, who practices medicine now in North Carolina, and how we treasure all our Lady Vol friends. Those are the friends I still have today.

Jasmin may not be competing professionally today as a runner, but her competitive spirit shines brightly when she talks about her determination to make a difference in

Jasmin Jones (Keller)

Postcollegiate Career Highlights (continued)

- First-place finish in the majority of Knoxville area road races, 1993–2005
- 5K best time, 16:24
- 10K best time, 35:04
- Ranked top ten in US (1500 and 300 meter) six years in a row
- Highest world ranking 800 top 50
- Ranked top 100 all-time in the world for indoor mile
- Competed/endorsed for Adidas
- Competed/endorsed for Nike
- Olympic Trials finalist, 800 and 1500 meter
- Competed on European Grand Prix track circuit (won several competitions in Europe)
- Member of the Indoor Track World Championship Team
- Six-time Expo 10K winner (Knoxville, Tennessee)
- Lady Volunteer Hall of Fame
- Licensed counselor in social work
- Mental health and disabilities coordinator, Head Start
- Family therapist for Covenant Health Care, Peninsula Center (seven years)

the lives of children through her work as a mental health and disabilities coordinator for Head Start:

I meet with families and children with disabilities to help with their needs. I love my job. It is so fulfilling to see what you can do

boy with serious mental issues. He is very bright, but he saw scorpions, devils, and something wasn't right. He has a diagnosis that schools won't recognize—antisocial behavior. I had to do a lot of legwork—go to the doctor with his mom to identify that he was also ADHD [attention deficit hyperactiv-*

story. I hope that I can do that. When you think about things, the older you get the more you think about what you have done. When I leave this world, what do I want to have accomplished? I want my children to be successful. I want them to remember Mom as doing what she could to make their dreams come true. As I wrote in a letter to my high school coach Edward Church, "If I can inspire any young person the way that he has inspired me, it would be a blessing." That is truly how I feel in terms of what he has instilled in me. If I can do that, with someone reading this story, then that would be wonderful.*

Our children and families need advocates. As we grow older, we try to become wiser and not cynical.

for a child. So many children haven't been exposed to the same opportunities as others—who at four years old don't even recognize a letter of the alphabet. I look at their records and think, "Where was the doctor in this case?" They were passed over before now. These kids are missed because they are poor. My job is to get them the help they need. If they didn't have me at this point in their lives, they would be lost to us. Now as a parent I know I am going to give 200 percent. I know what parents are feeling. When I do training for the teachers at the beginning of the school year, I share my experiences as a parent. I tell them not to be judgmental and that these children aren't necessarily lazy or stupid. No one wants anything to be wrong with their child. These parents just don't know what they need. I am really passionate about this. My boss sometimes gives me this look—I can be persistent when people don't get what they need. You have to be compassionate when you do the kind of work I do. Unfortunately, a lot of people are overlooked or not taken seriously. Recently I saw a little

ity disorder]. This is a diagnosis that schools will accept. Doctor signed his diagnosis, and now this child is in school. He needed to be in class—otherwise he would have been passed by, thrown away. Our children and families need advocates. As we grow older, we try to become wiser and not cynical. The bottom line—someone has to advocate for our children, so if I am too overbearing or pushy, it is OK. I am that parent—if my child needs a service, I will get it. I believe this has been my calling in this helping profession. This is where I belong, and I wouldn't want to be doing anything else.

Jasmin Jones Keller is still running. Her race venue is different now, and she has stepped into different shoes and taken on a larger team with her purpose—that same purpose that she envisioned at the young age of eight. She says:

I tell young people today, "GO FOR IT and you can definitely do it." I hope that I can inspire someone from just reading my

Being a Lady Vol is not just about athletics—it's so much more than that. Being a student-athlete is so much different from being just an athlete—people are depending on you, relying on you—the friendships, the sadness, the happiness. I don't think I could have gotten this experience anywhere else. I got the whole package—the education, the friendships, the role models. When I was inducted into the Lady Vol Hall of Fame, I was so emotional. I had my head down, saw Pat Summitt, and I said, "Oh, I was just a mess." She said, "Look at me. I'm just as nervous when I go and do my things." I said, "No you aren't." She said, "Yes, and you know what the big difference is? They don't know it."

I have been blessed to be able to run and do all these things. I am going to take full advantage of all that has been given me.

Jasmin Jones Keller continues to lead her life with purpose and determination. And we will all do well to follow in her tracks.

Patty Wiegand

Patty Wiegand's competitive speed earned seven All-America accolades and the 1991 NCAA Woman of the Year for the state of Tennessee.

Pitter Patty

The pitter patter of little feet often brings up a visual of a little child running lightly through the house. When Lady Vols hear the words, "Pitter Patty," they think of something quite different. Patty Wiegand (Pitcher) earned her nickname as a top cross country and track and field competitor at the University of Tennessee. Among her many honors, she was 1991 NCAA Woman of the Year for the state of Tennessee and top-ten national finalist. That's quite a "pitter patty" of little feet!

Patty grew up in Canastota, New York, a small town approximately thirty miles outside of Syracuse. She learned her work ethic at an early age, recalling:

I grew up in a lower-middle-class family with a single mom who was struggling with four kids. She was determined that we all would go to college. I was the youngest of the family, so by the time I turned a teenager, I knew I needed to earn a four-year scholarship. My mom's resources were running low. The way I found a scholarship through running was a true blessing. I had a paper route from the time I was twelve, and I always wanted to get the papers out early. My brother and I would get our papers and put them in a stack. He had his, and I had mine. And we would race our paper routes. Whoever got home first won. I think that is how I got my endurance. My brother was two years older and I did whatever he did. He was on the track team, so I said I was going out for the track team.

Patty started running track, and the school coach, Andy Pino, who had been her sixth-grade teacher, recognized her abilities. By eighth grade Patty was competing in national meets. Her school followed the national physical fitness program that called for all students to run a mile, and Patty ran faster than all the boys. Because of a paper route, her older brother, her mother's focus on college, and a dedicated coach, Patty found her speed and endurance that became her trademarks.

In high school Patty was All-League five years, All-East, and All-State four times and a two-time All America. In 1986 she participated in the US Olympic Elite Distance Camp and was a member of the US National Junior Team that toured Kenya and China. At the end of the 1987 indoor season, Patty was ranked in the top five in the country in five events: 800 meter, 1000 yard, 1500 meter, and the mile.

Patty's competition was the best in the country. She particularly recalls two young stars, Jasmin Jones (Keller) and Valerie Bertrand:

In high school I competed against Jasmin Jones (Keller) and Valerie Bertrand. When I was in eighth grade and Valerie was in ninth, we were in a New York state meet. In a picture of us on the podium, I think I got sixth place, and she got fourth. I didn't know Valerie, but we knew each other as competitors.

Jasmin and I competed all through high school. One time we competed in the 1000 at the Easterns, an indoor track meet in the Northeast. And it was three of the best one thousand runners at the time. And I said

Patty Wiegand (Pitcher)

Sport Stats

- Academic All-America, 1989
- NCAA Woman of the Year for the state of Tennessee and top-ten national finalist, 1991
- H. Boyd McWhorter SEC Female Scholar Athlete of the Year, 1991
- Won 3000 meter at NCAA Indoor Meet in 1991 and was on victorious 3200-meter relay team
- 1991 NCAA runner-up outdoor in the 5000 meter
- Double SEC Champion twice in 1991, winning the mile and 3000 meter indoor and taking the 3000 meter and 5000 meter outdoor
- Seven-time All-America in track and field
- Fourteen All-SEC certificates, including nine for victories
- School record holder, indoor and outdoor 3000 meter and 5000 meter, and with the 4x1500-meter relay
- Earned cross country All-America accolades in 1989 with fifth-place NCAA individual finish
- Three-time All-SEC performer in cross country, including a first-place personal result in 1990 (16:45.10)

Academic Stats

- B.S., Engineering, University of Tennessee 1991
- M.D., College of Medicine, University of Tennessee Memphis

Postcollegiate Career Highlights

- Member of the USA Eco-DenT Travel Road Racing Team; traveled to China, South Korea, Portugal, 1992–95
- Top five, US National 5k Championships, 1995
- Pediatrician
- Volunteer assistant coach, community's high school women's track and field team
- Organized nutrition and exercise program called "Recess Run" for children
- Continues to compete in road races
- Lady Volunteer Hall of Fame

1990 Cross Country SEC Champions: (front row, left to right) Dina Spagnoli (34th), Patty Wiegand (1st), Kristen Permakoff, Michelle Strothers (23rd), Jasmin Jones (5th), Alicia Johnson, (back row, left to right) Cindy O'Bryant, Lisa Richardson (56th), Lynne Collazo (49th), Megan Thompson (4th), Monica Olkowski, Celeste Susnis (8th), and Christy Crawley.

to her, "*You know, you kicked me off the track.*" *It was when she started to kick, and she knocked me into the infield. And she said, "I did not!"*

So I was always very afraid of Jas because she was very physical.

Andy Pino, Patty's high school coach, was central to her development. He paced her mileage so that she would achieve well in high school but still have room to grow at the next level. "If you bring a girl's effort to certain miles, like 60 or 70 a week, she has nowhere to go in college," she says. "Coming out of high school, if you ask about mileage,

you would think that fifty miles per week is a good answer. But thirty miles is a better answer. At fifty miles you have burned out. You have taken everything you have to work with, and now you have nothing. It takes a considerate high school coach to do this. He could have made me better in high school if he had pushed me to higher mileage. So when I went to college, I had room for improvement."

Not surprisingly, Patty was highly recruited. Texas, Villanova, and Penn State were knocking on her door. Coach Andy Pino was a graduate of the University of Tennessee. When signing time came, Patty considered her mentor's advice. He had been low-key, but it was his advice that moved Patty's decision to pursue her career at the University of Tennessee. And Patty was in for a surprise.

"I learned that Jasmin Jones (Keller) was also enrolling at the University of Tennessee," she says. "By no means did we mean to be teammates. She was ranked number one and I was two, and I did not intend to end up on the same school with her because we were going to be competitors. So when I found out that Jas was going to UT, I said, 'You have to be kidding. She is very aggressive.' Jasmin and I were supposed to be roommates and I was afraid of her, so I had my mom call to request that she not be my roommate. I got out of being her roommate."

Patty soon grew to appreciate her teammates and became especially close to Jasmin and Val Bertrand. She realized that having such outstanding teammates helped to push her beyond her limits. They all made each other better.

Patty thrived on the top-quality resources available to student-athletes. "We had endless opportunities," she recalls. "And we were told about those opportunities. Any talent we had, they just explored completely. They made you reach beyond your potential. I don't think I was supposed to be a National Champion. I don't think I am talented enough. And I would tell friends, 'I'm really not talented enough to be a National Champion but UT made me one.' They gave me the trainers. They gave me the nutrition. They gave me the coaches. And all this support . . . I really don't think I was the best runner on the track. I think I had the best support on the track that made me a champion."

The Lady Vols find a sense of family in the women's athletic department, and this helps new student-athletes especially to have a personal sense of belonging in spite of the large size of the University of Tennessee. "I had a family," says Patty. "I had friends. I had tutoring. I had meals. It was such a blessing to walk into a family. These people were automatically my friends."

The genuine care of her coaches continues to inspire Patty:

I remember when we were first introduced to Missy Kane (Alston Bemiller) as our coach. Here she was—this beautiful, fit Olympian, and I thought, "She is going to make me run into the ground." She took us to the mountains on her own personal time to become a team before cross country started. And, it was seven days of training—but wonderful experiences, and Missy was truly being a friend. Missy did so much. She sacrificed a great deal for us girls. One Easter we were at a track meet, and she bought surprise Easter baskets and put them outside the doors of our hotel rooms. When there was a challenge at home, Missy was always there. I am just so proud to know her and say she is my friend. She was my coach the whole time.

Missy was amazing. She was such a good coach because she got in our heads. We could be dying, and she would say, "You were the smoothest one out there." Then I would think, "Really? I guess I am OK." And she would say that for the last lap I was going to run 65. Now granted, she would train us to do that. But she instilled that confidence in us.

Patty's speed set records and captured national attention throughout her collegiate career. Her final year of competition for Tennessee stands clearly in her mind:

When I was a senior, I was one of the favorites for cross country. It was my time. I should be in the top five. The meet was in Knoxville, and my coaches and family were there. In retrospect, I must have gotten influenza or something. I was totally wiped out the week before and did not run a good race. I truly was exhausted. So that was the only race when I was expected to do something, and I didn't get the desired results.

So then came indoor nationals, and I got a cold. And I was thinking that I had crashed in cross country and couldn't crash at indoor nationals. I remember getting on the line for the finals in the 3000 nationals and deciding that I would just go to the end of the line for the first part of the mile and then slowly pass. And I still had to run the 4x8. Missy said that she was considering that I should drop out. But at the end, the gun went off, and I took the lead, and I was very fresh still, and I knew I wasn't dying. And I took the lead comfortably. I was just waiting for my turn to come. And I thought, "This is it—I'm really going to be a national champion! I can't believe this is really happening to me!" As I finished that race, I remember cooling down and calling my high school coach and saying, "I did it! I'm at nationals!" That was a goose-bumpy time. I had been one of the favorites but not the standout. That is probably my all-time favorite moment—winning indoor nationals with Missy Kane as my coach, and my 4x8 teammates Jasmin Jones (Keller), Monica Olkowski, and Alicia Johnson.

Academically Patty achieved top marks as well. She was the 1991 H. Boyd McWhorter SEC Female Scholar of the Year and in 1992 graduated with a degree in chemical engineering. At that point Patty set her goals even higher and decided to pursue medical school. "I came from a home where there were no physicians in our family," she says. "I didn't know much about medical school. So I told Joan [Cronan] that I was thinking about going to medical school, and Joan arranged for me to meet a female anesthesiologist. This physician encouraged me and said that I could do this. If Joan Cronan had not been a part of my life, I don't believe that I would have become a doctor."

As a physician, Patty has many opportunities to share her insights. And many of her lessons come from her Lady Vol track and field days. She comments:

I love to talk sports with young female athletes because being a student-athlete has taught me so much for my career and in my "mommy-hood." If I have a hard day at work, I think it was nothing compared to working on the track in Knoxville and knowing that I had to win a certain event. Being a student-athlete really teaches you. You have to work out when you are tired. You have to study when you are tired. You have to follow the rules. It just made me balance my time wonderfully well.

There are a number of pressures. For example, when I took my MCAT, I hadn't planned to go into medicine, so I didn't study. Nor did I have a lot of science in school. So I can remember sitting in MCAT and thinking, "This is nothing. I could be on the line at nationals." And whenever I think

Teammates and friends: Jasmin Jones Keller, Valerie Bertrand Bauchmann, and Patty Wiegand Pitcher. Courtesy, Jasmin Jones Keller.

about something a little strenuous in life, I just think I could be at nationals. It could be a lot more stressful. It could be a lot worse.

Today Patty Wiegand Pitcher still defines happiness to include running and being a team player. She says that whether she is happy or sad, a pair of sneakers and the road are just what the doctor ordered.

"People ask what I do all day, and I say that I give out hugs and kisses and stickers," she adds. "And get called everything but Dr. Pitcher. And they are dolls. I consider my group and my patients and my staff as phenomenal. It is a supportive thing. Like the University of Tennessee. We all work together to make everything go together in a wonderful environment. It is sweet. It is great. I do love going to work everyday."

Patty is following her dreams and goals, always with an eye on the special memories at Tennessee:

When I left UT it was like my five years of Christmas were over. And it was five years of Christmas. It was incredibly hard, packing up and leaving all of my dear friends. Twenty years later, here I am. I go to the UT campus often. I see Joan Cronan often. I remember being down when I left high school, but there was never such sadness as when I had to pack up from UT and go to medical school.

Now I get to be a mom, and it is such a different chapter in that book of life. But let me tell you, those were four years of being the princess. Tennessee is one of only two schools in the country that have separate men's and women's athletic programs. They were there just for me and the other women in the program. They were all for us. And they fought for us to make it the best that they absolutely could have.

When I've gone back to the Lady Vol Hall of Fame dinners, it is amazing to see how

indebted we all feel to the University of Tennessee women's athletics. Every single person becomes very tearful and very grateful and expresses that we would not be the people we are if not for the University of Tennessee. And it is really, really true.

It is absolutely possible, no matter what initial state we are in, to realize our dreams. We can get there with hard work. We need to remember everyone who helped to bring us there, and thank them as we pass through each stage of each success. And then we will look back and say, "That was the most wonderful experience of my life."

Patty is combining her passion for running and her dedication as a physician to inspire children to be healthier human beings. She has organized a race called "The Recess Run." The race is free for all children and includes preparation that teaches healthy nutritional habits while they train for the half-mile run. Being a true volunteer—this is just one of many ways that Patty contributes her time and expertise to the community.

Patty Weigand Pitcher is one of those rare individuals who truly teach by her words and her deeds. She once described herself as a "consistent" runner. She earned a scholarship through college by winning races. She was asked to run, and she simply responded by asking, "How fast?" Patty is now challenging others to step up to their own starting blocks. She is providing support, encouragement, commitment, and inspiration. A lot of children will pause one day and look back at their doctor, community leader, coach, or friend and say, "Thank you. That was the most wonderful experience of my life."

The Lady Vols cross country team is growing as a regular regional and national contender for top honors.

Spotlight
Daedra Charles (Furlow)
Basketball, 1988–91

Daedra Charles

USA

Daedra Charles led Tennessee to its third National Championship Title in five years and totaled 1,495 career points for the Lady Vols.

No Stops for This Train

Meeting Daedra Charles (Furlow) today, it is nearly impossible to believe that anyone would look her in the eye and tell her that she can't do something. But eighteen years ago in Detroit, that is exactly what her cousin did. This single challenge ignited Daedra's determined spirit to accomplish whatever she sets her mind to do.

Daedra vividly recalls her early years growing up in Detroit: "I have a cousin who is more like my brother, and he, my sister, and I grew up together. His name is Sean Hopkins. We loved to watch basketball. I clearly remember that we were watching the national championship when Magic Johnson in his sophomore year at Michigan State won over Larry Bird at Indiana State. At that moment I knew I wanted to play basketball. I had never played but just loved the game. I had heard about Cheryl Miller, the McGee twins from Flint, Cynthia Cooper—I said, you know, I want to play this game because it looks like a lot of fun. I had no idea how to approach it, but I wanted to do it anyway. I was eleven years old."

When Daedra turned twelve, her mother enrolled her in St. Benedict, a private school, because of the superior educational offerings, and here Daedra found her first real opportunity to play basketball, trying out for the girls' team. Even this early in life her determination and desire were evident. "I had no clue of what I was doing, but I wanted it," she says. "I suffered with asthma, so my mother didn't want me to play and didn't think I would be able to run. Every

Friday during the summer it seemed like I was in the emergency room—but the doctors told my mother, 'Look, she knows her limitations. Let her play.'"

Although her mother was always on "pins and needles," she supported Daedra's will to play. Daedra describes her first basketball year as a significant growth experience: "I always was in the key three seconds, my coach always made me run laps, and I couldn't shoot free throws. I would turn the ball over—my mother would be covering her face in the stands. I didn't know what I was doing. Even though in my mind I could do all these things, physically, I couldn't do them. I was learning."

It was then when her cousin suggested that Daedra might reconsider her choice of sports. She recalls, "My cousin was the one that told me, 'You shouldn't be playing basketball. You should be playing with Barbie dolls because girls don't play basketball.' He made me mad—and I said, 'You know what? I'm going to learn this game, and you know what? I'm going to come back, and you and I are going to play, and I'm going to kick your butt.' He responded, 'Yeah, yeah, yeah.' He was a really good basketball player, played at St. Benedict as well, and he went on to play at Shrine High School."

And Daedra played. And she became good. Daedra credits her grade school coach, Paula Artis, for much of her development that year: "My coach believed in me from day one. She would pick me up on Saturday, and we would go shoot. Sometimes she would have her cousins come—they were boys—and we would play one-on-one. Coach Artis really helped me develop my skills and gave me that confidence to know that I can be what I want to be."

Now when she went to the neighborhood basketball courts, boys, who previously wouldn't play with her because she was a girl, wanted her on their teams. Basketball camps and playing with boys helped Daedra develop her skills quickly. She had grown taller, and her skills and knowledge of the game had become stronger. Her growing self-confidence translated into a more aggressive attitude in the game. Always a staunch believer in her daughter, Daedra's mother told her that "because she was so much taller she should stand straight, walk tall, and that God gave her big hands and big feet for a reason." By the end of her eighth grade year, Daedra had the attention of nearly all the high school coaches in the Detroit area.

Sometimes chance seems to be well-placed. Daedra's plans to attend the same school as her sister changed in the spring of 1983 when that school unexpectedly closed. Daedra registered to attend St. Mary's High School with a teammate from elementary school. Her decision attracted the attention of Anthony Taylor, a coach at St. Martin de Porres High School. Coach Taylor had been on the losing side of Daedra's talents when he coached the team at St. Mary's Elementary School, archrival of St. Benedict. He invited Daedra to visit St. Martin de Porres. Only five blocks from her home, de Porres offered a small, personalized environment. It was an immediate fit, providing Daedra with a high school community that really cared about her complete success as a person in the classroom as well as on the basketball court. Her coach, Fred Procter, was the kind of coach who understood the challenges and

The 1989 NCAA National Championship basketball team: (front row, left to right) Regina Clark (5), Melissa McCray (35), Bridgette Gordon (30), Debbie Scott (50), Dena Head (11), (back row, left to right) Tonya Edwards (33), Kelli Casteel (34), Sheila Frost (12), Daedra Charles (32), Debbie Hawhee (52), and Carla McGhee (24).

needs of young people and served as a significant adult role model for the team. He was also a coach who recognized the importance of the future.

When Daedra was a junior, Coach Procter called her into his office for a chat about college. Daedra had never really considered her future college options. She says:

I knew people went to college but I didn't understand really how to get there. I played basketball because I loved it—it wasn't to go to college. I didn't know about the scholarships. My coach said, "Look—you have a great opportunity to go away to school." He said, "I want you to think about going to college, and I have some things I want

to give you. I don't want this to go to your head, but there are over two hundred colleges looking at you. They have been calling me about you and they know about you." I am thinking, "What . . . me? Wow!" It was awesome. In his office were all these boxes—I thought they were equipment and supplies, because he was also the athletic director. Pointing to them, he said, "These are your boxes. You have been getting letters since your freshman year." There were six boxes of mail that had accumulated. I said that I didn't know how to go about this. He said to take my time, think about the top twenty-five schools I was interested in, then from there narrow them to fifteen, ten, and then by my senior year I needed to

Daedra Charles (Furlow)

Sport Stats

- US Olympic Festival, 1987
- ESPY Awards Co-Team of the Decade (1900s), 1988–91
- SEC Tournament Title, 1989
- Two NCAA Championships 1989, 1991
- US National Team, 1989, 1992, 1994
- Kodak All-America, 1990, 1991
- NCAA All-Regional Tournament Teams, (East) 1990, (Mideast), 1991
- SEC All-Tournament Team, 1990, 1991
- Wade Trophy Winner, 1991 (first SEC player to win)
- Naismith All-America Team, 1991
- All-SEC Team, 1991
- SEC Female Athlete of the Year 1991
- US Olympic Team, bronze medalist, 1992
- Scored 1,495 points, grabbed 858 rebounds and blocked 97 shots during her Lady Vol career
- Member 1000 Point Club with 1,495 career points
- Member 800 Rebound Club with 858 career rebounds

Academic Stats

- B.S., Human Ecology, University of Tennessee, 1991

have five schools that I wanted to visit. I was overwhelmed. I didn't really know how to get started. But he and Coach Taylor helped me. I pulled all the mail from those twenty-five schools that interested me. Coach Taylor said that if there were only form letters and no handwritten letters, to toss them. My mom, sister, and I went through the mail. At that time the recruiting rules were different. Tennessee was never, ever, ever, ever on my list. My early choices included University of Southern California, Kansas, Old Dominion, and Louisiana Tech. The letters from Tennessee were form letters—there were books—but I never really heard about Tennessee. If Tennessee was talked about, I just don't remember.

So I was getting ready to graduate my senior year—I had just become Michigan's Miss Basketball, All America, Gatorade—I can't even remember all the awards. I was decorated. I was happy about my achievements, and happy about Miss Basketball, but I was still trying to search where I really wanted to go to college.

I first seriously became aware of Tennessee when I was playing with Tonya Edwards in an AAU tournament in Connecticut. That was the first time I saw Pat and Mickie DeMoss [then UT assistant coach and recruiting coordinator] because they were at Tonya's game watching us. I remember Tonya saying, "They're looking at you," and I kind of blew it off because I hadn't thought about going to Tennessee. Tennessee had been sending me letters and calling all along, but this was the first time Tennessee captured my attention. I narrowed my final choices to Michigan State, Kansas, Iowa, and Tennessee. These were the schools that I visited.

I was having trouble with my ACT test. Pat said, "No matter what—we want you. We see you here. We believe in you, we can help you, and you are going to graduate in four years from here. I can guarantee you that." I thought, "Wow, that's impressive." After an official visit and unofficial visit, I loved it. The other schools I liked OK, but I never felt a fit. I felt an immediate fit with Tennessee both times I visited. But I didn't tell Pat that.

Tennessee won a National Championship in 1987. Pat called me after they won. She said, "Daedra, what do you think?" I said, "I am happy for you all. You all did well." She said, "Well are you going to come?" I said, "I don't know. I am still thinking." She said, "You don't know?" Now, signing day was coming up. So before she got off the phone, I said, "Pat, I'm coming. I'm going to be a Lady Vol." Oh man—she was happy! Holly [Warlick] got on the phone; Mickie [DeMoss] got on the phone. They were all screaming and laughing—and I knew that was the perfect place for me. Out of all the people who came to visit me at home—I think I had maybe fifteen people come—my grandmother only liked Mickie DeMoss. The tie there—and my grandmother didn't know this—Mickie is from Louisiana, and my grandmother is from Louisiana. My mother and father are from Louisiana, and there was something about Mickie DeMoss that my grandmother liked. My grandmother told my mother that she wanted me to go to Tennessee, but my mother said that it was my decision. But she was so happy that I picked Tennessee because my grandmother had such a good vibe about Tennessee, about Mickie and about Pat.

The 1991 NCAA National Championship basketball team: (front row, left to right) Jody Adams (3), Dena Head (11), Nikki Caldwell (33), Lisa Harrison (21), Regina Clark (5), (back row, left to right) Peggy Evans (20), Debbie Hawhee (52), Daedra Charles (32), Kelli Casteel (34), and Marlene Jeter (15).

Daedra Charles (Furlow)

Postcollegiate Career Highlights

- Competed professionally overseas in Japan, Italy, and France, 1991–97
- WNBA Los Angeles Sparks, 1997
- Fourth Lady Vol to have her jersey retired (number 32), 1991
- Tennessee Lady Volunteer Hall of Fame, 2001 Inaugural Class
- Assistant women's basketball coach, University of Detroit Mercy, 2003–06
- Color analyst for Comcast Local, 2004–06
- Named one of ESPN's Top 25 College Women's Basketball Players in 2005
- Assistant women's basketball coach, Auburn University, 2006–08
- Coached at her alma mater, St. de Porres High School, and worked as a supervisor for a center for abused, neglected and delinquent juvenile males
- Women's Basketball Hall of Fame
- Assistant women's basketball coach, Univerisity of Tennessee, 2008–present

So, what's this about a "Train?" In 1987 Daedra tried out for the Olympic Sports Festival. It was her coach, Leon Barmore from Louisiana Tech, who nailed her with a name that would stick:

One day before practice Leon Barmore said, "You know who you remind me of?" I thought he was going to say Erica Westbrook [or] Janice Lawrence because I enjoyed watching them play, and they play in his program at Louisiana Tech. And then he said, "Do you know a guy named Dick 'Night Train' Lane?" I am looking at him and thinking, "You are comparing me to a MAN?" He said, "Well, Dick 'Night Train' Lane was really before your time. He was a running back for the Detroit Lions. You know one thing about

that guy? Anytime he got the ball, he made it happen. They couldn't stop him. And that is you." I am thinking—football, basketball—I am trying to put that together, but I got the message because whenever I got the ball, something happened. That same day I bought a T-shirt and had "Night Train" put on it. The next day I wore it to practice, and never in a thousand years would I have ever thought that name would have stuck. My teammates to this day still call me "Train." Whenever Pat sends me a note, she calls me "Train." Even the people I played against say, "Here comes the Train—Train in the lane." They associate the "Train" with me.

Night Train left her mark when she came to Tennessee. As a Lady Vol she contributed her strong work ethic and unwavering belief in the possibility of reaching her goals. The journey was not easy. Her freshman year was spent sitting on the sidelines due to Proposition 48, which dictates standards for ACT scores and grade point averages for student-athletes. Having difficulty with standardized tests, Daedra knew that she would face the challenge of proving herself academically if she wanted to compete on the basketball court. Once again, it would be the words of her mother that provided Daedra with the confidence to overcome an obstacle.

"My mother told me that when I put my mind to something, I can do anything," Daedra declares. "She said that if I can learn basketball plays, I can learn academics. I understood her concept. She was right. When I studied hard, I did well. When you practice and you study, you get what you want."

Daedra did well academically her freshman year. That year it couldn't have been easy to sit on the sidelines. Yet, she seized the opportunity to learn how to balance her life at college. She learned to achieve goals through discipline, hard work, and a positive attitude. She grounded her life in something even greater than basketball. "I had an opportunity to settle into college life before basketball," she says. "So when it was time for me to play, the Train was ready. It was about learning how to balance both. That was my challenge. Guess what? I did it. If you are serious enough and want it, you can do it. You have to set your goals."

The Train brought passion to her game. Being a Lady Vol was hard work. Her love of the game and complete trust in her coaches were essential. She comments:

Daedra Charles-Furlow with husband, Anthony, and son, Anthonee Charles Furlow, 2007. Courtesy, Daedra Charles-Furlow.

I don't think I could have gone through all that if I didn't love it. If you're serious about it and you want it, it has to be a desire burning within you. I wanted it. If Pat said, "Run through that wall," I was going to run through that wall. She had been there and done that. She had gotten her teams to that level. I wanted to be one of those players. It wasn't a question of whether I believed her. That was never a question. I believed her. It was how willing was I to work hard to achieve that? She had a national championship. I wanted a National Championship. And these are the things I needed to go through to get it. Was it always fun? No. Did it hurt? Yes. But it was worth it. Because, guess what? They remembered. That 1989 Championship Team—they remember that we were all on that team. That 1991 national championship team—they remember that I was on that team. And nobody can take that

away from us, and we were on top of the world. In 1991 no one really believed we could do it but us. We knew if we got there, Pat had the game plan. All we needed to do was to execute it—X's and O's. We knew that Mickie, Holly, and Pat were masterminds. They were going to have it together. It was up to us to execute. And we approached it with the attitude that we are here to win— not simply to show up. And we didn't have all of this talent—we were good players, but we fought, we pushed each other, we didn't let each other give up. We wanted it—we had a taste of it—we liked it.

Sometimes the coach provided extra incentives for performance. Daedra has the dubious honor of being a member of the team that was evicted from the locker room in 1990. The team had just returned from a mediocre road trip through Indiana. Coach Summitt thought their play lacked discipline, as if the team took past wins for granted. Able to smile about it now, Daedra recalls the incident that made local and even national headlines: "Not only did Pat throw us out of the locker room—she put us in a room with nothing on the walls, no music, and when we brought in our own stuff, she took that away too. We wore the same practice clothes every day. She took all of our gear. It was for about a month. We learned to appreciate what we had. We earned what we had our own way rather than riding the coattails of the past team."

Daedra says that if she had to do it all over again, she would still choose Tennessee—not just because of basketball but because of what Coach Summitt brings to the table. "Her work ethic is unmatched," she

says. "She would watch game tapes until she was sick—if she had to watch all night, she would to figure out what we did wrong. When she first started out, she did everything. She took that program, embraced it, and made it what it is today. You aren't going to hear of many women who are going to do that. People—I mean men—listen to Pat. She is powerful. When she talks, she grabs you. You will leave there thinking, I can do whatever I want to do. She is sure of herself. She is confident and can get it done."

Daedra "Night Train" Charles (Furlow) is a student of her college coach. She shows the determined focus on quality that never stops short of reaching her goals. Her competitive spirit defies losing. She embraces the importance of individual integrity to the strength of the team. As a player she was always serious and intent to take care of the business at hand. She says:

People maybe thought I wasn't friendly—I was just focused. It wasn't time to smile or celebrate until the game was over. It was about business for me. Pat will tell you I am a competitor. Even in drills and practice, I didn't believe in losing. You can ask Jody Adams this. In the beginning I wouldn't put Jody on my practice team. It bothered her, and she came to my room after practice one day. Now Jody never came to my room. We just never hung out together. I said, "Hey Rat (I called her Rat), what are you doing?" She said, "Chooch (she called me Chooch), something is bothering me. I have one thing to ask you. What can I do to get on your team?" It bothered her. I said, "Well, Jody, one thing—if you will give me the ball, then I will pick you." At the next practice Pat paired us up, and Jody gave me the ball. So that trust was built, and from that point on, we were closer. I only know to be straight—to tell you the truth. In practice—and I learned this from Bridgette [Gordon], Sheila [Frost], and Melissa [McCray]—you can't always think of a nice way to say what you need to say—it just comes out. As a leader in order for us to play well, I would have to say it straight—it started with me. I wanted and embraced that responsibility. At the end of the season, Debbie [Hawhee] said, "In the beginning I thought you were a little bit too mean." I said, "Debbie, I had to push you all so that you could push me." She said, "I understand that now, and without you we wouldn't have had this national championship." I said, "Without the team there is no ME." We cried—it wasn't about liking each other. We were there to do a job—sometimes you may not like someone—but you learn to move on.

Reflecting on what she gained from being a Lady Vol, Daedra readily describes critical elements of living successfully: "Pat taught us how to be a person. We learned how to act, to go to class, to graduate. She held us accountable. We knew that when we left, we were going to be OK. Pat taught us how to be self-sufficient."

Daedra sees challenges facing today's youth and embraces her roles as a mother, teacher, and coach with her same infallible spirit and gusto:

You can be old school, but these are new millennium kids. We have to change with the times—these kids aren't on the same page. I am still doing what Pat tells me to do. Pat and I will always have a special relationship. I really believe that I would not have been as successful as a player and as a person had I not played for her. All the players take on her attitude. Even when I am coaching my kids, I find myself saying what she would have said. "Worry about the day I don't say anything to you," Pat said. I tell my kids that too. She believed in my abilities. She respected me as a player and as a person. I never thought I was going to be a coach—I didn't think I would be able to deal with all these girls' attitudes. As a player I really didn't have ups and downs. When I was on the court, I was focused on basketball. But when I coached my high school team, I realized that I liked it. I want to keep learning, further my education, and be a good example for my son. I love coaching. This is my way of giving back to young women, the community, people who embraced me, who pushed me. Our kids need strong support today. The environment is no excuse for not being successful. You can make it—there may be a teacher, aunt, or friend who can help you. No excuses—I can't even hear them. It is a struggle, but how bad do you want it?

Daedra Charles-Furlow began a new chapter in her life on May 19, 2008, when she returned to Tennessee as assistant coach for the Lady Vol basketball team.

Oh—one more thing. Remember that day eighteen years ago when Daedra was advised to play with Barbie dolls instead of basketballs? With a twinkle in her eye, the Train said: "My cousin and I did have that match. I want you to know that I kicked his butt."

Charting Her Own Course

Her name could be offered as the definition of a "well-rounded" individual. She is a surgeon, professor, speaker, researcher, community leader, and mother. In college she was an honor student majoring in engineering science and mechanics, recipient of the 1993 University of Tennessee Chancellor's Citation for Campus Leadership and Service, and one of only sixty stars named to *USA Today*'s list of the Best and Brightest. She earned the SEC H. Boyd McWhorter Post-Graduate Scholarship in 1992.

And she did a little swimming. Virginia McGrath (Weaver) was one of the most decorated swimmers in Tennessee history. She was fifteen-time All-America; 1990 SEC champion in the 200-yard individual medley; 1990 and 1992 SEC champion in the 200-yard freestyle relay; Tennessee record holder for the 800-yard freestyle relay (1989 and 1992), 200-yard individual medley (1990), and 200-yard freestyle (1991); and three-time Collegiate Swimming Coaches' Academic All-America. She participated in the NCAA Championship all four of her collegiate years. And that is the short list.

Most athletes have particular ways to prepare for competition. Jenny had her own special trademark. "I guess all swimmers have crazy routines that they go through," she says. "Certainly my routine included prayer. And I was always someone who was cold. Even at summer meets outside, I wore my parka and gloves. Everybody would make fun of me for wearing gloves. But my hands would always be cold. Like every-one else I would put on the Walkman and listen to my certain little songs. But probably the gloves were the weirdest thing I did. I didn't care if it was 90 degrees outside—I had my gloves on. It was definitely a strange trademark. And then I just tried to relax."

Jenny's premeet preparation may have added to her success, but years of dedicated practice made the biggest difference. Growing up in Knoxville, Tennessee, Jenny began swimming competitively year-round when she was nine years old. She swam for a number of clubs, including the Knoxville Swimming Association at UT, the Pilot Aquatic Club, and the Atomic City Aquatic Club in Oak Ridge. She also swam for Farragut High School. Jenny describes her swimming career as having a slow start:

When I was younger, I was always the kid kind of bringing up the last. I don't think I was born with that kind of competitive drive. I think it was kind of nurtured. I was told at a young age that I had talent as an athlete, but I wasn't even the best kid on the neighborhood swim team, much less anything else.

My parents were a huge influence on me. They were so supportive. Some parents throw their hands up in the air and say, "This is too expensive and I'm not driving you to all these meets." But my parents were just more than happy to do anything I wanted with swimming. I credit them. My coaches there at UT were wonderful. And my career just kind of took off in college. Several coaches I had growing up in various age groups were very helpful.

**Spotlight
Jenny McGrath
(Weaver)
Swimming and Diving,
1988–92**

Jenny McGrath brought honors to Lady Vol swimming as an NCAA Championships top-sixteen finisher in multiple events all four years.

Jenny McGrath (Weaver)

Sport Stats

- UT record holder, 800-yard freestyle relay, 1989
- Three-time Academic Collegiate Swimming Coaches Association All-America, 1989, 1990, 1991
- SEC Champion in 200-yard individual medley, 1990
- UT record holder, 200-yard individual medley, 1990
- SEC Champion 200-yard freestyle relay, 1990, 1992
- UT record holder, 200-yard freestyle, 1991
- UT record holder, 200-yard freestyle relay, 1992
- GTE/CoSIDA Academic All-America, 1992
- *Knoxville News Sentinel* All-SEC
- Fifteen-time All-America

Academic Stats

- B.S., Engineering, University of Tennessee 1993
- M.D. College of Medicine, University of Tennessee, Memphis 1997
- Completed general surgery residency at the University of Tennessee, Memphis, Department of Surgery, 2002
- Completed fellowship in advanced laparoscopy and bariatrics at the Ohio State University, 2003

By the time she entered the University of Tennessee, Jenny was definitely not the one coming in last. Freestyle and individual medley were her specialties, and she wasted no time pushing her competition. "As a freshman," she says, "I went head to head in the 50-yard freestyle with Florida senior Dara Torres, a world record holder and undefeated throughout her entire collegiate career. It was a dual meet, Tennessee vs. Florida at Florida in Gainesville. And I beat her. And she was the Olympic gold medalist and world record holder."

When Jenny was a sophomore, she came close to swimming another "first." In the SEC meet she attempted what no one has ever achieved, back-to-back wins in the 200 individual medley and 50 freestyle. After winning the individual medley, she missed first place in the 50 freestyle by only 0.02 second. It was close enough to mark that moment as one of her most memorable.

Her third-place finish in the 200 individual medley at the 1990 United States Championship meet generated a flashback of insight: "At the nationals my freshman year I was third in the 200 IM. They present roses to the top three finishers. And all these little kids would wait outside the swimming pool. When a swimmer came out with roses, they knew that she had been in the top three. It was the first time ever that I got bombarded with children wanting my autograph. And I remembered when I was a kid looking up to student-athletes. The role reversal struck me. And I remember thinking how you can have an influence on a child. I could tell the kids that it wasn't too long ago when I was here getting autographs myself. 'You can do it. This can be you one day.'"

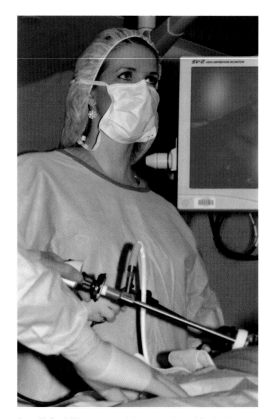

Jenny McGrath Weaver, general, laparoscopic, and Bariatric surgeon, 2007. Courtesy, Michelle East Photography.

Championship swimmers don't just happen. The Lady Vols practiced at 6:00 every morning and from 1:00 to 4:00 every afternoon. Their relentless workouts produced confidence with a competitive edge. "We had such good coaching at UT," she recalls. "We worked so hard. I clearly remember stepping up on the starting block and knowing that I had worked harder and put in more yards and more training than any other girl there. I knew that because we just worked hard. In high school I was afraid. In college I remember thinking, 'There is no way any other girl has worked harder than I have, and there is no way any girl up here is going to beat me.' And I am not the only one who felt that way. We would talk about it. That instilled so much confidence in all the girls on the team."

The student-athletes' confidence extended beyond the day of competition. Jenny cites others in the Lady Vol program as significant to her accomplishments:

The whole support of the Lady Vols from Joan Cronan to the assistant athletic directors to everybody—extends beyond the athlete to the student. They all provide help with education and everything you need. When you are there, you don't quite appreciate it. Then as an adult you look back and see how invaluable all of that was. Doing great in the sport was wonderful; we had great coaches there. I got where I was largely because of the college coaches. But now as an adult, now that the medals are lying in a closet somewhere, I see the greater value. I didn't have to take out loans to get through college. I had people there to help me with classes if I wanted it. And I developed lasting friendships. There are so many intangibles that are not medals or trophies. That is what I really appreciate now.

Numerous reflections on the past bring a smile. When she was a junior and preparing to compete at the NCAA competition, some fans surprised them with a special boost. "About a week before we left," she says, "David Keith (the actor from Knoxville who was in *An Officer and a Gentleman,* among many other films) made a home video with several other actors, including Brooke Shields and Corbin Bernsen. They all talked on the tape about what big Tennessee fans they were and how their blood ran orange! They wished us luck at nationals and said they were the biggest Lady Vol fans! After nationals, our team made a video to send back to them, spoofing some of their movies and thanking them for their support. Needless to say, none of us got any phone calls from Hollywood! It was embarrassingly awful, but we had fun!"

Jenny is a physician specializing in laparoscopic and bariatric surgery. She is proud to be associated with a hospital that was one of the first ten in the United States to be approved as a Center of Excellence by the American Society of Bariatric Surgery. Jenny's work focuses on weight-loss surgery and is truly rewarding:

The main thing I love about my job is that it is a "happy" job, for lack of a better word. So much of surgery and medicine involves giving people bad news. My surgery is working with patients who are morbidly obese, many of whom have all sorts of diseases related to being obese, such as diabetes and high blood pressure. These patients all say they can't play with their children or their grandchildren or they can't even fit in an airplane seat due to their weight. I operate on them, and the weight just starts falling off.

Six months to a year after surgery, these people return to see me, and their lives are almost unrecognizable from what they were before surgery. These are people who now exercise. They play with their kids. They have basically been given back their lives. And it is just so fun and rewarding for me to see these people be healthy, active adults. Many have struggled with obesity their whole lives.

I see people who can't walk across the room, and a year later they are doing triathlons. It is just great, and I love my job.

Jenny McGrath (Weaver)

Postcollegiate Career Highlights

- SEC H. Boyd McWhorter Post-Graduate Scholarship recipient, 1992
- Board-certified general, laparoscopic, and bariatric surgeon with Memphis Surgery Associates
- Assistant clinical professor of surgery with the University of Tennessee, Memphis
- Medical director of the Saint Francis Center for Surgical Weight Loss in Memphis
- Practices at one of the first ten centers in the country named a National Center of Excellence by the American Society of Bariatric Surgery
- Physician consultant to Ethicon Endo-Surgery for laparoscopic surgical device innovation and development
- Named to forum of top twenty female laparoscopic surgeons in the country by Johnson & Johnson
- Author of several medical journal articles and national speaker on laparoscopic surgery, robotic surgery, and surgical trauma
- Featured surgeon in multiple local outlets, such as *Memphis* magazine, the *Commercial Appeal,* and local news stations, including televised coverage of a gastric bypass done on the first adolescent in the mid-South
- Lady Volunteer Hall of Fame

Jenny McGrath Weaver is an inspiring person. To her patients, she is heroic. To her family, she is a treasured daughter, mother, and wife. To the University of Tennessee, she is a top scholar and groundbreaking researcher. To Lady Vol fans, she is a well-decorated swimmer who gave them many an occasion to cheer. To Jenny, she is simply a woman living her life as she was meant to do. In her own words:

Looking to people for motivation is fine, but ultimately you have to figure out what God put you on earth to do. For some it might be music; for some it might be to be a stay-at-home mom. I have developed great respect for stay-at-home parents. But I am also still trying to do what I think God put me here to do and that is to do a surgery that not too many other people can do. I would certainly tell any young woman that she needs to be exactly who God made and not be anybody else. Looking to other people to improve yourself is great, but never look at someone and say, "I want to be just like them." God made us all to do different things and be different people. And thank goodness He did.

Lady Vol swimmers raise competition another notch as they leave the blocks at a home meet.

Spotlight
Catherine Byrne (Maloney)
Swimming and Diving, 1989–92

Catherine Byrne

Catherine Byrne accepts the 1992 NCAA Woman of the Year Award. Courtesy, Michael Deane/Fine Photographs.

Championship Defined

When Catherine Byrne (Maloney) steps up, she brings with her the résumé of a champion. Known for her swimming accomplishments, one expects to see the trophies of an athlete. Her achievements in the classroom and her successful medical career also are not surprising when one considers her consistent top performance as a student. Add to these the Woody Hayes National Scholar-Athlete Award for Division 1, the 1992 NCAA Woman of the Year, and the University of Tennesee Torchbearer Award, the highest recognition presented to a UT undergraduate student, and one begins to realize that Catherine Byrne Maloney is a most unusually gifted individual. She is also kind, caring, humble, and the kind of person one would treasure as a friend.

Catherine's life began in Houston, Texas. Her two older brothers were swimmers, and her parents created the kind of home that nurtured and supported their children's interests. Until she was four years old, Catherine refused to put her face in the water. Four years later, though, when her oldest brother, Norman, came home from a swim meet with a green windbreaker, she was motivated to swim. "I really wanted that windbreaker," she says. "My mother said that he earned it swimming, and if I wanted one, I would need to earn it too. So I began year-round swimming and still have that green windbreaker today. It is covered with patches that mark the memories of many swim meets."

Catherine credits her parents for their commitment to their children. Even vaca-tions involved traveling to swim meets, and like many parents of swimmers, Anne and Robert Byrne worked volunteer positions at all their meets. The entire family enjoyed swimming and found many friends in the camaraderie generated at the events.

When Catherine was ready to enter junior high school, her family moved to Cleveland, Ohio. Connected to her team in Texas, Catherine suggested that she stay in Texas and live with her coach. Not surprisingly, her idea was answered with a one-way ticket to fly her from a swim meet in California to her new home in Ohio.

Upon arriving in Cleveland, Catherine discovered that high school swimming is well supported in Ohio, with pools in nearly all the high schools. Seeking additional training, Catherine joined a club team, the Lake Erie Silver Dolphins, and found a significant mentor in her coach, Jerry Holtrey. She remembers:

When you are in the water, you do lots of thinking on your own with your face down. Coach Holtrey tuned into the needs of all the swimmers. He knew when you were having bad days—he knew how to motivate you through the low times. He was a great coach—meeting emotional needs too. He was a very strong coach for me to have before and throughout college. For the Olympic Trials in 1988 and 1992, he was with me and helped me keep my perspective. Even after I enrolled at UT, I trained with him in the summers.

Coach Holtrey was my driving force—I had no problems working hard for him. The Olympic Trials happened before the school year ended, and I wanted both coaches—my

Catherine Byrne (Maloney)

Sport Stats

- Three-time Academic College Swim Coaches Association All-America, 1989, 1990, 1992
- SEC champion, 200-yard free relay, 1990, 1992
- GTE/CoSIDA Academic All-America, 1992
- Woody Hayes National Scholar Athlete Award, 1992
- NCAA Woman of the Year, 1992 (first Lady Vol to enjoy this distinction)
- As a freshman finished sixth at the NCAA Championships in the 100-yard backstroke and helped lead 200-yard and 400-yard medley relay squads to fourth-place NCAA finishes to help the Lady Vols to their best-ever NCAA Championship placing of fourth
- Fourteen-time All-America
- Tennessee record holder in the 50-yard, 100-yard, 200-yard backstroke; 200-yard free relay; and 200 and 400 medley relay events during her career

Academic Stats

- B.S., Education, University of Tennessee, 1992
- University of Tennessee Torchbearer Award, 1992
- Master of Physical Therapy, Emory University, 1995
- M.S., Healthcare Administration, Central Michigan University, 2003

Catherine Byrne Maloney with husband, Pete, and children, Teresa and Kyla, 2007. Courtesy, Catherine Byrne Maloney.

college coach and Coach Holtrey. He was so supportive. When I didn't achieve what I had wanted, he said, "Life goes on. You can move on to your career. You have achieved much." He was such a great coach. He was direct, constructive, not personal. [He] helped me find the balance, to recognize that swimming is important and that I have a life too, whatever it is—academics, community activities, or other endeavors. I don't think I ever told him how much he meant to me.

In addition to swimming, Catherine excelled in cross country running and the high jump event in track and field. By the end of her sophomore year at Solon High School, Catherine's schedule was filled with sports practices, competition, and academics. Concerned that his daughter would tire of the pace, Catherine's father suggested that she focus on one sport. It was a difficult decision. Realizing the training benefits in cross country running, Catherine continued cross

country with swimming through her junior year. In her senior year, she focused primarily on swimming, with the backstroke and sprint freestyle as her specialties. Her motivation to work hard in sports transferred to all aspects of her life.

"I always wanted to emulate what my brothers did," she says, "whether it was in swimming, at school, SAT scores—I had to do what they did or better. No one pressured me to perform—that was my internal drive. I was the youngest and wanted to be more than the baby sister. I realized that whatever you do, you need to put all your time and energy into it—so why not give it your best effort and see what can happen? Experiencing success in sports gave me positive reinforcement and carried over into academics too. I can't settle for a 'B.' I need to look for that 'A.' I am very goal-oriented and need to have goals in my sights."

It is not surprising, then, that Catherine had specific goals to guide her college selection. She desired the warmer climate of the South, a large school, and one that offered enough academic options to provide the latitude to change her mind about majors and also assure solid preparation for graduate work in a medical field. For her athletic interests, Catherine was looking for a swim program where she could make a significant contribution as a backstroke and freestyle swimmer. She says, "My parents and I were looking at the University of North Carolina, University of Iowa, and the University of Tennessee. Dave Roach, the Tennessee women's swim coach, came to my house in Ohio after UNC had visited. He let me know that Tennessee was honestly interested in me as a person. He knew that I had a strong place on this team and said, 'We need you for what you can do for us.' That really factored into my decision."

The University of Tennessee fit Catherine's selection criteria. On her campus visit, she saw a strong team environment with the cohesiveness of the coaching staff and team. She liked that women had a program separate from men but also liked that they swam in the same pool together and had some swim meets together. She felt drawn to the spacious campus and especially liked the strong support on athletics with an emphasis on academics. Joan Cronan made it clear that Lady Vols are student-athletes, with classroom success being a number-one priority. Catherine says:

Lady Vols are special. Because we were tall, most people would assume we were the basketball team. We would correct them, but the success of Pat Summitt and media attention to the basketball program helped with all the sports. Swimming itself doesn't get much media attention. Being a Lady Vol is tremendous. Community support is amazing. To me it was phenomenal to see community members come to a swim meet on a Saturday. The Boost-Her Club made distinctions between sports and did things for each team/sport. The Boost-Her Club made strong efforts to help us know our importance, and Joan Cronan did a great job to assure that swimmers were in the media. You are recognized as a Lady Vol—even just walking on campus. I felt very proud. People knew we were working hard—seeing us walking with wet hair, wearing big parkas. They knew we were dedicated, getting up early. We saw a lot of pride in what we did. Whatever your sport, people were behind you. On the football weekends—I loved the excitement and energy of all the people. Even football fans supported Lady Vols—women get so much play at UT, more than anywhere else. To see fans wearing shirts or hats supporting the Lady Vols—it's unbelievable! Women don't get second billing.

Catherine loved being a part of a team and especially enjoyed the camaraderie of being around other people with similar aspirations, goals, and strong work ethics. Her freshman class included twelve freshmen, with four from Ohio. She recalls:

We had a big freshman class. Eleven of us graduated together. We were so close and had lots of talent. Seven or eight of us were at Olympic Trials in 1988. After our sophomore year, Coach Dave Roach left UT to become athletic director at Brown. Switching coaches requires a mind shift to a new

Catherine Byrne (Maloney)

Postcollegiate Career Highlights

- US Olympic Trials competitor—swimming, 1988, 1992
- Physical therapist: Grady Health System (1995–99); Piedmont Hospital (1999–2001)
- Medical staff for Paralympics, 1996
- Liaison, Athletes & Coaches for Canoe/Kayak Venue for Olympics, 1996
- Allied health consultant, Emory University School of Medicine, Division of Physical Therapy, 1997–present
- Physical therapist, PRN, Wesley Woods Hospital, 1998–2001
- Community volunteer, Central Presbyterian Shelter, 1999–2005
- Coordinator of clinical education of physical therapy, Piedmont Hospital, 2001–04
- Operations manager, Rehabilitation Services, Piedmont Hospital, 2004–07
- Outreach committee member, Vision Class, Embry Hills United Methodist Church, 2005–present
- Director, Center for Rehabilitation Medicine, Emory Healthcare
- University of Tennessee Swimming Hall of Fame
- Lady Volunteer Hall of Fame

coach. Our new coach, Pete Raykovich, new assistants, and the team dealt with the challenges and issues that come with change.

She also learned that success can be defined differently—by the pride generated just from being a part of the Lady Vols team. "I was amazed to see people who would have been top swimmers at Division II schools but chose to come to Division I," she says. "It blew my mind that people would be on a team even when they knew they couldn't make the qualifying times for regional or national competition. Their best wouldn't be good enough. Those people really motivated me—teammates who chose Tennessee because they wanted to make contributions and be part of an elite group—they really motivated me to contribute even more."

Team spirit evolved from the rigorous practice schedule and special opportunities to be together. Catherine recalls a training trip to Florida during winter break her freshman year: "During winter break we would get a little less than a week off. Classes would end, and we would stay on campus about two weeks. We cooked our own meals and had two or three training regimens a day. We went home for a quick break and then returned before school started and trained some more. For one of those weeks our freshman year we went to Boca Raton. It was great—really nice—we trained but had so much fun. We didn't have training trips any other years. Team building really happened with that trip, and our spirits ran high. In an entire year the swim team is off about two weeks—that is all."

Despite all the accolades Catherine earned throughout her collegiate years, it is the time following graduation that really sticks in her mind:

Swimming was such a huge part of my life, and 1992 was such a special year for me because of the support that I felt. I had actually completed graduation and found that I wasn't "out of sight, out of mind." I was nominated by UT for a number of awards. That year I received the Woody Hayes Scholar Athlete Award and the NCAA Woman of the Year Award. It was such a whirlwind year—1992. It was phenomenal to be rewarded for swimming, academics, and community service. I saw that all the work over all those years paid off—not just my work, but my parents' sacrifices, the choices that we all made. At the NCAA Award ceremony my father had tears in his eyes. I had never seen him choked up before. My mother had a charm replica of the award made for me. They were so proud and have been my support all the way. When you are a Lady Vol, the University of Tennessee is committed to you. Joan is still interested in what I am doing now.

Six months after graduation, Catherine entered Emory University where she earned a master of physical therapy degree and met Peter Maloney, a competitive swimmer who shared her same professional goals and became her husband. Both are now parents of two young girls and make their home in Atlanta, Georgia. Catherine's career has grown to the top of her profession as an administrator in a Solucient Top 100 Hospital.

Would her life be different if she hadn't had swimming? "A health career would have happened anyway," she says. "My mom is a nurse, one brother is a doctor, another brother is a chemist—my family is medically involved. Without swimming I might not have moved as far away from home for school. I don't think I would be as outgoing, people-focused, able to tune into people as I do now. You have time to think when you are swimming, so I developed listening skills. I don't think that athletics and fitness would have been as important to me."

When asked what advice she has for young women today, Catherine doesn't hesitate to respond:

Make sure you find balance in your life. Stay committed to what is important to you. Rely on your family and friends to help you through when things don't go as you planned. So many pressures come from the outside—if you listen to everyone's opinions about certain things, you can get pulled away from your own purpose. You can get too involved in athletics too soon. It is important to find that balance—what works for you, academically, athletically—but also what I am trying to instill in my kids: the importance to give back to the community. We have to give back at some level. We can't be so single-minded to think that there's not something else out there. Stay committed to what is important, but find balance. Recently, my daughter looked at me and said, "I don't want you to go to a meeting tonight, Mommy. But I know you are helping the homeless people so it's OK."

Catherine Byrne Maloney pursues a life consistent with her goals. And she does so with passion. She is a true champion.

Spotlight
Abby Pearson
Golf, 1992–94

Abby Pearson

Abby Pearson at the U.S. Women's Open, 2003.
Courtesy, Abby Pearson.

On the Greens with a Big Orange T

If you were in Florence, South Carolina, and happened to see eleven-year-old Abby Pearson, you would have agreed with the notion that she would become the best swimmer in the world. In fact, anyone who witnessed her competitive nature knew that Abby would post many points in the win column of whatever venture she took on.

Abby and her sister Amy had discovered their love for swimming at a friend's pool. When her parents learned that they were swimming without adult supervision, they joined a local club so that Abby and Amy could swim safely. Every summer morning their father dropped them at the pool to play all through the day. One day Abby and her sister arrived to find the pool closed for repairs that would extend into August. At the clubhouse they discovered that a junior golf clinic was beginning. So to fill their time, they enrolled for lessons. Abby vividly recalls those days: "We went to the clinic from 8:00 a.m. till noon every day and played all afternoon. My first club was a 5 iron with a red grip. I'll never forget that club. When the pool reopened, Amy and I returned to swimming. Later in August the club held a Junior Golf Championship, and we signed up. My sister won. I couldn't bear losing to her, and with a vengeance I traded in my goggles for golf clubs and never swam competitively again."

While her determination to beat her sister might have initially drawn Abby to golf, she quickly realized her deep passion for the sport. Even though her parents were not golfers, they became her avid supporters, taking her to competitions, and many times her father served as her caddy. Enthusiasm fueled her skills, and Abby's talent drew notice. In 1990, at age sixteen, she was named South Carolina's Junior Champion, and in 1990 and 1992 Abby achieved the honor of South Carolina Women's Amateur Champion. "I played on the boys' high school golf team and was the number one player my junior and senior year," says Abby. "I also was selected to the All-Conference teams both years. In 1992 I played in the US Women's Amateur Championship and was defeated in the quarterfinals by Annika Sorenstam."

Not surprisingly, college recruiters were knocking on the door. Abby spent every weekend at the golf course and was hesitant to let anyone divert her from doing what she loved most. Recruiting trips were not high on her list of weekend activities. When Auburn University offered a scholarship, Abby verbally committed largely because she had previously visited the campus, found it to be acceptable, and was eager to turn her full attention away from college recruiters and back to playing golf. Then Ann Furrow called.

The University of Tennessee was building a golf program for women. Ann Furrow, an extraordinary scholarship athlete who had played golf for Tennessee through the men's program, was on a mission. She and Athletics Director Joan Cronan together had raised $1.5 million to create six fully endowed scholarships for golf. Along with Linda Franz (Sowers), a new coach snagged from a high-powered advertising and marketing position, they were pursuing the best players of the world for the inaugural class.

Abby Pearson

When the call from Tennessee came, Abby's father strongly urged her to schedule a visit. Abby saw the campus, met the people, and was hooked.

The minute I met Ann Furrow, my decision was made. She is truly amazing and has been the heart and soul of the UT golf program. At that time Ann was our volunteer coach. She traveled to many tournaments and was a great supporter for us all. I remember that she gave us food with special treats like cookies and candy in the bottom of the bags. Our coach always stressed healthy food, so when we found a few treats in the bottom of the bag, we all had a sigh of relief.

When she arrived that fall, Abby remembers first meeting her teammates.

We all met for the first time at the 'Rock' [campus landmark] I was impressed by the level of competition we had among us. We were all driven to be number one. I recall at some point Ann Furrow had told me about an especially strong player, Katharina Larsson, who was transferring to Tennessee. Ann whispered, 'Katharina will be our number-one player, and you are our number two.' That was all the motivation I needed. I was not going to be number two! Well, we all brought out the best in each other because of the level of skill we each had. We really respected one another.

Abby's determined spirit rose to the challenge. She could be very single-minded and admits that at times she might have caused a little stress for the coach.

The first time we played at Cherokee Country Club in Knoxville. I was on a par 5 with a 3 wood in my hand, trying to reach the green in two. I hit three or four balls out of bounds. Coach suggested I use an iron, which didn't suit me because I was determined to prove to her I could pull off the shot. I said, 'No, I can do it.' I finally did get the ball on the green, but I had to do it my way.

Abby's passion and work ethic led to top honors in the sport. She was UT's first-ever women's golf All-America after being named to the second team in 1993. She was declared 1993 Southeastern Conference Co-Freshman of the Year and set a course record at the 1993 NCAA Championships in Athens, Georgia, with a score of 67.

Abby attributes her success to the people and family of the Lady Volunteer program:

The Lady Vols' support system is unbelievable. From the coaches to the trainers, to the academics, to the leadership—their care and dedication are real. I was never alone. Being a Lady Vol taught me how to be a team member. It's not all about me. When I didn't do as well individually as I wanted to, I learned how to cheer for the team.

Abby made her professional debut in 1995 when she joined the FUTURES Golf Tour. Over the course of the next five years she won three tournaments and tallied five second-place finishes and twenty-one top-ten showings. She ranks twenty-second on the all-time money FUTURES list. In 2003 she qualified and competed in the US Women's Open. Abby has worked as a golf instructor

First-day arrival of the Lady Vol premier golf team, 1992. Left to right are Head Coach Linda Franz, Susan Conger, Shelley Kinder, Katharina Larsson, Abby Pearson, and Angie Boyd. Photo by Bill Pearson; courtesy, Abby Pearson.

LPGA. The Duramed Futures Tour is the official developmental step between college and the LPGA. We are the "stepping stone" between college and the LPGA.

Abby works with coaches to teach collegiate players how best to prepare themselves for a successful professional career. She stresses that women need to finish their education and then learn how to build their own support systems for independent living. Her passion to strengthen women for success is loud and clear:

I believe everyone has a passion—you just need to find it. I found my passion in golf; I just love the game! Now I feel so fortunate to be in a position that enables me to give back by creating more opportunities for women to chase their own dreams of playing on the LPGA Tour.

and served as assistant women's golf coach at Ball State University and Western Michigan University.

Having completed her undergraduate study in communications at Ball State University, Abby is now tapping into her experiences and giving back to women in golf. Abby manages the sponsorship between Duramed and the Duramed FUTURES Tour. Focused on women's health care, Abby's company promotes a mission that is consistent with her own commitment to support active, healthy women's lifestyles. Abby manages many initiatives on the tour, including one called "Foundation 4 Success." One component of the program is a college initia-

tive. The tour strongly believes in the importance of helping college players with the transition from collegiate to professional golf. Abby says:

The transition between college and professional golf can be very difficult. All of a sudden your support system is gone, without your coach to plan and help manage your daily schedule. You are totally responsible for every aspect of your life: living expenses, health insurance, and golf requires special clothing, equipment, practice, entry fees, and many other expenses. It can be overwhelming to make the transition, and student-athletes don't go straight from college to the

At the 2007 NCAA tournament, Abby spent a little time with the Lady Vol golf team. When the student-athletes gathered around her and showed their obvious admiration, Abby was struck by the shift in roles:

A couple of the UT players came up to me said that they had met me when they were young and had always looked up to me. They were so excited and couldn't believe that we were meeting again now. Not long ago I was standing in their shoes.

Abby Pearson has come full circle. Her energy and commitment are enough to assure us all that with help, determination, and preparation, our dreams are just a few swings away.

Spotlight
**Tracy Bonner
(Headecker)**
**Swimming and Diving,
1992–97**

Tracy Bonner

**Tracy Bonner seems to be flying as she dives with
perfect precision.**

She Dives through the Air with the Greatest of Ease

Have you ever wanted to join the circus? Tracy Bonner (Headecker) did just that. As a star performer for the Cirque du Soleil, this Lady Volunteer discovered that life after college doesn't mean life without diving.

Tracy's journey growing up took her just about all around the world before she landed in Las Vegas, Nevada. Born in Webster, Texas, Tracy enjoyed her childhood in Houston with her brother, Chad, and parents, Charles and Laury Bonner. Until she was in the eighth grade, her sports focused on gymnastics and swimming. In eighth grade she began diving and then in high school dropped gymnastics and added cheerleading to the mix.

While Tracy was a strong, well-rounded athlete, she began to realize her gifts for diving. Looking back to the early years of diving, Tracy is especially grateful for the sacrifices that her parents made to support her passion:

When I was young and had just found diving, my dad's job was going to require that we move to another state. I was in the groove, getting better all the time, and didn't want to be taken away from my great coach and team. I remember saying, "I am not leaving my high school or diving team or coach. Unless you find me a good program that has a coach that I like, I will not leave." I put my foot down. Looking back on it, I can't believe that I spoke up like that. Well, we stayed in Houston. My dad moved by

himself and came home on weekends to see us. I don't know if I was the total reason we did it that way or not. I was certainly a part of it, though.

Wow—what a sacrifice and how understanding my family is! They got me to every training practice as a kid. I remember a time when I was upset with them because I wanted my own car. I said, "I earned this college scholarship, so you can give me a car." They responded, "Well, actually we paid for your college but you were much younger at the time." Traveling to all the competitions, lessons—all those weren't cheap. My parents had to sacrifice to make that happen. What a perfect answer! They invested so much in my athletic career so I could get to where I needed to be. As a little kid you don't realize all that goes into it.

Tracy did have remarkable guidance and direction in Houston. She had found Dave Parrington, a talented coach, whose move to coach women's diving at the University of Tennessee greatly impacted Tracy's future decisions. When it was time to consider colleges, Tracy looked everywhere. She reflects:

Selecting a college is a challenging process as a kid. It is a huge step in life—at the time it seems as if your life is depending on it. For an athlete a good fit can make a significant difference for competition and opportunities.

When I was being recruited, that was the last year when athletic directors could make home visits [NCAA regulations]. Joan Cronan came to my house to recruit me. She is a special part of why I came to Tennessee. We always joked that I was going to take her

Tracy Bonner (Headecker)

job one day. I used to say, "That sounds like a fun job—I think I would like to do that some day."

The presence of her diving mentor, Dave Parrington, the community spirit of the women's athletic department, and the campus as a whole proved to be just the right match for Tracy. Whenever she had questions or concerns, she knew that she could go to her coach for help. Given that Coach Parrington had been at Tennessee for only a year, Tracy was his first full college recruit. It was a perfect fit.

Tracy came to Tennessee with the eagerness and the determination to be her best. She found challenges every day. "I tell people that I was born in Texas," she says, "but I think I grew up in Tennessee. I was living several states away from home for the first time and making decisions about my life that up to now had been supervised by my parents. I definitely grew up in college."

Balancing the commitments of being a student-athlete requires strong discipline. Divers are the "early birds of campus," up for practices at 6:00 a.m. when few people are awake, trudging through the freezing cold and then getting wet by plunging into a pool. Tracy says:

Our lives were a bit different. I couldn't go out partying because I had to get up so early. I was not such a social person. It took lots of discipline. We don't have what people think of as normal college routines. Athletes are usually self-motivated to do their best all the time. I put pressure on myself—set my own higher standards in everything I did. I concentrated a lot on school work and athlet-

Tracy Bonner Headecker in "O," a Cirque du Soleil performance. Photograph by Tomasz Rossa; costumes by Dominique Lemieux, © Cirque du Soleil, Inc.

ics. That is what I chose to do. I was mostly with student-athletes. The Lady Vols create a close community that is nurturing. It is wonderful to have so many great friends who are athletes.

I did join a sorority. They understood that I couldn't be at many of the meetings and functions. I really enjoyed having that "family," too. Lots of girls made signs and came to competitions. They were great—cheering loudly and having fun. I was so fortunate to have a great circle of friends. I love Tennessee, and it became my home.

Many memories stand out for Tracy. She recalls one time when she nearly changed the career for a well-known Tennessee quarterback: "I was driving on The Hill [oldest part of campus]. The road is narrow, one-way, and curvy. I was going back to the dorm from an engineering night class, and it was dark. As I was driving around the blind curve, a student was walking in the wrong direction right in the middle of the street. It was Peyton Manning! I almost hit him—Peyton Manning! I can't even imagine if I had injured him—thankfully, I had quick reflexes. He and I joked about that forever."

Tracy might have turned a few heads that night when she was driving on The Hill, but when she stepped up as a diver, she caught the attention of the world. Setting school, SEC, and NCAA records on the 1-meter springboard, 3-meter springboard, and platform, she established new standards for women's diving. International competition also took her to numerous venues, including Australia, Germany, Mexico, and one of her favorite places, Moscow. She says:

I have always had a fascination with Russia. I hadn't met Russian people except in diving competitions. The language is so perplexing. I love Moscow. I was so taken aback by Red Square. I went there two years in a row, and the second time it was cleaned up so much. Moscow is a beautiful city.

It is so ironic that now working at Cirque du Soleil I sit in a dressing room with so many Russian speakers. I have always had this big admiration in my heart and soul for the country and people. I don't know how my sense of connection with Russia developed. I grew up so differently in terms of lifestyles.

My first roommate here was a woman from Russia. She is now a great friend, and we teach each other. It is fascinating to see how life presents experiences to us.

Diving seems to be a sport that particularly challenges personal fears. Tracy acknowledges that fear can be a factor and is best overcome by the trust that grows through training: "When you are younger and learning, you don't think about the risks the same way you do when you get older. Yes, there can be fear. I had fears and Dave was able to teach me in such a way that I learned to trust. Knowing that you trust completely in the person who is teaching gets you beyond your phobias. It is a learning process, and it takes time to get to the bigger tricks and dives. Especially at Tennessee we have the greatest support from all sides—strength and conditioning, training, coaching—on a day-to-day basis, they give you everything you need to make you the best you can be."

Mental preparation is an additional component of training. Classes in sports psychology added visualization and imagery techniques to Tracy's skills. She learned to follow a routine that began with a musical headset to escape the announcements of scores set by previous divers. Staying away from the diving well, Tracy focused only on the dive she was about to perform. When her turn came, she would have a word with her coach, dive, and then return to her coach for quick feedback. Then it would be time to prepare for her next dive. Sometimes that would be only a matter of a few minutes, and other times hours would remain between events.

On one occasion, Tracy was competing in an NCAA competition where noted diver

Tracy Bonner (Headecker)

Sport Stats (continued)

- SEC Champion, 1-meter springboard, second on 3-meter springboard, fourth on platform, 1997
- US National 3-meter synchronized diving Champion at US Spring National Diving Championships and earned spot to compete at US World Team Trials, 1997
- Earned berth on US National Diving Team by placing sixth at US National Spring Diving Championships, 1997
- US Diving National Championships, two-time gold medalist (with Lady Volunteer Kathy Pesek), 3-meter springboard synchronized diving, (winter and summer) 1997
- Earned US National Team member place, finishing second on 3-meter springboard at US Outdoor Nationals, 1997
- Finished fifth on 1-meter springboard, highest finish on this event in career history at US Nationals, 1997
- Member of US National Team competing at World Diving Cup in Mexico City, Mexico; finished fourth on 3-meter synchronized diving event (with Kathy Pesek), 1997
- NCAA Woman of the Year for the state of Tennessee, 1997–98
- NCAAA Women's Enhancement Scholarship Award, 1997–98
- NCAA Postgraduate Scholarship Award, 1997–98
- Pi Beta Phi Senior Focus Graduate Study Scholarship Award, 1997–98
- Ten-time All-America

Academic Stats

- B.S., Education, University of Tennessee 1996
- M.S., Education, University of Tennessee 1997

Tracy Bonner (Headecker)

Greg Louganis was commentating for television. At a break, Louganis joined the divers and performed his trademark dive that had tragically resulted in a career-ending head injury. "I was still young in my career—learning my ways of the sport—and was amazed that I was even on the same platform with this phenomenal diver," she recalls. "After I did one of my dives, my coach called me to his side and said, 'Tracy, how many times do you think he has dived since his injury?' I thought that the number had to be pretty high if he was willing to dive with us that day. Well, he had actually only done a total of eight dives since his injury. He did it flawlessly. I couldn't believe how strong he was—so mentally strong. There will never be another diver like him."

When she thinks of her collegiate years at Tennessee, Tracy's first thoughts go to the people who have made such a difference in her life:

Teammate champion Kathy Pesek joined Tracy Bonner to claim five gold medals in women's three-meter springboard synchronized diving at U.S. Diving National Championships.

What is special about the Lady Vols? So much—now having been gone for a number of years, I really see the family entity that the women's athletic department is. You know that the people you need are going to be there. Joan Cronan, Pat Summitt. Pat isn't just about Lady Vol basketball—for me that was apparent. She is always thinking of every sport and every athlete. It doesn't matter what team you are on—athletes are equally important. You can see Joan anytime—what company has the president available to everyone? Her door is always open. You wouldn't find that anywhere else.

Jenny Moshak and all the athletic training staff members are the top in the country. Jenny and her staff do whatever it takes to assure that athletes are at their prime. In 1996 Jenny turned down other opportunities to accompany me to the Olympic Trials. It was just after I had surgery, and physically it was a hard time in my career. Her dedication is unmatched. I owe so much to Jenny.

So many people played a huge role. I am so fortunate and grateful for having met all these wonderful people—the fans, the Boost-Her Club. There is no way to duplicate the Lady Vol experience or even express completely what it is—the awe of what it is.

On one of her many international journeys, Tracy and her teammates had some time before flying home. They were in Australia, and the Cirque du Soleil just happened to be performing there. Tracy and her friends went to see the show and ended up with front-row seats, and there Tracy discovered her future. Having completed her bachelor of science and master of science degrees, she announced that she was going to join the circus. Today she stars as a professional diver in a show unlike any other. From sixty feet above, Tracy spins and climbs in a large metal hoop and dazzles the audience with her skills and magic.

"I love what I do," she declares. "I get to perform for over 1,800 people twice each night, touching the lives of so many people. I get to do what I have trained for my whole life. This is the only place where you can dive for a career. It is absolutely fabulous. Our diving competitions were never seen by so many people. Except for the Olympics, diving is not something people come to watch. It is great to have this opportunity to show people what diving looks like."

What is Tracy's message to young women today? "Always work hard toward your dreams and goals," she says. "I believe if you want something, you can do it. It's just a matter of figuring out how to make it happen—about making choices. We get knocked down so often that we start thinking we can't do it. That saddens me. We can accomplish our dreams if we just look for another direction over the roadblocks. Try it a different way. We need to work hard to be who we are. Look to your heart and soul for your own desires. In this crazy world that we live in, there is so much beauty if you look past the negatives and find the sunshine."

Tracy Bonner Headecker has a rare and joyous spirit. In five seconds of sheer precision, she takes our breath away and fills us with amazement. That's quite a splash.

Spotlight
Adrienne Walker (Chery)
Softball, 1996–2000

Adrienne Walker

Adrienne Walker pitched the first no-hitter in Lady Vol history against Cleveland State on February 24, 1996.

"Build It and She Will Come"

She was one of the most sought-after recruits in collegiate softball. She came to the University of Tennessee before the softball program even existed. Her given name is Adrienne, but to anyone who knows her, she will always be "Buffy."

"My mom and dad reside in Carlsbad, New Mexico," she says. "It is a fairly small town. My mom is a nurse. When she was pregnant with me, someone repeatedly called our house and asked to speak with 'Buffy.' It happened so often that after I was born, my parents decided to call me 'Buffy.' After mom returned to work at the hospital, she met a woman who was chatting about her Aunt Buffy. As it turned out, her aunt's telephone number was just one digit off from ours. She was the one who had been calling our house!"

Buffy grew up with a strong sense of family and faith. She listened to stories about her grandparent's faith and learned to believe that nothing is impossible. She flourished at sports and was especially talented as a softball player. She was a born pitcher, and her skills matched her passion for the game. As she was completing eighth grade, her future as a ball player looked bright until the barrier of prejudice appeared and steered Buffy's life onto an unexpected course. She recalls:

Basically, word got around to my dad from the coach that I would never pitch high school softball for their program. So I went through a very difficult time in high school. It was hard because I was used to being on the same team with my friends and playing games with them. We had been doing that for years until we all reached high school. Eventually, it got to the point where basically the coach said that anyone who played with Buffy Walker in the summer (because my dad did coach me in the summer) would not play for him during the school year. This coach had led a successful high school softball program for a number of years and therefore carried quite a bit of power in his position. So a lot of my friends were put in a position where they could not play with me in the summer because they wanted to play in college and the coach had promised he could get them scholarships. And then there were other friends who said that they were going to play for whomever they wanted in the summer. They said, "I'm good. You need me during the school year." They were definitely brave and bold enough to stand up to the coach. And that is a hard thing to do especially at such a young age. None of us should have ever been put into that kind of a situation—forced to make that kind of decision. I just wanted to play softball. I just wanted to play with my friends. I just wanted to pitch.

After her eighth-grade junior varsity season, Buffy never played high school softball again. She did go on to play for the high school basketball team but could pursue her real love, softball, only in the summer. The coach's words left their mark on the summer league, though, with some of her friends and the more competitive softball players feeling too intimidated to join her team. With recreation league play having limited competition and exposure, Buffy's father knew that they would have to make a change. She joined an ASA fast-pitch travel team based in Phoenix, Arizona. "My dad always tells me a story about when we were in our back yard playing catch," she says. "We were practicing pitching and he said to me, 'I don't know how we are going to do this,' when all the high school softball problems were going on. 'We can't afford to send you to school ourselves.' I turned to him and said, 'Dad, that's why we pray.' I actually used to pray to God that I could get a scholarship. I didn't know at the time why I was going through all that. I would say, 'Why is this happening to me? I didn't do anything to anybody.'"

Reasons for her high school experiences will never be justified, but Buffy's family support and her own confidence and commitment leave no question of their love and championship spirit. Knowing that Buffy's opportunities for achieving a college scholarship in softball required that she play where she would be seen, Buffy's father sought a solution. He found an answer after meeting with Phoenix Head Coach Phil Kemmer at several tournaments during the summer of 1993. Buffy would live in Phoenix with the Kemmer family for the following two summers while in high school. The coach paid for her to fly between El Paso, Texas, and Phoenix, Arizona, and her parents drove to see her play at all the tournaments. It was an early separation from home and a situation that reflected a tremendous belief in the future.

"For me being away those summers was like going through my freshman year at college," she remembers. "That really helped me when I did go to Tennessee. I had already gone through that process of being away from family and not really knowing anybody. That definitely made me stronger. It was an experience."

Adrienne "Buffy" Walker-Chery and her husband, Yves Reginald Chery, 2007. Courtesy, Adrienne "Buffy" Walker-Chery.

The decision to spend summers in Phoenix proved to be fortuitous. While on the Phoenix travel team, Buffy caught the eye of Jim Beitia, then head coach for women's softball at the University of Oklahoma. Beitia watched Buffy at a number of tournaments and visited her at the Kemmer household in Phoenix. Early discussions of Oklahoma shifted her sights to Tennessee when he announced that he was taking the head coaching position at the University of Tennessee to initiate a softball program for women. Buffy was so impressed with Coach Beitia and the opportunity to be a part of the inaugural women's softball team that she did not hesitate to commit to Tennessee. She says:

Adrienne Walker (Chery)

Sport Stats

- NFCA First-Team South Region, 1997
- First-Team All-SEC, 1997
- SEC Pitcher of the Week, 1997 (April 8), 1998 (April 14)
- All-Tourney, Lady Vol Classic, 1997
- All-Tourney, Lady Vol Spring Invitational, 1997
- First no-hitter in school history, 1996 (February 24 vs. Cleveland State) All-Tourney, Great Smoky Challenge, 1996
- All-Tourney, Tennessee Tournament of Champions, 1996

Academic Stats

- B.S., Communications, University of Tennessee 2000

Postcollegiate Career Highlights

- Advertising and marketing recruiter
- Marketing manager, Fireman Property Group (California)
- Director of acquisitions, Coaches' Choice (California)

Carlsbad, New Mexico, is really close to the Texas border, and Carlsbad sits in the middle of the desert. Growing up in New Mexico, when I was playing ball, we would always have tournaments in Arizona, California, or Colorado. I had never at any point made it [to the] South or to the East Coast. So when I had the opportunity to see Tennessee on my recruiting visit, I fell in love with it because it was so different from anything I had known growing up.

I remember flying to Tennessee in September, and it was right around the time the leaves were changing colors. Flying over the mountains you could see an orange tree here, a red one there, and it was so pretty. It was so different from what I was used to seeing—cactus, sand, and tumble weeds.

Once I set foot on campus I was sold. I could have gone to play for other established programs, and my parents would have loved for me to be closer. I remember when I told them that I wanted to go to Tennessee. They said, "Are you sure? They don't have a women's softball program yet."

But that was part of the lure—an opportunity to start a new program. One of the main reasons I went to Tennessee was because they didn't have a program. That was one of the big deciding factors. It was an opportunity of a lifetime to be a part of the first program. I knew that everyone doesn't get this opportunity. I just felt very strongly that it was where I was supposed to go. I knew the history of the women's athletics department and how much they put into the women athletes. Not to take anything away from the highly respected men's athletics department, but the women's program at Tennessee stands on its own. And

you can't say that for every program out there.

Buffy opened Tennessee's first season, and on February 24, 1996, she pitched Tennessee's first no-hitter. Throughout her career as a student-athlete, Buffy Walker set records and marked first-time events. Most precious to her, though, are the memories of the people—the fans, her teammates and the university community:

The moment that I have hung onto from UT was our very first home game. I think that was a game against Purdue. And it was snowing that night. It was freezing, and my parents were there but they weren't in the stands. They were in the car. In fact, most of the West Coast parents were in their cars. Tyson Park has a wooded area, and every now and then you would see them come up to the outfield and then go back to the car and sit and peek up over the dashboard. I remember that game so vividly. I remember the snow falling. I remember we had kerosene heaters in our dugout. When I think about the game, it was like slow motion to me. I remember having those little hand-warmer pouches in our back pockets. Jackie Beavers and I both pitched. We would pitch and then stick our pitching hand in our back pocket and keep it there the whole time. Wiping off the mound with our hand in our pocket, taking our time, and trying to keep warm, we would keep it in there until the very last possible minute. And I remember Lisa Wyatt. She played first base for us, and she got too close to one of the kerosene heaters and the back of one of her uniform pants legs burned. We were all joking and saying

we would just tell coach that she cleated herself. We were freezing but so entertained in the moment and loving the game. That is one thing I will never forget.

Buffy Walker loves softball. She has followed her heart and believed in her vision despite obstacles along the way. Her journey underscores her message to young women:

You can do this. Scholarships are not easy to come by, but there are always other options. One thing I want young girls to know, whether it is softball or another sport or talent, there are always options for you. I think many girls say, "Oh well, I'm not going to get a scholarship," and they get discouraged and start to question why they are playing. But when I got to Tennessee and started looking around, some girls were there on academic scholarships. Some had transferred from junior colleges. So there are a lot of ways for girls to get an education while doing what they love. Today there are more and more opportunities to play at the collegiate level. Don't ever let anyone tell you that you can't do something. I am a firm believer that all things are possible. You just have to have faith and believe. You can be anything you want to be. If you believe in yourself, you can do it. That is what I would stress for young girls. Believe and you can be successful.

Buffy Walker could have played collgiate softball almost anywhere. Instead of joining a program with an established winning record, she chose to set the standard. She brought to Tennessee the pioneer spirit of the West and her belief in possibility. And her contributions are here to stay.

Tyson Park, adjacent to the University of Tennessee campus, was the Lady Vol softball home playing field until 2008.

A Tennessee Original
Donna Thomas

Donna Thomas

Donna Thomas, senior associate athletics director

Guardian of Tradition

Some might know her as "The Enforcer." When Lady Vols are summoned to her office, it could mean trouble. Donna Carol Thomas is a disciplinarian and a stickler for the rules, fiercely protective of Lady Vol tradition and never hesitating to say what she thinks. She can be a force intimidating to face, but beneath her exterior there is a heart of orange, white, and pure gold.

Donna easily articulates her responsibilities as senior associate director of women's intercollegiate athletics. Her role is to assure that all actions connect to four basic goals:

Student-athletes are students first.

Athletic performance in every sport results in a top-three position in the Southeastern Conference and in the top ten nationally.

The Lady Vol program is one of integrity.

Wearing the orange jersey is a point of pride, and Lady Vols are an active part of the community.

Donna's oversight ensures university compliance with NCAA/SEC rules. She interprets policies, educates the UT community, and monitors all aspects of operations: recruiting, enrollment, scholarship administration, academic advising, alumni involvement, and other areas. She pays close attention to every student-athlete to maintain eligibility requirements. Donna's reminder of boundary lines may not always be happy news, but her attentiveness enables all sports to compete fairly and appropriately according to regional and national guidelines. Angela Kelly, head soccer coach, points to the sig-

nificance of this function: "Donna Thomas has the thankless job of policing our institution from a compliance and administrative standpoint. I can honestly say that there is no one better. That is my personal opinion. We are all grateful that Donna keeps us all so well informed and guided in our paths toward excellence."

Donna is involved in nearly every aspect of women's athletics. She approves budgets, authorizes contracts with sponsors, approves purchases, and supervises the daily work of support staff. On any given day she may be helping individuals to resolve conflict, addressing staff performance issues, providing staff education and professional development, or preparing job tools for coaching staff. Rob Patrick, head volleyball coach, depends on Donna's direct answers and reliability. "Donna has been one of the best people that I have known to work with on a daily basis," he says. "The best thing that I like about Donna is that she will shoot straight with you all the time. You will know exactly where you stand with her and her position on any subject. She is a very steadying and constant force within our athletic department."

A responsibility daunting to many is just second nature to Donna. She supervises event management for basketball and provides leadership for a staff who must remain one step ahead of customer needs and crises. When one considers that the arena hosts over 20,000 fans at a single event, and then realizes that overlapping sport seasons can often lead to simultaneous events, the job seems nearly impossible. Yet, when teams arrive, they may not even pause to consider the hours that someone gave to prepare for their needs. When fans arrive, rare would be the individual who notices anything other than the action of the game. The event almost looks as if it runs itself effortlessly. That is the result of an extraordinary leader. Carrie Cole, assistant golf coach and former student-athlete, recognizes the diligent work behind the scenes: "As the 'team captain' of the department, Donna keeps everyone moving in the right direction at all times, and like any great captain, will do everything in her power to help you reach your goals and be there to congratulate you when you do."

Donna is always noticing the distance student-athletes grow from their freshman to senior years. The Lady Vol program strives to prepare young women for life. Their experiences as student-athletes are not unlike those of life after college. When Lady Vols graduate, Donna shares their pride and joy. She feels the poignancy of saying "good-bye." Donna never really does put closure on a graduating student. Lady Vols are always Lady Vols. Donna follows their careers, life events, and ups and downs. To celebrate their accomplishments, Donna spearheaded the establishment of the Lady Volunteer Hall of Fame. Each year a class of distinguished graduates is inducted and celebrated for accomplishments during and after their collegiate careers. Judi Pavon, head golf coach, admires Donna's enthusiasm and generous spirit to honor others: "Donna is the lady behind the scenes in Lady Vol athletics. Things would not operate as professionally or efficiently without Donna dotting the i's and crossing the t's. She is a great lady who supports coaches and student-athletes but doesn't seek recognition for her hard work and dedication."

Donna sees her "invisibility" as a measure of success. She asserts, "It is my job to take care of everything necessary so that all coaches have to do is coach." Loud and clear are her own words vowing her commitment to operate with integrity as a responsible steward of resources: "We have been given incredible opportunities—financial gifts, support of fans, alumni, the university, and the community at large. We will have done a great disservice to all if we don't manage well and work effectively together."

never faltered. From day one the values of the Lady Vol program have held strong: (1) the importance of a degree, (2) the high caliber of competition, (3) responsibility to the community, (4) a commitment to do things in the right manner."

Donna describes her role as one to assure that each student-athlete graduates from the University of Tennessee "with a degree in one hand and an opportunity for a fistful of Championship Rings in another." Limited opportunities and limited duration for

It's our job to help students understand that the degree is number one. If they don't go to class, they don't play. Someday they won't be able to play their sport. It is our job to prepare student-athletes for "someday."

Donna's dedication to the Lady Vols found its beginning in 1978, when she first joined the staff as the head manager of the Lady Vol basketball team and continued to serve while working as a student toward her goal to complete an undergraduate degree. Donna has great memories of the early days of women's athletics and still marvels at the distance they have come. When asked about what changes have occurred over the years, Donna responds with a question: "The important question is: What has not changed? The evidence of change is apparent when we consider facilities, travel, expansion and fan support. What makes the Lady Vols special is to understand what has

professional playing careers underscore the importance of completing college. "It's our job to help students understand that the degree is number one," Donna says. "If they don't go to class, they don't play. Someday they won't be able to play their sport. It is our job to prepare student-athletes for 'someday.'"

Head Coach Pat Summitt of the Lady Vols basketball program values the experience and depth that Donna brings to the department. She observes that "Donna Thomas's administrative skills, her knowledge of women's athletics, and her compliance and day-to-day operations proficiency cause her to be our point person in the department.

She's our All-American—the one we search for when we need the 'go-to' person."

Student-athletes are college students. Like all college students, they sometimes make poor choices. When Lady Vols need a reminder of the values that they represent, Donna does the deed. Professional basketball player and Lady Vol Tamika Catchings is aware of Donna's role as disciplinarian. "Donna has always been the one that we tried to avoid having to see because of something that we did wrong," she says. "But, there weren't many instances of that. She is very good at what she does and always makes sure that everyone in the Lady Vol family abides by the rules. She is strict when it comes down to it, but we loved her for that in the long run."

While student-athletes may feel as if they are at the other side of the table when they face the corrective discipline of Donna Thomas, it is her very experience as a student that motivates her to invest her life energy in their success. "Most of us here have somewhat grown up with athletics," she explains. "I have a huge desire to do this because someone did it for me. I want us to be difference makers for our student-athletes. We are molding the future by teaching these young women."

Donna has been working with women's athletics since 1990, when she returned from serving as the director of recreation ministries for a 5,000-member church. She completed a master of science degree in recreation and athletic administration and is an adjunct professor and lecturer in two colleges at UT. The University of Tennessee is one of the few institutions that positions men's and women's athletics as separate and equal

departments. Donna cites this as a strong statement of the administrations' commitment to women's programs: "The separation of departments allows both areas to concentrate on young women and young men with equal attention."

Sonia Hahn-Patrick, co–head tennis coach, views the organiztional structure and Donna's role as a key to success: "Donna has strived to give the Lady Vol department the respect it deserves as a separate athletic department, and there are few in the country. She continually challenges us as coaches to raise the bar and to strive for excellence on and off the court."

Joan Cronan, director of women's intercollegiate athletics, says that "Donna Thomas is the most efficient person with whom I have ever worked. She has a lot of pride in the total athletic program."

Every organization has unsung heroes, those individuals who silently and willingly handle whatever is required to ensure excellence. The Volunteer symbol of the University of Tennessee depicts the Torchbearer and displays the words: "One who beareth the Torch shadoweth oneself to give light unto others." Donna holds the torch for the Lady Vols as they each enter the university and inherit the legacy others have created before them. With the light that Donna shows them, they honor, respect, and strengthen the traditions for all who follow.

Donna Thomas is a Tennessee Original.

The Lady Vol rowing team passes new competitive levels, moving Tennessee forward as a top rowing school.

03

Ringing in a New Century, 1997–2007

Eleven Sports, Countless Champions

As if marking the turn of the century, Lady Volunteer basketball players provided NCAA National Championships Titles as bookends for the 1997–2007 decade. During these ten years basketball achieved another National Championship title, bringing a total of seven trophies to Coach Pat Summitt's Tennessee teams.

All eleven sports added markers to the Lady Volunteer's history. The 2005 volleyball team competed in the NCAA Final Four Tournament. The soccer team emerged on the national scene as a serious Sweet 16 contender in 2002, 2003, 2004, 2006 and 2007. Track and field popped to the top in 2005 when they captured both the NCAA National Championship (Indoor) Title and the NCAA Mideast Regional (Outdoor) Title. Joining the other nationally recognized Lady Vol sports, rowing achieved a first-ever bid to the NCAA varsity 8+ Championships in 2003. Swimming and diving, cross country, and golf teams continued on the upswing. Rocking the decade were the Lady Volunteer softball teams, posting back-to-back-to-back trips to the NCAA Women's College World Series, 2004–07.

It's All about Fun
Marketing and Promotions

Wanted: Individual to direct marketing and promotions for the Women's Intercollegiate Athletics Department, the University of Tennessee. Must be willing to generate at least ten new ideas each hour; supervise a large cadre of student interns, graduate assistants, and staff; operate three different telephones simultaneously; assure that crowds of no fewer than 15,000 are having fun at all times; be willing to wear strange costumes, including a hot dog suit; take small children to the center of a standing-room-only arena to perform amusing tricks and competition in under one minute; monitor the safety of special effects including indoor fireworks; develop marketing plans and brand management of the Lady Vol organization; plan, develop, and implement all entertainment for all Lady Vol events; drop cows from the rafters; perform any and all other duties as needed. At all times remain calm, congenial, and cooperative with others.

Sound impossible? Not only are those expectations possible, they are simply "all in a day's work" in the life of the marketing and promotions department. Dedicated to "providing a great environment for student-athletes and for fans," the staff of this area brings out all the bells and whistles that frame an event and keep it moving throughout the athletic action. Planning and preparations begin well before the gates open and last long after the lights go off.

Jimmy Delaney, director of marketing and promotions for the Women's Intercollegiate Athletics Department at UT, understands fans, tradition, and the Lady Vol way: "Our fans are incredibly loyal. We have such a strong tradition of performance and winning." Delaney's work is not unnoticed. Head Coach Pat Summitt of the basketball program is keenly aware of his role in creating a fun venue for the Lady Volunteers. She says, "Jimmy Delaney has generated, with his talented mind and creative ideas, a successful marketing plan to generate interest and enthusiasm for thousands of Lady Vol fans. It's more than just a Lady Vol basketball game to Jimmy—it's an event."

Above: All-America Tonya Callahan, hailed as "the best all-around player we have ever had" by Co-Head Coaches Ralph and Karen Weekly, completed her 2005–08 Lady Vol career as the school's all-time leader in home runs (51), RBIs (241), total bases (492), walks (154), slugging percentage (.646), and on-base percentage (.487).

Left: Candace Parker turned eyes to a new century as the first woman to dunk the basketball in an NCAA Tournament game.

Above: Named 2007 Sportswoman of the Year by the Women's Sports Foundation, pitcher Monica Abbott led the Lady Vol softball team to the Women's College World Series for the first time ever in 2005. Left: Lady Vol volleyball team huddles before the match.

1997

Basketball: NCAA National Champions (Tennessee 68–59 Old Dominion)

Golf: NCAA East Regional—2nd; NCAA Championships—6th

Rowing: NCAA National Championship, Varsity 4+—9th; Petite Finals—3rd

Softball: overall—45–22; SEC—20–7; Eastern Division—2nd

Swimming and Diving: SEC—3rd

1998

Basketball: SEC Champions; SEC Tournament Champions; NCAA National Champions (Tennessee 93–75 Louisiana Tech)

Cross Country: SEC—3rd; District/Region—3rd

Soccer: SEC record 5–3; Eastern Division—4th

Softball: overall—37–31; SEC—13–15; Eastern Division—3rd

A single athletic event requires 24/7 attention. Delaney and the marketing staff plan event agendas down to the minute. Well before the doors open, staff members spend hours rolling T-shirts, banding posters, and gathering miniature game balls and other treats to stir crowd participation.

The work team reviews the "play-by-play" schedule of fan seating arrangements, student cheering sections, special accommodations, music, pep bands, special guest performers, and pizza give-away. Every event is planned with the unexpected in mind. Inevitably an eleventh-hour cancellation of a half-time program calls for activation of "Plan B." Staff members throw out their ideas, schedules shift accordingly, and the clock is always moving. Every person carries individual duties and flawless dedication. Even one miss will affect the event. Delaney spends at least two hours with technicians to finalize the lights. In his pocket is a compact disc containing two and a half minutes of opening music to add razzle-dazzle to the introductions. Preparing the music took six to eight hours. Many events have fireworks at the opening, half time, or closing. Other special effects may be warranted depending on the event. Perfection is essential. Each minute is planned and builds to the next

Jimmy Delaney encourages a fan to lead the crowd in "Rocky Top" at a basketball halftime program.

moment. The production elements must blend to provide background to the event and at the same time stir the excitement of the fans. Delaney says that they "always have a set of eyes on everything. I have a little bit of butterflies in my stomach before every event."

Ideas for event activities come from brainstorming sessions, observing other venues, and suggestions from the general public. Ideas always begin with the question, "What would be fun?" The marketing staff considers the demographics of the fan base and builds from there. They are always challenged to find what they can do that is different. Some of the more memorable activities have not been the most lasting. Delaney laughingly remembers the idea to use an air gun to launch hot dogs into a hungry, happy crowd at a basketball game. He dressed up like a hot dog and fired the gun. The hot dogs emerged and blew into pieces just over the bench of the visiting team. That was the end of the flying hot dogs.

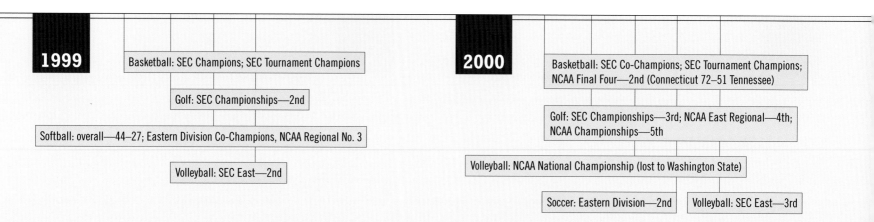

1999

Basketball: SEC Champions; SEC Tournament Champions

Golf: SEC Championships—2nd

Softball: overall—44–27; Eastern Division Co-Champions, NCAA Regional No. 3

Volleyball: SEC East—2nd

2000

Basketball: SEC Co-Champions; SEC Tournament Champions; NCAA Final Four—2nd (Connecticut 72–51 Tennessee)

Golf: SEC Championships—3rd; NCAA East Regional—4th; NCAA Championships—5th

Volleyball: NCAA National Championship (lost to Washington State)

Soccer: Eastern Division—2nd

Volleyball: SEC East—3rd

Fans of all ages have a place in Lady Vol festivities. These future Vols are honored by the community program "Character Counts."

Sometimes keeping the fun in the game can be a challenge. When the score is down, it is the job of the marketing staff to keep the fans there. Let's say it's just before half-time at a basketball game and the Lady Vols' lead has slipped away. The marketing staff gathers in the hall, and Jimmy gives the pep talk: "We can't do anything about the score. We all want our team to win. But we can do this: it is our job to see that every person here has a great time and goes home feeling happy about being here tonight. So smile and have fun!"

When the final buzzer sounds, and the fans leave, the marketing staff forms a small bunch around their director. Delaney, thanking them for their hard work, says, "Great job—not a person here can say they didn't have fun, and everyone stayed through the end." Jimmy Delaney turns to consider final needs for the day, and his thoughts are already moving ahead to the next venue.

Half-time entertainment at another Lady Vol basketball game highlighted a UT student fraternity performing a step show. This was a first, and Delaney said that they really didn't know what fan reaction would be. The students stepped to "Rocky Top" for their closing number, and the fans went crazy. "That was a real example of a total grassroots entertainment. It was a huge hit," Delaney says.

Especially popular with fans is the Chik-Fil-A cow drop. Chik-Fil-A, the popular fast-food chain, provides stuffed cows, and marketing staff poised on catwalks drop the cows from the rafters to cheering fans. Delaney will never forget the first time they dropped the cows and the reward he felt when he saw and heard fan reaction. "My job is just great," he declares. "It's all about people having fun."

When asked what he does to keep his staff so motivated, he smiles, reaches out his arms, and says, "I just tell them to think about all that—the tradition, the fans, the student-athletes, and coaches, everything that is so special about Tennessee. And then think about all of that without you."

The conductor is truly a master.

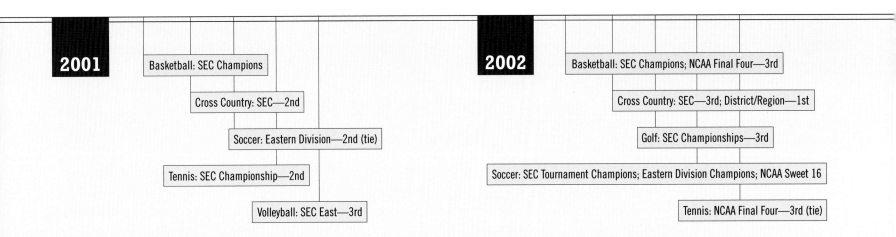

2001
- Basketball: SEC Champions
- Cross Country: SEC—2nd
- Soccer: Eastern Division—2nd (tie)
- Tennis: SEC Championship—2nd
- Volleyball: SEC East—3rd

2002
- Basketball: SEC Champions; NCAA Final Four—3rd
- Cross Country: SEC—3rd; District/Region—1st
- Golf: SEC Championships—3rd
- Soccer: SEC Tournament Champions; Eastern Division Champions; NCAA Sweet 16
- Tennis: NCAA Final Four—3rd (tie)

Students before Athletes
Thornton Athletics Student Life Center

The University of Tennessee Women's Inter-collegiate Athletics Department recruits student-athletes first to be students who will graduate with a college degree. The consistently high graduation rate stands alone as evidence of academic priorities. Since all students experience challenges during the transition to college and throughout developmental stages of growth, the Thornton Athletics Student Life Center offers comprehensive services in advising, counseling, and time management to support the academic success of student-athletes.

The center provides tutoring and houses a computer lab as well as group and individual study areas. Assistance is available for special needs, including test anxiety and learning disabilities. All freshman student-athletes are required to spend at least six hours in the center each week. The staff assures that student-athletes are on schedule academically and that they learn how to manage the many demands of their time.

Lady Vol softball stand-out Sarah Fekete found the services to be especially helpful in preparing her for life beyond softball. "When you go to school at the University of Tennessee," she says, "you are going to get an edu-

cation. I know firsthand that you can't make a living just playing professional sports. It is important to be able to support yourself when you get out of college. I learned from the staff at the Thornton Center that you need to be self-sufficient and use time-management skills. They guided me through the steps to prioritize my schedule demands."

The staff of the center report directly to the provost's office. They work closely with advisors in every college to assure a top-quality academic experience for student-athletes. The center is located in the heart of campus and is always a hub of student activity.

Top: The "Lady Vol Lunatics" are a standard fixture in the student cheering section at volleyball games. Bottom: Student-athlete Felicia Guliford (track and field, cross country) seeks academic guidance from Eric Brey, director of Thornton Center.

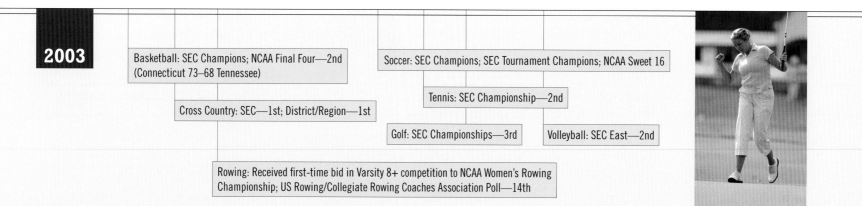

2003

Basketball: SEC Champions; NCAA Final Four—2nd (Connecticut 73–68 Tennessee)

Soccer: SEC Champions; SEC Tournament Champions; NCAA Sweet 16

Cross Country: SEC—1st; District/Region—1st

Tennis: SEC Championship—2nd

Golf: SEC Championships—3rd

Volleyball: SEC East—2nd

Rowing: Received first-time bid in Varsity 8+ competition to NCAA Women's Rowing Championship; US Rowing/Collegiate Rowing Coaches Association Poll—14th

Beyond Orange Borders

Road Trips

Travel to competition has undergone many changes since the early Lady Vol days. Building competitive seasons required traveling to other venues, and distance had a direct impact on expenses. Schedules dating before the early 1970s reflect that consideration, with many events occurring within the state or immediate region.

Transportation usually consisted of rented station wagons, vans, or even personal cars with coaches and team managers driving. Many Lady Vols still remember times when their teams were nearly lost driving in a caravan of cars through unknown territory to find an arena or playing field. Often student-athletes brought their own money for food, and when overnight accommodations were needed, several piled into each room. Lady Vols sold doughnuts, washed cars, and conducted other events to offset travel expenses.

As the Women's Intercollegiate Athletics Department began to establish a budget and address Gloria Ray's early priorities of funding coaches and scholarships and building credible competition, travel was an important component. Ray was determined that Tennessee would be on the national map.

"Early on we traveled where we needed to meet competition," Ray recalls. "As we grew better, we went further."

Twenty-first-century student-athletes enjoy the comfortable travel of van, bus, or plane, depending upon time and distance. Their room accommodations and food provide what they need to be comfortable and focused on their competition. The expenses are supported through the departmental budget. Coaches determine season schedules based on goals for their sports. The Lady Vols of thirty years ago would be amazed by the ease of today's travel. They would be excited to see that Lady Vols have a national and even international presence in the sports world.

An essential part of off-site competition will never change, however. Lady Vols still laugh, tell stories, work hard, and treasure memories of their travels on the road.

On the Road with the Lady Vols

Sue Flamini, a member of the Lady Volunteer soccer team from 2001 to 2004, wrote a journal on her team's trip to Florida to play in the 2003 SEC Conference Tournament. The Lady Vols were the ones to beat, having won the Conference Championship the previous year. The tournament promised to be exciting, and the Lady Vols were filled

with anticipation. Here's what Sue had to say about that memorable trip.

Wednesday, Nov. 5, 2003

After a long bus ride last night to Orange Beach, Alabama, we finally made it to our destination, and we found it to be much more than expected. The bus ride included all kinds of old-time favorite movies such as *Dirty Dancing* and *Dumb and Dumber*. We've taken so many long bus trips lately that we have already seen all the new movie releases.

We arrived at 2 a.m., and Ange [Kelly] let us sleep until 11 a.m. today!! I love sleeping in, so that had already made the day great. When we awoke, we found that our bedroom balconies overlooked the ocean, and we were pretty amazed by the sight. This morning Keeley [Dowling] and I actually took a trip down to the water before breakfast. It was great to smell the saltwater and walk through the sand.

Our beloved coaches, Sam [Baggett], Ange and Scott [Blount], personally delivered our breakfast. We all hung out until around 12:15 p.m., when we had to meet downstairs for a jog/stretch. Ange took us around the parking lot twice, and then we

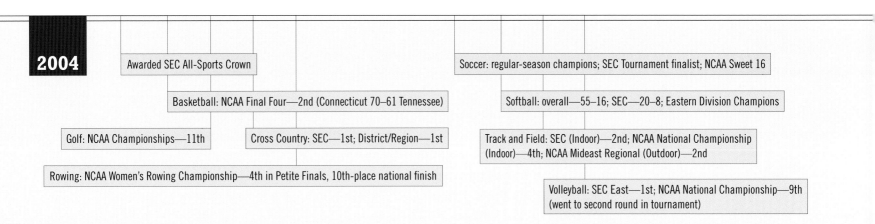

2004

- Awarded SEC All-Sports Crown
- Basketball: NCAA Final Four—2nd (Connecticut 70–61 Tennessee)
- Golf: NCAA Championships—11th
- Cross Country: SEC—1st; District/Region—1st
- Rowing: NCAA Women's Rowing Championship—4th in Petite Finals, 10th-place national finish
- Soccer: regular-season champions; SEC Tournament finalist; NCAA Sweet 16
- Softball: overall—55–16; SEC—20–8; Eastern Division Champions
- Track and Field: SEC (Indoor)—2nd; NCAA National Championship (Indoor)—4th; NCAA Mideast Regional (Outdoor)—2nd
- Volleyball: SEC East—1st; NCAA National Championship—9th (went to second round in tournament)

all headed straight to the beach. We all took off our shoes and ran about a quarter of a mile down the beach, where the coaches were setting up a soccer/volleyball court. We always play freshmen/sophomores and Kim [Patrick] vs. juniors/seniors, and today, of course, we [juniors/seniors] won! After we finished our game, our entire team sprinted to the water and dove head-first into the ocean. The waves were strong, but luckily no one was taken away by the tide. Ange allowed us to swim for a total of about three minutes before we were called in. It was a fun time because our entire team was swimming and riding the waves together.

In the afternoon, everyone took a trip to the movies. We usually go see a movie at least once per trip. Some of us saw *Runaway Jury*, while others saw *Matrix Revolutions* and *School of Rock*. We headed to a restaurant after the movie, where we saw the usual "Oh my God, I can't believe an entire team just walked into our restaurant" look from the people behind the counter, but they did a good job.

Well, now everyone is getting primped and ready for the annual SEC banquet. We usually have a good time getting dressed up, mostly because we're usually in soccer shorts and tee-shirts rather than skirts and dresses.

I will check in tomorrow, which is our first game day against South Carolina. I feel a great vibe from everyone on the team so far, and our team chemistry seems brilliant. Let's hope it carries to the field for our first victory in the tournament tomorrow.

Thursday, Nov. 6, 2003

This morning we started early, up at 8 a.m. for breakfast. The team looked ready from the moment I walked into the breakfast room. I was very excited to play, and I think we all were. Because we were coming back to the tournament as SEC Champs, we have been feeling a little bit of pressure. Other teams see us as the team to beat this year. I think we were ready to finally get things started.

We left for the game around 10 a.m., and arrived at the fields soon after. On the bus we watched a great music video that our video coordinator Ethan [Mayers] made for us. He always inspires us with videos before the games, and at the end of the season, he compiles them to make an awesome video that summarizes all of the highlights of the season.

The game started, and we came out strong, having about five shots in the first 10

Sue Flamini shows the determination and talent that collected top honors in her four years playing for the Lady Vols.

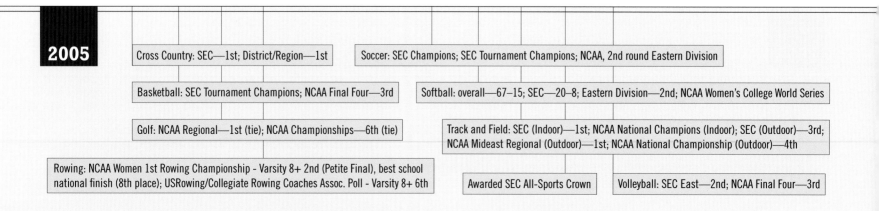

2005

Cross Country: SEC—1st; District/Region—1st

Soccer: SEC Champions; SEC Tournament Champions; NCAA, 2nd round Eastern Division

Basketball: SEC Tournament Champions; NCAA Final Four—3rd

Softball: overall—67–15; SEC—20–8; Eastern Division—2nd; NCAA Women's College World Series

Golf: NCAA Regional—1st (tie); NCAA Championships—6th (tie)

Track and Field: SEC (Indoor)—1st; NCAA National Champions (Indoor); SEC (Outdoor)—3rd; NCAA Mideast Regional (Outdoor)—1st; NCAA National Championship (Outdoor)—4th

Rowing: NCAA Women 1st Rowing Championship - Varsity 8+ 2nd (Petite Final), best school national finish (8th place); USRowing/Collegiate Rowing Coaches Assoc. Poll - Varsity 8+ 6th

Awarded SEC All-Sports Crown

Volleyball: SEC East—2nd; NCAA Final Four—3rd

minutes or so. Unfortunately, we went into halftime 0–0, a position that did not match the ideals we had set in our pre-game talk. We went out in the second half with a vengeance, putting high pressure on South Carolina, but unfortunately we kept coming up short. Finally, Keeley made an amazing run and dribbled the ball up the entire field, then passed it to LP [Lyndsey Patterson]. LP was about to score until she got tripped up in the box. Ali [Christoph] was confident in her penalty kick, and she put us up 1–0 to win the game. Of course, we felt that we should have scored a lot more goals, but sometimes teams just can't find the back of the net. We were excited about the victory, however, and we will certainly take this win to help motivate us for tomorrow's game against Ole Miss.

After the game our team went to eat at an Italian restaurant near our hotel. My dad and brother Chris are in town, and Ange is always happy to have them join us for meals. After lunch we headed back to the hotel, where the injured players got treatment, the studious did their homework and some of us . . . ha-ha . . . went to the pool and beach for some rest and relaxation. Unfortunately, for our team, rest and relaxation means throwing me in the pool with all of my clothes

still on. I was looking for back-up and for some help when I was getting thrown in, but instead all I got was laughter and clapping while I was about to be submerged underwater. We also watched the sun set over the Gulf of Mexico, and we watched dolphins swim in the Gulf as well. Besides having a great soccer day for Tennessee, we also enjoyed our surroundings immensely. I realized today that we are very lucky to be here surrounded by great scenery and also great teammates, coaches and family.

Tonight we ordered in. Sometimes it is nice to go out to dinner, but just eating in our rooms can be relaxing. I visited Ashley [Dawes], Erica [LaShomb], Melissa [Amado] and Talia [Wright] in their condo, and we discovered board games such as "Guess Who" and "Connect Four," which can always help to provide some good, clean fun. After the games I packed up and headed back to my condo for some much needed rest. Tomorrow will be a great day to get revenge on the only SEC regular season team that we lost to: Ole Miss. Go Lady Vols!

Friday, Nov. 7, 2003

11:45 a.m.—Game day!! We woke up at 10 a.m. to dolphins once again swimming

in the Gulf, right outside our bedroom window. We had the usual breakfast, and Ange ordered us to get 15-minute massages from a teammate and hang our legs for another 10 minutes. Because we played games back-to-back, it is important to get our legs ready for action today. We ate lunch today at an international market, and we coincidentally ran into Ole Miss also eating there. We gave each other the "rivalry stare" and then continued to eat.

Five o'clock—game time! Excited and ready to go, we loaded the bus. We watched the video again; it just seems to get us pumped up so well! As we got off the bus, we were greeted by our marketing director, Carolyn [Wares] and our NCAA compliance person, Todd [Dooley], while they were blasting "Rocky Top" from their car speakers. It was a good feeling, because everyone was screaming the words at the top of their lungs. It personally made me even more pumped up to play, and to represent UT.

The game itself was a battle, and we went into halftime scoreless. The shots were about even, but I had a good feeling about the game. A little bit into the second half, we managed to find the back of the net. I actually received the ball in the midfield and played it to Rhian [Wilkinson] while she ran at the

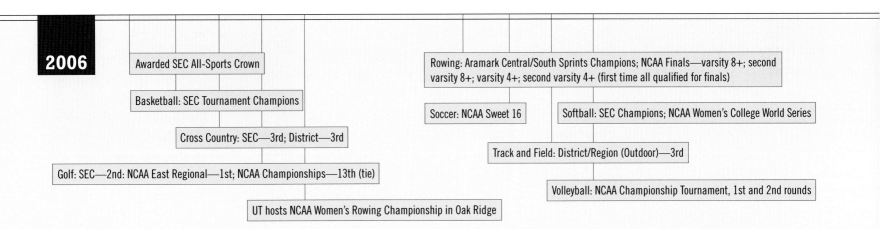

goal. She slid the ball away into the corner to put us up 1–0. The second goal came a little bit later in the second half, when Rhian beat a pair of defenders down the end line to play a perfect ball to Ali, who placed the ball directly past the goal keeper for our second goal. From then on out, there were about five minutes left, and our main concern was to keep the ball out of our end. We were successful, and we cried "victory" the entire way back to the hotel.

We ate at a seafood restaurant later that night, and everyone was very happy and excited about the opportunities that were ahead of us. We couldn't wait to play in the final and hopefully become back-to-back SEC Champs.

Saturday, Nov. 8, 2003

Today was what we like to call a "Happy Saturday." During our season one of our motivations to win games on Friday night is so we can have a great Saturday and all be in good moods around each other. We started with breakfast once again, and then got to hang around the hotel and watch UT beat Miami in football!! We also took this time to study for all of the schoolwork that we have been missing. Around noon, Buddy

[Marie-Eve Nault] came into our room and announced that we would be doing partner massages poolside, followed by a 45-minute swim in the pool/ocean. We headed downstairs for the festivities.

I was partners with Ali, and we had to massage each leg for 10 minutes. It's great to get a massage, but it is hard work to give one. When we were finished, we all headed straight to the ocean to enjoy the sun and the water. We brought our mini-football down to the water and pretended that we were football players for a while. Then we headed to the pool for a rinse-off, where Kayla [Lockaby] and I were still in the football player mode. I would throw a pass to Kayla as she jumped off the side of the pool, head first into the water. I must say, she does have some stellar receiver qualities for a soccer player.

After the pool, we had time to relax and shower before heading off to the marina to go on a Dolphin Cruise!! This was such an incredible experience. We took a chartered boat out on the Gulf and searched for dolphins as they swam around. Then our boat would start going really fast, and the dolphins would ride along the boat's wake, just like a surfer rides waves on top of the water. The dolphin would come astonishingly close

Lady Vol soccer captured the SEC Championship in 2002. Pictured here (left to right) are teammates Kim Patrick, Jen Laughridge, and Sue Flamini.

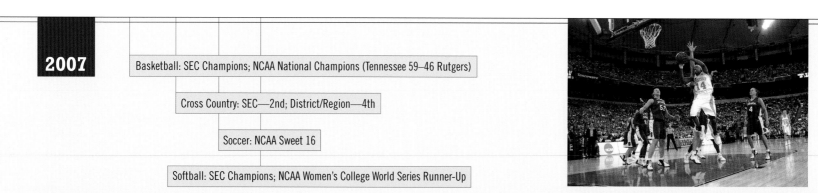

2007

Basketball: SEC Champions; NCAA National Champions (Tennessee 59–46 Rutgers)

Cross Country: SEC—2nd; District/Region—4th

Soccer: NCAA Sweet 16

Softball: SEC Champions; NCAA Women's College World Series Runner-Up to the boat, gain speed, and then jump up as high as it could to impress everyone watching. They were so smooth and sleek; it was truly a beautiful sight to see. Then we watched the sun set over the water and noticed the moon rising on the other side. Once the sun went down, the party really started as we danced the rest of the night away on the boat deck.

That night our coaches prepared dinner for us. It was what Ange likes to call a "progressive" dinner. We would have appetizers in the managers' room, salads and soups in the trainers' room, our main course in the guys' room and the dessert in Ange and Sam's room. I'm pretty excited about some good home-cooking before the SEC Final tomorrow against Florida!

We came into this tournament very excited to repeat last year, and we also felt the pressure from all of the teams around us. Tomorrow is the Championship game, and we are extremely excited to do our best and take home first place again. I can't wait to play!

Sunday, Nov. 9, 2003

Today we woke up at 10 for breakfast in the manager's room. We definitely get to sleep in a lot more on these soccer trips than we do while we're back at school! After breakfast we had a meeting in Ange's room to discuss Florida's style of play. We all learned who will be starting, and who we'll be marking to start off the game. After the meeting, we had to pack up and get ready to leave our beloved beach condo that we enjoyed extensively throughout the week. It will be sad to wake up tomorrow morning and not see dolphins outside my bedroom window!

We loaded the bus and arrived at the field for the SEC Championship game. I was excited yet nervous at the chance to become SEC Champs once again. Then I tell myself that I play my best when I am nervous. I know it is just a mind game, but usually it works!! When our pre-game talk was over, we headed to the field, where Florida was already warming up. We began our warm-up to one of the most exciting and memorable games I have ever played as a Lady Vol.

The game started, and once again I felt that we came out strong. We were pressuring Florida with our unique style for the first 10 minutes. We had several quality scoring opportunities, but once again we went into halftime scoreless. I had a great feeling about the second half. We were playing well, and Ange let us know that she was happy about what she was seeing out on the field. We headed out for the second half, when we found our first and only goal of the game. It was off a corner kick, when Ali placed the ball to Keeley's head, who extended and hit it far post to LP. LP then tapped it in for a wild Lady Vol celebration. Unfortunately, with 15 minutes left in the game, Florida was awarded a penalty kick (PK) after a takedown in the box. Dena Floyd scored to tie the game, 1–1.

After two sudden-death overtimes, the inevitable PKs would decide the fate of this year's SEC Champ. However, after a nerveracking and nail-biting 2–1 score, we came away with the victory. It was a bittersweet victory, because we would have liked to win in regulation time. We ended the celebration with the complete drenching of our three coaches, Sam, Ange and Scott. Sam thought she was sly and avoided our first attempted

Sue Flamini
Soccer, 2001–04

Sports Stats

- First-Team All-SEC, 2001
- Soccer Buzz All-America honorable mention, 2001
- Soccer Buzz Freshman of the Year finalist, 2001
- Soccer Buzz First-Team Freshman All-America, 2001
- NSCAA Second-Team All-Central Region, 2001
- Soccer Buzz First-Team All-Central Region, 2001
- 2001 Soccer Buzz Central Region All-Freshman Team, 2001
- SEC Player of the Week, Sept. 10, 2001
- 7 shots vs. Kentucky, Nov. 8, 2001
- 2 goals vs. Kentucky, Nov. 8, 2001, and vs. Furman, Nov. 15, 2002
- SEC Academic Honor Roll, 2002–05
- 3 assists vs. Kentucky, Oct. 26, 2003
- SEC All-Tournament Team, 2003

Academic Stats

- B.S., Business Administration, University of Tennessee, 2005
- Graduate assistant in Women's Intercollegiate Athletics marketing and promotions
- M.B.A./M.S., sport management, University of Tennessee, 2008

Postcollegiate Career Highlights

- Intern, NCB Sports, January-May, 2008
- Fox Interactive Media, May, 2008–present

drench; however, Tracy [Swibas] and I sneaked up behind her and tried for a second time—this time successful. We always like to show our appreciation for our coaches after a victory by getting them as wet as possible. Mission completed.

Well, now we are traveling back to Knox-ville, with the SEC East, Regular-Season, and SEC Tournament Trophies sitting on the front seat. We're pretty proud to have ac-quired the Triple-Crown of the SEC. We will have to work hard this week to prepare for this weekend—the first and second rounds of the NCAA Tournament. Go Lady Vols!

Lady Vol Erica Griffin anchors a strong Tennessee defense.

Lady Volunteer soccer teammates give "high-five" greetings during introductions.

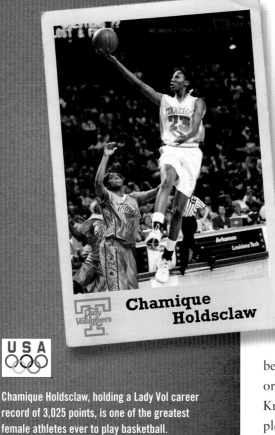

USA

Chamique Holdsclaw, holding a Lady Vol career record of 3,025 points, is one of the greatest female athletes ever to play basketball.

Mique

In 1995 Tennessee Lady Vols added a new word to their vocabulary: Mique. This word has not yet entered the dictionary, but anyone who knows basketball can define it.

Mique (meek) n. [orig. *Cha + mique* < Mique] **1.** standard setter **2.** one who dazzles with gold **3.** a champion among all champions **4.** one who causes amazement and wonder **5.** one who scores many points, rebounds, assists, and steals **6.** one whose very presence evokes cheers and the music of "Rocky Top."

Upon the arrival of Chamique Holdsclaw at Tennessee, Mique immediately became a household word. She has been called "the greatest player ever to play the game," and when her number 23 jersey was retired on February 1, 2001, Chamique became the fourth Lady Vol to be so honored. She is the only Lady Vol to have a Knoxville street named for her; at the completion of her collegiate career she held the record as UT's all-time leading scorer (3,025 points) and rebounder(1,295); and she holds the NCAA Tournament career record for points (479 points, 21.8 ppg) and rebounds (198 rebounds, 9.0 rpg) in tournament games.

Chamique has achieved and keeps achieving. When she reaches one record, she sets another by claiming it twice. Her name is often followed by the phrase "the only woman ever to be awarded …" Chamique has brought new fans to women's basketball,

and her extraordinary career in the WNBA has expanded the fan base even more.

She is an icon in women's basketball, but that is what Chamique does—not who she is. Chamique Shaunta Holdsclaw was born in Flushing, New York. She has one younger brother, Davon. After her parents divorced, her grandmother June Holdsclaw raised her in New York City. Chamique cites her grandmother as her role model, mentor, and the person whom she most admires. Her grandmother worked hard and dedicated her life to providing Chamique with every opportunity to get a good education. Chamique learned the importance of a college degree and set it as one of her goals. "My grandma told me that once I left home for college, not to come back home unless I have my college degree in four years," she recalls. "Coach Summitt challenged me and helped me to stay on track. I was motivated to work hard as a student-athlete. I really wanted to be the first in my immediate family to graduate from college."

Before dazzling Big Orange Country, Chamique achieved notice in New York. While attending Christ The King Regional High School in Queens, New York, she played for the school's women's basketball team and led them to four straight New York State Championships and one National Title. She was already beginning to gather "firsts," as evidenced by being the first among females and males to be recognized as New York City's Player of the Year for three consecutive years. By the time she graduated from high school, Chamique had accrued a daunting list of honors and achievements.

The 1996 NCAA National Championship basketball team: (front row, left to right) Laurie Milligan (11), Michelle Marciniak (3), Latina Davis (5), Misty Greene (13), Kim Smallwood (10), (back row, left to right) Brynae Laxton (31), Pashen Thompson (44), Tiffani Johnson (4), Abby Conklin (52), Chamique Holdsclaw (23), and Kellie Jolly (14).

Chamique Holdsclaw

Sports Stats

- US Olympic Festival, 1995
- ESPY Awards Co-Team of the Decade (1900s), 1995–99
- SEC Freshman of the Year, 1996
- All-SEC Freshman Team, 1996
- NCAA All-Regional Tournament Teams, (East) 1996, (East) 1999, (Midwest) 1997, (Mideast) 1998
- All-SEC Team, 1996, 1997, 1998, 1999
- Kodak All-America, 1996, 1997, 1998, 1999
- NCAA All–Final Four Team, 1996, 1997, 1998
- SEC All-Tournament Team, 1996, 1997, 1998, 1999
- USA Basketball Player of the Year, 1997
- Honda Cup Winner 1997, 1998
- NCAA Tournament Most Outstanding Player, 1997, 1998
- NCAA Regional Tournament Most Outstanding Player, (Midwest) 1997, (Mideast) 1998
- Naismith All-America Team, 1997, 1998, 1999
- US National Team, 1997–2000
- US Basketball Writers Association Player of the Year, 1998
- Honda-Broderick Cup Athlete of the Year, 1998
- Associated Press All-America Team, 1998
- Sporting News Player of the Year, 1998, 1999
- Sporting News All-America Team, 1998, 1999
- Sports Illustrated Player of the Year, 1998, 1999
- WCBA Player of the Year, 1998, 1999
- SEC Female Athlete of the Year, 1998, 1999
- SEC Tournament Most Valuable Player, 1998, 1999
- Naismith Player of the Year, 1998, 1999
- Associated Press Player of the Year, 1998, 1999
- ESPY Awards Women's Basketball Player of the Year, 1998, 1999

Responding to the recruiting efforts of Coach Pat Summitt, Chamique and her grandmother agreed that Tennessee would be a good college fit. Mique especially liked the fan enthusiasm, tradition, and family-like closeness of the team. For fans, it was love at first sight. The 6'2" freshman became an immediate favorite when she scored a team-high 16 points against the 1995–96 US Women's National Team in a November 22, 1995, preseason game. Her first season at UT was complete when the Lady Vols became 1996 NCAA Champions. The Lady Vols added 1997 and 1998 National Championship wins to the record.

Mique points to the 1997 NCAA championship victory as one of her most memorable Lady Vol moments. She recalls chest bumping and hugging teammate Niya Butts in celebration. That image captures the heart of what Mique especially values from her

Tennessee times: "Looking back, I treasure the people most of all. I had the opportunity to meet some incredible lifelong friends."

Basketball opened the world to Chamique. Her abilities and talent earned her a spot on the USA Basketball's 1997 World Championship Qualifying Team. It was her first of what would be many trips out of the United States, and the younger Chamique was surrounded by eleven professionals. With Nell Fortner as the US head coach and four-time Olympian Teresa Edwards as her roommate, Chamique flourished. Chamique finished as the team's leading scorer (19.0 ppg) and rebounder (6.2 rpg). Her US Team claimed the silver medal and a berth in the 1998 World Championships.

Chamique points to Teresa Edwards as an individual that she truly admires. Coach Nell Fortner recognized the value of pairing the two as roommates on their travels. A

Chamique Holdsclaw

Sports Stats (continued)

- Sullivan Award, 1999
- Kodak 25th Anniversary Team, 1999
- Naismith Player of the Century (1900s), 2000
- UT's all-time leading scorer and rebounder
- Holds the NCAA Tournament career record for points and rebounds in tournament games
- Member of 3,000 Point Club with 3,025 career points
- Member of 1,000 Rebound Club with 1,295 career rebounds

Academic Stats

- B.S., Arts and Sciences, University of Tennessee 1999

Postcollegiate Career Highlights

- WNBA Rookie of the Year, 1999
- WNBA Washington Mystics, 1999–2005 (first overall draft pick)
- Six-time WNBA All-Star, 1999, 2000, 2001, 2002, 2003, 2005
- US Olympic Team, gold medalist, 2000
- Author: Chamique on Family, Focus, and Basketball (New York: Fireside, 2000), My Story (New York: Fireside, 2001)
- Fourth Lady Vol to have jersey retired (number 23), 2001
- International Career: Ros Casares Valencia, 2004–05; TS Wisla Can-Pack Krakow, 2006–07, championship, MVP of the finals
- WNBA Los Angeles Sparks, 2005–07
- Honorable mention WNBA All-Decade Team, 2006
- One of five players named to NCAA 25th Anniversary Team, 2006
- Three-time All-WNBA
- Only Lady Vol basketball player to have Knoxville street named after her

The 1997 NCAA National Championship basketball team: (front row, left to right) Chamique Holdsclaw (23), Brynae Laxton (31), Laurie Milligan (11), Niya Butts (3), Misty Greene (13), (back row, left to right) Kyra Elzy (5), Tiffani Johnson (4), LaShonda Stephens (34), Abby Conklin (52), Pashen Thompson (44), and Kellie Jolly (14).

biographical sketch of Chamique that appeared on the USA Basketball Web site included this quote from Fortner: "Last summer [1997] Chamique was surrounded by great players like Teresa Edwards. I think they were really good for each other, the 'grand dame' and the rookie. She brought some excitement to Teresa, who in turn gave some wisdom to Chamique. She played all over the world, leading the team in scoring and rebounding the whole time. That's a lot to ask from a young player, but she handled it like a pro and did a fantastic job. She's still getting better, and there's no telling where her game is going to end up."

Future international play would take the college star to countries including Berlin, Canada, Slovakia, Germany, and Brazil. Each time Chamique returned with medals and standout recognition for her extraordinary play. Future experiences would include bringing home a gold medal from the Olympic Games in Sidney, Australia, in 2000.

Mique continued to delight fans throughout her collegiate career under the tutelage of Pat Summitt. Of the lessons she learned as a Lady Vol, she especially points to "accountability and sacrificing for others." Mique attributes her success as a student-athlete and her continued achievement as a professional player to her "drive and passion for the game and to not being afraid to fail."

Chamique has many memories from Tennessee, and one especially brings a smile. "Everyone knows that Coach Summitt is a great dresser," she says. "Well, one day I told her that she was GQ. For the younger generation, this means that you look like a million bucks—really sharp. Time passed, maybe weeks. Coach grabbed Semeka Randall's and my attention, and she called out, 'Hey Guys, do I look QT?' We laughed so hard.

At the end of her collegiate career, Chamique Holdsclaw's 3,025 career points set a new basketball standard for both women and men at the University of Tennessee.

It was hilarious. We said, 'No, Coach. It's GQ.' Coach always tried to keep up with the things we would say, and this was great because she had to stay connected and be able to relate to 18–21 year olds. That was too funny."

As Mique considers her greatest life challenge, she says that "remaining true to one's self in a world that is trying to change you" is particularly important. Her inner strength shines through her motto: "Tough times don't last but tough people do!" When asked what advice she would share with youth who are at the beginning of their life journeys, Chamique's words come from experience: "It is important to stay focused and dedicated. You must learn to sacrifice for others, but the key is perseverance. When you fall, you must be able to pick yourself up and keep going. That's the mark of a true champ."

Chamique became a visible role model even at a young age in college when most people are seeking answers to their own "coming-of-age" issues. Her high profile as a WNBA superstar has only increased her public presence. Fame carries with it excitement, sometimes fortune, and unique opportunities. It also heightens one's responsibility as a role model for children and youth.

One of the most well-known Lady Vols, Mique has always given her Tennessee family reasons to be proud. It is rare when she is not mentioned by commentators when they are covering women's basketball. She is the measure for quality, character, and accomplishment. The world may know her as "Chamique," but to Tennessee fans, she will always be Mique. And we know what "Mique" means.

Spotlight
Laura Lauter (Smith)
Soccer, 1997–2000

Laura Lauter

Forward Laura Lauter Smith garnered honors that included All-SEC and All-Region.

She's All Lady Vol

Some people just seem to be born with focus and determination. When Laura Lauter (Smith) was six years old, she told people that she wanted to be a soccer star and earn a scholarship to college. With the support of loving parents, outstanding coaches, and her own strong spiritual faith, it wasn't long until she had the credentials to be convincing. "The very first time I played organized soccer was in a little indoor league in Philadelphia," she recalls. "I was in either kindergarten or first grade, and my sister, two and a half years older than I, played in the same league. My sister claims credit for my soccer success, because that very first year, each player got to vote on a player to be on the all-star team. I was number 0, because I was so little, and I was really bummed because I didn't get picked. I was sure I should be on the all-star team with all those third graders. So, my sister said that was my motivation, because at that point I decided I was going to be great."

Laura continued to play indoor soccer until fourth grade when her family moved to Fort Wayne, Indiana. There she found an outdoor recreation league that was co-ed. Laura immediately grabbed the attention as a star player. She says:

There were just three girls on the team, and we were the best three players on the team. At every game the parents on the other team would yell to their sons, "Don't let that girl get the ball from you." My parents would just laugh and say, 'Who is that girl?' But

next year they asked me to play on the traveling league team, and that is where soccer really started for me, I guess. My parents said, "OK, if we are going to put the money into your playing, you are going to have to work hard on your own." Knowing that I had their commitment to help me achieve my goals was so internally motivating that I told my mom and dad, "I am going to get a soccer scholarship. I'm going to get a full ride to college." I told them that.

Laura's confident spirit was natural in a family that encouraged participation without gender barriers:

I grew up with a dad who played college football, so when I was a kid, my dad would say, 'Get out there and play with the boys.' Taking my dad at his word, I played football on the playground at school. School uniform regulations required skirts for girls. I remember one day when the principal said that I should not be playing tackle football in my skirt. I responded, 'Well, they never catch me.' That was in fourth or fifth grade.

My mom was a good athlete too. We would challenge my older cousins to a football game—mom would be quarterback. We still all go out and play football together at Christmas.

With her parents as role models, Laura drove herself to practice every day. As her passion for soccer grew, so did her motivation to excel. She remembers:

I would go outside and train on my own. My parents would call me for dinner, and I would say, "Just five more minutes, Mom." I was hard on myself and pushed myself harder than anyone else ever would. I think I knew that if you want things to happen, you have to work hard. My dad told me his stories about working hard in the summers. He grew up really poor. His father was a Philadelphia fire fighter. He got to college by earning a scholarship. The only way he was able to go to college was to work hard. He instilled in me the idea that to accomplish things, you have to work hard. And so, I was completely willing to do that.

I had friends who would ask, "What do you want to be when you grow up?" I never thought that far. I just knew I wanted to be a star in soccer. I'd say, 'I'm going to get a college scholarship, and my dad is going to buy me a car.' (I don't think he had planned on that.) I knew early on that my sport was soccer. I just knew that was one of the things in life that was going to happen or that I was going to work and make happen. It must be something about the way God wired me. I never thought that I was better than anyone else. I was using the talent and drive that God gave to me.

Laura capitalized on her gift of speed. She was fast and able to go for the winning goals. Even when she played with others who were better coached or more skilled, she would shine with her speed on the field. "I was always really fast," she says, "and I loved scoring goals. Even in high school, you could put me at defense but you were going to find me at forward because I wanted to score goals. So, I was a forward. Some people are naturally born to play a certain position. For the most part that's what I was

best at—scoring goals. There is just something thrilling about being able to score goals as the 'go-to' person."

Following her freshman year in high school, Laura's family moved to Knoxville, Tennessee, and it was love at first sight: "I loved the feel of the South. I had trouble understanding my coach's southern accent, and we would laugh about that. Even though my parents moved back to Indiana, I chose to stay in Tennessee to complete my senior year at Farragut High School. I had found a community at my church and people who supported me. I loved this area."

Laura had achieved her goal to be a top competitor for a collegiate scholarship. She also had learned from her parents that living many places can be fun and energizing. She was drawn to the opportunities that come with new adventures. Her standout accomplishments and academic successes made enrolling in a college with a highly credentialed soccer program a clear possibility. The University of Tennessee women's soccer program celebrated its first year in 1996. Though she was sought by schools with more well-established soccer programs, including Vanderbilt, one of the top fifteen in the country at that time, Laura was drawn to UT:

An assistant coach at Vanderbilt had coached me in Olympic development. I knew he would be great. But my attention turned to the University of Tennessee when Joan Cronan called me. She was on the Board of Directors for the Fellowship of Christian Athletes. She said, "I want you here obviously because of your athletic gifts—but I also think you can add something to this program and this school as a person and as a

Forward Laura Lauter Smith earned 1998 All-Central Region and All-SEC accolades.

Christian." I thought, "Wow—for her to think of me as more than an athlete—this is where I am supposed to be." I was drawn to the excitement of building a new program. I would be one to help build the first building blocks—we all would have an opportunity to create the culture of Lady Vol soccer. To this day our team is such a tight group of girls even though we are so different individually. Other schools didn't offer this opportunity to create something new. Both of my parents really have that entrepreneurial spirit, and so the idea of playing it safe has never been a big temptation for me. At Tennessee I would get to be a part of something that is really amazing. Seeing where Tennessee soccer is now, I think I was able to do that. Because of great coaching, amazing parents, supportive teammates, and an unwavering faith in an unwavering God, I found success as a Lady Vol.

Laura's expectations of the excitement and fun that would result from being a part of the soccer team's early years proved true. These Lady Vol teammates became a close-knit group whose bonds played out in dance and song. "Our pregame ritual—we all put on rap 'booty' music and would dance," she says. "If we weren't dancing, we weren't connected as a team. We had hilarious times—made up dances. That was pregame for us—we dressed and danced in the locker room. That was our dynamic all four years—we didn't start that way, but we grew to be that. I always said a silent little prayer before the game started, then the whistle blew, and we played. We were ready."

This team, characterized by loyalty, respect, and positive thinking, was especially

Laura Lauter Smith and husband, Brian Smith, 2007. Courtesy, Laura Lauter Smith.

significant for Laura when she was injured during her junior year. She recalls:

I was on crutches for two months and not able to do even mild practice until about six months. It was a total of nine months before I could play again. It was such a challenging time. Jenny Moshak [athletic trainer] used to show the video of my injury in her classes because it was such a terrible injury. I looked as if I had been in a car wreck, and recovery was really difficult. At the beginning of my senior year I started to get back into practice. I had always been the fastest. All of a sudden I was in the middle of the pack. In soccer we have a fitness

test called "the cooper"—seven laps around the field, one and three-quarters miles in eleven minutes and forty seconds. My body wasn't going to do it. The first day I didn't pass. The second time I didn't pass. If I didn't pass it, I couldn't play. I remember Lisa [Tipton Wiles], Rachael [Newkirk], Kelly [Berrall], Kim [Sgarlata], and Tori [Beeler Watson] were out there running with me to help me keep pace—they dropped back, and they held me and pulled me through to keep pace. I will never ever forget that and will always feel so connected to those girls. At my weakest moment I wanted to be so strong—but in the midst of these moments when I wasn't those things, they said, "WE ARE GOING TO HELP YOU DO THIS." For me it was such a humbling moment and beautiful picture of our friendship and what that team created—the sisterhood we had to do that for each other. I don't think there is another team in the country that has a team whose members would do that for each other.

In life we need people and community around us. The Lady Vols created that community. We knew we would be there for each other when we were having a tough time. We knew that we succeeded as a team and we failed as a team. I learned as much from our failures as our successes. I think that is important. We were such a diverse group of girls—I am a Christian—there were girls who disagreed with my faith, but I knew they loved me and they knew I loved them. We respect each others' views and have a bond that time isn't going to break.

The University of Tennessee had also promised Laura that she would flourish in areas outside of her sport. As a speech communications major, Laura was challenged and motivated by the faculty and academic experiences. "I guess at any school you get out of it what you put into it," she says, "but I think UT provided me with a great education. I had such a wonderful experience across the board—professors who were supportive of me being an athlete and coaches who stressed the importance to keep up with academics. In speech communications Dr. John Haas was my mentor. I taught communication studies in high school after graduating, and we even talked about doing some graduate work together. I learned so much from him. I have gone back and spoken to some of his classes."

Involvement in the greater community through church, service projects, the Fellowship of Christian Athletes, and friends outside of athletics provided balance in her life. Without hesitation, though, Laura is certain that her Lady Vol experience is pivotal in opening her career opportunities after college:

Being a Lady Vol prepared me so well for the real world. I got two jobs for which I had no experience, but I could show that I knew how to be successful. From living the daily regimen of a student-athlete—weights, conditioning, class, practice, study, compete— I know what it takes. I know how to work hard, to be committed, how to communicate, how to be a member of a diverse team, time management, how to learn and grow from mistakes. Having the background of a Lady Vol provides the best job experience. I believe I could have achieved any job I wanted because of the confidence I gained as a Lady Vol.

Laura's career paths reflect the same assertive planning and motivation that she displayed as a young girl. After graduating she moved to Texas to work while her husband, Brian, pursued a graduate degree in seminary. Eager to combine her passion for athletics and speech communications, Laura researched to identify an opportunity ideal for her. She found a high school that needed someone to teach speech communications and coach girls' soccer. Teaching certification would be available through a summer program. Laura focused her energies on teaching and coaching in Fort Worth, Texas, a hub for women's soccer programs. As a coach, Laura was proud of those girls who went on to compete as student-athletes in Division I programs. Even more significant, though, were the lessons of fairness and confidence that she taught every student by example. She says:

In Texas they do a really good job supporting high school sports. Soccer was included as a class offering, so I got to coach throughout the school year. We had six soccer fields: girls got three, and the guys got three.

One day the girls needed more space for team practice, and the guys said that they didn't know we were going to be out there. They were in the middle of something. I was determined that my girls were going to do their planned practice that day, so I told their head coach that we had been training inside doing strength conditioning and now needed to work outside. He said, 'Well, you girls haven't been out here this spring,' and he was looking at me with this attitude, so I said that Title IX ensures that we get the goals that we need.

Laura Lauter (Smith)

Sports Stats

- Career Highs: 11 shots vs. East Tennessee State, Sept. 19, 1997; 3 goals vs. South Carolina (Sept. 13, 1998); 2 assists vs. Georgia (Oct. 25, 1998); 9 shots (SEC high) vs. Georgia (Oct. 25, 1998)
- 1998 Third-Team NSCAA All-Central Region
- 1998 Second-Team Soccer Buzz All-Central Region
- 1998 Second-Team All-SEC
- 1998 SEC Player of the Week (Sept. 28, 1998)
- 1998–2000 SEC Academic Honor Roll

Academic Stats

- B.S., Communications, University of Tennessee, 2001

Postcollegiate Career Highlights

- Family hot tub business (with father and husband)
- Pharmaceutical sales representative
- Public high school, Fort Worth, Texas: teacher, communications studies; women's soccer coach
- Played soccer on traveling amateur team

I was not trying to be a jerk. I just did not want my girls to feel that they were not as valuable—for them to think that because we are girls we had to wait until the guys were done. I did not want to instill that in them. I believe that no girl should ever feel like a second-class citizen because of her gender. She needs to know that she has value and opportunity because she is a human being.

He finally said, "Well, I know. I have daughters." And I said, "You would not want your daughters to feel that we put them second." I felt that I needed to stand up for my girls. There is something so valuable to having a girl play sports and to let her know that there is more value to her than what her body looks like.

Laura continued to play soccer for a traveling women's amateur team, and just as in college, soccer generated new friendships and opportunities. A teammate suggested that she consider a career in pharmaceutical sales. Intrigued, Laura put together a résumé that indicated how her experience as a Lady Vol was the ideal preparation for success in a competitive environment that involves pressure to perform and earn the confidence of others. A rigorous interview process resulted in her selection from a pool of experienced candidates even though Laura had never worked in sales or in a medical field. "This was just one more instance," she says, "when I was able to convey that I could do the job—that I don't let people down—that I can handle pressure and people can count on me. My confidence came from being a Lady Vol. And even before that—from my early years on—from the constant support of my par-

ents and my belief that God provides us all with our talents, drive, and opportunities."

Laura's faith and connection to her family led her to recognize and trust opportunities for change when her father began a new company. Joining the family business, Laura and Brian worked together in roles that enabled them to travel throughout the world. Throughout this period their circle of friends grew even wider, and their experiences allowed time to affirm their values as a family.

Laura and Brian moved once again, returning to Tennessee where Brian as a youth minister and Laura as a mother direct their energies to building family and community. Laura would still like to coach, even more now as a mom. She says:

I never felt pressure from my parents to have to be something. I don't ever want to do that as a parent. I have seen so many athletes whose parents pushed too hard, and by the time they are freshman in college or even in high school, they are burned out.

Now I think my greatest life challenge is finding balance between being a mom, wife, and still contributing to people outside our family. I don't want get bogged down in the doing of life. I don't want to feel scattered. I want to create a home that is a refuge and source of strength for our family—my husband and children.

Laura has shown that she has a winning record in meeting great challenges. Her advice to young women?

I would tell future Lady Vols that to play at Tennessee is one of the greatest honors they

could have as an athlete. To play at a place with such integrity and tradition—don't take it for granted. To be a Lady Vol requires a lot of work and sacrifice. You have to know who you are. If you are going to be successful, you have to be grounded in who you are and know that this is something that YOU desire. Being a student-athlete is not for everyone; it's gut-check time—do you have what it takes to handle this kind of schedule, pressure from coaches, teammates, and professors? If so, it is incredible. If you stay connected to other people, it really makes it worth it.

I never thought, "I can't do this." We all just did it—off season, then training, then preseason, then season—then cycle all over again. I can't thank the community and the UT women's athletic department enough. We have people everywhere who give so much. The women who endowed the scholarship for my position are from New England. They just love University of Tennessee sports. I love Tennessee sports—all sports, football, orange. As Lady Vols, "THANK YOU" is all we can say. People know that if you are Lady Vol, you are special. That is for life. It is great to remember our team and know that we were all able to be a part of building the UT Lady Vol soccer tradition.

Laura Lauter Smith's achievements themselves are stunning and made history for University of Tennessee record books. She is quick to say that her successes are tributes to what is far greater—that her story is one about faith in God, family, and community. She is right. It is her passionate spirit—her dazzling and unwavering belief in possibilities—that makes the Lady Volunteer tradition even more special.

Spotlight
Tamika Catchings
Basketball, 1997–2001

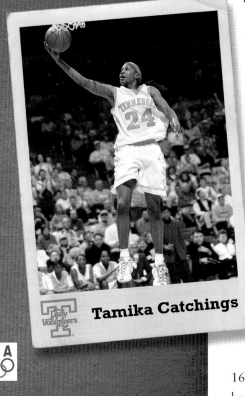

Tamika Catchings

Tamika Catchings joined the Lady Vol record books with 2,113 points, 1,004 rebounds, 311 steals, and 140 blocked shots.

What a Catch!

The number 24 was retired December 2004 and will never be worn by another Lady Vol basketball player. This jersey is the fifth to be retired, honoring the extraordinary contributions of Tamika Catchings. Known as "Catch" to her teammates and Tennessee fans, this Lady Vol is legendary for her athletic prowess, service to the community, and academic achievements.

Tamika was born in Stratford, New Jersey, and basketball has always been a strong presence in her life. Her father, Harvey Catchings, played in the NBA for eleven years for the New Jersey Nets, Milwaukee Bucks, Los Angeles Clippers, and Philadelphia 76ers. He was also member of the Chicago Bulls' broadcast team during their 1996 Championship season. Tamika's older sister, Tauja, was a 1996 Nike/WBCA High School All-America who as a freshman and sophomore led the University of Illinois to Sweet 16 appearances. Tamika also has an older brother, Kenyon, who was an All-America basketball star in high school. Her mother is Wanda Catchings.

Because of basketball, Tamika's family traveled and moved quite a bit throughout her childhood. When she was small, the family moved to Milwaukee. Five years later they spent a year in Italy. Tamika was in second grade when her family returned to the United States to live in Abilene, Texas. The years from third grade through her sophomore year in high school were spent in Deerfield, Illinois. Tamika's final high school move was to Duncanville, Texas, to complete her junior and senior year of high school.

As a little girl Tamika's first sport was soccer, and she thought that she would be a soccer player for life. She and her sister enjoyed a variety of other sports as well: basketball, softball, track and field, gymnastics, and even bowling. In high school she excelled in track and field, volleyball, and basketball. Her skills and talents could have taken her in any direction, but Tamika was especially enthusiastic about playing basketball. She had been playing on an organized team every year since the third grade, when her father was her coach. "Because my dad played in the NBA, I was constantly around basketball," she told writer Dee Ebersole-Boukouzis. "Seeing my dad play heightened my interest because I wanted to be like him. He was my role model."

Tamika's high school basketball career soared. As one of the top young players in the country, she earned a résumé full of honors, including Gatorade Circle of Champions Southwest Regional Player of the Year as state winner for Texas, two appearances in *Sports Illustrated*, four-time Parade All-America, and Miss Basketball in Illinois as a sophomore, the only player in state history to receive this citation before her senior year. She was also named Miss Basketball in Texas as a senior, becoming the first player to receive Miss Basketball honors in two states.

Tamika played for the silver-medal-winning US Junior World Championship, qualifying in Mexico in the summer of 1996. On that same trip she scored a team-high 22 points in the COPABA Tournament title game against Brazil. Tamika continued her international play the next year as a

Tamika Catchings

Sports Stats

- US Junior National Team, 1997, 1998
- ESPY Awards Co-Team of the Decade (1900s), 1997–2001
- US Basketball Writers Association Rookie of the Year, 1998
- SEC Freshman of the Year, 1998
- Honored by the Eleanor Roosevelt League for the Hard of Hearing for being a special role model for youngsters and adults with hearing impairments, 1998
- NCAA All-Final Four Team, 1998, 2000
- SEC All-Tournament Team, 1998, 1999, 2000
- Kodak All-America, 1998, 1999, 2000, 2001
- All-SEC Team, 1998, 1999, 2000, (Second Team) 2001
- NCAA All-Regional Tournament Teams, (East) 1999, (Mideast) 2000
- Sports Illustrated All-America Team, 1999, 2000
- Naismith All-America Team, 1999, 2000
- Associated Press All-America Team, 1999, 2000, (Second Team) 2001
- Naismith Player of the Year, 2000
- Associated Press Player of the Year, 2000
- US Basketball Writers Association Player of the Year, 2000
- SEC "Good Works" Team, 2000
- WBCA Player of the Year, 2000
- NCAA Regional Tournament Most Outstanding Player, (Mideast) 2000
- ESPY Awards Women's Basketball Player of the Year, 2001
- Member 2,000 Point Club with 2,113 career points
- Member 1,000 Rebound Club with 1,004 career rebounds

member of the 1997 US Junior World Championships Team, which captured a silver medal at the FIBA Junior World Championships in Natal, Brazil.

Although Tamika was accomplished and involved throughout her elementary, junior high, and high school years, she faced difficult challenges during these times. She says:

My greatest life challenges came when I was growing up. I had to wear glasses, had a speech problem, and had a hearing problem for which I had to wear hearing aids. Needless to say, I had a lot of struggles within and outside of myself. There wasn't a day that went by without my coming home crying. I just wanted to give up. I didn't want to go back to school because I hated being different from everyone else. I hated the rude comments and being the object of cruel jokes. But my parents picked me up every day, brushed me off, and placed a new challenge in front of me. They wouldn't allow me to give up, and they constantly pushed me to achieve more and not to let words hurt me. It took a while, but I succeeded.

When it came time to select a collegiate program, Tamika decided that she was partial to orange. She entered the University of Tennessee in 1997 and grabbed immediate attention as a stellar student-athlete. This freshman earned recognition that included All-America honors, citation by the USBasketball Writers Association and the *Sporting News* as their Freshman of the Year, SEC Freshman of the Year, selection to the All-Tournament teams at the Northern Lights Invitational and the Marriott–Big Apple Classic, and selection as Rookie

Thrilling Indianapolis Fever fans as Rookie of the Year in 2002, Tamika Catchings is among the WNBA league's top players. In 2006 she was the top vote-getter for the WNBA All-Star game and finalist for WNBA Defensive Player of the Year, an honor she won in 2005. Courtesy, Pacers Sports & Entertainment.

of the Year by her teammates. And there is one more accomplishment to note. Tamika's Lady Vol team went undefeated at 39–0 and claimed the NCAA National Championship, with Tamika earning a spot on the All–Final Four Team.

Tamika's Lady Vol team was a particularly stunning group. Chamique Holdsclaw (a junior), Semeka Randall (a freshman), and Tamika made up a threesome known as the "Meeks." Before their college days, each one had been tagged with the nickname, Mik (pronounced "Meek"). With Coach Pat Summitt and their teammates, they decided on nicknames that would differentiate them. Chamique remained "Mique" since she was a junior, Semeka was called "Randall," and Tamika became known as "Catch."

Tamika's family members have always been role models for her.

My mother, father, sister, and brother have always been by my side through "thick and thin" and have allowed me to be ME, Even when I was in college, they were constantly there for me when I needed to vent or anything else. They always pushed me to be better than I was the day before. Knowing that they were behind me no matter what has allowed me to blossom into the person that I am today.

That person today is even more decorated. Tamika's accomplishments speak volumes to her substance. Always involved in community service, Tamika capitalizes on her public visibility to make a difference for others.

She values the lessons that she takes away from the basketball court. As she commented to Ebersole-Boukouzis, "Playing basketball has taught me the importance of teamwork, hard work, dedication, commitment, sharing, love, and friendships. Basketball has also been a guide to keep me away from bad influences. You don't have to become a professional or even play at the college level to let sports teach you how to be a better person and how to help you reach your goals."

Tamika put her words into action when she established the Catch the Stars Foundation in the spring of 2004. The foundation's mission is to motivate youth to achieve their goals and dreams by providing effective academic and fitness related programs. The

programs focus on fundamentals including reading, study skills, organization, and goal setting.

Many of the Catch the Stars programs operate throughout Indianapolis, but Tamika has also hosted events in Dallas, Chicago, and South Carolina. Through mentoring, the foundation is "preparing our youth to catch their dreams one star at a time." Tamika is very dedicated to the community.

Tamika finds her inspiration in many individuals on and off the court. She particularly respects the work of Oprah Winfrey, who, she says, "is an amazing African-American woman who has changed the lives of so many people, young and old. One of my dreams has always been to be influential in the lives of everyone I come across. Oprah is doing that every day through her shows and all that she does in the community. She is my definition of a phenomenal woman!"

Playing basketball at Tennessee provided a learning ground for Tamika to identify the qualities and values that are most important to her:

Being a Lady Vol taught me more than just being a basketball player. Yes, we got scholarships to play on the basketball team, but I think we learned more about becoming great people—great women more than anything. Pat made sure that we carried and presented ourselves professionally—which is something that has carried over to post-college life. We learned outstanding life lessons while we were there. I know I never once doubted that Pat wanted anything but the best for each of her players. I know there were players that she was tough on, but I think we all look back on certain situations

Tamika Catchings

Academic Stats

- B.S. sport management, business minor, University of Tennessee, 2000 (graduated ahead of her class)
- M.S. sport studies, University of Tennessee, 2005

Postcollegiate Career Highlights

- WNBA Rookie of the Year, 2002
- WNBA Indiana Fever, 2002–present
- All-WNBA, 2002–07
- Member of bronze medal US World Championship Basketball Team, 2002, 2006
- Member of Olympic gold medal US Basketball Team, 2004
- WNBA Defensive Player of the Year, 2005, 2006
- Named to the WNBA All-Decade Team, 2006
- Leading vote-getter in the 2006 and 2007 WNBA All-Star game
- US Senior National Team, 2007–08
- Fifth Lady Vol to have jersey retired (number 24)
- President of the WNBA Players Association
- Five-time WNBA All-Star
- Named to US National Women's Basketball Team for 2008 Olympic Games in Beijing, China

in our lives after the fact and are thankful for the things that we went through. We each have learned the discipline we need to go through changes and to shape our perspectives on life as we push forward.

Looking back, Tamika sees some of those learning moments in a different light:

Before I came to UT, I never really had a coach that yelled at me or told me that I did anything "wrong." So, coming in I assumed

that has made plenty of magazines and is the talk of everyone who has heard her name: that intense glare that makes you sweat on the spot and wish you could just disappear right away.

After practice I went up to the office to face Pat one-on-one, and she asked me if I was going to be one of the players that she was going to have to wear lace gloves to deal with. From that first practice to where we are today I have never had another run-in with Pat. To this day I remember my first prac-

The lessons Tamika gathers from the basketball floor apply to any venture. Her advice to youth as they find their own goals and talents applies to everyone:

The biggest thing to learn is to accept and love yourself for who you are. Each of us is God's unique creation. We aren't meant to look, act, and be just like everyone else. This is something that I struggled with in my younger days. I wore hearing aids, glasses, braces, and had a speech problem. I didn't fit in and was often the butt of jokes. I found something that I was good at—basketball— and used that as my escape. I set goals and worked hard every day to achieve each of the goals I set. I encourage young people to dream big and not to let anyone discourage them from doing whatever it is they want to do!

Pat asked me if I was going to be one of the players that she was going to have to wear lace gloves to deal with. To this day I remember my first practice as a Lady Vol, and I will never forget it.

I knew all that I could about basketball, and I was pretty confident about my skills. I remember at my first practice Pat was yelling at me about my hands and my feet and my positioning on defense. Now, not only was this the first time that I had been truly critiqued on the basketball court, but there were also quite a few people in the gym, and I refused to be embarrassed in front of them. I ended up saying something back to Pat, and I know all my teammates, coaches, and everyone in the gym must have thought I was crazy. I just wasn't used to criticism or interested in learning a new style of defense since I had experienced success up until then anyway. Pat continued to ride me about defense that practice, and at the end of the practice it seemed that she was about to give up on me. Imagine the look that she gave me—the one

tice as a Lady Vol, and I will never forget it. It wasn't funny when it happened, but it is funny now. That is the story I always share with people when I speak, and it just seems so funny when you look at it after the fact.

Tamika attributes her success as a basketball player to her will to win the "TEAM" way:

I think that I always was the chameleon of the team who would do anything and everything that I could do to help my team win. If I needed to be the scorer, I could do that. If I needed to be the defensive stopper, I could do that. I figured out a way on every team that I played on to be a valuable part of what that team needed. That is what continues to make me successful.

Tamika completed her college degree ahead of her class in December 2000. That achievement itself is a testimonial to her ability to set goals, organize her priorities, and work hard to achieve success. She went on to earn her master's degree in sports studies in May 2005. She is determined to meet every goal that she sets for herself. There is no doubt that Tamika Catchings will not only reach every star she seeks but also will most certainly inspire and enable everyone she touches to find their own places in the universe.

The 1998 NCAA National Championship basketball team: (from bottom left, clockwise to right) Kristen Clement, Teresa Geter, Niya Butts, LaShonda Stephens, Brynae Laxton, Chamique Holdsclaw, Kellie Jolly, Semeka Randall, Misty Greene, Kyra Elzy, Tamika Catchings, and Laurie Milligan.

Spotlight
Young-A Yang
Golf, 1998–2002

Young-A Yang

Young-A Yang set the Lady Vol program record for best individual 72-hole NCAA Championship finish after carding a 75-73-71-69=288 total to complete the 2001 NCAA Tournament in fifth place overall at even par.

A Pretty "Fairway" to Make a Living

As an LPGA Tour player, Young-A Yang travels the world over. While that might present a challenging transition to many college graduates, travel is second nature to this Lady Vol.

Young-A was born in South Korea and spent her first fifteen years living in Tae-Gu City. As a child she swam competitively locally, figure skated a bit, and enjoyed table tennis. Her parents played golf, and when she was ten years old, her father invited her to play the game. She recalls:

It just started as a fun activity. It was not my intention to turn pro. It just started as something fun to do. Then I went to a tournament, and after that I got a little more serious. But my parents said that I could not turn pro until I graduated from college. That was one of the reasons that they wanted me to come to the United States—so I could go to school and then play golf. It is very tough to do both of them at the same time. You have to spend a lot of time in school, and it is kind of unrealistic.

Young-A came to the United States in 1995 and entered high school at Saddlebrook Academy in Wesley Chapel, Florida. Her skills were apparent as she achieved a ranking of fourth nationally among juniors, earned numerous accolades in her sport, and excelled academically. After graduating in three years, she was ready to attend college.

I looked at Florida and Arizona, but Tennessee just felt right. Part of the reason I picked UT was the support of the women's program. I also felt that I could make a bigger impact on the team because it was a pretty new program [established 1991]. I liked the climate a little colder so that when I turned pro, I could be used to playing in all kinds of weather. And the grasses are different. In Florida you are pretty much limited to Bermuda.

Even though Young-A guided her decisions with a professional golf career in mind, she also considered other factors that would assure her happiness:

Another reason I picked Tennessee was that it just felt a lot like home. I know this was a business decision, but it would have been difficult to make without looking at the personal part. Coming to UT made a great difference in my life. I like the people. Tennessee just felt right after my campus visit. So I just went with what my heart and mind told me.

Psychology caught Young-A's interest for a major that would be fun and give her insights to help her golf game. If golf had not been her career choice, Young-A might have been an artist. Her mom went to art school, and Young-A enjoyed drawing.

Being a student-athlete gave Young-A experiences that are unique for golfers.

Being on a college team is a very unique experience. Golf is an individual sport, and when you are in college there is a team emphasis. Here you travel with a team, and they are the

The 1999–2000 Lady Vol Golf Team placed fifth in the NCAA Championships—the best finish for golf up to that point. The team included (back row, left to right) Anna Umemura, Erin Simmons, Young-A Yang, Rosanna Zernatto, Nicole Cavalcanti, (front row, left to right) Tina Schneeberger, Caroline Cole, and Stacey Bergman.

people you see the most. They often become your best friends. I know that is not always true. It is hard to get along with somebody you see all the time, but we did OK.

As a contributing member of the Lady Vol golf team, Young-A did better than OK. Among her many achievements are school records for the most top-ten finishes in a season at nine (2001–01), most top-ten finishes in a career with twenty-six, most tournaments as top UT scorer with thirty-one, most rounds of par or under in a career with thirty-six, lowest single-season stroke average with 73.06 (2001–01), and lowest career stroke average with 74.37.

Young-A values what she has gained from being on the Tennessee team.

I got a lot out of being a Lady Vol. I don't think I would have stayed in Knoxville if I didn't feel that this was home. Knoxville has become my second home. I got to know a lot of different people. I think that [UT head coach] Judi Pavon and Luis, her husband, really adopted me as part of their family. I still have Thanksgiving with them and see how they are doing. I have gotten a lot of good advice from the people I have known at the University of Tennessee. I am still benefiting from my Lady Vol experience.

Young-A Yang

Sports Stats

- SEC Tournament, second place, 1998
- SEC Freshman of the Year, 1999
- NGCA All-America honorable mention, 1999
- All-SEC First Team, 1999–2002
- NGCA Academic All-America, 2000
- NGCA All-America Honorable Mention, 2000
- Holds school record for most top-ten finishes in a season at nine, 2000–01
- Holds school record for lowest single season stroke average with 73.06, 2000–01
- GTE Academic All America (later known as Verizon/CoSIDA Academic All-America) District At-Large Team, 2000–01
- NGCA All-America First Team, 2001
- Won the Betsy Rawls Intercollegiate Tournament with a score of 218 (74-73-71=218), 2001
- Lowest round was a 65 at the Bryan National Collegiate Tournament, 2001
- NGCA All-America Second Team, 2002
- SEC Tournament, tied for third place, 2002
- Holds school record for most top-ten finishes in career with twenty-six
- Holds school record for most tournaments as top UT scorer with thirty-one
- Holds school record for most rounds of par or under in a career with thirty-six
- Holds school record for lowest career stroke average with 74.37
- Four-Time All America (a first in Lady Vol history)

Academic Stats

- B.S., psychology, University of Tennessee, 2002

Postcollegiate Career Highlights

- Currently on the LPGA Tour
- Volunteer coach, University of Tennessee women's golf team, 2008-present

Young-A attributes her ability to balance her life and manage responsibilities to lessons learned as a student-athlete:

Sometimes I think it is hard to keep life balanced. That is one thing you learn from college. You learn how to balance activities. Student-athletes have to maintain their grades. They have to perform at the expected level. I had a little struggle in my third year. I was really excited after my second year. I played a lot better my second year than my first year. I really didn't take much time off. I was always practicing golf. But then my junior year, my result was not that great. I had to learn when to take time off to enjoy life. Golf is definitely my life, but then I like to go to movies, and I like to go shopping.

That is one thing that I just learned recently in the last couple of years. I cannot play golf all the time. I have to enjoy other things. It is one of the things Judi [Pavon] said to me in college. She said that I need to learn to enjoy other aspects of life. I need to have friends other than golf people. Even being with my sister helps to balance my life. I do what she likes to do. I do something that is not related to my interests. It is great putting in hard work on what you do, but you have to take a break. It is a big thing. Some great athletes say they get burned out, and then they never come back to their sport. One of the reasons is that they were not able to enjoy their lives fully.

As she considers how she has grown since college, Young-A points to a desire to become a little more flexible:

I think my personality has changed. I think that I was a lot more stubborn in college than I am now. If I don't like something, I don't like it. I'm very extreme—from one end to the other end. There is no medium. I'm trying to improve that. My sister is trying to help me with that. I was fairly flexible with things about the team. I have strong opinions on issues that relate me as an individual and golf.

Young-A has found mentors in family, friends, coaches, and other athletes. She says:

I get help from different people. I probably talk to my mom the most. Since she has come to the states I have gotten closer to her. She travels with me most of the season. I probably talk with my mom and my sister who lives with me the most. I depend on my sister a lot, especially for help at home. I talk to Judi [Pavon] a lot, too. I talk with Ann Furrow [UT volunteer coach]. I keep in touch with the people I am close to all the time.

There are a number of different people that I ask for advice. There are things that my mom would not know how to handle related to American culture. She could give me a general idea of what to do, but the way things are handled might be very different here.

I also talk with my high school coach, John and his wife Linda.

I like Se Ri Pak [LPGA Tour player with twenty-three career victories as of 2006 among her accomplishments] because of what she has done for women's golf. I think any Korean girl would look up to her just because of her impact.

Young-A Yang set the Lady Vol program record for best individual 72-hole NCAA Championship finish after carding a 75-73-71-69=288 total to complete the 2001 NCAA Tournament in fifth place overall at even par.

In addition to having strong support of her friends and family, Young-A covers all the bases to help her succeed.

I am superstitious, I don't know if there is anything to it or not, but I am going with it. I always carry with me three tees. If I lose one, I have to replace it. If I get into an argument with my mom before I play, I never play well that day. If I eat a particular breakfast and then don't play well, I don't want to eat it again. The same rule applies to clothes. If I play badly in certain clothes, I probably don't wear that outfit again.

Whatever she does, it works. Following her collegiate career, Young-A is successfully pursuing her professional goal, entering her fifth year as an LPGA Tour player. She says:

I am pretty excited about this season. This is my fifth year on the LPGA. I have had some ups and downs, but this year maybe I can really improve. Last year was better. It was a little more consistent than my previous three years. I am excited.

I was lucky that I knew what I wanted to do. Golf has been my life since I was nine or ten. Even if I had not turned pro, my life would have been something relating to golf. So in that way, I think I am lucky. It would be hard to do something when you are not enjoying it.

Young-A encourages others to find their dreams and work to make them come true:

Follow your heart. That is what you should do. That is basically the reason I came to Tennessee. When I was talking to my friend about where I wanted to go to college, she said that it sounded as if I already knew where I wanted to go. So the next day I just called the coach and said that I am coming to Tennessee.

My brother is just starting college, and he is trying to figure out what he wants to do, what we want him to do, or what my parents want him to do. I tell him, "You have to do what you want to do."

Being independent and self-reliant are important. That might make you stronger. It might help you grow up more, but it would also be difficult living life without appreciating others and growing from the support they can give you. It is important to follow your own desires and still engage your family, friends, and the people who care about you.

When Young-A retires from the professional circuit, she intends to coach so that she can return to others all that she has gained from her experiences. Her life so far has been right on course. "When I put my mind to something," she comments, "I can do it well. My parents did not force me to play golf. They actually were not very happy about it. They just wanted me to study and not be an athlete. In sports you have to be the best. And you have to be tough. I guess that is why they wanted me to wait until I graduated from college."

Young-A Yang's extraordinary accomplishments speak volumes about her dedication, discipline, and drive. Keep your eye on the sports page. This Lady Vol is far from finished.

Grace Harrington

Grace Harrington was a member of the first Lady Vol rowing team (2001) to claim victory in the Club 8+ race at the Head of the Charles in Boston, one of the largest and most prestigious regattas in the world.

This Grace from Memphis Rocks and Rows

Grace Harrington (Houser) was discovered. Lisa Glenn, coach of the UT women's rowing team, was scouting the campus for talent. The minute she saw Grace, she snagged her as a student-athlete. As it turns out, Coach Glenn was right on the money.

A freshman from Memphis, Grace had enjoyed sports all her life. With an athletic father, Grace grew up swimming, playing basketball, and just playing ball in the back yard. She earned high school letters in swimming, volleyball, and basketball. In basketball she found a coach she especially admired and played under somewhat unusual circumstances. As she recalls:

I only played basketball for two years when I went into high school. The men's basketball coach at the time was a terrific coach. He was a great man. The men's basketball team went to the state tournament several years when I was in high school. During my sophomore year I wasn't being coached very well on the basketball team, and he took me under his wing a little bit. He would give me some pointers when we were having a shoot-around in the gym. Then after I quit the team, a group from my calculus class wanted to put together a recreation team. They wanted to prove that the "nerds" could play, and they invited me to play with them. So I went back to this coach my junior year and asked if they had ever had a girl play before, and he said, "No, but if you
want to play, you can." So I played basketball with the guys in my senior year in high school.

Grace especially excelled in volleyball. She played on the Junior Olympic Team and experienced great success during her senior season. She says:

My senior year the volleyball team made it to the state tournament for the first time in fifteen or twenty years. We were just really fired up about the game we had won against a rival to make it to the state tournament. Our high school had a tradition to hold a big pep rally in the gym with the band whenever the football or basketball team made it to the state tournament. And we were determined that we wanted a pep rally because we were going to state. But the principal wouldn't let us. They said it was going to take too much time away from academics. They said they already had too many things scheduled that week. And so the boys' basketball team got a pep rally when they went to state but the girls' volleyball team didn't.

Grace considered seeking a collegiate scholarship to play volleyball at a small college. She was more inclined to take a break from organized athletics, though. A friend encouraged her to visit the University of Tennessee. Even though she thought a smaller school was her preference, Grace scheduled a tour. Grace was attracted to the campus, the diverse academic offerings, and the many opportunities for campus involvement. She qualified for an academic scholarship, and so there she was—enrolled as a freshman at UT and capturing the eye of women's rowing head coach, Lisa Glenn. Grace recalls:

At some point after being up at UT for a week or two, I was going through sorority rush with my roommate on campus. We were walking down some stairs, and there was this woman walking up the other side looking at me. And that was kind of weird. And she stopped and turned around and came up to me. And she asked, "Are you an athlete here at UT?" And I said, "No." She said, "Are you interested in rowing?" It was Coach Glenn. She was walking around campus recruiting for the novice program. She said I looked tall and athletic. We talked about it for a few minutes, and I got a flyer about an informational meeting. I ended up dropping out of rush. And a week or so after the rowing meeting, which I thought I had missed, some of the assistant coaches were staffing a booth at an activities session. So I talked to them and asked a few questions, and they said, "Why don't you just come down to our facility, and we will put you on a rowing machine and see what you think?" And that was that.

I had never even seen rowing before. When I had visited UT in the summer, we had been in the bookstore, and I had bought a T-shirt that said "Tennessee Crew" on it. At the time I had no thought of being on the rowing team. I had just liked the shirt.

Grace found rowing to be physically demanding. Individual strength and skill contribute to the overall team performance. It is a sport that leaves no room for even one individual to weaken. Grace explains:

If one person is off, it throws the entire boat off. It is a total team sport. You have to be so perfectly matched with the rest of your boat. You can't have a standout even in a good way because the boat works best when everyone is using the same technique at the same level. And then, there are no substitutions. It isn't like swimming where you are off doing your own thing. In basketball or volleyball if someone gets tired, you can take them out. Rowing doesn't work that way.

Each boat has a position called the "coxswain" whose role is to serve as a coach, cheerleader, and athlete. One of her major jobs is to watch for the safety of the boat and the team. The coxswain is also in charge of steering. She watches the rowers' technique and keeps the rowers focused. The coxswain tells the crew where they are in relation to the other boats. The crew doesn't have the view of the boats ahead, and the coxswain can affect motivation by keeping the team updated on positions.

When the crew is in perfect synchronization, the effect is absolutely beautiful. The boat appears to fly effortlessly along the river, and the team members are moving as if they were one being. An observer finds the spectacle, with its steady, smooth rhythm, breathtaking, even lyrical.

Grace acknowledges that when the team is working perfectly together, the feeling is indescribable: "You know the feeling when you've got it. But it is hard to describe. As the team works together, it can be very beautiful. When we are at that place of 'not thinking,' just doing our jobs, matching our technique and power, we all know it. The feeling is sensational."

Grace Harrington (Houser)

Sports Stats

- Recorded a time of 6:29.89 in varsity 8+ boat semifinal at Midwest Championships, 1999
- Held her spot in varsity 8+ boat, finishing first and second place at several events, 1999–2000
- During fall season captured seven medals, including four gold, 2000
- Boat finished first in a dual meet vs. Louisville, 2000
- Collegiate Rowing Coaches Association All-South Region, Second Team, 2001
- Collegiate Rowing Coaches Association National Scholar-Athlete, 2001
- Maintained her spot in varsity 8+ shell, winning gold at Chattanooga Head Race and Head of the Charles, 2001–02
- Crew finished sixth in Grand Final of the Lexus Central Sprints, 2001
- Crew finished second in Cal Cup at the San Diego Crew Classic, 2001

Academic Stats

- B.S., Engineering, University of Tennessee, 2003
- M.D., College of Medicine, University of Alabama, Birmingham, 2007
- Completing residency at the University of Alabama, Birmingham

Postcollegiate Career Highlights

- Working to complete medical residency in pediatrics
- Enjoys reading, gardening, running, and swimming
- Married to Matthew Scott Houser, tax attorney

The spring of her freshman year Grace made a significant move from novice level to varsity. A member of the varsity 8+, her position was usually right in the middle of the boat on seat 3, 4, or 5—the section called the power house. Even with her athletic strength and quick learning, Grace found her varsity assignment challenging:

It was an intimidating jump. It was not easy being around all these athletes who had rowed in high school or for several years in college. One of the team members, also a freshman, Jenny Bradley, became one of my very best friends. She was right in front of me in the boat that season. (She is currently coaching the novice program at Lewis and Clark College in Portland, Oregon.) Well, she just really helped me through a lot that first season—through even the very basic things of where to go and where to be when.

That first spring the varsity 8+ boat recorded a time of 6:29.89 in the semifinal at the Midwest Championships. Grace was named to the Lady Vol Honor Roll and every following year consistently achieved the highest grade point average for her class. In 1999–2000 Grace was named to the SEC Academic Honor Roll with a perfect 4.0 grade point average. She maintained her spot on the varsity 8+ boat and saw improved finishes every year, winning the gold at the Chattanooga Head Race and Head of the Charles (Boston) in 2001–02. She remembers:

One of my most memorable moments was when we went to the Head of the Charles and we were in the club eight event and won

The Lady Volunteer rowing student-athletes develop strength, endurance, and teamwork to compete at a high level with teams from throughout the country.

for the first time ever. But as we were going down the course, we didn't know we had won, because it was a race against the clock. We knew we ran a good race, but we didn't know that we won. But as we went back to the dock, there was a man in a polo shirt at the finish line who came out of a little tent and said, "Congratulations, Lady Vols! That's the fastest time!" And we were just thrilled! We were so excited. And then we got back to the dock, and Coach was there and she was so excited, too. But it was thirty minutes later before they posted the official times, and sure enough, we won. It was a great day and we got medals; we were interviewed and loved the celebration.

A sport that depends on efficiency and synchronization of a team requires special preparation. Student-athletes follow extensive strength training and conditioning on land and water. They work out by running,

swimming, and utilizing rowing machines and bicycles. Preparation focuses on developing muscular and technical strengths to generate the most power and speed possible for every stroke.

Before a race the rowers talk through the race with the coxswain. They discuss any points in the race where they may need to focus on a certain type of technique or any points when they might try to put on a lot of power for ten to fifteen strokes in response to an approaching boat. They might need to talk over the curves of the river or places where the water might get choppy. Almost always the team does a practice row of the race course. Prerace routines also call for mental preparation. Grace says:

It was my major time for mental preparation. When we are out there racing, I try not to think about anything. I am a thinker naturally, and I would try to think too much. I would try to make my own judgments about what was going on. And I really had to learn to turn that off. We used to talk about giving our brain over to the coxswain during the race and stop thinking and row. That was a challenge for me. One of those profiles you take to see how you work as a team showed that mine was the role of a challenger. I was the person who looked at a situation and tried to figure out a way to make it better. That was the part of me that I had to put aside for a while.

Many benefits of rowing seem obvious. The physical conditioning itself leads to better health. The process of growing as a team instills valuable lessons about working effectively with others. Grace says:

I am not a morning person. But rowing is a morning sport. I had to learn how to deal with that. I had a roommate my sophomore year, and I would give her a ride to the boat house every morning. We had a system set up so that we didn't actually have to talk to each other, because neither of us are morning people. We both knew what time we were going to leave. We had this morning routine. One would say, "Are you ready?" The other would say, "Yes." Usually we were at the boat house before we had to talk.

In my junior year I was in more of a leadership position. I not only had to learn how to function at an early morning hour but to be positive and encouraging to other people, even though what I really wanted to do was sit in the corner and not talk to anybody. So that was good, having to be a leader but also to step out of my shell. That has also come into play in medicine where I have to get

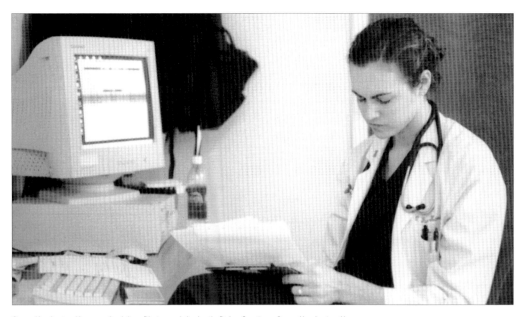

Grace Harrington Houser, physician. Photograph by Justin Duke. Courtesy, Grace Harrington Houser.

to the hospital early and communicate well with others.

Rowing also presents opportunities to learn much about oneself, and these insights are perhaps the most valuable of all. According to Grace:

You just have to trust that the person in front of you and the person behind you are putting their all into the race just as you are. It's not something you can measure on an individual level when you are in a boat and out on the water. Coach Glenn could often tell if someone was not doing so well in a race. But as a rower in a boat, you just have to trust that everyone else is giving her all.

Learning to trust has been really helpful to me in medical school—just to be able to trust what I am being told to do, even if it doesn't make sense to me, and to know that my job is to do it.

Grace has many great memories of her Lady Vol rowing years. The common thread of them all is people—her parents, her teammates and her coach:

My dad's favorite phrase when I was swimming was "swim hard and have fun." Then when I switched to volleyball, he switched it to "play hard and have fun." And then when I was rowing, he said, "row hard and have fun."

For my very last race for Tennessee, spring of my senior year, my goal was to race in the fastest boat. And all three of us close friends, Jenny Bradley, Shannon McMahon, the coxswain, and I were all in that same JVA [boat]. My dad came up to me as we were carrying the boat down the dock. Parents are not supposed to come up to the rowers. And the race was getting ready. But my dad came up and gave me a hug and a kiss on the cheek and said, "Row hard," and his eyes were tearing up. It was so encouraging and supporting.

I cherish friends and so many shared experiences from the Lady Vol years—especially in something like rowing, which is physically demanding. My best friend from college, Lindy Herzog, was my matron of honor at my wedding. She rowed her freshman and sophomore years, and we were roommates for three years. I don't know if we would have become such good friends if we had not done the rowing together. Jenny [Bradley] was also in my wedding. I just treasure those women and the time we spent together in college.

Grace's favorite competitive course is the Head of the Charles in Boston. Time has passed, and now as she pursues a career in medicine, Grace finds little time for rowing. Her youngest brother rows for West Point, giving her good reason to attend the event in 2006. She says:

I told Coach Glenn that I was going to be there, and she got me in the boat out on the course. And we placed twenty-fourth out of fifty boats in the race. It was a testimonial to the program to see how strong we had become. I had not rowed in four years. It was amazing to see how much we remembered and how well we worked together. The technique that Coach Glenn is teaching has been so successful and consistent over the years that we all just kind of knew each other and knew the same stroke. Coach Glenn really stands out as an excellent coach. She is somebody who has done a fantastic job of taking the Tennessee rowing program and building it into one that is nationally known and respected. And she is very personable and really cares about her student-athletes.

Grace feels special pride in the Tennessee program. She enjoyed being a part of the entire sports atmosphere and laughingly remembers a time when she encountered a fan:

I was at an auto parts store getting something for my car. I had my Lady Vol sweats on. And an elderly lady came up to me with big wide eyes and said, "Are you a Lady Vol?" And I said, "Yes, ma'am. I am a rower." And she said, "Oh, I thought you were going to be a basketball player."

It was neat being a part of that kind of atmosphere. Not only in rowing but in the bigger picture—it was cool to be part of something so much bigger than I was. I felt that I was able to contribute in some little way. It was great to be around such wonderful people.

Being a part of the Lady Vol organization was very special. Being around people like Joan Cronan and her excitement for women's athletics was special. They were passionate about building rowing even though we were the only SEC school with rowing as a varsity sport. But they really believe it is worth the investment. And seeing Joan Cronan come to our meets was so inspirational. We felt extremely supported by everyone in the Lady Vol organization—even the people in the weight room.

One day, seemingly out of nowhere, a coach with an eye for talent beckoned to a freshman and said, "You can do this." Grace Harrington Houser stepped up to the challenge with a performance that remains forever a hit on the record charts.

Spotlight
Vilmarie Castellvi (Crews)
Tennis, 1999–2003

Vilmarie Castellvi

Vilmarie Castellvi began the 2003 season with a number-one national ranking and held it throughout the season.

A Good Match: UT and Vilmarie

Before she picked up a tennis racket, Vilmarie Castellvi was always on the run. This little girl loved to run, ride a bike and play. She was naturally athletic and envisioned herself as a gymnast. Considering the possibilities of injuries in gymnastics, Vilmarie's mother suggested that she choose another sport. A tennis camp was scheduled for that summer, so at age nine Vilmarie decided to try tennis.

She loved it.

Recognizing the talent of their daughter, Luis and Vilma Castellvi supported every opportunity for Vilmarie to develop her abilities. They sent her to Florida during her high school sophomore and junior years to develop her skills for competition. During her senior year at school in Puerto Rico at Academia San Jose Villa Caparra, Vilmarie served as team captain. She was a three-year member of her country's Federation Cup team and the first Puerto Rican to be invited to participate in the Challenge Cup as a USTA Player, and she was ranked among the top ten in the fourteen and sixteen age groups. And she wasn't even in college yet.

Vilmarie knew of the Lady Vols at the University of Tennessee and was definitely interested in the program.

I knew Sonia [Hahn-Patrick] before I went to school because she worked in the tennis academy where I was. I traveled with her a little bit and got to spend some time with her. I liked her as a coach. I met Mike [Patrick] when he came down to see Sonia, and once or twice he saw me play. He talked

to me then. And I knew some of the Tennessee players. Knowing some players and the coaches helped me make the decision. I know they treat their student-athletes very well. That was my main criterion. I had some other scholarship offers, but I felt as if they really wanted me at Tennessee.

Vilmarie entered UT in the fall of 1999 with a major in marketing. She experienced challenges of time management, balancing her life as a student-athlete, and just learning her way around a new community. She remembers:

My freshman year I had a hard time adapting to going to school and playing my sport. I thought tennis was my first priority, and I was forgetting about school. And then I wanted to have a life at the same time. But then, going to school, I didn't like my classes. There were just so many difficult factors. My personal life was low; tennis was going downhill. I was trying to concentrate the same amount on everything. And I wasn't sleeping. I was just not very happy.

Somehow, something clicked and I made myself do it. I started taking better classes when I could choose. So I was smart enough to get my classes early for the spring, and I tried to play around with my schedule for tennis. I started doing a lot better. And I did well in school after I balanced it out. I was not going out much. But I started focusing on school and tennis.

It is a challenge to do all these things. And it was something that I was not used to. My high school was not that difficult. I mean it was a good school; there weren't as many challenges as in college. And of course in high school I wasn't doing as much. It was easier to get a day off from tennis. In college, you have a team and coaches who depend on you. You have more responsibilities.

It wasn't long before Vilmarie caught the spirit of Tennessee:

I remember wearing the orange. And every time we played, all the stands were packed. The support was great from people from other sports and staff. And I was amazed at the involvement of the community. Every one, even our athletics director, Joan Cronan, came. That kind of support makes it easy to be a student-athlete.

The community of friends and teammates grew, and Vilmarie was a top performer. "They started calling me 'Speedy' because I was fast," she says. "I remember one year they got us T-shirts and printed 'Speedy' on the back of mine. That was pretty funny. It was the first time they called me that."

Vilmarie says that her game completely changed throughout college. She came to Tennessee with a strong commitment to play tennis, but she really had not learned the regimen of steady hard work.

When I first came to Tennessee, I didn't really know what working hard was all about. And I remember my coach saying if you do an

extra something everyday, then that will pay off at the end. My work ethic became completely different from start to end. This made my tennis change completely. I changed my forehand. I was a completely different player with a different mindset. It was more my mind and my competitiveness that made a difference. I was improving what I had, and the results showed.

Many great moments come to Vilmarie's mind when she pages through her Lady Vol years. She remembers beating the University of Georgia in Knoxville on April 13, 2001, after a twenty-year losing streak against Georgia at home. Hers was the game that clinched the win. Postseason tournaments also kindle some great memories: "I remember getting to the semi-finals of the NCAA [2003], a first for the Lady Vol team. And individually, I got to the quarters of the NCAA the same year [2003]. Of course, getting to the finals was not as memorable since I lost in the finals. But still, that was a good memory."

Before a tennis match Vilmarie had an individual routine and then followed regular team preparation as well. She says:

I would shower and try to wake myself up. If we were playing at 10:00 a.m., I would get up three hours before so that I would be really awake. There were always certain things that I did but nothing outrageous. I would have breakfast. I would want to take my time. Then when it was time to go to the courts, I would run there.

As a team, we always had certain routines. I always loved jumping rope. Our coaches had great routines for us. And for some reason I always wanted to include jumping rope in my routine. So I always did it. We played doubles first and then singles. Before doubles I would jump rope just a little bit, and then I would jump rope again between doubles and singles.

Vilmarie earned a stunning array of honors as a Lady Volunteer. In her senior year alone (2003), she earned All-America singles and doubles, All-SEC First Team singles and doubles; SEC Player of the Year; ITA National Senior Player of the Year; ITA Southeast Region Senior Player of the Year; ITA National Player of the Month, January and March; NCAA Singles Championship runner-up; Tennessee Sports Hall of Fame Female Amateur Athlete of the Year; El Nuevo Dia's Puerto Rican Women of the 21st Century; and winner of the Honda Sports Award.

Graduation marked a time for transition when Vilmarie stepped away from collegiate competition and into professional tennis. Just like the step from high school to college, this change presents new challenges:

The level of tennis between college and pro is completely different. It is a completely different game. College was great. You play some individual tournaments, but you are always with a team. You play for yourself but you are held accountable. When you play pro, it is more individualized. You are there by yourself. No one is with you. You are on your own. You do the best you can. And sometimes there is not one person in the

Vilmarie Castellvi (Crews)

Sports Stats

- Lady Vol Tennis Most Improved Player, 2000, 2001
- Second-Team All-SEC Doubles, 2000, 2003
- First-Team All-SEC Singles, 2001, 2003
- Lady Vol Tennis MVP, 2002
- NCAA Doubles Championship Second Round, 2002
- Second-Team All-SEC Singles, 2002
- Singles All-America, 2002, 2003
- Honda Sports Award, 2003
- ITA National Senior Player of the Year, 2003
- ITA Southeast Region Player of the Year, 2003
- Doubles All-America, 2003
- SEC Player of the Year, 2003
- ITA National Player of the Month, January and March 2003
- NCAA Singles Championship runner-up, 2003
- Tennessee Sports Hall of Fame Female Amateur Athlete of the Year, 2003
- El Nuevo Dia's Puerto Rican Women of the 21st Century, 2003
- Singles career record: 140–51 (first all-time)
- Doubles career record: 97–63 (fifth all-time)

Academic Stats

- B.S., Business Administration, University of Tennessee, 2003

Postcollegiate Career Highlights

- Currently plays on the Women's Tennis Association Tour
- Has been ranked as high as number 146 in the world

stands cheering for you. It is very lonely. So you do it on your own.

My tennis has changed. It is a faster-paced game. I am hitting the ball differently, and my thought process is very different.

I want to be the best I can be. That is all; that is really it. And I mean that in tennis, and I mean that in life. I think that no matter what you do, you can always improve. Life is a series of challenges. It is not like a mark that you have to reach. In tennis, I would love to be in the top ten, so goals can be specific. But if something holds me back and I put everything I can into it, then I leave happy.

In life, always be better. Everyone can always do better. I would say be the best you can be. And practice makes perfect. If you truly love something, you will work hard at it. And you put mind, soul, everything into it. I think you will find a way to succeed.

Vilmarie Castellvi Crews, competing professionally, shows her power, 2007. Photograph by Matt Billips and courtesy of Vilmarie Castellvi Crews.

To hear Vilmarie talk about her life, one can't help but smile. While tennis is her passion, her enthusiasm extends well beyond the sport, and she embraces a broad spectrum of interests. She loves fashion and is very quick to confess to being the world's worst packer, often traveling with enough different shoes for every day of the week. She is quick to trade in her tennis gear for dress-up clothes with dangles and dazzling jewelry. She likes to explore and meet different people, and she lists Korea, Japan, Beijing, and Thailand among her favorite trips.

This energetic, accomplished Lady Volunteer offers her prescription for success:

Whatever you do, have an awful lot of fun. And do it for yourself. Don't do it for anyone else. If you are going to be a tennis player or whatever you are going to be, it is you and the ball—no one else. Do it for yourself, not because someone else wants you to. And keep your life balanced. You can't sleep, eat, and dream tennis. You need to do other things so you can stay motivated and keep tennis, or whatever your vocation is, exciting.

Vilmarie says that people are the difference. She describes her parents, Luis and Vilma Castellvi, as heroes who amaze her with the strength they have shown throughout their lives. Her older brother, Carlos Cernuda, works as a systems consultant in Puerto Rico and is one of her favorite people in the world. Vilmarie also found an extra-special friend in Tennessee: her husband, Andy Crews, who was a student-athlete for the University of Tennessee men's tennis team. Her coaches—Juan Carlos Escudero in Puerto Rico and Sonia Hahn-Patrick and Mike Patrick at Tennessee—inspire a work ethic and dedication that have moved Vilmarie's game to a different level.

When we think of competitive tennis, we think of mental fortitude, coordination, physical agility, drive, dedication, and focus. When we think of Lady Vols, we think of passion, pride, and tradition. When we put all that together, we find Vilmarie Castellvi and a whole lot of fun.

Spotlight
Kara Lawson (Barling)
Basketball, 1999–2003

Kara Lawson

Kara Lawson brought a fierce competitive focus to Lady Vol basketball. With 1,950 career points, she helped take her team to to four SEC Championship Titles and three NCAA Final Four Tournaments.

Don't Change the Channel— Kara's On!

Kara Lawson has always been an avid sports fan. Some of her former roommates joke that they didn't want to room with her in college because they knew the television would always be tuned in to the sports network. She was goal-driven with a proven record of knowing what she wanted and then achieving it. She was completing a college degree in finance, planning to play professional basketball and attend law school during the off-season.

So it might be understandable that she thought the telephone message was a joke. It was something that she never really imagined doing. Opportunities don't simply fall from the sky. National sports television networks don't make cold calls. Kara recalls:

The week after I took the LSAT for law school application, I got a call from ESPN to come and audition for an analyst position with them. I thought it was a joke. I thought someone was playing a joke on me because I never heard of anyone getting cold-called to be on TV.

I went up there and apparently did well on the audition. I had never taken any communications classes or anything like that. I do think playing at a high-profile program like Tennessee prepared me because I was well versed in the media from the other side of the camera. I understood how to do interviews and be on TV from being at Tennessee. That alone helped me. I had never taken any formal TV training at all.

But I did well enough to get the job. It kind of snowballed a lot faster and farther than I ever thought it would have. So, here I am—four years later and I'm still doing it. It has kind of taken turns I never would have expected.

Kara Lawson was not a "cold call." Even as a freshman she showed her talents with top academic honors and as one of the most decorated SEC student-athletes. Her consistent and remarkable play on the court was matched by her mature, objective analyses of her performance in postgame interviews. Kara's memory bank is uncanny and could probably give a computer game a good run. She voraciously reads all newspapers, watches sports network news, and remembers just about everything she reads, hears, or sees. In a story for *Sports Illustrated for Women* (October 30 2000), Kelli Anderson marvels that "at age three Kara had memorized all the US presidents, at age four she could list all the NFL quarterbacks and could spout statistics on running backs who played in the Big Ten 15 years ago." Kara's analytical mind, intelligence, confidence, physical strength, and unwavering competitiveness create a talent that can flourish in the board room as well as on the boards. Her professional polish and integrity complete the package.

During her childhood, Kara left no stone unturned. She played soccer, basketball, and even football. In Little League baseball, her defensive play was so intense that, according to the *Sports Illustrated for Women* article, "she would field the ball and then chase down the base runner herself. That resulted in the establishment of a local chapter policy

Kara Lawson (Barling)

known as the 'Kara Lawson Rule' requiring fielders to throw the ball to teammates when the situation called for it."

Kara grew up with the expectation that physical activity is an essential part of life.

My parents exposed me to athletics at an early age. We were expected to play a sport every season. It was a rule but we weren't forced to do anything we didn't like. You could pick any sport you wanted to play, or activity, like dance or something. My older sister picked that. So, I followed that rule, and I tried to do different sports every season. I wanted to see what sport I liked, what I enjoyed the most, and also which sport I was the best at.

She did not see gender boundaries, and simply tried every sport she could, including football. "When I was trying to play football," she remembers, "there were parents that didn't want me to play. But that is something that my parents dealt with. I can't say when I was seven or eight that there were people that didn't want me to play. None of the players ever expressed that they didn't want me to play. I was kind of oblivious to all of that."

Kara was one who set goals, and as she tried out different sports, she naturally considered what it would be like to play in each one as a professional. The absence of professional leagues for women did not deter her interests. She just thought that she would be playing with men:

When I was growing up, there was no WNBA. If you were going to play basketball in the pros, you had to do it with the men.

Kara Lawson brought a fierce competitive focus to Lady Vol basketball.

So, I just decided that was what I wanted to do. I wanted to be an NBA basketball player. I always played with guys in other sports growing up and was successful. So I figured that would work when I got older.

Kara's parents' encouragement of their children to be active and find their own points of passion developed a strong foundation for Kara's approach to life. With the disciplined work ethic and values that she learned from her parents, Kara knew to build her goals in a way that allows her to use her best talents and skills while at the same time to have fun in what she is doing. She had learned how to use her short-term experiences to articulate long-term goals with vision. That was quite an insightful sixteen-year-old mind! She says:

I'm a big believer in trying a bunch of things. That's the way I grew up, just doing what you like. Play what you enjoy. And I never had pressure from anybody to narrow down to one sport and focus only on that. I actually made that decision myself when I was sixteen. I was playing both basketball and soccer for my high school, and in the soccer season my sophomore year, I decided I just wanted to focus on basketball. That was my decision, and it was a time when I said to myself, "I want to see how good I can be if I just do one sport." All my life I had done so many sports and had been pretty good at all of them, but I wanted to see how far I could go in basketball. And coincidentally that was also the same year that the WNBA started. I'm sure that played a factor in my decision. I saw that this is one female sport in which I can actually be a pro. So, I thought, "Let's

try it. I know I can go to college with a basketball scholarship, because at sixteen I have already gotten many letters from colleges." I knew I could play in college. I thought, "Let's see if I can make the pros." So that is when I decided to focus on basketball, but up until that point I still played everything. And I think it is important just to let kids be kids, enjoy different sports, and see what they like. That's what I did. Don't get me wrong—I was competitive in every sport and I wanted to win and I wanted to get better. But there is a natural progression when something springs forth that you really like.

When the time came to commit to a college, Kara chose Tennessee over other choices that included Duke, Stanford, and Virginia. The straight-A student had the academic credentials and athletic abilities to go just about anywhere. She was the Naismith High School Player of the Year and highly touted. Kara was drawn to Tennessee because of the depth and breadth of academic offerings and the strong commitment to women's athletics. She knew that Tennessee consistently set their goals to achieve National Championships. After enrolling, Kara was even more convinced that she had found the right fit:

The University of Tennessee was the perfect place for me to come. Everybody always asks, "Looking back, if you had to make the same decision, would you do it?" And I say, "Yes," without hesitation because it is a great place, and the people are just great people. When you go to Tennessee, you are always part of the family. I think that is the thing that I appreciate most. The relation-

Kara Lawson (Barling)

Academic Stats

- B.S., Business Administration, University of Tennessee, 2003 University of Tennessee Torchbearer Award, 2003

Postcollegiate Career Highlights

- Member of 2003 WNBA Select Team that came in second in FIBA World Cup
- Western Conference Finals, 2003, 2004
- WNBA Sacramento Monarchs, 2003–present (1st round pick, fifth overall, in 2003 draft)
- SEC Community Service Post-Graduate Award Winner, 2003
- ESPN game analyst, 2004–present
- Studio analyst for Sacramento Kings Local TV, 2004–present
- WNBA Championship title, 2005
- Featured on Wheaties cereal box, 2005
- ESPN studio analyst, 2005–present
- ESPN NBA Sideline Reporter, 2006–present
- Member of WNBA Select Team in FIBA World Cup, 2007
- US Senior National Team, 2007–08, gold medalist, FIBA Americas Championship
- Named to US National Women's Basketball Team for 2008 Olympic Games in Beijing, China

With 1,950 career points, Kara Lawson helped take her team to four SEC Championship Titles and three NCAA Final Four Tournaments.

ships that you build there are something that you will always have. At Tennessee you are not off on your own. There are so many people there who can help you along and guide you and help you make the right decisions. I never felt like I was lonely or alone when I went off to college because I had a whole group of players that were my teammates. I had roommates. I had academic advisors, coaches, and anyone that I could go talk to about anything. I learned about leadership, accountability, and teamwork. I had great examples from upper-class players when I was a younger player. And when you become an upper-class student player, you try to set the example as well.

The rigorous practice, values, and structure of the Lady Vol program provided an environment that cultivated and enhanced Kara's competitive spirit and mental fortitude. Playing required the willingness to work hard every day at every practice. As much as players learn from the coaches and teammates, Kara points to an element that is intangible but essential in every athlete:

There is an element—a competitive edge—to every athlete that you can't allow a coach or other players to touch. That's yours, and that's what makes you unique. It's what allows you to press on and not believe in critics and not allow someone to break you. I have always maintained that internal competitiveness and just worked hard. So many people say they are working hard, but it is amazing how many people will allow you to outwork them. At any level, collegiate or pro, everyone has a limit. Everyone has a limit where they say, "I am not willing to go a step farther." I have always tried to see where everyone else's point is and not let anyone see where mine is.

Kara Lawson: professional basketball player in the WNBA, ESPN game analyst, ESPN studio analyst, ESPN NBA sideline reporter, studio analyst for Sacramento Kings local TV. This is the stuff of which fairy tales are made. Make no mistake about it, though. Kara Lawson made this journey by setting goals, studying, practicing, sacrificing, and doing all those other things that define determination and focus. She makes it look easy because she loves it. But as she points out, the journey has not been without challenges:

Pro basketball was definitely a change for me on a number of levels. People say college is the first time you kind of go off on your own. You don't have your parents around, and you are kind of in charge of yourself. And you have to make decisions about how you are going to do certain things. I think that is true, but I think the biggest adjustment is going off on your own from college to pro. I had to figure out how to live by myself—pay bills and all that stuff that you don't have to figure out in college. That was probably the biggest adjustment for me off the court.

On the court, it is just a different dynamic. There is not as much camaraderie at the pro level as there is at the collegiate level. You don't do as many things together as a team.

You mostly just practice together. There is no weight training together. There are no team meals together—no pregame meals. So just like a job, you go to practice, and then everybody goes her own way. Your relationships with your pro-team members are a lot different. You go from off-season workouts to practicing with your team, trying to blend with ten, eleven, or twelve, depending on how many you have on your team and dealing with different personalities, skill sets, and learning how to play with one another, growing together, and of course, rising to the competition. I like to win.

Kara does like to win. She sets her challenges, measures the gaps, and then moves forward with agility. Her motivation shines every day. She says:

I figured out pretty early on that I loved to play basketball. And that is what I wanted to do. And so for me I just set my mind to seeing how good I could be. I set a lot of goals; I wanted to play; I wanted to do this; I wanted to do that; but at the end of the day I just wanted to see how good I could be as a player in the sport. That is kind of a neat challenge for me as I continue to get older and improve in my game. You never want to shortchange yourself, to think back and say, "If I had worked harder or if I would have lifted weights more or run more or changed

my diet. . . ." I never want to look back and say that I didn't give it full effort in any area or say I wish I had done that.

I just want to see how good I can be. And to me that is exciting—to see how much you can improve on a day-to-day basis, on a year-to-year basis. So just find something that you enjoy doing, something that

Just find something that you enjoy doing, something that you love to do. Some days I wake up and it is funny to me—my job is to play basketball.

you love to do. Some days I wake up and it is funny to me—my job is to play basketball. It's crazy. So I wake up and I say, "The only thing I have to do is work out." So that is fun.

It is amazing how far you will go. I sometimes watch my teammates in practice, and I marvel that I am playing with these people; they are 6'5" and have unbelievable skills, and I'm just this short, slow kid—but you just keep working. It is amazing how you can look back, see where you have come from and how much you have improved. A lot of my putting it together came from playing at Tennessee.

Kara Lawson is everything but typical. Perhaps there is something to be said for chance and the laws of probability. In this Lady Vol's case, the K-Law rules that when possibility meets capability and determination thrives on passion, the person at the top will be a champion. That person will be Kara Lawson.

Keeley Dowling

Keeley Dowling sent the Lady Vols to their third straight NCAA Sweet 16 with her tenth career match-winning goal in the 1–0 win over UAB.

The Journey Makes the Goal

When soccer star Keeley Dowling considers what advice to give young women today, without hesitation she says that experience outweighs the prize. Given the remarkable accomplishments of this Lady Vol, her suggestion is worth noting.

Keeley grew up in Carmel, Indiana, just twenty minutes north of Indianapolis. At the age of four she began playing soccer. Living in a state famous for basketball, Keeley's talents also were on the court, but it was soccer that really drew her passion. She loves the skills and quick, strategic thinking required for what is dubbed "a player's game." Encouragement from her parents, coaches, and other adults provided Keeley with the opportunities to play, develop her skills, and learn the value of hard work and commitment. She says:

My role models are my parents. They have been extremely supportive of everything that I do, especially of soccer. The morals and values that they instilled in me define the character that I have today. You don't forget those principles when you leave home to go on your own. I value what they taught me, particularly when I meet people who never really had that kind of guidance and support.

Recalling a parent who worked to build a soccer program for children, Keeley acknowledges that involvement in soccer provided a framework to learn much more about herself and life around her:

When I was little, I wanted to grow up to be a doctor. This goal was largely inspired by a teammate's father who was an orthopedic surgeon in sports medicine and was chiefly responsible for putting my club team together when I was nine years old.

Significant adult role models continued to be a key factor in Keeley's life in high school.

In high school I had an athletic trainer who really helped me a lot. He built confidence in me at a time when girls are often struggling with self-identity issues. He said that I had talent and that I could go far competitively if I worked hard. I was so fortunate to have his encouragement. It is big to have self-confidence instilled in you at a young age.

Her confidence-building high school years were marked with achievements and accolades. In 2000 Keeley and her team won the state championship. She was named a *Parade Magazine* All-American, named to the 2000 NSCAA/Adidas High School All-America team, and was a member of the Carmel Cosmos club team, which, having claimed the state crown every season since 1993, achieved National Runner-up in 2000 after bringing home a regional title.

Keeley captured the attention of collegiate coaches throughout the nation. After visits to Santa Clara University, the University of Arizona, Southern Methodist University, the University of Virginia, and the University of Tennessee, she narrowed her choices to Virginia and Tennessee. Keeley recalls:

Defender Keeley Dowling shows the skill that earned her three All-America, four All-Region, and four All-SEC honors.

Keeley Dowling

Sports Stats

- 3 goals vs. Alabama, Oct. 7, 2001
- Soccer Buzz Central Region All-Freshman Team, 2001
- Second-Team Soccer America Freshman All-America, 2001
- Second-Team Soccer Buzz Freshman All-America, 2001
- College Soccer.com Honorable Mention All-America, 2001
- All-SEC: Second Team, 2001; First Team, 2002, 2003, 2004
- Soccer Buzz All-Central Region: Second Team, 2001; First Team, 2002, 2003, 2004
- First-Team NSCAA All-Central Region, 2001, 2002, 2003, 2004
- SEC Academic Honor Roll, 2002, 2003, 2005
- Three-time First-Team Soccer Buzz All-America, 2002, 2003, 2004
- SEC All-Tournament Team, 2002, 2003, 2004
- SEC Good Works Team, 2003
- Second-Team SoccerTimes.com All-America, 2003
- Two-time Missouri Athletic Club Hermann Trophy semifinalist, 2003, 2004
- Two-time Soccer Buzz Player of the Year finalist, 2003, 2004
- Three-time NSCAA All-America: First Team, 2003, 2004; Second Team, 2002

When Coach Angela Kelly came to my house on her recruiting visit, she introduced Tennessee to me with a binder of printed materials. She laid it all out—I am a visual person. Ange was passionate and personable. Then on my campus visit I met Pat [Summitt]. Pat wrote me a letter. It was really personal, saying that they really wanted me to come to Tennessee. I hung her letter on my wall. I knew that the Lady Vols would invest in me. Tennessee stood apart as truly unique because of Ange and the university's high level of commitment to women's athletics. That's why I came to Tennessee.

The University of Tennessee proved to be a great fit. Keeley continued to be challenged and to develop on and off the field. She comments:

Being a Lady Vol taught me tradition. Through Ange I learned more about char-

acter and integrity. As an athlete you want to be out there playing. I am thankful that playing was my major role. I had the support of everyone. I never felt like I was alone. I treasure most the friendships I have formed, the memories of being together. Even though I don't see my teammates very often now, I know that when I do see them, we can pick up where we left off. We will have a bond forever as Lady Vols.

That bond grows because of tender memories and laughter:

There were so many funny moments. I remember one time just before practice we duck-taped a teammate, Sue Flamini, to the goal post. When the coaches arrived to start our regimen and couldn't find Sue, we all had a good laugh. I think Sue thought it was funny. Our team also created an ongoing tradition that always kept us laughing. Ange

Keeley Dowling

had a big puffy jacket that she wore when it was cold. Ange is small, so the jacket really caught our attention. Every single time she wore it, we would run over and tackle her to the ground. We always took her out.

Other memories remind Keeley of the great lessons learned from the highs and lows that athletes experience:

The way that you are perceived as a player isn't always how you really are. A lot of my teammates got to see that during my sophomore year. I was traveling a lot with the US Under-19 National Team. We had won the world championship, and I was on top of the world. I returned to UT, and we were getting ready to play Mississippi State—not a great weekend. Every single emotion was rock-bottom. I think that was a moment when I felt the epitome of what a team should be. Ange knew what I would be experiencing—coming down from such a high. She was there for me. My team was there for me. I was trying to be tough and competitive, especially because I wanted to be a leader. When things happen, and you don't know why, you feel vulnerable. I realized that even though I don't like being vulnerable, I can't control life all the time. The support they gave me was like a family. They were incredible.

What is it that Keeley wants young women to know?

I was almost at the point when I was going to stop trying out for this team. If I had stopped trying, my story would probably be a little different. Even when you feel like

Defender Keeley Dowling helped the Lady Vols to three straight NCAA Sweet 16 Tournaments during her collegiate career.

giving up and no one believes in you and you're hearing all these things, don't stop. Don't ever give up. Hard work pays off. Even if you may not get the results you are seeking, you are still going to impact people along the way. That is what's most important. If you can keep sight of the people along the way and not the prize of what it's going to look like, then you're going to be successful. Whatever happens, it's really the journey that is important.

Keeley Dowling declares her most memorable Lady Vol moment as her freshman year, when her goal-winning point marked a first SEC Soccer Championship for the University of Tennessee. That was just the beginning of her collegiate journey. Look at the people she has impacted along the way.

Spotlight
Dee Dee Trotter
Track and Field, 2002–04

Dee Dee Trotter

Dee Dee Trotter hit the ground running, earning distance medley relay and 400-meter national titles.

Dee-termined to Be a Tennessee Lady Vol

When Dee Dee Trotter turned ten, she declared that she was going to be a Lady Volunteer at the University of Tennessee. Having moved from Phoenix, Arizona, to Atlanta, Georgia, this spunky, energetic little girl was ready to take on the sports world.

In Phoenix Dee Dee's athletic activities began with baton twirling and a little karate. Even then her confidence and enthusiasm were apparent. "I remember marching in a big parade on St. Patrick's Day," she says. "I don't think we really had a routine, but we were all twirling our batons and excited. There was a live horse painted green—really! I will never forget that green horse!"

Atlanta presented a wider choice of sports activities, and Dee Dee immediately signed up to play basketball. She was new to the sport, but the coach, Jonathan Merritt, took her under his wing and taught her how to play. Dee Dee and Merritt's daughter, Danielle, soon became best friends and were known throughout the area as a fearsome twosome. Dee Dee recalls:

I was number 3 and Danielle was number 12. We would run scores up—I was so fast and Danielle was so good—the girls wouldn't know what to do with us. We conducted massacres on the court. We destroyed our age group—scores would be so lopsided. So they put us on the bench and kept us on separate teams until our last year together. Then that year we smashed the whole

thirteen-to-fourteen age group. That was FUN—the best time ever!

Even today Dee Dee attributes her athletic success to the relationships formed in these early years:

I am still affected by the people who started me in basketball fourteen years ago. I didn't know anything about basketball. I didn't know anyone. Danielle's dad—I think of him as Uncle Johnny—he is the reason I was introduced to sports at all. He taught me to know that I can do it.

Dee Dee's dreams turned to Tennessee when she and Danielle were selected to play on an all-star team in a tournament annually held at the University of Tennessee in Knoxville. Thrilled by the experience of playing in Stokely Athletic Center and seeing Coach Pat Summitt, the best friends at age ten made a pact to become Lady Volunteers. Ironically, when they played in the thirteen-to-fourteen age bracket for their final tournament year, their all-star team was named "Tennessee." Dee Dee recalls, "I was ten years old when I decided that I wanted to come to UT to be a Lady Vol. Danielle did too. We had hoop dreams—I never changed that goal."

Dee Dee and Danielle went on to different high schools, and with different schools came different opportunities. Danielle stepped away from the court, but Dee Dee continued to play her number-one favorite sport, basketball.

Basketball? Well, Dee Dee did run a little bit of track on the side. She says:

Dee Dee Trotter

Sports Stats

- Member of SEC runner-up, 4x400m relay, 2002
- SEC Outdoor champion, 400 meter, 2003
- NCAA Outdoor runner-up, 400 meter, 2003
- World Championship gold medalist 4x400-meter relay, 2003
- As a sophomore, she ran US 4x400-meter relay in prelims at IAAF World Championships, 2003
- AOPi Lady Vol Athlete of the Year, 2004
- NCAA Outdoor champion, 400 meter, 2004
- NCAA Indoor champion, distance medley relay, 2004
- Helped UT return to NCAA top five Indoor (fourth) and top ten Outdoor (seventh), 2004
- SEC Outdoor runner-up, 400 meter, 2004
- Ran on UT sprint medley relay unit that broke twenty-year-old collegiate, meet, and UT records at Penn Relays, 2004
- US Olympic gold medalist, 4x400-meter relay and fifth-place finisher in 400 meter, 2004
- US Olympic Trials bronze medalist, 400 meter, 2004
- First Lady Vol to turn pro prior to completion of her collegiate eligibility (did so after junior year)
- Eight-time All-America
- Two-time NCAA champion
- UT record holder Indoor and Outdoor, 400 meter

This is how things were for me—I was going to play basketball for Pat Summitt. I was so determined to do it that it didn't matter if it seemed impossible. If Coach Summitt didn't see me play in high school, I would show her what I could do when I got there. I applied on my own to UT and was accepted. Then I was recruited.

Myrtle [Chester Ferguson, then UT track and field coach] recruited me the same year my high school basketball team went to the state finals. We lost in the second round. Basketball season ran well into track season, so I had only five days before my first track meet. I broke the Georgia state record in the indoor 200. I don't know why Myrtle was there, but she made herself known. At that point I had been the State Champion in the 100 and 200, but track came third. I always got a late start in track. My priorities were cheerleading, basketball, and then track. I would miss most of the meets. I don't know if I was fast or if other competitors were slow—the real competition didn't really show up until the state meet anyway. Well, maybe I was fast.

Dee Dee arrived on campus as a track scholarship student-athlete determined to use her freshman year to adjust to the rigors of academic life and to perfect her basketball skills until she could try out for Coach Summitt. As she recalls:

I told Myrtle that I was already coming to UT and that I had a dream of going to Pat Summitt to have a tryout. I knew I was good and knew that I had simply been overlooked. Myrtle respected that and said she had girls double-up on sports in the past. I

guess most people said, "She [Dee Dee] can try out, and she probably won't make the team." I didn't have a problem with that. We are talking about the best coach in the country. Later I knew that if I were that good, Pat would have seen me. I didn't let anyone deter me. Pat told me, "I don't make mistakes usually. But if you say you want to try, you can." That was all I needed to hear. That year Pat had four athletes who weren't returning. That opened a huge door for me—she could have picked up anybody that time and hadn't held a tryout in many years. I told her that I wasn't interested in trying out my freshman year—I needed to dedicate time to track and work on school. I wanted to get under college scrutiny and wanted to take it slow. But I told her that I wanted to try out the next year.

So, Dee Dee focused her immediate sights on using her freshman year to establish firm footing academically, with track as a temporary sports home until she could move to the basketball team, where she thought her talents really belonged. Just as Dee Dee captured the attention of coaches, almost immediately she claimed the spotlight among her teammates:

We gathered for our first team meeting. All team members, coaches and freshmen were there. None of the freshmen really knew the other people. I came into the meeting—I won't say that I had an attitude when I got here, but I was kind of distracted as a big city–life kid from Atlanta coming to Knoxville. I was hanging out with Danielle, my best friend—so the track team found me to be a little antisocial. I really didn't know them and didn't have anything against them—I was just staying with the person I knew best. The meeting was very structured with designated speakers. Nearing the end of the agenda, the captain stood up and said that there was one more team rule: when we traveled by bus, freshmen were required to give up their seats to upper-class teammates. She sat down. I held up my hand—no one had spoken except the captain—and said, "Excuse me. I have a question. Why is that?" The distance coach said that it was just one of those unwritten rules—that was just how we did things—by seniority. I said, 'Is that right? Well, when I am captain that will be the first rule to go.' The room was so silent that we could hear the crickets chirping. Then some of the freshmen fell out laughing, saying, "That girl is crazy!" The giggles started passing through the room. Myrtle [Chester Ferguson, coach] was over there laughing. They were just stunned. I never got bumped. They respected me and kind of stayed out of my way. When I wanted to share, I did— that rule just wasn't right.

I did have an ego thing going on, though. I thought I was better than all the other women. I wasn't, but I thought I was.

That first year Dee Dee competed in nearly every event. She wasn't used to running every day and was motivated, she says, solely by the assurance that she would have her basketball tryout:

I would secretly go in to watch basketball practice. I was going to play for Tennessee— even if I rode the bench for victory, even if I never got out of the warm-up suit. There would be a day when Pat would play me—I would be that good.

Finally, I got the phone call from Myrtle [Chester Ferguson]. Pat was going to have the tryout in the fall. Elated, I went home for the summer, traded my track spikes for basketball shoes, and worked out all summer. I trained so hard. That summer a new track coach, J. J. Clark arrived at UT. Coach Clark called me to introduce himself and asked when I would be back to campus. He expected me to return early for training. I said, 'Well, I will be back when school starts. Basketball tryouts are in four weeks.' He said, 'Well, when you get back, we will talk about it.'

When I returned to campus, Coach Clark and Coach Caryl [Smith Gilbert] called me into the office. I told them that basketball tryouts were in three weeks. They said, "What? Basketball tryouts?" I told them that the previous coach and I had an agreement that I could try out. I had done lots of preparation, and Pat Summitt was holding a tryout for the first time in years, and I had to be there. They said that I had two options: I had to decide between the two sports.

I felt like I had been shot with a gun. This was my dream—they really didn't know that had been my dream since I was ten years old. They only knew me as "Dee Dee Trotter, All America, her freshman year." I was faced with a problem. Here I was the inner-city kid, wanting to go to college. I had no student loans, and I couldn't risk losing financial stability by trying out for something that wasn't guaranteed. I couldn't do that. I cried and called my mom—I was frantic. I wanted to try to live the dream. It was dramatic, and it shattered me. I built a wall up against

Dee Dee Trotter

Sports Stats (continued)

- Was previous school record holder Outdoor, UT's 4x400-meter relay
- Previous school record-holder Indoor, 200 meter
- Member of school-record distance medley and 4x400-meter relays indoor

Academic Stats

- B.A., Arts and Sciences, University of Tennessee, 2005

Postcollegiate Career Highlights

- World Championships (400m), fifth place, 2005
- World Championship gold medalist 4x400-meter relay, 2007
- World Championships (400 meter), fifth place, 2007
- US Outdoor Champion (400 meter), 2007
- Named to US National Women's Track Team for 2008 Olympic Games in Beijing, China

track and field. I could not find the love in the sport—I felt it took something from me. I came; I fought; I almost conquered.

This is why I had trouble finding my way into this sport. It probably worked out for the best. I believe that Pat would have seen me as a good player—I had been encouraged by all the basketball team players—but maybe if I had played, I wouldn't have had the success that I have now.

Dee Dee's successes in her sport are stunning, and while she has grown accustomed to being a track athlete, her motivation comes from a place quite different from the field. She explains:

What I love isn't so much the running part—that can be discouraging. I want to be the best I can be in everything. The reality is that you are going to win and lose—no one is going to win all the time. You might have a stretch when you win a lot and then the next year drop. You have to win the ones that count—get the gold. That time, when I got the gold [2004 Olympics], I found that there are a million little people out there that absolutely do not know anything about me—but they think Dee Dee Trotter is awesome. They just come to me—little kids. If I can inspire someone else to follow her dream, there isn't anything better. I want them to know not to be discouraged from following their dreams. You have to drive as far as you can down that road until the road changes direction. That's what I did. When the road hit rocks and changed direction, I kept on driving. Don't let any hurdles or people discourage you from doing that. Some people may tell you that you're not

Dee Dee Trotter (far right) and teammates (from left to right) Sanya Richards, Monique Henderson, and Monique Hennagan ran the 4x400-meter relay in 3 minutes, 19.01 seconds, to capture gold for the United States at the 2004 Olympiad in Athens.

good enough or that this isn't going to make you happy. You can't listen to that. Follow your heart with determination, and trust where the road takes you.

Dee Dee's own determined spirit and willingness to follow that road in spite of disappointments along the way led her to this place today. More than a face and a name, Dee Dee Trotter shows a deep commitment to creating a healthy and positive community. Her nonprofit venture, TEST ME—I'M CLEAN, challenges young people to achieve their goals drug-free. Her conviction is reminiscent of the same fire that pushed that ten-year-old little girl in Atlanta, Georgia, to see her dream and go after it. She says:

I do as much as I can to let people know the truth about me—to show that I am not the person they see on television or on a bill-

board. When an athlete falls out with drugs, we all go down with them. Then everyone thinks we all do drugs to be at the top of our game.

I want to give back. I started the TEST ME—I'M CLEAN program to promote the right way to succeed. I don't profit—I am the first donor. I think we should make a big deal out of things we do that are positive. I am hoping that this effort will get everyone involved to have fun and to inspire integrity. If you win—if you are one of the fortunate few who win—you want to be able to get up at the age of thirty-five and not worry about somebody—maybe your daughter or your son—finding you in a coma. That might sound overly dramatic, but it's not. It's reality.

Not surprisingly, Dee Dee sees many years of competing ahead. Now running is her number-one focus. And D-Trott is running with purpose.

Spotlight
Sarah Fekete (Bailey)
Softball, 2003–07

Sarah Fekete

Sarah Fekete, showing her strength as a clutch player, always dreamed of being a Lady Vol.

Stepping Up to the Plate, Fekete-Style

She grew up in the small town of Maryville, Tennessee, at the base of the Great Smoky Mountain National Park, twenty miles down the road from the University of Tennessee. Her dream was to be a Lady Vol. Her motto is: "Don't tell me what I cannot do." She stepped right out of her comfort zone and put on the cleats of an All-America star.

Sarah Fekete is living proof that with perseverance, focused goals, and defiant optimism, an individual can achieve her goals. The achievements marking Sarah's four years as a Lady Vol softball player are noteworthy in themselves, but the challenges along the way tell the real story of a championship spirit:

When I was preparing to go to college, a number of smaller schools were trying to recruit me. I had always dreamed of being a Lady Vol. My lifelong goal was to play for Pat Summitt, but I wasn't good enough in basketball. Fortunately, I found an opportunity to stick my foot in the door with softball. Up until the last minute when I signed with UT, I was just going to walk on. Then at the last minute Tennessee offered me scholarship money for books. I declined full scholarships at several other state universities.

Halfway through my freshman year, Ralph and Karen Weekly turned me around from being a right-handed hitter to being a left-handed slap hitter to utilize my speed. It was really frustrating to go from something I have always done successfully my whole life

to doing something that is not natural. The biggest lesson that I learned from my time at the University of Tennessee is that you have to get out of your comfort zone if you want to be successful. Sometimes you have to take two steps back before you can take one step forward. And I think that is the way it is in life, too.

My junior and senior years as a Lady Volunteer I was a First-Team Division I All-America. I want my experiences to show other little girls that they can achieve their dreams too. Success didn't come easily, but I got there through many sacrifices. Don't ever let anyone convince you that you can't do something. I am proof that you can.

Just as Sarah was adapting and growing her skills, so was the team as a whole. She observes:

I think my freshman year we were very naïve. We would come to practice without any incentives or team goals. We had fourteen freshmen in my class. As we matured as women and as players, each of use began to see that we were working for something special. We found a strong sense of togetherness. We really pushed each other and strived to work hard in practice. When you are competing everyday, it makes you better. So when you face real competition, you are ready. You have already prepared against great pitchers and hitters hundreds of times. As a result our team confidence grew higher and higher.

As teammates working hard together, they began to feel the bonds that come from shared experiences. As Sarah recalls, many of those times brought laughter:

Sarah Fekete hit in the number-two position in the lineup and played center field in 2006.

One of the first funny moments we shared as a team happened at our first home game my freshman year. We were all taking our positions for the game. Senior Kristi Durant was catching, and when she ran out, she tripped over third base, fell, and messed up the chalk line. Field maintenance had to redo the line before the game could start. We were playing at home, and Kristi just stood up, did a little bow and went back to catch.

Sarah is known for her determination to improve her skills. She attributes her relentless spirit to her parents, Fred and Mary Ann Fekete:

My parents were the drive behind my work ethic. I never had a chance to get comfortable. I believed I could always play better and it was expected. My parents really pushed me my whole life in school and in athletics. I was expected to play at the highest level and would not be satisfied with anything else. At times I put tremendous pressure on myself to be perfect, but sometimes a little motivation is needed. One of the best values that my parents instilled in me was respect for others. Any of my teammates would tell you that they could count on me no matter what. I always wanted what was best for the team.

Sarah's parents were involved in her softball pursuits and participated to support her development. "I feel tremendously lucky that I had parents that were willing to spend their time and money on me," she says. "Our family vacations were spent going to the ball park and catching a couple days of sightseeing wherever our tournament was being held. One of my parents attended every collegiate game I ever played in. I am so glad that we were able to share this experience and make memories we will always treasure."

Once Sarah entered college, her parents remained involved and attended nearly every game. Teammates whose homes were far from Tennessee found a welcome second home with Sarah and her family. She recalls:

Teammates would go to my house even when I wasn't there. We would have girls home for Thanksgiving dinner. My parents were like foster parents for the girls from out of town. One of our teammates lost her mom to cancer. Her father called my parents first, and they drove to her dorm room to be there for her. She had a place of refuge if she wanted to get away from everything.

Strong work ethics, effective teambuilding, and hard work paid off in results. The team captured its first Southeastern Conference Eastern Division title since the 1999 season and earned a bid to the NCAA Tournament for the first time in five years. That was a defining moment, and the team knew they were moving Tennessee softball to a new level. By the middle of her junior season, 2005, Sarah was leading the country in hitting. Then she was injured. As she remembers:

I was hit by a pitch and broke my jaw. At the time I was wearing a wire face mask. It didn't work, obviously. I had two plates and eight screws surgically placed in my jaw. My mouth was wired shut for four and a half weeks. I lost twenty pounds very quickly. My doctors were really concerned about my overall health. I was forced to take time to recover. The hardest challenge was watching my teammates play when I could not. The rest of my body was fine, but because I could only breathe through my nose, I couldn't even get my heart rate up.

I came back about two weeks before I was cleared to play. I was just healthy enough to get back in the lineup. I finished the rest of the season, but my performance declined. Additionally, not being able to work out for four and a half weeks made playing more tolling on my body.

The 2005 season marked another historic step for the Lady Vols when they moved through NCAA regional competition to earn a spot at the Women's College World Series. For the first time the University of Tennessee softball program was front and center as a serious National contender. The trip to Oklahoma City gave fans cause to be proud and stirred excitement throughout the country. The Lady Vols' first victory of the series came over the third-ranked Arizona Wildcats.

"Beating Arizona [1–0] in the World Series was one of the most exciting moments in my athletic career," says Sarah. "We weren't really on the map yet, and it was just an unbelievable feeling. I knew at that time a new diamond dynasty had been born. It was very special."

A loss to UCLA positioned UT to battle their SEC foe, Alabama, for a spot in the semifinal round. A win over Alabama placed Tennessee eye-to-eye with number-one Michigan. Fighting to advance to the championship series, Tennessee scored a victory over Michigan after playing for almost eleven full innings until 1:21 a.m., central time. In their final meeting with Michigan, the Lady Vols were just one run short of victory. Fans everywhere were talking about the nail-biting series. Sarah says, "ESPN drew the highest ratings and numbers for a women's softball event during the period of our games at the World Series. It was amazing that we had drawn that much attention."

The first trip to the Women's College World Series put fans and competitors on notice: the Lady Volunteers are serious about softball.

The 2006 softball season began with the upswing momentum of the previous year. The Lady Vols were ready to compete, and Sarah was prepared:

The next year I wore an Emask. It is clear plastic face mask, made of the same material as bullet-proof glass. I wore it all season

Sarah Fekete (Bailey)

Sports Stats

- Set a rookie record with 13 stolen bases and led Tennessee on the base paths with a 13-for-18 effort, 2003
- Only rookie her year to see playing time in all 70 games, 2003
- Completed career as all-time Tennessee leader in batting average (.398) on base percentage (.456) and stolen bases (85) while rating second in UT runs scored (189) and hits (296)
- Broke the SEC single-season record for hits with 110
- SEC All-Tournament, 2003, 2004, 2006
- All-Tourney, Lady Vol Classic, 2004
- SEC Player of the Week, March 21, 2005, March 13, 2006
- First-Team All-SEC, 2005, 2006
- Academic All-SEC, 2005, 2006
- Division I National and SEC Batting Champion hitting .500 (110/220), 2006
- Led Lady Vols in hitting with a .414 average, third best single-season total in UT history, 2005
- Singled against Arizona and UCLA in the Women's College World Series, 2005
- All-Tourney, Georgia Southern Invitational, 2005
- Led Tennessee with 63 career stolen bases, 2005
- Tennessee Hall of Fame Female Amateur Athlete of the Year, 2006
- Gold Medal Winner for Team USA Softball in the World University Games, 2006
- Played with the National Pro Fastpitch Team Philadelphia Force, 2006

Academic Stats

- B.S., Arts and Sciences, University of Tennessee, 2007

Postcollegiate Career Highlights

- Southeastern sales representative for Emask
- Spokesperson for Emask
- Married to Chad Bailey, 2007

and led the nation in hitting with a .500 average. I played awesome in it, and it is a lot lighter than the wire mask that I had previously worn. I felt more confident because I felt protected.

Postseason found the Lady Vols once again heading for the Women's College World Series. With one experienced year at Oklahoma City, the team knew what to expect and was eager to play. Once again, Sarah found herself in harm's way:

I was hit in the face again in the World Series. It was the same place where I was hit the first time. If I had not been wearing an Emask, the doctors said my face would have probably been shattered because of all the reinforcement I have from the previous surgeries. I was really lucky and am really grateful to Jeff Evans for creating a facemask that allowed me to continue to play at such a high level. I am now the official spokesperson for the company.

Sarah is passionate about her cause. Her experience with injury shifted her understanding of individual needs, ignited her conviction to give back to the community, and raised her awareness of her role as an aspiring teacher. She comments:

Joe Whitney with the UT sports psychology department worked with me to overcome the impact of being hit by that pitch. As an athlete, you don't ever want to admit that you are scared. Coping with such a serious injury made me a stronger person. It was probably the most defining time in my life because of the rehabilitation challenges.

When I broke my jaw, it was very hard to communicate with my mouth wired shut. I was in a lot of pain. When I talked, others couldn't understand me. My teeth were clinched together. When people that I know were around me, they thought it was funny at first. But to me it wasn't funny at all. It really opened my eyes to be more aware of the needs of others.

Sarah puts that lesson and all her experiences as a Lady Vol to task to help others in the community. She loves to work with children and wants to make a significant difference in their lives. She says:

I am a hometown girl. It is really special for me to be able to give back to the community that gave so much to me—to the coaches and adults who have been there for me and to the girls that want to be like me. I give hitting lessons to children. My favorite students are the kids who are in the middle-skill range. These are kids that don't portray much confidence. When they build their athletic confidence, it helps their overall personal confidence and self-worth.

Sarah's Lady Vol experience has given her occasions to celebrate and challenges when she chose to grow. She believes that she is more prepared for life after college with a better appreciation of how she can have an impact on others:

I will take with me the importance of respecting other people and the importance of hard work and determination. There is a sense of community in the Lady Vol program, and no matter where I am, I know I could

come back and find the same level of care and concern. If I blew my knee out, Jenny Moshak [assistant athletics director for sports medicine] would still rehab with me. Joan Cronan [director of women's athletics] would do anything for me. She knows the student-athletes here on a personal level. I will try to make a difference in someone else's life the way they the coaches, staff, and supporters of the Lady Volunteers have made a difference in mine.

Looking back on her four years with the softball team, Sarah feels proud:

We started a new era on the campus of Tennessee. I am extremely proud to say that I was a part of that. After the last game that I played for UT, I was asked how I felt now that my career was over. Teary-eyed, I said, I will always be a Lady Vol. My blood will always run orange. And no matter how old I get and how far away I get from the softball world, my teammates and my coaches will know that I was a part of something. We started a dynasty.

Sarah Fekete exemplifies the "can-do" spirit of a Volunteer. Her determination to surpass even superior performance to become the best she can be redefines the meaning of "improve." Sarah is a standard-setter whose energy has ignited support for University of Tennessee softball and inspires optimism. The dynasty has begun, and champions are sure to follow.

Spotlight
Tianna Madison
Track and Field, 2004–05

Tianna Madison

Tianna Madison earned six All-America accolades in just two years.

World Champion

What makes a world champion? Some people will tell you it is all about numbers. That is what makes you best. Tianna Madison is proof that there is a little bit more to it.

Tianna grew up in the small town of Elyria, Ohio, and it wasn't until high school that Tianna discovered that she had a natural talent in track and field. She says:

I didn't really gravitate towards track until high school. I realized that I was kind of better at that than I was at volleyball and basketball. I had three people who encouraged me—my father, my coach, Carl Below, who passed away in 2003, and his wife, Jackie Below. When my dad could not drive me to a summer track meet, Mr. Below would take me.

Tianna's skills and hard work would pay off. Her record-setting performances distinguished her throughout the nation. She was a member of the 2003 *USA Today* All-USA High School Girls' Track Team; named 2003 Gatorade Ohio High School Girls Track and Field Athlete of the Year and 2002 American Track and Field Outdoor All-America; charted a Lorain County record with nine career state championships, including seven in individual events; and became only the third athlete in Ohio history to win four events at a state championship meet two years in a row (2002 and 2003). Tianna appeared in the "Faces In The Crowd" section of *Sports Illustrated* (July 7, 2003). And these are just a small portion of her high school decorations. She met challenges off the track with equal vigor, achieving academic Distinguished Honor Rolls all four years.

"I got serious with summer track," she recalls, "and an opportunity opened for me when I was jumping at Nationals, my first big national-type meet, in Palo Alto. I jumped fourteen feet, which was not a good one for me at the time, but I was invited to the Olympic Development Center because of the potential that I had shown."

At the Olympic Development Center, Caryl Smith Gilbert, then on the coaching staff at the University of Alabama, was leading the clinic for track and field. Tianna was so impressed with Coach Smith Gilbert that she told her father that her college choice would be wherever the coach would be:

I remember thinking that Coach Caryl Smith Gilbert really knows what she is doing because I was getting results right away. So in the van on the way back to the airport when she got a phone call offering her a coaching position at Tennessee, I said, "That's it. That's where I'm going."

But my mother made me take all my college visits anyway before officially announcing that I was going to go to Tennessee. I visited Ohio State, Illinois, Purdue, and then Tennessee. I liked the environment at Tennessee. It was a place you could just walk into and immediately feel warm and fuzzy inside. I came to Tennessee on a football weekend, and there was so much support and love and so much orange. Wow! I also liked that Knoxville had a small-town feel and felt good to me coming from a small town.

Tianna Madison

Sports Stats

- SEC Outdoor Freshman Field Event Athlete of the Year, 2004
- SEC Indoor and Outdoor runner-up, long jump, 2004
- Indoor All-America, 2004
- Ran on UT sprint medley relay unit that broke twenty-year-old collegiate, meet, and UT records at Penn Relays, 2004
- Member of runner-up 4x100-meter relay at SEC Outdoor meet, 2004
- Member of SEC Academic Honor Roll, 2004 and 2005
- IAAF world champion, long jump, 2005
- NCAA Indoor and Outdoor champion, long jump, 2005
- SEC Indoor and Outdoor champion, long jump, 2005
- SEC Indoor Field Event Athlete of the Year, 2005
- AOPi Lady Volunteer Athlete of the Year, 2005
- Helped Tennessee win NCAA Indoor National Championship, 2005
- Also a member of UT outdoor school-record 4x100-meter and 4x200-meter relay units
- School record holder Indoor and Outdoor, long jump
- Ranks number two on school's Indoor performers list, 55-meter dash

Once at Tennessee, Tianna experienced the adjustments common to freshman students. Even though her grades were high, she was accustomed to performing even better. She says:

Academically speaking I did OK my first semester. I was not especially happy with my grade point average. I think it was a 3.2. I was stressed about that because I came from high school where I had a 4.5. I was getting used to a new program where I really needed to work and discipline myself. . . .

I was no longer the star. You know, you have to adjust and check your ego at the starting line—just really humble yourself and start from the beginning. That was what my first year was about because if you would ask me, I would say that I did not have a very remarkable year at all. But a lot of people said I did pretty well for a freshman. We would look around at our new teammates and someone would say, "I was the state champion." And I would think, "Well, I was a state champion, too. OK, now we are all on the same level."

Unquestionably, Tianna was also a star performer as a Lady Vol. She earned top distinctions at indoor and outdoor events. She matched and surpassed all-time records, was selected as the SEC Freshman Outdoor Field Events Athlete of the Year, named Academic All-SEC, and a member of the Lady Vol Academic Honor Roll. Not bad for a freshman. Always seeking to go faster, jump farther, and achieve more, Tianna never rested on her laurels. She is quick to identify ways that she grew and learned at Tennessee:

Being a Lady Vol taught me how to be a team player. And it taught me a different kind of discipline—the kind that makes us responsible for each other. I became more aware of what you have to do to make it better for the next person, and this ties in with being a team player. We had this thing in practice where we would all feed off of each other. If I didn't go to bed at 10:30 and get up at 6:00 a.m., I kind of cheated my teammates out of being a little bit better. I helped the rest of my team get better just as they helped me. We really were proud to be Lady Vols. Anywhere we walked in as a team in that orange, we just made everybody stop and look. I loved it.

Tianna says that she "learned cause and effect as a Lady Vol," and her goals and preparation demonstrate her belief that deliberate effort brings results:

To know where you want to go or what you want to be, you have to know where you started. And for most of us, that means starting from scratch. You have to pull out the paper and write down your goals. You have to write where you want to be and give yourself a timeline. And do those things and don't let up about achieving those goals. Just keep chipping away at it.

Tianna follows her goal-oriented model when she specifically prepares for competition. She says:

Preparation depends on what meet I am going to. Mentally preparing for a race and mentally preparing for a run are two different things. For the race, there is less pressure

Tianna Madison—undeniably the 2005 world champion long jumper. Courtesy, *The Tennessean*.

on me because no one is going to expect me to show up as one of the top two or three sprinters because I am a long jumper. My preparation is just to execute and have fun because this really isn't my event. Whatever happens is going to happen as long as I give it my best.

Now, preparation for the long jump is very different. Maybe a few days before the meet, I go through videos and visualization—almost a kind of meditative state where I just zone out completely. And usually I don't speak to anyone for a while and that is when I start to focus, because technique is so important. Sometimes I run down the runway so fast that my technique is sloppy. And because I am moving so fast,

it does not matter. But right now I am working on becoming a technician. So I repeatedly drill and go over it in my head, and that is how I prepare. I design my warm-up so that the muscles I need to use are being warmed up. A lot of times in the past we would jog two laps and call it a day. Now I have a really specific warm-up. And then I have a really specific play list depending on the meet.

In August 2005 Tianna Madison won the IAAF World Championship in Helsinki, Finland, with a 22 feet–7.25 inches distance in the long jump. She was just under twenty years old and just completing her sophomore season at Tennessee. She comments:

If you had asked me during my freshman year, what my sophomore year was going to be like, I would have said, "Well, I don't know. We will just have to see." I would have never imagined that I would lose only one jump competition and then win the world championship. To go from 20 feet to 22 feet in one year—I never would have thought that would happen.

I think I relaxed a little bit. I had one year of experience under my belt. The SEC championships no longer scared me. I was not shaking when I got on the runway. Just that extra year gives you a little more confidence. I thought, "How about this year I just leave it all on the track?" That was just me putting it all out there.

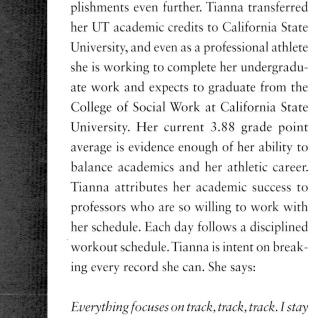

Tianna Madison

Postcollegiate Career Highlights

- US Outdoor runner-up, 2006
- World Indoor silver medalist, 2006
- US Indoor runner-up, 2006
- Third at Nike Prefontaine Classic, 2006
- First at DecaNation, 2006
- Ranked number two in the world (number one in United States) by Track and Field News, 2006
- US Outdoor, fifth place, 2007
- World Outdoor, tenth place, 2007
- Modesto Relays, first place, 2007
- Madrid, seventh place, 2007
- Second Lady Vol to turn pro prior to completion of her collegiate eligibility (did so after sophomore year)

Enthusiasm and focus continue to define Tianna's drive. Turning professional provided Tianna with the opportunities and total athletic training regimen to extend her accomplishments even further. Tianna transferred her UT academic credits to California State University, and even as a professional athlete she is working to complete her undergraduate work and expects to graduate from the College of Social Work at California State University. Her current 3.88 grade point average is evidence enough of her ability to balance academics and her athletic career. Tianna attributes her academic success to professors who are so willing to work with her schedule. Each day follows a disciplined workout schedule. Tianna is intent on breaking every record she can. She says:

Everything focuses on track, track, track. I stay motivated by setting high goals and knowing that every day brings me a step closer to my goals. Burnout means you really don't have any more hunger or desire or you probably don't have a goal at the moment to shoot for. But I have goals in every single part of my life. So, I never get burned out. I work really close to Jackie Joyner-Kersey right now. I have her records to chase. I will not sit down.

Tianna is also motivated by the people in her life. Her parents, Robert and Jo Ann Madison, are, in her words, "phenomenal." Tianna speaks with obvious pride when she mentions that her younger sister, Christina Madison, is on a full track and field scholarship at Purdue University. Tianna's older sister, Adrianne Madison, ran high school track, and their growing friendship as adults gives Tianna a special outlet when she wants to take a mental break from track. Countless athletes also inspire Tianna, and she particularly appreciates her friendship with Jackie Joyner-Kersey and her husband, Bobby Kersey.

Tianna is also by impressed by people whose accomplishments usually don't make the headlines:

I admire the "unsung heroes" as I call them. I admire my older sister for being a single mother and making it work. I admire all of the people who live from paycheck to paycheck because they have a discipline with their finances that I don't have.

Aside from her astounding athletic feats, it is this compassion for others that adds a special sparkle to Tianna's spirit. While she has traveled throughout the world, her thoughts are never far from the people who live in her hometown, Elyria, Ohio:

I want to build a neighborhood center and establish a foundation to keep kids off the street, to keep them active. Because, every time I go home, my heart is broken, feeling for these children who are not doing anything. They just stay at home, and the teenage pregnancy rate is so high. It is so sad. I just want to make sure that, because I am a household name in my hometown, I can come back and create something that would be conducive to brighter futures.

So, what makes a world champion? The record books tell one big part of the story. Tianna Madison tells the rest. Tianna Madison cares about people. She wants to leave this world a little bit better than she found it. That is a real world champion.

Spotlight
Monica Abbott
Softball, 2004–07

Monica Abbott

USA

Monica Abbott's pitching and leadership put Lady Vol softball in the national spotlight with advances culminating in the finals of the Women's College World Series in 2007.

"Sudden Impact"

Is it a plane? Is it a bird? It's Super-Abbott! When Monica Abbott winds up for a pitch, fans collectively draw in their breath and fix their eyes to the pitcher's mound in anticipation. A moment later the crowd raises voices in admiration of a wonder to behold.

Longtime women's softball fans have been watching Monica Abbott for years with expectation, and now this amazing pitcher has pulled into the sport a growing base of new fans who at one time never imagined they would stand in line for hours simply to see the wonders of Monica Abbott. They have become dedicated-for-life fans cheering for Monica, Tennessee Lady Vols, and women's softball in general. And we haven't even mentioned the young female players who are newly inspired to try out the fun of softball.

The opportunity to support and to help build a relatively new softball program (established 1996) to National-Championship caliber is exactly what drew Monica's attention to the University of Tennessee. She says:

I narrowed my college choices down to a top two, UCLA and the University of Tennessee. I knew Tennessee was going to build the softball program. They just needed some key players. So for me it was a question of being part of developing a program or going to an established one and adding to an already great roster as just one more person. I could have gone to UCLA to win several championships. Or I could have come to Tennessee
to help the program have the opportunity to compete for a championship. For me the greatest feeling comes from knowing that the Tennessee softball program has succeeded and will most likely continue to be successful. That is the greatest reward for me. That is also what sold me as a recruit— the opportunity to develop a program. It was a leap of faith. And it was really hard at times, especially my first year. I know I was meant to be at Tennessee.

When I came on my campus visit, I absolutely loved it. I wanted to go to a school that loves athletics and supports student-athletes. UT is in a college town and it fit exactly with what I wanted. There is so much community support. I wouldn't change it for the world.

Lady Vol fans agree that Monica was meant to be at Tennessee. Monica surpassed virtually every career and single-season pitching record at Tennessee. While here the team made UT history as the first Lady Vols to battle for the National Championship at the Women's College World Series in 2005, 2006, and 2007. "I have poured my heart and soul and more into this program," she declares. "I wanted to be able to end on a high note, and I can leave this program knowing that we have raised the bar to expect a National Championship."

Monica's ability to see the big picture and to feel the rewards in the building stages of a program reveals uncommon maturity. Her tenure on the team gave future Lady Vols the assurance that they can know the reality of the World Series. She takes pride in the progress her team made, and at the end of her senior season she reflects on what is really lasting. "This year has been awesome,"

Monica Abbott

Sports Stats

- All-Tourney, NCAA Regional No. 6, 2004
- SEC All-Freshman Team, 2004
- Lady Vol MVP, 2004
- All-Tourney, Compass Bank Invitational, 2004
- All-Tourney, New Mexico State Pick-Off Invitational, 2004
- Selected to US Softball National Elite Team, 2004
- SEC Pitcher of the Year, 2004
- SEC Freshman of the Year, 2004
- First Team All-America Pitcher of the Year, 2004
- Most wins and most strikeouts in a season by a freshman: 45 wins and 582 strikeouts (2004)
- SEC pitcher of the Week, 2004 (Feb. 9, Mar. 29, Apr. 5, Apr. 12)
- US Softball National Collegiate Player of the Week, 2004 (Feb. 10); 2005 (Feb. 14)
- UT Daily Beacon Athlete of the Year, 2004, 2005
- Edamerica Lady Vol Athlete of the Month for February and April, 2004, 2005
- Louisville Slugger/NFCA First-Team All-America, 2004, 2005
- Most games pitched in a season: 69 (2005)
- Women's College World Series First Team, 2005
- SEC Co-Pitcher of the Year, 2005
- First Team All-America Pitcher of the Year, 2005
- SEC All-Tournament, 2005
- All-Tourney, Georgia Southern Invitational, 2005

Lady Vols send encouraging cheers from the dugout to their teammates.

Monica says. "It was probably one of the most fun seasons I've had playing. We just had so much fun together. Our team this year had a true genuine love for each other; we were a family. I left the softball field with twenty lifelong friends and a bunch of people that care for me."

How did this noteworthy left-hander develop such insight and generosity? Monica grew up in Salinas, California. Known as "Monie" to close friends and family, Monica is especially close to her family. She says:

My mom and dad are always very encouraging, and I admire my grandma and grandpa. My family started a fast-food restaurant called Foster's Freeze. Grandma and Grandpa helped to grow that business through a lot of hard work. I like the passion that my grandpa puts into things. He

builds things with his own hands. He is so persistent and dedicated. They are so loving, and yet, they are also not afraid to speak their minds. They have both been to the World Series.

I am the second oldest of four sisters and one brother. Jessica is my older sister. My brother, Jared, played football in high school. My younger sisters, Gina and Bina, are twins. Gina plays volleyball, and Bina plays softball and basketball.

Monica started playing softball in second grade and enjoyed playing T-ball and sports with her sister, Jessica. She began pitching in fifth grade and batted until her junior year in college, when she concentrated solely on pitching. Monica's high school and summer league coach, Keith Berg, provided mentoring, and his guidance particularly supported

Monica through the college selection process. She says:

My mentor outside my family was Keith Berg. He was my high school coach the last two years and my summer ball coach. He talked to Co-Head Coaches Ralph and Karen Weekly and was very supportive of my decision to come to Tennessee. His help really made a difference for me, because I was being recruited by many people.

Family, coaches, and playing experience taught Monica the value of working hard to achieve goals:

I believe my work ethic has made a difference for me. I'm always trying to get better. No matter what happens, I always try to find something that I can do better. I tell myself that I am not out here just to get through this day if I have had a long day. I say that I am out here trying to get better today. The ability to focus myself on each day has come with time.

Monica's pregame routines help her to focus on her job ahead:

Before we get on the bus to go to the field, I always lay my uniform out with everything that is on it. If the game is the next morning, I lay it out the night before. I put everything out that I need to wear the next day. My roommate and I would turn on music and just get ready. I visualize two or three times before the game. That's my routine. I just stay focused. I am not one of those people who are out there laughing. I'll talk, but I am not super talkative. I get a nervous

rush before every game. I don't get as nervous anymore, partly because my mental game is better. But I definitely get a little nervous.

Once she gets out on the softball field, Monica is very careful about where she steps. "I don't step on the chalk lines," she says. "I just can't. I jump over the line every time I go out to the mound. When the game is over, it doesn't matter, but during and before the game—no way will I step on a line."

Monica equates the perception people have of pitchers as similar to that of quarterbacks in fooball. When pitchers do well, everyone celebrates. When they do poorly, they carry the blame. Sometimes she just needs a short time to refocus. She explains:

If I start out really slowly, maybe I have walked a batter and I look really nervous, my teammates will come up to me. And usually, Shannon [Doepking], my catcher, will say something like, 'Hey, calm down a little bit. Why don't you try breathing? That might work.' Sometimes I will just forget to breathe. Oops, I don't need oxygen. Sometimes they will tell me a little joke or something; it helps lighten the mood so we are able to refocus. They usually say, "We are right behind you. Don't worry." They are encouraging.

Of all her remarkable record-making achievements, two stand out as Monica's favorite Lady Vol moments:

This year when we played Alabama [April 21, 2007], the first strike-out broke the strike-out record [first NCAA Division I pitcher

Monica Abbott

Sports Stats (continued)

- SEC Pitcher of the Week, 2005 (Feb. 7, Mar. 7, Mar. 14, May 3, May 10)
- Louisville Slugger/NFCA National Player of the Week, 2005 (May 4)
- US National Softball Training Team, 2006
- Women's College World Series First Team, 2006
- First Team All-America Pitcher of the Year, 2006
- Roy F. Kramer SEC Female Athlete of the Year, 2006–07 (first Lady Vol non-basketball student-athlete to receive award) SEC Pitcher of the Year, 2007
- Honda Sports Award, Top Collegiate Softball Player, 2007
- US Softball Collegiate Player of the Year, 2007
- Pitched forty-two consecutive innings without allowing an earned run at the Women's College World Series, 2007
- Most strikeouts in a season: 724 (2007)
- Women's College World Series First Team, 2007
- First Team All-America Pitcher of the Year, 2007
- Only player with more than one fifty-win season in a career (two)
- Only player with four 500-strikeout seasons (and two 600-strikeout seasons) in a collegiate career
- 2,440 career NCAA Division 1 strikeouts (first all-time)
- 189 career NCAA Division 1 wins (first all-time)
- 112 career shutouts (first all-time)

Monica Abbott

Sports Stats (continued)

- 253 career games pitched (first all-time)
- 206 career games started (first all-time)
- 1448 career innings pitched (first all-time)
- 178 career complete games (second all-time)
- 11.80 career strikeouts per seven innings (third all-time)
- .848 career win percentage (tenth all-time)
- 16 career saves (tied eighth all-time)
- 23 career NCAA Division I no-hitters
- 6 career NCAA Division I perfect games

Postcollegiate Career Highlights

- Named 2007 Sportswoman of the Year (team sports) by the Women's Sports Foundation (highest award ever received by a softball player in the SEC)
- Selected Championship Game MVP of National Pro Fastpitch (NPF) Softball League, 2007
- US National Softball Team, 2007, finishing international season 20–0, with Abbott posting a team-best 6–0 record as a member of the rotation
- Named to US National Women's Softball Team for 2008 Olympic Games in Beijing, China

Monica Abbott returned to Tennessee on April 12, 2008, this time wearing red, white, and blue as a member of the USA National Team that will compete at the 2008 Olympics in Beijing, China. Photo by William Ewart; courtesy, William Ewart.

to punch out 500 hitters during each of her four collegiate years]. Having all the fans get so excited and Shannon [Doepking] jumping up—that was really a great moment for me.

My sophomore year when we made it to the World Series for the first time, we came in third place [June 6, 2005, losing to number-one Michigan]. Sitting with the team in a circle after that game—just talking about what we had achieved that year and realizing what we had done—was pretty awesome. That was the first time we had experienced really good success.

Monica has dedicated her heart, talents, and focused spirit to the Lady Vols. She is especially appreciative of the bene-

fits she has gained as a student-athlete at Tennessee:

The support of all the coaches is great. The coaches are competitive in a way. They all push each other to do better. But the support of the community for the Lady Vols is really good, as is the support of the University for the Lady Vol athletics department. It helps when you have all that support. It makes it easier to concentrate on your discipline.

Marty McDaniel, the pitching coach, is in the background a lot. I think that he is such a good coach. Pitching-wise he has helped me so much. He played men's fast-pitch. He brings different aspects of the game of softball with him. He makes you think about

The Women's College World Series softball team, 2007: (front row, kneeling, left to right) Tiffany Baker, Alexia Clay, Jennifer Griffin, Erinn Webb, Danielle Pieroni, Co-Head Coaches Karen and Ralph Weekly, Lindsay Schutzler, Natalee Weissinger, Liane Horiuchi, Nicole Kajitani, (back row, standing, left to right) Manager Audra Hendrix, Volunteer Coach Stephanie Sayne, Assistant Coach Marty McDaniel, Shannon Doepking, Megan Rhodes, Allison Fulmer, Anita Manuma, Monica Abbott, Caitlin Ryan, Tonya Callahan, Lillian Hammond, Tiffany Huff, India Chiles, Administrative Assistant Ashlee Goble, and Director of Softball Operations Kendal Rainey.

the game in a totally different light than you would ever think about it. He is lighthearted. He is fun but very serious at the same time. He lets you know that you are doing well without putting stress or pressure on you. He is the perfect complement to Ralph and Karen [Weekly]. He is usually in the dugout. He has been here three years. People don't realize he is there, but he is working with the pitchers all the time. He has taught me so much about pitching. He brings out the best in us.

When she considers what advice she would share with youth, Monica stresses that no matter what goals you have, fun and hard work should go hand in hand:

Work hard and always have fun. Live it. Dream it. Achieve it. If you are not having fun, don't do it. Work hard and enjoy that you are working hard, but don't let people take your fun away. There are going to be days when you are not having fun, but live for the moment and enjoy every step of it.

I love softball. For me going to the softball field is what I imagine it is like for Oprah Winfrey going to the studio. I love so many things about it. I love the opportunities it has given me. I love the team aspect. I love that it is instantaneous. You can just be going along, and something happens, and it is exciting. I love being a pitcher; you are kind of like an artist painting a scene. I just love being with my teammates. I love being

outside in the sun. I get to play in the dirt like a little kid.

I love all the hard work we put into it. There are so many things you can do to get better. It is not about one thing. With softball, there are so many different parts to the game. There is always something new that you can learn about it. Even though I am a pitcher, I love learning about different positions on the field. I love this game.

Monica Abbott has goals. She will represent the United States in the 2008 Olympic Games. Long-term aspirations include working as a sports analyst. As far as champions go, Monica Abbott is already there. The rest is icing on the cake.

Candace Parker, the "total package," rewrote the Lady Vol record book with her extraordinary talent, intelligence, and versatility.

CP3: Perseverance, Character, and Hope

She out-sparkles. She out-dazzles. She out-dunks. And she stands beyond words. Candace Parker has reset the game. And we all have taken notice.

In fact, Candace drew attention well before national eyes were upon her. By the seventh grade, she was six feet tall and in love with basketball. That same year an eye-level encounter with Coach Pat Summitt turned her thoughts to orange:

When I was in the seventh grade, Tennessee was playing DePaul in Illinois. I know Tamika Catchings because she is from the same area where I grew up. We went to the game to see her play. After the game, I asked Tamika Catchings's father, Harvey Catchings, if I could take a picture with Pat Summitt. He grabbed Pat and took the picture. I was already six feet tall. Pat asked, "How tall are you? I'm going to take you home and fatten you up." I thought that was the greatest thing ever. I still have that picture.

Before Candace grew into basketball, her dreams were on the soccer field, and then she took a brief side trip to volleyball. She says:

I actually was a die-hard soccer player when I was younger, and I told my parents that I didn't want to play basketball. They said, "You are going to be over six feet tall. Why would you not want to play basketball?"

I wanted to be an Olympic soccer player. Then I got to seventh grade and started play-ing basketball. And I fell in love with it. It happened overnight. I have always played YBA. But I did not start seriously until seventh grade. That is when it just took off. I started playing and would always be in the gym. I would always be with my father and beg him to take me to the park on Saturday.

In high school I played volleyball too. My first recruiting letter from Tennessee was to play volleyball. I played varsity volleyball my freshman and sophomore years. Then my junior year I really wanted to focus just on basketball. I had it in my head that I was going to go on and play basketball in college on scholarship.

Candace's family provides a strong foundation for athleticism. Her oldest brother, Anthony Parker, plays professional basketball for the Toronto Raptors. Marcus Parker, the next older brother, played point guard in high school and is a physician at Johns Hopkins Medical Center in Baltimore. Her father, Larry Parker, lettered at Iowa under Lute Olson, and her mother, Sara Parker, was a pre-Title IX vocational player. Each family member contributed particular skills to help Candace improve her skills. Her brothers served as practice players, her father as coach, and Candace's mother broke down tapes. Candace credits her parents for teaching her the importance of finding her own individuality, prioritizing goals, and developing a strong work ethic.

"I am very fortunate because, obviously, I'm blessed with long legs and long arms," Candace observes. "But when I was younger, my dad always pushed me to be different. My dad and my mom encouraged me to focus on what is important to me. They helped me set priorities in my life and said that if I work hard now, it will be easier later. I definitely know that I am reaping the benefits from all that hard work."

Sometimes plans take an unexpected turn. As her junior year was drawing to a close, Candace was playing at the top of her game and drawing the attention of nearly all the colleges in the country. She was looking forward to a great summer of basketball:

On July 11, 2003, I went up for a rebound, came down and tore my anterior cruciate ligament. It was the worst feeling ever because I knew it was torn. After I got over the initial shock, I just set goals.

On July 29 I had surgery to repair my knee. The doctor said it was going to be between six and nine months before I could play. In my head I already had my comeback planned for December. He cleared me to play in December, and I probably played a little bit sooner than I should have. But I would do it over again. Our team ended up winning the state championship again that year for back-to-back years.

Collegiate programs courted Candace. She recalls:

During recruiting I received a lot of information from different schools. Coach Summitt visited me in Illinois. She poured a glass of water and said, "This is what I want you to see." The water was clear; I could see through it. Coach Summitt said, "You see everything. This is what I want Tennessee to be." Then she said, "This is what people can do. They can cloud your mind." She dropped

an antacid tablet in the water. It bubbled up and fizzed. I couldn't see through it. My dad looked at me and smiled. And that was on my home visit.

When she came to pick me up at the airport for my Tennessee visit, Coach Summitt was dressed in the Jason, scary mask for Halloween. I didn't know who she was when I walked into the airport. So I walked away. She came over to me and asked, "Are you here to visit Tennessee?" I was standing away from her. Then I looked at her eyes and saw it was Coach Summitt. She just does funny stuff like that.

It was the good fortune of Tennessee that Candace decided to be a Lady Volunteer. She says:

I committed to Tennessee the day before signing day. I felt that it was the best fit for me. It encompasses everything that I want in a school—fan support, the best coach in the game, playing against the best practice players, having the best teammates to play with and practice against, and tradition. The city of Knoxville is really behind basketball at Tennessee.

Candace graduated from high school and was eagerly anticipating the experiences of college. The news came early and would once again test Candace's strength and determination. As she remembers:

I entered my freshman year at UT, and they noticed that I had a lot of swelling in my knee. We did an MRI and discovered a bad hole in my cartilage. So I had to have more surgery, basically a reconstruction of my

Candace Parker

Sports Stats

- US Junior National Team, 2004, and led team to a gold medal in Puerto Rico with a 5–0 record
- Academic All-SEC: 2005, 2006, 2007
- SEC Freshman of the Year, 2006
- SEC All-Tournament Team, 2006
- All-SEC Freshman Team, 2006
- Earned spot on the five-member All-Opals World Challenge Team, 2006
- US Senior National Team (youngest member selected since 1994), 2006; guided Team USA to a bronze medal in Brazil and set a new American record for blocks in a tournament (14)
- Kodak All-America, 2006, 2007, 2008
- NCAA All-Regional Tournament Teams: 2006 (Cleveland), 2007 (Dayton)
- Associated Press All-America Team (Second Team), 2006, 2007
- All-SEC Team, 2006, 2007
- ESPY Award nominations, 2006, 2007
- NCAA Final Four Most Outstanding Player, 2007
- NCAA All–Final Four Team, 2007
- NCAA National Championship Title, 2007
- Naismith All-America Team, 2007
- John R. Wooden All-America Team, 2007
- ESPN the Magazine Academic All-America, 2007
- SEC Player of the Year, 2007
- Academic All-America (Second Team), 2007

Candace Parker

knee. Doctors said that I would be out a year. I was really fortunate because I had a lot of really great friends who hugged me and were there for me to cry. My friends, my coaches, everybody was just great.

I had a Bible verse that I lived by. It was Romans 5:3. It says that we should not only rejoice in our sufferings, but our sufferings produce perseverance, character, and hope. And that is what I wear here on my wrist always—PCH—for perseverance, character, and hope. [Candace writes "PCH" on her wrist under her wristband for every game.]

It just reminds me there are going to be times when we suffer and go through adversity, but God puts adversity there, and we can do it. I think that is the heart of my story. Winning the National Championship this year [2007]—everyone sees how great it is, but there is a lot of suffering that goes into it.

Players guarding Candace might suffer at times too. One of her crowd-favorite shots is the dunk. On March 19, 2006, Candace entered the record books as the first woman to dunk in an NCAA Tournament game and then topped her record (and those of the pros) by doing it again, netting two dunks in one game. She says:

I did my first dunk when I was fourteen years old. My father told me that I could dunk. I had been touching the rim since I was in eighth grade. So my freshman year, I started getting a little higher and first dunked a tennis ball, then a volleyball. My dad said, "I really think you can dunk a basketball." He told me that there is not that much difference between a volleyball and a basketball

and that I have big enough hands. I didn't believe him. I tried it a couple of times and failed. One day we were in Naperville [Illinois] at the gym. I remember it. It was on a Saturday morning. The first time I tried to dunk, the ball hit the back of the rim. I was wide-eyed because I almost did it. I tried a second time and I got it down. I was so excited and told my brothers, and my dad said, "She dunked at an earlier age than you guys did." My brothers were all upset, but Dad said that dunking was not all of my game: "That is not all that you can do."

Candace continuously focuses on all that she can do to be better:

I am my biggest critic. I look on the court and say, "That is great, but this summer I want to do this, this, and this. This is how I want to get better." I think that is what keeps me hungry.

Honestly, winning is definitely addictive. The more you do it, the more you want it. After we won the 2007 National Championship, I was thinking, "I want to do it again." And we had just won it. [Candace's thought would prove to be prophetic. The Lady Vols won their eighth National Championship in 2008.]

I think the drive always to stay on top and always to want to be the best are what make me who I am and what make Tennessee who we are. Pat Summitt is the most intense person. She wants to outwork you and to be successful. When you have a leader like that, you always want to get better.

Our coaches and our team are very close. So we tease. We joke. We are very laid back. But when it is time to go to work, we get to *business. Coach Summitt respects us enough to be able to turn it on and turn it off. We are laughing at the shoot-around before games, but in between the lines it is business.*

Candace respects and learns from her coaches and teammates and has found role models in Lady Vols who have come before her:

I am very fortunate, and I attribute this to Tennessee. Strong tradition and past athletes set the tone for what we are expected to do in the Lady Vol family. We have so many role models. Daedra Charles-Furlow is on speed-dial on my phone. She is an amazing person and an amazing mentor. She is always there—no matter what—with whatever I need. I am the godmother of her son, Anthony. I am so happy for her accomplishments as a student-athlete at Tennessee and also for what she is doing with her career in coaching.

Obviously, Tamika Catchings is one of my long-standing role models. We grew up in the same area. Her parents are my friends. She was my mentor when I played internationally on the US Women's Senior National Team. I have really gotten to know her.

Also, outside of the Lady Vol family is Tina Thompson. She really impacted me as a teammate on the US Women's Senior National Team. She is the nicest person. She talked to me just like a little sister. She would say, "Look: this is what you need to do." She understood my youth and inexperience at the international games.

Candace finds inspiration from women off the court as well. "I would like to in-

Top: Joined as teammates on the USA National Team, Candace Parker and Kara Lawson celebrate gold at the 2007 FIBA Americas Championship, qualifying the team for the 2008 Olympics in Beijing, China. Bottom: Candace and her canine pal, Fendi. Images by Design/Wade Payne.

terview Oprah Winfrey," she says. "She is a strong African-American woman who has been successful and has given back with her time and money. She has broken barriers that no other woman has even touched. I grew up watching her on television. There is not a book on how to be Oprah Winfrey. I would just love to pick her brain."

When asked to speak to young women who may see her as their role model, Candace has special advice:

I had many heroes when I was growing up. My brothers, my dad, and my mom were some of them. Be who you are. Take pieces of your heroes and construct yourself. Take different qualities that you like and put them together. Don't be like me. Be who you are. I hope that I can make a difference. My parents and Coach Summitt taught me that. Those people were role models for me. And you have a responsibility to those people who are role models for you.

At a young age Candace Parker has accomplished a lifetime of achievements in basketball. She is the center of media attention and draws respectful admiration wherever she goes. She is quietly humble about her accomplishments and focuses on what she can do for others:

My brothers keep me grounded. When I might be a little too focused on an achievement, they knock me right back down. A verse in the Bible says: "Talent is God-given; be humble." I have this quote: "Fame is man-given; be grateful. Conceit is self-given; be careful." I think these thoughts encompass everything. Conceit is not something that I would like to have.

I want to do something with basketball. I want to give back to basketball. I love kids, and I look forward to being married, having kids, and teaching them. I think what is important to me now is that little boys are looking up to girls as role models. I think that is so special. I know that my sons are going to respect women athletes across the board. My job is to teach them that everybody deserves respect.

While her fans always see her competitive determination to win, people who know Candace might see a little bit more. Whenever Candace attempts a free throw, she touches her heart to honor her fiancé, Sheldon Williams, a Duke graduate and professional basketball player with the Sacramento Kings. He does the same for her. Something extra happened at Sheldon's games, though. When the fans in Atlanta, where he formerly played for the Hawks, learned of his relationship with Candace, they started wearing Tennessee orange to his games. Candace comments, "Lady Vol fans are everywhere. Sheldon said, 'I didn't go to Tennessee. Why are they wearing orange?' I told him that is how deeply dedicated our fans are."

Candace was especially happy to deliver the 2007 NCAA National Championship Title to Tennessee fans. "My favorite moment would probably be when we won the National Championship," she says. "We were standing on the podium, and it was almost unreal. It felt like a dream. It still hasn't hit me that we won the National Championship."

Candace Parker and her Tennessee team turned the dreams of Lady Vol fans into reality. Every day this Tennessee team puts forth hard work, sacrifice, and the determination to make the next best performance even better. It is only fitting that Candace experience the dream after all that reality.

Common Ground, Oceans Apart

The University of Tennessee women's athletics program has experienced change and significant growth throughout the years. The turn of the century has brought the Lady Volunteers into a new era. In 2006 four Lady Vols, two recent graduates and two veterans, shared their memories. Spread throughout the world from Australia to Sweden, California to Tennessee, these four women shine as testaments to the values of the Lady Volunteer tradition.

Sidney Spencer played basketball for the Lady Volunteers from 2003 to 2007. She and her teammates were two-time SEC Champions and two-time SEC Tournament Champions. They twice made it to the NCAA National Championship Final Four and won the NCAA National Championship Title in 2007. Sidney's awards are plentiful on the court and in the classroom, where she was an honor student and graduate with a B.S. in Education. She came to Tennessee from Hoover, Alabama. Called Sid-Vicious or Sid-Ville by her teammates, Sidney won the hearts of all Lady Vol fans. She currently plays professionally for the WNBA Los Angeles Sparks, where she completed a stunning rookie year.

Whenever Sarah Blum ran onto the volleyball court, she was greeted by Tennessee fans with a loud "Blooooooom!" This Lady Vol from Tulsa, Oklahoma, dominated as a middle blocker for Tennessee from 2003 to 2007. She claimed the school records in total blocks (674), blocks per game (1.55), and achieved the fourth all-time hitting percentage in Lady Vol history (.315). Like Sidney, Sarah added

academic honors to a never-ending list of athletic achievements. Sarah's B.S. is in Business Administration, and she plans to complete a master's degree in sport management.

Crystal Cleveland (Mahoney) competed as a Lady Volunteer tennis player from 1999 to 2003. Growing up in Delray Beach, Florida, today Crystal and her husband call Melbourne, Australia, home. Crystal's tennis prowess earned her third all-time records in singles (125–36) and doubles (119–34). She was named Lady Vol Tennis MVP in 2001. In 2002 her team competed at the NCAA National Championship Final Four, and in 2003 she played in the NCAA first round, singles. Like Sidney and Sara, Crystal was an academic standout, graduating with a B.S. in Human Ecology.

Golf was a way of life for Katharina Larsson even when she was a small child growing up in Skoghali, Sweden. She competed in her first national golf tournament when she was seven years old. A member of UT's first women's intercollegiate golf team from 1992 to 1995, Katharina's skills brought immediate attention and success to the program. In 1992 she won the True Temper/Memphis Tournament, had fourteen top-ten finishes in her career, and won the individual championship at the1994 SEC Championships. This 1994 SEC Player of the Year was equally competitive in the classroom, completing her B.S. in Communications at the top of her class with a perfect 4.0 grade point average. Today Katharina works in the golf profession as an instructor, writer, and competitor throughout Europe and the United States. She also enjoys family life with her husband, Peter, and their daughter, Maia.

Sidney Spencer shows the toughness that earned her "Athlete of the Week," one of many standouts.

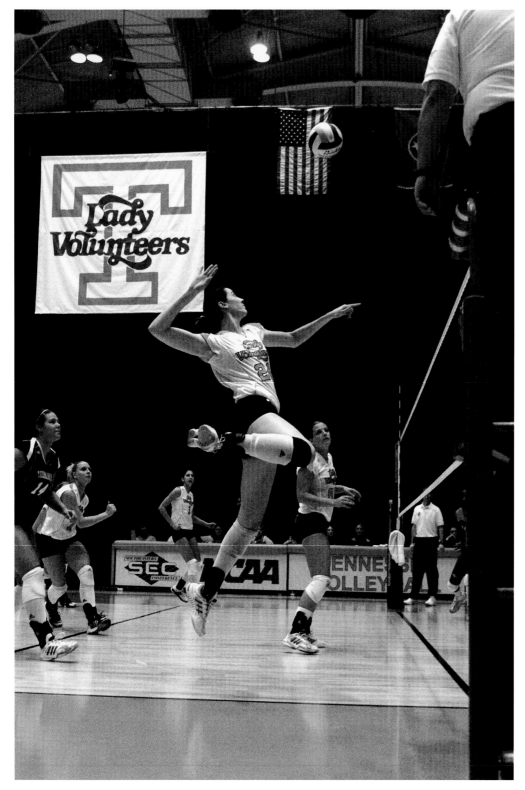

Sarah Blum set records every year of her Lady Vol career.

Even though these four women are at different points in their careers and lives, memories of their Lady Vol experiences bring them together to a common ground. From their own corners of the world, the first memories that come to mind are of great victories:

Crystal: I remember our tennis team making it to the Final Four in 2002. I will never forget the sheer excitement we all felt in that moment as a team. We were jumping up and down, hugging each other like little kids. We had made Lady Vol tennis history and did it as a unit.

Sarah: I will always remember November 14, 2004, when our volleyball team beat Florida at Florida for the first time. It was great—we were so excited, jumping up and down, screaming—it had been our goal and is my favorite moment by far. Of course, we were on their home floor, so the entire place was dead silence except for us cheering!

Katharina: I remember winning the SEC in 1994. Our Volunteer coach, Ann Furrow, had geared us up for that particular tournament the entire spring, and we were really prepared. When we arrived at the venue, the course was fantastic. I felt like it was my time to play fantastic golf, and I did. I played forty-eight holes without one single bogey. I had never done that before or since.

Sidney: Winning the NCAA National Championship Title in 2007 was definitely a high point. During that six-game run, just hearing my teammates saying that they were doing this for the seniors really touched me.

When needing encouragement and motivation, Crystal turns to her parents "who taught her the greatest life lessons and are her greatest mentors." Sidney agrees that family played a large role in the development of her basketball interest. "My family encouraged me," she says. "Since I have two older brothers who played sports and a father who played every sport possible, it was almost inevitable that I was going to do the same. We always had driveway games of horse, two on two, or three on three, depending on how many neighborhood kids were there. I am grateful that I was never forced or pressured into playing sports. It was always my choice, and that is what has made basketball so enjoyable."

Sarah, as well, points to her parents and to her club coach for making a significant difference in her life direction: "My club coach, Dane Hendrix in Oklahoma really took me under his wing my sophomore year in high school. He taught me the mental part and told me that I could be an amazing player with a lot of hard work. He gave me the love for the game that I have now. I admire my parents the most; they have been great supporters and never missed my games."

Sidney found role models in teammates and others at UT. "I have several mentors at the University of Tennessee," she says. "Shanna Zolman (Crossley) was by far the one who took me under her wing both on and off the court. She has been such a faithful prayer and accountability partner for me. I am inspired by Tamika Catchings because she works so hard and Cait McMahan because of her commitment to the team despite adversity in life. Also my Bible study teacher, Reagan Womack, and the football

chaplain/Fellowship for Christian Athletes director, James Mitchell, gave me guidance and direction for my life throughout all four years."

Moving far from home were early personal challenges for Sarah and Katharina. Crystal faced the same hurdle after college graduation. As they comment:

Sarah: When I first came to UT as a freshman, I was homesick. All the seniors said it would be OK, and of course, I was fine eventually.

Katharina: It was a big challenge to leave home and go to college in a country completely unknown to me. When I arrived in the US, it took me one hour to read one page in my biology book. I had to look up every third word in the dictionary. Fortunately, my English improved quickly. During our tournaments I met other Swedish golfers, and it was therapy for me to speak to them about my joys and troubles.

Crystal: Moving to the other side of the world with my husband in November 2006 was a big step for me. We relocated to his home country of Australia. Leaving my comfort zone and moving to a city I had never before seen was a huge challenge. It has been a terrific experience for us, and I think it was important for me to take this leap of faith.

Most Lady Volunteers discover that the lessons they learn in their sports are metaphors for the greater experiences in life. When considering the elements of her athletic success, Sidney says that she is always

challenged by learning her purpose in life and reasons for playing basketball. She adds that "first and foremost God is the reason for my success; second, knowing my priorities; and third, always working hard. You never know who is watching and when your hard work will pay off."

What do they treasure most from their collegiate days as Lady Volunteers?

Katharina: I liked everything about my UT experience. I admire the professional approach to everything in the women's athletics department. I have always felt that our university cares as much about the female athletes as the male. I liked my teachers, teammates, and classmates.

Sidney: I love the opportunities basketball and being a Lady Vol give for women in careers after the sport. I have gained so many life skills from being on the court, under the pressure, and in the heat of a game.

Crystal: I treasure the friends I made. Four of my teammates were bridesmaids in my wedding. These are people I will always have in my life. If I had not gone to UT, I would have missed out on some of the greatest friends a person could have.

Sarah: I treasure the friendships. I also had a lot of fun doing community service. The twins [Jessica and Kristen Kinder, graduate assistants] in the strength and conditioning department started a physical education department at a local school. The Lady Vols helped and had so much fun. I was on the jumping station and taught kids how to jump.

When asked what they learned from being Lady Vols, Sidney and Sarah both agree that time management skills are a valuable outcome:

Sidney: At first I had no time management skills at all. I did not even know when I was going to be able to eat. Coach [Summitt] sat down with me, and we mapped it out. As I became older, I learned how to separate basketball and my life. When I stepped onto the court, it was time to work and focus on the team to become better so we could win a championship. However, once practice, rehab, film reviews, etc., were over, I learned how to do other things such as enjoy my friends and family. I even learned how to cook and play Scrabble and spades.

Sarah: I learned that I can do anything now. Commitment, time management, having a positive attitude, and working with other people showed me that if you have shared determination, you can do anything. We weren't always as tall as other teams, but our legs were always fresh. Working hard made a difference and kept us going. We had a strong work ethic and the desire to win. We set team goals and worked as a unit to achieve them. Every one of us stayed motivated.

Before competition, Crystal would take a moment to pray. Sidney also prayed and played spades while watching the UT men's team practice. Sarah says that relaxing and focusing on what she was supposed to do helped before a game: "I never got nervous before the game. I tried to pump everyone else up, and we would dance and jump around in the locker room."

Katharina Larsson shares her expertise as teacher. Photograph by Peter Samuelsson.

Every Lady Vol has her own favorite funny stories:

Crystal: We had some very funny team meetings after matches. Our coaches even had a laugh or two at some of those meetings. Meetings usually started out seriously and turned into something else by the end. I remember having a very long team meeting in Wisconsin after we had lost a match.

It was late, and we had been meeting for a while when I looked over and saw that one of our teammates had fallen asleep. Two of us nudged her to wake her up before our coaches caught her sleeping. We thought that was really funny at the time.

Sidney: One time we were scrimmaging in practice against the practice players, and we had been working for a while. One of the players was dribbling the ball and clearly stepped out of bounds, but Coach [Summitt] didn't want play to stop. She wanted to push us to go harder. We all were saying, "He was out!" Coach [Summitt] said that she was getting old and maybe a little senile because she "didn't see so well anymore." We all laughed at that.

What advice do they have for today's young women?

Katharina: *Work hard and focus on your individual goals. You cannot do your best in everything at once, but you can be your best at one thing at a time.*

Crystal: *You can't please everyone and if you do your best, then that is all anyone can ask. In the end, the people who matter the most will be there for you.*

Sidney: *People always told me that I would never go to Tennessee because I wasn't good enough. Then when I signed with Tennessee, they said I would not get playing time and would transfer within two years. Ever since I was a young child, I wanted to play for Tennessee and then play for the WNBA. Now I play for the WNBA Los Angeles Sparks. People are always going to have opinions and say you can't accomplish your dreams. I say you use those people to motivate you and work hard to achieve your goals to prove them wrong. It's not about them!*

Sarah: *Stick to your dream. It is hard work, but being happy makes it all worthwhile. There will be ups and downs; do it and love it.*

A Tennessee Original
Jenny Moshak

Jenny Moshak (center), assistant athletics director for sports medicine.

A Lot of Comfort in a World of Hurt

On April 24, 2006, Jenny Moshak dipped the wheel of her bicycle into the Pacific Ocean to mark the beginning of a journey across America. Twenty-seven days and 2,905 miles later, she arrived in Savannah, Georgia, and greeted the Atlantic Ocean with the same wheel dip but a new set of memories, feelings, and dreams. The cyclist had successfully achieved a lifetime goal. Jenny calls it her "National Championship."

Few people know as well as Jenny what it really takes to be a champion. Jenny has celebrated championship victories with hundreds of Lady Volunteers. Her role as assistant athletics director for sports medicine is critical to the success and well-being of the student-athletes. She oversees sports medicine, athletic training, rehabilitation, strength and conditioning, and direct medical care for the basketball team. Joan Cronan, director of women's athletics, is dedicated to assuring number-one commitment to the student-athletes. She is quick to say that "Jenny is one of the most outstanding athletic trainers in the business, and she cares so much about the student-athletes. Our coaches and staff depend on her."

A day in the life of the athletic training room is never the same. At any given time an observer may see a student-athlete on an examining table with a staff athletic trainer checking her knee. Team members may be having therapy in the whirlpool after practice, staff may be preparing equipment for a visiting team, a coach may be consulting with an athletic trainer about the readiness of a student-athlete, an athletic trainer could be assisting a student-athlete with a session of rehabilitation following an injury, or a team may be preparing for practice and student-athletes need their ankles taped.

The athletic training staff works with the student-athletes before, during, and following competition, as well as in the evenings, weekends, early mornings, and throughout every day. And that is just the tip of the iceberg.

At every athletic event there will be one person who is not really watching the score. In fact, that individual may not even know who has the ball, baton, or any other essential of that particular sport. That person will definitely be paying attention, however; those eyes are following the jumps, runs, falls, turns, and all the other actions that use muscles, bones, joints, and every other part of the body. The eyes belong to the athletic trainer—the person who is always the first to see an injury and who sometimes even anticipates it a split second before it occurs. The athletic trainer is working all the time to oversee physical needs and assure healthy play.

Jenny Moshak has transformed the sports medicine program for Lady Vols. Her knowledge, skills, and competence are recognized throughout the athletic world—collegiate and professional. Her reputation is so widely respected that Jenny is often the person professional athletes seek for rehabilitation following injury. Head Basketball Coach Pat Head Summitt recognizes Jenny as "the best athletic trainer in the country. Her knowledge, work ethic, communication skills, and dedication to the Lady Vol program set her apart from all others."

Lady Vol Tamika Catchings, WNBA player, still considers Jenny her mentor and friend:

JMo, as we call her, has had a special place in my heart since my early years at the University of Tennessee. She always went out of her way to take care of us. She made sure that we got all of the proper care and attention that we needed. For me she also became a mentor—someone even to this day that I can call and ask for an opinion on different situations that I'm going through. She is, simply put, an awesome friend.

Lady Vols are quick to spot Jenny as a person who genuinely cares about their well-being and advocates in their best interests. She is available 24/7 and rarely gets through an hour without several telephone calls. She consults with physicians on a regular basis, often responding to their inquiries for advice regarding the best plans to recommend to their patients for rehabilitation. Always willing to roll up her sleeves and work the "front lines," Jenny inspires her staff and is a mentor to students in her field. She is called upon to lecture, write articles, facilitate workshops, and share her knowledge with the community at large through television and other media forms. Health professionals call upon her regularly to speak at seminars and conferences. Tina Bonci, codirector of the Division of Athletic Training/Sports Medicine at the University of Texas, acknowledges Jenny's expertise:

Jenny Moshak has worked tirelessly to provide the Lady Volunteer athletics program with the medical resources and expertise required to build consistent winners.

Jenny Moshak celebrated her own personal championship when she completed a 2,905-mile bicycle journey of the United States from the Pacific to the Atlantic shore.

Through her innovative programs, Jenny has been able to keep student-athletes in the game, maximize their health and performance, and expedite their recovery from injuries. She is a master clinician who keeps up with the latest in medical, psychological, social, nutritional, orthopedic, and rehabilitative concerns of the female athlete. Student-athletes and coaches alike have been able to capitalize on her knowledge, experience, and collaborative problem-solving skills to meet the challenges associated with a sports system that is committed to performance excellence. The Lady Vols are fortunate to have a certified athletic trainer of Jenny's caliber and level of commitment and dedication who knows how to consistently get the job done.

What Jenny knows and what she does are significant, but it is her heart that

makes her a standout. When basketball star Candace Parker was facing surgery to repair her knee and red-shirted her freshman year, Jenny gave her the emotional and physical support that she needed to stay positive, strong, focused, and healthy. Candace says:

Jenny Moshak is the reason I am playing basketball. Without her, my knee would still be causing difficulties. I probably wouldn't have even scratched the surface of being the player I am today. You can tell her how you are feeling, and she will give you a hug. She is a great person. She is more than a trainer.

Tracy Bonner Headecker, a Lady Vol diver and now professional diver for Cirque du Soleil, remembers Jenny's tenacious dedication:

Jenny pioneered treatment for me. I had a bad injury just after my freshman year. A student-athlete that young in the program doesn't usually get ongoing personal care directly from the head trainer. This is normal routine in the Lady Vol training room, though. The regular medical techniques weren't working for me. Jenny took classes to learn alternative techniques to help me work through my injury. If she hadn't been willing to learn, I don't think I would have been able to come back as a competitive diver. Jenny is a top athletic trainer.

I really admire her willingness and ability to teach her student-interns and staff. That way everyone gets to learn, and student-athletes are better served. In the training room freshmen are equally special, and all sports are equally important. Jenny is willing

THE PROGRAM

by Jenny Moshak

A place where a young girl talented,
becomes a young woman skilled;
Where dreams are fulfilled.
Where honesty, hard work, integrity and
commitment are preached;
The top of your game is reached.
Where life long teammates
and friendships develop;
The teachings of coaches envelop.
An abundance of support and resource;
Media Relations assists with discourse.
Sports Medicine provides the ability to heal;
Team ENHANCE the power to feel.
Strength and Conditioning stride
to reach performance peak;
Academics guide the degree that you seek.
Marketing promotes the play;
Development secures means to pay.
Sport Psychology heightens mental training;
Administration provides the structural framing.
Performing in front of an orange sea;
Cheering and applauding,
no place they would rather be.
Rocky Top the song known nationwide;
Wearing Lady Vol orange with pride.
Women's Athletics holds the creed;
The University of Tennessee,
the place to succeed.

to "get down and dirty" to do whatever it takes to help athletes be at their prime. I owe a lot to her, and she will always have a special place in my heart.

Head Volleyball Coach Rob Patrick also recognizes Jenny's commitment to every student-athlete and sport: "Jenny is always available to spend time with my student-athletes and me. She is available any time of the day or night and puts the student-athletes' well-being as top priority."

Carrie Cole, assistant golf coach and former student-athlete, has observed Jenny's role from both perspectives. She praises Jenny's priority for the student-athletes and her persistent thirst for education: "Jenny always puts the student-athlete first. She is constantly looking for ways to educate herself in her profession and to make student-athletes healthier, stronger and better in every way."

When asked about her work, Jenny is quick to educate others about the unique student-athlete experience: "Many people don't realize the energy these young women put into their sports. The student-athletes are exceptional individuals but they are people with the same needs as others. Whether they win or lose, they are still great people. An injury can feel devastating to an individual who has so much focus and drive to be her best. Our job is to provide care, prevention, rehabilitation, evaluation, and referral needed for a healthy recovery."

Typically, the majority of student-athletes are between the ages of eighteen and twenty-three. Many are living away from home for the first time. Developmentally, this age period can be a transforming time as stu-

dents explore their interests, independence, confidence, relationships, and coping skills. Student-athletes are no different from others except that additional pressures, expectations, media attention, and time demands can add anxiety and challenges for even the most capable individuals. First-year student-athletes bring with them the confidence of having been at the top of the talent in their high schools, only to discover that they are starting over with teammates who are equally talented or even more accomplished. Throughout their collegiate careers, student-athletes encounter the same issues and hurdles as other students, but they are carrying the additional responsibilities of their sports.

Recognizing that physiological and emotional needs are interrelated, Jenny believes that student-athletes need support as they navigate their lives. When a student is unhappy or struggling with a difficult issue, the impact can manifest itself through weight-management problems, physical pain, sleeplessness, and many other ways. Conversely, a physical injury can cause emotional responses including depression, fear, or a drop in self-confidence. An athletic trainer is often the first individual who spots a problem. Jenny knew that she needed to construct something new that would treat the whole person.

Her vision led to the development of a unique program, Team ENHANCE, to help student-athletes with the nutritional, mental, and emotional aspects of performance. Team ENHANCE combines the resources of university staff, coaches, and medical experts from the community to offer comprehensive services. As Jenny explains, "When a student-athlete has an injury, the impact and rehabilitation process can affect her outlook and all the aspects of her college experience. Just as we need physical attention, emotional well-being and optimism can have significant impact on rehabilitation. Team ENHANCE enables us to provide comprehensive care."

Of all the endeavors she has spearheaded, Jenny is most proud of Team ENHANCE. The program has seen meaningful results and has become a prototype for similar services throughout the nation. Lady Vol Sarah Fekete found that Team ENHANCE played a significant role in her return to the softball field after an injury:

I had some very serious injuries, and I found help through Team ENHANCE. You deal with different issues as a student-athlete. There are specific issues that go along with sports like fear of failure, strength conditioning, and about how hard it is mentally and emotionally. If you have a problem and don't know how to deal with it, the problem just escalates. It can be difficult for student-athletes to talk with a coach or teammate about these issues.

Head Golf Coach Judi Pavon recognizes that Team ENHANCE is an essential component of student-athlete care:

Jenny works tirelessly to keep all student-athletes performing at the highest levels. She is an expert in her field and has surrounded herself with a capable staff to assure top-quality care for all sports. She not only cares for the physical well-being of the student-athletes, but also for the mental and emo-

tional sides. I think her efforts have really helped elevate performance of all Lady Vol sports at Tennessee.

What does it mean to be one of the best? Angela Kelly, head soccer coach, believes that it means passion:

Jenny is an inspiration to us all, and is so passionate about the complete student-athlete, her health, well-being, and development into a healthy, confident young lady. She is on the cutting edge of her profession, and we are all, as Lady Vols, so fortunate to have her with us at Tennessee.

Danielle Donehew, former assistant director of women's athletics for basketball operations and currently executive vice president of the WNBA's Atlanta Dream, suggests that the best means innovation and competence:

Jenny is always on the forefront of medical support for student-athletes. Her hard work, dedication, professionalism, and thoroughness are top-rate. The quality of medical care for every student-athlete at the University of Tennessee is exceptional because of the athletic training program that Jenny has built.

Clearly, the best means Jenny Moshak.

When Jenny was in high school, one of her friends had a foot injury that affected her ability to compete in sports. The care and healing of the injury was difficult, and Jenny saw firsthand the challenges and frustrations that her friend experienced.

When a student-athlete has an injury, the impact and rehabilitation process can affect her outlook and all the aspects of her college experience. Just as we need physical attention, emotional well-being and optimism can have significant impact on rehabilitation.

She decided then that she would pursue a career in sports medicine and athletic training. After completing undergraduate study in physical education with a coaching emphasis and minors in athletic training and health education at Western Michigan University, Jenny completed a master of science degree in exercise physiology at the University of Tennessee. During her graduate study she was a graduate assistant, serving as assistant athletics trainer for the Lady Vols. She has worked with athletes throughout the United States and the world. In 1989 she joined the University of Tennessee Women's Intercollegiate Athletics Department as head athletic trainer.

Jenny Moshak gives complete dedication to everything she does, all the time, with every individual. She inspires, encourages, challenges, and listens with a genuine desire to make a difference. She is a Tennessee Original.

"Beyond the Win"

Women of Purpose

In her first book, *Reach for the Summitt* (1988), Pat Summitt relates stories of games and victories. The pages are filled with remarkable accomplishments of student-athletes and their coaches. Summitt concludes with the insight that while victories are special, what we do "beyond the win" points to the true significance of our experiences. That is what really defines the champion. The Lady Volunteer tradition has remained focused on values set more than thirty years ago. The pride and passion of the women who have cared for this legacy are the essence of the "Beyond the Win" experience. Lady Volunteers have honored their predecessors, treasured the tradition, and passed it on to the next generations. They have gone "beyond the win" with honor, gratitude, and humility.

The Lady Volunteer history tells stories of determination, persistence, and dedication. Women who had vision, dreams, and purpose have challenged every woman to step forward and put her own special signature on this world. With each class comes another generation to add to the legacy.

Pat Summitt
The Tallest Summitt

In 2002 Tonya Hinch, executive vice president of operations for Edison Schools, pulled her car to the side of the airport terminal and opened the door for Pat Riley, coach of the Miami Heat and former coach of the Los Angeles Lakers. They were headed to a national education conference, and Riley, the keynote speaker, was given the charge to motivate, energize, and inspire over one hundred school principals who were struggling with impoverished, low-performing public schools. As they discussed the meeting ahead of them, Tonya smiled and said, "You know, you were my second choice for a speaker." Coach Riley turned sharply and asked, "Who was your first choice?" Tonya replied, "Pat Summitt, but her schedule was already full." Riley chuckled and said, "She would have been a fantastic choice!"

Pat Summitt is extraordinary. Her accomplishments are astounding; her accolades endless. She has met four US presidents and is a household name throughout the nation, perhaps even the world. This Tennessee favorite garners fierce loyalty from fans and absolute respect from those in the sports industry and wider business arena. She receives a seemingly endless number of requests for her time, attention, and talents. Amidst all the demands, she always has time for her extended Tennessee family. Her successes are clear by any measure—winning seasons, National Championships, total game wins, trophies, and awards. But Pat Summitt measures her successes one person at a time, by the young women who allow her to enter their lives, discover their best, and believe they can be even better.

Coach Pat Summitt celebrates her Lady Vols' seventh NCAA basketball championship title, 2007.

Pat in Her Own Words

I started playing basketball in the third grade. We were at recess and the principal, Mr. Davis, came out and said he wanted me to stay after school. He coached the team. That was the sport my brothers played. We had a basketball goal in the hay loft, and that's what we did after we finished all our chores or homework at night. We had lights up and would go play. For me, that was the game that I just fell in love with. I don't know why—I mean, I played softball in college, and I played some volleyball. But the one constant sport in my life was basketball. I just really enjoyed it more than any other sport. As an "up-and-down" game it was exciting. I played the half-court style for a while. I primarily played on the offensive end at that time.

And then, having the chance to play USA Basketball and go to the World University Basketball Games in 1973 was great. That's when I dislocated my jaw. That was pretty traumatic, being that far from home, and I remember going to the hospital on Sunday, and the hospital was closed. They didn't take emergency patients. So some USA doctors actually put their thumbs in the back of my mouth and popped my jaw back in and told me to have it checked when I returned home. I lost fifteen pounds on that trip before I came home. I got home early and knocked on the door. When my mother opened the door and saw me, she just started crying. She couldn't believe her little girl looked like that. She didn't know about my jaw. Back then you didn't have cell phones and calling home from Russia wasn't an option. So, I just made it through and went home.

NCAA national championship banners mark the Lady Vol basketball legacy in Thompson Boling Assembly Center and Arena.

What was your first year at Tennessee like, and how have you grown?

It was the 1970s. I was just finishing undergraduate college days and getting started in my career. The first year I coached at the University of Tennessee, my initial goal was to get student-athletes on campus to try out. I knew the team the year before I started had an undefeated season. They were good. I had gone up to watch them at James Madison when they played in the regionals. But I just wanted to see what would result from open tryouts. We wanted to try to see if we could get some other players. Girls' basketball in the state of Tennessee was basically very sound. It had been for years. I was hopeful that we might recruit some people that would walk on. We had some people come in and help us. It really wasn't even recruiting. They were students already in school here.

I still remember because of my age (twenty-two) being so close to the age of our seniors who were twenty-one that I really was conscious about gaining and maintaining the respect of the student-athletes. I was still competing but I never wanted them to see

than 40 depends on the team. Each year the team is going to be a team different from the year before. They may be stronger in certain areas and not as equipped in certain areas. And so I think you have to be realistic as a coach and coaching staff to say, "Here is what we want from you individually, and here is what we want from the team collectively."

And I have learned over my career that it works better if it is their idea. If you have goals but if you, the coach, are gathering information from the team, getting their feedback as to what they think they should do about their shooting percentage, about their defense, when it is their idea, it works better. Then you can always turn it back to them and hold them accountable. We didn't set these goals; you set these goals. It is your team. And when a team takes that kind of ownership, it just works much more efficiently. It is so much better—because they put their footprint on it.

That is something I have learned over the years. At first I think it was my way or the highway. I was still trying to establish who I was as a coach. I knew I was a disciplinarian. I always have been a disciplinarian, but I wanted to always be fair. I think you have to be fair, firm, but consistent. That was the approach I took.

I have been really fortunate because I have been able to learn from so many people and then establish my own philosophy. You know, you can gather a lot of information, no matter what profession you are in from some of the top in the profession. But then you have to do what you are comfortable with and what fits the people you are working with. Just being around people that could break down the game from the team concept

me as a player. And I never played in front of the student-athletes I coached. I would go quietly at night to the PE building and play with a bunch of guys.

The late 1970s period was a great turning point for us. We were gaining commitment on behalf of the administration and beginning a time when we certainly started to be able to recruit. In 1982, when the NCAA took over, it was the defining moment for women's athletics from a competitive championship opportunity. That gave women's athletics instant credibility and national exposure. And so the resources were put in place

throughout the country, although some at a different level.

Now our goal every year is to win a National Championship. But I didn't start out that way. At first the goal was to build a successful team. And then our goals focused to what we wanted to do on the offensive end and the defensive end. Something that you can measure statistically is good for our team rather than just stating the big goal of winning the national championship.

Whether you define your goals to out-rebound your opponents by plus-10 or hold them to a field goal shooting percent of less

Left: Coach Summitt and Lady Vol Kara Lawson discuss strategy courtside. Right: Coach Summitt consults with Lady Vol Sidney Spencer.

to the fundamental aspects of it helped me gain more confidence over time. That expanded my knowledge.

Whom do you especially admire?

I admire great teachers. I had some great teachers and some who were not into it—what a difference. As a teacher or coach you try to reach every person. There is a variety of personalities, and you don't reach every person. There have been players who have come and gone, and I never felt that I got the most out of them. And I think that is my job. But for the most part I think when our student-athletes leave here, they are confident young women. And they know the game

of basketball. But they have also learned a lot about the game of life. And so it is an incredible platform. And I feel incredibly blessed to be able to work with these young women. Because, let's face it, we live in a male-dominated world. And I was dominated by three older brothers. But it has been a joy for me to see young women mature and leave here and have that feeling that they can do whatever they choose. [Lady Volunteers have graduated to continued successes in many professions. In the sports field alone, Pat Summitt has produced media professionals, coaches, athletic program administrators, Olympians, and professional players throughout the world. In 2008 all five graduating seniors were draft picks for the WNBA.]

You seem so tuned in to each individual player on the team. How do you know just how to motivate each one?

To reach every person, I think you have to make the effort to get to know each individual that you are working with, whether it is your assistants, your managers, or your student-athletes. One incredible tool has been the personality profiles instrument. That helps me more on the court than off the court. It can help you off the court if you are trying to dial someone up or calm them down. But it tells you a lot about where their strengths are—and what motivates them, how competitive they are. If they are not that competitive, how are you going to dial them up and get them to play at a different level? And if you know what really motivates them, then that is the key.

Interacting with the team, on and off the court, gives me a better gauge—from the beginning of the year until the end of the year. I learn to recognize attitudes and character traits in each student-athlete. This year [2007] when watching some of the playoff games, I noticed that I was very patient with Shannon Bobbitt. But the reason I was very patient with Shannon was that she is one of the most coachable players. She is like a sponge. She wants to soak it all up, and to me she is one of the most special point guards we have had. We have had some good ones, of course—Holly Warlick and Kellie Jolly, two great ones. When Dena Head and Tonya Edwards were here—you think about those teams that won championships. But for Shannon to come in here from a junior college, have the confidence, want the communication, and want the feedback that allowed her and us to be very successful. I never felt that she was one of those players who are insecure or defensive. Student-athletes can be defensive. It is hard for them to open their minds and really listen and take in your message. I was calm with her but at the same time I think I challenged this team. They were not the kind of team that you had to ride, because they were motivated. With a few exceptions, every day I would go in and see Nicky Anosike and Alexis [Hornbuckle] picking up and providing leadership and everyone else following along. It was a team with whom I enjoyed the journey so much. I can't remember when I enjoyed a team like that.

The Lady Volunteer basketball team celebrates their 2007 NCAA National Championship Title in Quicken Loans Arena, Cleveland, Ohio. The team included (seated, left to right) Dominique Redding, Sidney Spencer, (second row, left to right) Elizabeth Curry, Cait McMahan, Shannon Bobbitt, (third row, left to right) Assistant Coach Dean Lockwood, Assistant Coach Nikki Caldwell, Nicky Anosike, Alberta Auguste, Alexis Hornbuckle, (fourth row, left to right) Alex Fuller, Candace Parker, Head Coach Pat Summitt, and Associate Head Coach Holly Warlick.

Do you believe that today's collegiate student-athletes appreciate how far women have come in sports?

Do they realize the value of everything they are given? You know, sometimes when these kids have had so much, I think they do take things for granted. But I think it depends so much on the backgrounds of these young women. Some of them grew up in more of a challenging environment. Not many of them had a silver spoon in their mouth. So for the most part, they appreciate it. And you don't want them to take it for granted. And sometimes you have to remind them.

But most of these young women understand and appreciate what they have.

What do student-athletes' parents expect?

The one thing that parents know is that I am going to care about their daughters—on and off the court. And I am here for them 24/7. I feel a tremendous responsibility for their well-being, their successes or failures. I know you can't reach all the people all the time but you keep trying. I try and establish our policies. I don't think they are unrealistic. Class attendance is mandatory, and they are required to sit in the front three rows in class. I think they eventually realize that this is good for them. They do pay attention. The professors know who they are. If they are not in class, it should be only because we are on a road trip.

Your ability to change with the times and varying natures of generations of players is a real strength. Many people resist change. You seem to embrace it.

I think if you are secure with who you are and if you also trust the people that you work with, change is easier. For example, if my assistants tell me that I need to back off here, or I am being too tough on this particular player, or we need to shorten our practices, I'm not saying that 100 percent of the time that I am going to do it, but I do want to listen. And most of the time I am going to do what they ask me to do.

I trusted this team this year [2006–07]. I gave this team more days off and shorter practices because they went after it. We only had ten players. So, am I willing to adapt in that situation? Absolutely, I am.

I don't think you could have a game plan and go in a game and then when something happens that doesn't fit your game plan, be too stubborn to change. The same is true day to day. You may have a practice; you may have everything mapped out for the week. We may go to play at LSU, and I intended to come back and practice the next day. And the players say, "Coach, we really need a day off." And I would say, "OK, but you better come back ready to go."

There are definitely times. The team told me in postseason that they wanted the day off

after we played. And I said, "You have to understand that I am concerned about our preparation." And they promised that they would be ready. And actually, that was between the Regionals and the Final Four. It wasn't necessarily a day that I wanted to give them off—because I wanted to taper the day before. But I just felt like this is a time in which if this is what they need, this is what we would give them.

People might resist change because they are set in their ways with their system. And it could be that they are inflexible. They are not willing to change. I think it is all about the team. You have to listen to your team.

Do you feel pressure to win?

I don't feel pressure to win for myself. A lot of people have asked me about this seventh Championship. My comment is that it is not about me winning seven. It is about it being the team's first. Maybe when I started out, I felt pressure because we had been to seven Final Fours and played in four Championships before we won one. [On April 6, 2008, the Lady Volunteer basketball team defeated Stanford University to win their eighth NCAA Championship Title.]

But the only reason I think we probably won one then was (1) because we had the talent to win, and (2) I had realized when Mickie DeMoss came in as our recruiting coordinator, that someday we were going to cut down the nets. And it just happened to be that year. So I think when you just focus on the end result, and you are not really focusing on the daily process and progress that you can make, you make a mistake.

How do you personally stay motivated?

I stay motivated because I love what I do. Teaching is my passion. Working with young women is my passion—seeing more in them than they see in themselves and trying to bring out the absolute best. And my absolute frustration is that I couldn't accomplish that with everyone.

I don't live in the past. I have thought from time to time back to the earlier teams that I coached. There were some players over the years that I was pretty tough on. And the people that I think I have been the toughest on were players that were stubborn and wouldn't totally commit and buy into the system.

The one thing I have done all my life is work. And that is all I know. And I just love it. And I am a high-energy kind of person. And when I try to work with someone who has a low work ethic, and they are low energy, that is a huge misfit.

What do you think is special about the University of Tennessee women's athletic program?

Because of the exposure and the attention on women's basketball over the years, with all of the TV games, I feel that we are a program that people recognize. And obviously now, you look across the board, and other programs are gaining national exposure.

Through the years I've just wanted to see us build the best women's athletics program in the country. We have a commitment from the president right on down. The university has stepped up from a budget standpoint to support women's athletics. We are a role-

The Lady Vol 2007 NCAA National Championship basketball team is honored by President George W. Bush at the White House, September 21, 2007.

model program. We have expanded our sports. We have brought in coaches across the board who are secure in themselves—and inspired by the success of our program. They know that if we can do it in basketball, we can do it in every sport.

What do you do right before a game?

Before each game, I usually get a thirty-minute massage. And I take a short nap. I really am a nap person. Before the North Carolina game in the Final Four [2007], I slept two and a half hours. I couldn't believe it. Before the Rutgers game I slept two hours. Before a big game, I can go in and

typically sleep thirty minutes to an hour. But before those two games, obviously, I was wound up. I had been watching films late at night and getting up early to watch film. But I felt so much more refreshed and ready to go in those two games. I am lucky in that regard.

Tell us a defining moment for Tennessee.

The defining moment for Tennessee was in 1987, winning our first Championship in Austin, Texas. We had been knocking on the door for years. Everybody across the country knew the Lady Vols, but I don't think they knew that we were here to stay.

What is your favorite memory?

My first favorite memory is the birth of my son, Tyler. Aside from that time, I would say it was the first National Championship.

Winning the Olympic gold medal in 1984 was big because I felt an enormous amount of responsibility and pressure to win in Los Angeles. Obviously, when we won the gold medal game it was really something. It was a very special moment. It was special when we won in 1976, when I was co-captain, and to be a part of history as the first women's Olympic Team for basketball.

Do you have a funny story?

One summer we came back for the start of school. I was walking through the hall and noticed a student-athlete. I challenged this young student-athlete. She looked like she was not in shape and had not worked hard. And it turned out she wasn't a player; she was a manager. And we got into the team room, and she started talking about what she did over the summer. And she said, "I'm a manager, I think." But she looked so much like this girl who had walked on. And I just blew it. That was the early 1980s. I just thought, "I am losing my mind."

What is your most unexpected result?

I would say that the loss to Michigan State in Indianapolis [NCAA Final Four, 2005] was one that has really stuck with me for a long time because we blew an 18-point lead. I can't remember another situation in a Final Four where we have just fallen apart.

Left: Bruce Pearl, head coach of men's basketball, shows his colors at the Lady Vols game against rival Duke, January 22, 2007. Right: "Pat's Payback": Coach Pat Summitt leads the cheering section in an enthusiastic chorus of "Rocky Top" during the Tennessee men's game with Florida, February 27, 2007. Providing extra support are Holly Warlick, associate head coach, and assistant coaches Nikki Caldwell and Dean Lockwood.

The "Rock," a well-known landmark on the University of Tennessee campus, displays the sentiment of Lady Vol fans.

Of all the Championship games that we have lost, I would say that was the one hurt more than any other. Having two players from Indiana probably added pressure for everyone.

What have been some of your life lessons?

I think there have been many situations where I have learned. The players have taught me a lot of life lessons. With Michelle Marciniak, the lesson was "less is more" . . . back off. Sometimes the people who appear to be the most confident can be the most fragile. And I think in that situation I needed to give her more positive feedback. I was tough on her. And I was tough on Holly Warlick. I think you expect a lot more from your point guard. They are like your quarterback. But the lesson is knowing when to step away. To learn that this is not working, now try Plan B.

What about the Lady Volunteer tradition is so special?

I'm proud of the Lady Volunteer tradition. It is more than just basketball. This logo is known around the world. I think in the sport of basketball right now with all the wins and the championships and the high-profile players, this program is as respected as any in the history of the game. But the success and the success of the student-athletes and the teams and the longevity—that is why people recognize our place in history.

And we're not done. I see women's athletics here across the board becoming the most successful program and maintaining that. I

Coach Pat Summitt and Candace Parker discuss strategy.

really do. I see it as a role-model program. There are always hurdles. I think we have just got to continue to promote and market our product. Obviously, revenue is always a concern. We have to continue to generate revenue. Our ticket is not that of men's football or basketball. But hopefully we can continue and put out a great product and hopefully generate more revenue year in and year out and get our other sports to do the same.

How do you want to be remembered?

I want to be remembered as a good mother to my son, Tyler. And I want to be remembered as someone who made a difference for young women.

And your message to young women today?

You can be whatever you want to be. You have to have vision. You have to have goals. And you have to be willing to work hard to reach those goals. But don't let anyone tell you that you can't do something. The mind is incredibly powerful. And the passion for something is a way to make a difference. If you are passionate about something and you've got that vision, then pursue it. Go for it. Don't let the fear of failure keep you from being successful. A lot of people don't try because they think, "If I don't make it, I'll be considered a failure or a loser." Stick your neck out. Have the courage to compete.

What Others Say

Tamika Catchings (Lady Vol, 1997–2001; professional, WNBA): What can I say about Pat??? Everyone on the outside sees one thing, but when you get up close and personal with her, there's not a negative thing about her. Yes, Pat is intense and sometimes can look like she's burning a hole through someone just by that single glare, but it's only because she loved each and every one of us and knew what we were capable of. To this day Pat and I still speak, and it's amazing how much I have taken away from my days at UT. She taught us more than just basketball and how to become better players. She taught us about being women and about taking care of ourselves, about responsibilities and consequences. She taught us more things than we thought we were learning while we were there in college. But I sit back and look at all of the wonderful things that

she has added to my life, and I thank God every day for putting her in my life!

Candace Parker (Lady Vol, 2004–2008; professional, WNBA): Everybody knows Coach Summitt as the head coach of women's basketball. And a lot of people ask, "Is she mean?" She is intense on the court. Is she mean? No. She expects greatness out of you and will accept nothing less. However, many don't see the side of her where her door is always open. She is always going to be there. Whatever you are going through, her door is always open. She is like our mom, and I love her to death. She is a very special and influential person in my life.

Billie Moore (coach of the first U.S. Olympic Women's Basketball Team, 1976, and first

women's coach to lead two different schools to National Championships: California State–Fullerton, 1970, and UCLA, 1978): Pat stands out certainly for what she has accomplished—her record is likely one that won't be broken. She started out so young in coaching. What really makes her great is the way she has done it—within the rules, always taking care of her student-athletes, and never compromising principles and integrity. I think of her as I think of John Wooden—a great role model professionally. They have put themselves in a profession that very few individuals experience. I think that people see Pat from the outside as a kind, nice person. On the inside, she is the person that we hope she is. Pat genuinely cares as much today about the single, individual fan as she did when the fans

numbered under four hundred. She has not changed her values and character. She is the ultimate professional.

A defining moment: the Lady Volunteer basketball team defeats Louisiana Tech to win their first NCAA National Championship Title on March 29, 1987.

Joan Cronan
The Pride, Passion, and People

Joan Cronan decided that she wanted to make the world a different place for women's athletics, and her stunning works speak to her achievement. What is especially amazing is that she recognized her destiny at the young age of twelve.

"I grew up in Louisiana in a house that was right next to the city park," she says. "When I was twelve years old, I went to try out for Little League, and they said 'no girls allowed.' And it made me mad. And I was as good as all the other little boys, and they wouldn't let me try out. So I really knew from that time on exactly what I wanted to do."

Cronan's first experience as a Lady Volunteer came when she served as head basketball coach (1969–70) while her husband Tom was completing graduate study. Coach Cronan led her team to an alternate berth in the first-ever National Invitational Collegiate Basketball Tournament. She remembers:

That time of life was exciting. I had a mission, and I had a goal, but I was really green. We came to Tennessee for Tom to get his doctorate. I simply wrote a letter saying that I would like to teach and coach women's basketball. My résumé was very short because I was twenty-three years old. I had coached one-half year of high school basketball (to win the state title), and I had coached volleyball, basketball, and tennis for one year at Northwestern Louisiana University. I had my master's degree. The College of Education wrote back to say that I was hired to teach full-time and coach

Joan Cronan's leadership has brought the Tennessee Lady Volunteer program to national prominence in eleven intercollegiate sports

women's basketball. I think I made $3,600 that year coaching and teaching a full load in the physical education department. I was low on seniority, so I taught a lot of bowling, tennis, and fitness fundamentals. That was my agenda. But it was an exciting time.

In 1969 women's sports were still organized as clubs. Joan experienced support for women's athletics but knew the program could be greater. "Helen Watson was very supportive," she says. "To me she was a very classy lady. Actually basketball was a club sport then, and we worked out of the intramural sports clubs. They had played just two games the year before I came here. I am too competitive to settle for that, so we expanded our schedule. Nancy Lay turned into a huge supporter but wanted women's athletics to stay under the physical education model. I knew I had a little work to do. My vision was that one day we would have a collegiate state winner. And to see what has happened thirty years later is just unbelievable."

Joan continued teaching for two more years but stepped away from coaching to give time to her small children. After Tom completed his doctorate, they moved to Charleston, South Carolina, where Tom accepted a position at the Citadel. Joan still had her dream. The next year she went to the College of Charleston and knocked on the door of the president. She told him that they needed to have a women's athletics program. He readily agreed and informed her that she could coach volleyball, basketball, tennis, and serve as the athletics director. In 1981 the College of Charleston was selected as the number-one women's athletics program in the country by the American Women's Sports Foundation.

It was a visit from Pat Summitt and the urging of her husband that convinced Joan to agree to be a candidate for the director's position at the University of Tennessee. She says

Pat had come into Charleston to recruit a student-athlete, and we had gone to lunch. She said, "The AD position is open at UT. Why don't you apply?" We were really happy in Charleston. We discussed it as a family, and I decided I would throw my name in

the hat. I give Tom credit for that because he kept saying, "You have got to go and make a difference in women's athletics. You can make it better from the platform at Tennessee than you can at Charleston." I love Charleston. It will always be near and dear to my heart. Tennessee just offered a bigger platform. So I applied, interviewed, and they offered me the job. I remember taking about a three-mile walk because it was

affecting more than just me. It was affecting Tom's job and the kids. We were very fortunate that Tom had a sabbatical from the Citadel the next year. The College of Charleston said to go try and see if I like it. And if I didn't, they would have me back. And so it was as if God said it was OK to go. I told Dr. Boling that we came here with the notion that we were going to stay. And twenty-four years later, it has worked out pretty well.

Joan Cronan became the director of women's intercollegiate athletics in May 1983. Gloria Ray had laid a strong first foundation and established a community presence for the Lady Volunteers. The early years had focused on hiring coaches, gaining funding for scholarships, and expanding com-

petition. Progress had been made. Joan identified her first goal to strengthen the internal support staff and then to step up the presence of Tennessee women's athletics in the community.

"We had very few support staff," Joan recalls. "The salaries were substandard. When you are building a corporation you have to take care of the people. So that was my first charge—to get everybody's salary

> I knew I had a little work to do. My vision was that one day we would have a collegiate state winner. And to see what has happened thirty years later is just unbelievable.

to a competitive level for that time. Then the next charge was to reach out to the community and let them know who we were, what we were doing, and what we wanted to do. I made a commitment that I wasn't going to add any more sports until we were funded in the top ten in the country in all of the sports that we had. We had a dream, and I knew we could have a strong national presence."

Joan Cronan's vision became a shared vision as she began to speak throughout the community and show her genuine commitment to women's athletics. Her sound stewardship of resources and firm belief in future growth drew support and gained attention. The university administration had supported the early women's athletics initiatives. Now they were even more visibly involved. "I give a lot of success of our program to the administrators," Joan says. "There aren't many programs where fans in the stands include the current president and three presidents emeritus who all truly care about you. It is not just that they feel like they have to be there. They really love the Lady Volunteer program."

The University of Tennessee Women's Intercollegiate Athletics Department is one of only two in the nation that function separately from the men's department. Cronan has seen the benefits of this organization:

This structure has afforded the opportunity to be a model. There are many wonderful senior women's administrators at other institutions, but there is a difference in my opportunity in reporting to the president. I didn't think it would happen in my lifetime. It is happening now, and that is significant.

I have always liked our structure. I have liked the opportunity that Tennessee gave me. I have had opportunities to look into jobs where I would be the athletics director over men and women, but always felt that this is my calling; this was my goal.

I am most aware of the separate structure when I see the perspective through others. I see it when the coach is recruiting the student-athlete. They are talking about the advantages, the strength of commitment to the women here, the separate weight rooms, athletic trainers, and all the other components of the student-athlete's daily life. I hear it in the exit interviews of graduating Lady Vols who realize the advantages they saw as directly related to being separate from the men.

To have this structure and be successful, I think you need three things: (1) you

The 2006 Lady Vol softball team brought Tennessee even closer to a National Championship at the Women's College World Series.

need to work together and like each other; (2) you need to be efficient and effective; (3) you need to win and to make money. And if we can do that, I think this structure is very good. I think the more things we can do efficiently and effectively, the better off we are going to be.

Joan Cronan leads according to management consultant Tom Peter's principle of "wandering around." She hires great people, clears the way for them to workand trusts them to do great work. She is always learning, always growing, and always showing her appreciation and gratitude for every single person. One Lady Volunteer softball player, Sarah Fekete, expresses the views of many

in her assessment of Joan: "We call Joan 'the Mayor.' She is everywhere. I know she has so many obligations, but she always finds time to go to our games. Then she will go to rowing and tennis and soccer. That says a lot about how she respects us and why we respect the program. She is there for us."

Joan recognizes the ways that everyone in the program is interconnected. She sees her role as one who supports the success of the people that she serves:

Everybody has their responsibilities, and they are accountable. I think that is important. But as far as the coaches, I never feel that I need to put pressure on them because they are already so competitive. So it is my job to make their job the best it can be to make the student-athletes' experiences the best they can be. So we go about that every day. When I hire coaches, I tell them we are going to do everything we can do, and we are going to say "no" sometimes; or we are going to say, "Wait, but you know we are going to do everything we can do to support you."

Rob Patrick, head volleyball coach, draws encouragement from Cronan's leadership style. "I can never thank her enough for giving me the opportunity to join the Lady Vol family and be a part of such an incredible athletic department," Rob says. "Joan trusts her coaches, and she allows me to manage the volleyball program the best way that I see fit. The one thing that becomes evident once you get to know her is that she is as competitive a person as anyone that I have met—Joan hates to lose."

When student-athletes come to the University on their recruiting visits, a meeting with Joan is always on the agenda. Joan always requests for each one to ask her a question. The questions vary from serious to outrageous. "It is fun to hear what they come up with," she says. "One of the most unique questions for me was, 'Why wouldn't I come to Tennessee?' My answer was, 'One, if you don't like orange (but it is a good fashion color these days); two, if you don't want to work hard, because our goals are very high (the only place in which success comes before work is in the dictionary); and three, if you don't want to take the responsibility that goes with being very visible.' Luke 12:48 is my favorite Bible verse. It says 'to whom much is given, much is expected.'"

Smokey, the Tennessee mascot, relaxes with the Lady Vol swimming and diving team following a community service event.

Joan is frequently asked what she likes most about her job. She responds that meeting with recruits, enrolling them, and then watching them mature over the next four years is what is most amazing.

Joan stresses to staff and student-athletes always to remember the significance of representing the University of Tennessee. Lady Volunteers carry an allegiance to integrity, honor, pride, and passion. Current student-athletes keep these values in the forefront for four years and then pass the legacy on to the next freshman group. "Just recently I sat at the all-sports banquet and watched the leadership of our student-athletes," she remarks. "It made me as proud as winning any game."

Fans love the Lady Volunteers. From the first small core of backers to sell-out crowds, the programs have grown well into a community of pride. Winning programs grabbed the headlines, and Joan Cronan grabbed hearts. At any given Lady Volunteer event, Cronan is always on the move, always on her feet, greeting and thanking fans. She says:

The loyalty of Lady Vol fans is unique. They really do consider themselves a part of our family. When we were recruiting Candace Parker, I asked her why she would get excited about committing to Tennessee. She said, "Where else in America would they be scalping tickets outside the arena?" It's the loyalty.

Joan Cronan and Pat Summitt enjoy a moment with Lady Vol supporters: Kathy Bolze (center) and her daughters, Angela Kauffman (left) and Valerie Kauffman (right).

And it just didn't happen overnight. We continually reach out to the community. We meet with civic organizations, partner for community service, and do all we can to involve the fans. We are truly a Lady Volunteer community.

We never want to forget who got us here. It rained last week, and we couldn't play softball. The Lady Vols stayed and signed autographs because the fans were there. And to me that was reaching out. We could have just told everyone to go home.

When asked to identify her favorite sport, Joan is quick to say, "whatever is in season." Her reply may seem evasive, but Joan's enthusiastic presence at every event, her unbending support of her coaches, and her strong

message of Lady Volunteer Pride leave no doubt of her sincerity. Joan Cronan's scrapbooks of memories could fill a library. Some moments are special standouts:

Winning the first National Championship [1987] in basketball has to be one of the most special because it was something that we had come so close to for so many years.

At the Final Four games, televisions in the arena lobby areas show the history of past games. Tom and I were in a lot of those pictures, and that was really special to us. It is hard not to think about the trips to the White House. Those have been very special.

I am proud of raising the funds to endow a golf program. That was huge.

I will always treasure our first trip to the Women's College World Series in softball.

The 2005 volleyball team trip to the Final Four was incredible. The National Championship in Indoor Track and Field made 2005 a banner year, and the tennis team generated excitement with a great 2008 season, advancing to the Final Four.

And I am so proud of the great progress and championship spirit that we see in soccer, rowing, outdoor track and field/cross country, diving, swimming—and most of all I am proud of the Lady Vols who carry with them the determination to go to the next level. They are all inspiring. Watching the student-athletes grow—to go to their weddings, see them have babies—the maturity that comes. Nothing thrills me more than

The 2005 volleyball team made Lady Vol history as finalists at the NCAA Final Four tournament. Pictured here are (back row, left to right) Assistant Coach Mike Minnis, Assistant Coach Cindy Noble, Milan Clarke, Amy Morris, Heather Harrington, Kristen Andre, Sarah Blum, Jackie Ramsdale, Kelsey Fautsch, Head Coach Rob Patrick, (bottom left, upper row) Mindy Flynn, Lauren LaFlamme, (bottom left, lower row) Annie Sadowski, Chelsea Noble, (bottom right, left to right) Julie Knytych, Yuliya Stoyanova, Joselyn Johnson, and Jasmine Fullove.

Regular-Season Crowns, and nineteen SEC Tournament Championships. Cronan was the National Association of Collegiate Women Athletics Administrators Athletic Director of the Year in 2005, inducted into the Fellowship of Christian Athletes Hall of Champions, the LSU Alumni Hall of Distinction, the College of Charleston Hall of Fame, and the Tennessee Sports Hall of Fame. She has made a significant difference in women's athletics and a lasting imprint on women's abilities to go after their dreams.

What Others Say

Tracy Bonner Headecker (Lady Volunteer, 1993–97; cast member, Cirque du Soleil): During my year of being recruited, the athletics director could still make home visits. She came to my house to recruit me. She is a special part of why I came to Tennessee. We always joked that I was going to take her job one day—I used to say, "That sounds like a fun job. I think I would like to do that some day—maybe not your job, but on your staff."

Pat Summitt (head basketball coach): Joan is what I call a mover and a shaker. She loves to be out in the community. Her PR skills are tremendous. She is well respected nationally for her leadership in women's athletics. She is a great role model for us and for the university. She has done her best to provide for all of us the resources we need—obviously depending on the budget. She has a tremendous influence on this community in its attitude toward the Lady Vols. She has been out and talked and sold Lady Vol athletics with great passion.

to have a call from a former student-athlete, and she says, "Joan, I am applying for a job. Would you make a call for me?" That is a neat thing to be able to do.

Family has always been important to me, and I guess what has been nice is that we have been able to make our family part of the Lady Vol family. I remember when the kids were in middle school, and they said, "Mom, we don't take a vacation like other kids do." And I said, "Let's talk about where we have been—Europe and the Olympics and a lot of wonderful places." So to be able to have a family that could grow through Lady Vol experiences has been very good. And now it is fun to call my grandsons and granddaughters and say, "Let's go to the Final Four!"

When I think of all the memories, I so appreciate the donors who have really meant something to the program. They have given and given and given. Some people spend a large portion of their income supporting us. And we appreciate that. We appreciate everyone who generously gives in all the ways that they do.

Joan Cronan inspires individuals to join the Lady Volunteer family. She upholds the priorities and values of the program. The student-athletes who become Lady Volunteers learn the importance of hard work, the honor of tradition, and the strength of education. Rarely does a twelve-year-old child truly recognize her vision. Rarer still is the one who grows up to achieve it. Under Joan's watch (and as of spring 2008), the Lady Volunteers have won nine NCAA Titles, had forty-four top-five NCAA Finishes, seventy-four top-ten NCAA Finishes, twenty-seven SEC

let me know about it! She represents the Lady Volunteer athletic department with constant class and tons of energy.

Deb Dyer Handy (Lady Vol student-athlete, 1967–68): Joan is one of the special people that I hold as a role model. She is always willing to give her time and believes in encouraging. She lives the positive, reinforcing a positive belief in the human spirit. She equally supports all. I am so proud to know Joan Cronan.

Tamika Catchings (Lady Vol student-athlete, 1997–2001; professional, WNBA): Joan was always around to support us and to acknowledge all that we did on and off the court. She was part of our families just through her continued support and belief in the things some of us may or may not have thought possible.

Candace Parker (Lady Vol student-athlete, 2004–2008; professional, WNBA): Joan Cronan is very supportive of our program. She has been a huge part of the university's commitment to Lady Vol athletics. She is at all the events and cares about each of us as an individual.

Sonia Hahn-Patrick (co-head tennis coach): Joan has always instilled in us the resposibility to respect our student-athletes as someone else's children and to treat them as the young ladies that they are. She cares about the student-athletes as individuals, not just student-athletes.

Angela Kelly (head soccer coach): Joan Cronan is the ambassador of the University of Tennessee Women's Intercollegiate Athletics Department for nearly three decades. Her leadership and vision have been a catalyst in developing one of the top women's athletic departments in the country.

Judi Pavon (head golf coach): Joan Cronan and Lady Vol athletics go hand in hand. I can't think of a better representative to be out in the community to spread the word about women's sports at Tennessee. She is always supportive of the teams and coaches and has done a great job to put together such a strong department.

Carrie Cole (assistant golf coach and Lady Vol student-athlete, 1998–2002): On my recruiting trip to Tennessee I will never forget my meeting with Joan Cronan. She was my first encounter with a person overflowing with Tennessee pride and passion, and she

Ann Lee Sprouse (member of the 1969 Lady Vol basketball team coached by Joan Cronan): Joan's persistence, competitive nature, and positive outlook are daunting. She simply refuses to look at the negative. She has always had a vision of what women's athletics could be. She is grounded in a value system of honesty and integrity. She does the right things the right way.

A New Season

Considering the astounding accomplishments in women's athletics over the past thirty years, it is no wonder that change punctuates the momentum of today. The eighteen-to-twenty-two-year-old student-athlete of the twenty-first century has a life defined by features difficult for previous generations to grasp. Just think about it:

These young people have been sending email messages to their friends since the first grade.

This generation has never heard a busy signal on the telephone.

This generation has never bought a record or eight-track tape, and even a cassette recording is a brief memory.

The media cover virtually every sport, opening worlds of possibilities that previous generations might never have known.

Medical advances, research, and continued education are presenting more ways to strengthen, repair, and lengthen playing lives in sports.

Athletes are stronger, bigger, and faster than ever before.

It is another year, a new season. The student-athletes are expected to arrive by the end of the week. The sun is barely up, but the University of Tennessee women's athletics staff is already preparing for the day.

Pat Summitt steps onto the practice court of Pratt Pavilion and reviews her schedule for the first fall workout of her basketball team. On the other side of campus in Alumni

Head Coach Matt Kredich and Assistant Coach Jennifer Arndt cheer for their winning swimming team.

Memorial Building a faculty member drops her key and notices the old, wooden floorboards of a former time. For a moment she almost thinks she hears the bounce of a ball. Shaking her head, she enters her office and begins to prepare for her freshman class.

Angela Kelly unlocks the doors of Regal Soccer Stadium and begins to walk through the hallway lined with photographs celebrating the Lady Vols in action. When she reaches the end of the hallway, she hears a young voice calling. Turning quickly, she sees a young girl with a soccer ball. "Hey Coach, can I have your autograph?" Coach Kelly smiles, signs the ball, and the girl looks up and says, "I will be a Lady Volunteer someday."

J. J. Clark is sitting at his desk and jotting down training workouts for his teams. Cross Country competition is now upon them, and they spent the summer competing throughout the nation and Europe. The engraved sign in the name plate holder on his desk catches his eye: *I Conquer Circumstances.* For a moment he stops and feels the power of his father's words—his discipline, his persistence, his determination to overcome obstacles. Coach Clark moves his eyes to the photographs of his sisters, Joetta and Hazel, and his wife, Jearl—all Olympians. His thoughts turn to the Lady Vols and the moment in 2005 when Nicole Cook won the 800-meter run in a record time of 2:00.75 at the 2005 SEC Indoor Championships. The Lady Volunteers went on to win the Indoor National Title that year, and Clark received 2005 USTCA National Indoor, USTCA South Region Indoor, and SEC Indoor Coach of the Year honors. Clark turns back to his notes, smiles, and resumes writing.

Rob Patrick is searching intently in the storage area of Stokely Athletic Center. Back in California, Coach Patrick had started a career path that was another world from women's athletics. After college he had entered the real estate business and quickly excelled. Although financially solvent, he had known that something was missing. When Rob was fifteen years old, his father tragically died. At an early age Rob had learned the value of every day. He had found early success in a business career but felt no lasting satisfaction. Rob resigned his job, went to Stanford, and accepted a women's volleyball assistant coach position. It was a

Left: Sherri Parker Lee Stadium. Above (left to right): Jones Aquatic Center. Tennessee Boat House. Below (left to right): Pratt Pavilion Practice Facility. Goodfriend Tennis Center.

Tom Black Track/LaPorte Stadium, with its eight-lane Olympic-style oval, serves as a premier track and field venue.

major lifestyle change but exactly what he had needed. His journey brought him to the University of Tennessee, and as head volleyball coach he was motivated to build a winning program. Now with determination he moves volleyballs, boxes, and other sports materials, and suddenly a glitter catches his eye. He reaches down and pulls out a framed photograph of the Lady Volunteer Volleyball Team at the 2005 NCAA Final Four. Blowing off the dust, he smiles and carries the picture to his office. He places it on the corner of a shelf, gazes at it, and returns to work.

The water of the state-of-the-art swimming pool in Jones Aquatic Center is still. Head Swimming Coach Matt Kredich looks out over the pool, and the silence of the building stirs his excitement and expectations for the season. He thinks of swimmers he has known, his first few seasons with Tennessee, and the people who had come before him. Just yesterday he had told a friend how special it felt to coach the Lady Volunteers. They were stewards of tradition, and for him the pride translated to a deep sense of responsibility to teach student-athletes the

standards that others had set before them. Coach Kredich dives into the still water and swims a steady lap. He is ready.

Head Diving Coach Dave Parrington hears a splash in the pool and glances in to see his fellow coach moving through the water. Coach Parrington returns to his desk and considers the divers who would be arriving in a few short days. Water is in his blood. Parrington had grown up in Rhodesia, now known as Zimbabwe. His parents were swim coaches, and from the age of fourteen he had been teaching people how to dive. Over the

Left: Lady Vol track and field teammates April Thomas (left) and Shanna Dickenson (right) carry Coach J. J. Clark in celebration of their 2005 SEC Indoor Championship. Right: Head Coach Rob Patrick advises the volleyball team during a timeout.

years he had seen changes in female divers. They were now more athletic, dedicated, and much more powerful. The bar had definitely been raised, and his sense of competition was heightened by the challenge. Opening his email, Coach Parrington sees that he has a long list of messages. Sighing, he begins to scroll through the list. His eye catches a familiar name, and he clicks open the message. Tracy Bonner Headecker, his first Tennessee recruit, is sending a good luck note for the new season. "Are there some good prospects in the new class?" she wants to know. Coach Parrington smiles with anticipation and answers her note.

Co–Head Coaches Karen Weekly and Ralph Weekly are sitting in the common area of the softball offices and discussing their schedules for the upcoming weeks. The previous evening they had stopped by the Sherri Parker Lee Stadium. The lights were on, and when they stepped onto the field, they chat-

ted with excitement and anticipation of opening day. Driving home, they both had grown quiet, each lost in thoughts and memories of players past. The pitching mound, each base, and the field had brought images of eager, determined young women—women who had been intent on building a dynasty. And in a very short time they had done so. The coaches stop for a moment as they review their plans. They look at each other, smile, and nod. It's time to play ball.

The Goodfriend Indoor Tennis Courts are silent. Co–Head Coaches Sonia Hahn-Patrick and Mike Patrick are looking over their preparations for the tennis team. Everything is set: skills practice, workouts, match schedules. Sonia recalls her father's words to her when she was young and just entering the tennis world. He had just seen tennis legend Arthur Ashe win the US Open. "Sonia," he said, "you will never get a more equal opportunity than playing a sport, especially

in tennis." She draws in a breath and thinks about the impact that playing tennis has had on her life. Now they would be teaching others and hopefully the Lady Vols would see that tennis is a small window to life. The student-athletes arriving that week would be on the beginning of an incredible journey. Mike is asking her something. She brings her attention back to the present and asks, "What did you say?" He smiles and says, "It is going to be a fantastic year."

Head Golf Coach Judi Pavon hears knocking on the door. She closes her eyes and thinks, "I know that door is going to open." The women's golf program is relatively young, but with the financial foundations built by Ann Furrow and Joan Cronan, and the devoted leadership of first Head Coach Linda Franz (Sowers), the Lady Volunteers are strong. Coach Pavon thinks about Tennessee's first team—Katharina Larsson, Abby Pearson, Susan Conger, Shelley Kinder

(Anderson), Sofi Stromgren, and Angie Boyd (Keck), who works in the office just down the hall. That team was a little before Judi's time, but their stories and achievements were well known to her. "I know that door is going to open." Coach Pavon jumps with a start. Someone is knocking on her office door. She opens it to see a freshman golf student-athlete with a pile of suitcases behind her. "Coach Pavon? I am lost. I just arrived from the airport but have no idea where I am going." Judi Pavon reaches out to greet her first arrival and says, "I know where we are going. We are knocking on the doors of the top five golf teams in the country. Come on. I'll take you there."

The sun is just beginning to show over the Tennessee River. Heavy mist rises over the water, and Head Rowing Coach Lisa Glenn is standing on the balcony of the University of Tennessee Boat House. She hears them before she sees them. The voices of young women singing grow louder and more distinct. Lisa peers into the distance and sees four boats moving swiftly and steadily through the currents. As the boats draw closer, she sees that the women are rowing and keeping together by the cadence of their song. Lisa smiles, remembering that singing used to be a regular custom in the time-honored sport. The boats are approaching now, and

Coach Glenn realizes with a start that the crews intend to disembark on the University of Tennessee dock. The Lady Volunteers are still a week from the start of their practices, but she begins to walk down to the dock to direct them to the public area. The rowing crews expertly maneuver their boats to the dock. One at a time, each rower steps onto the dock, and the sight stops Lisa sharp in her tracks. The women are wearing long dresses buttoned up to their necks, and high-topped buttoned shoes. They proceed up the dock and pass Coach Glenn without even a glance. The sun is getting higher now, and occasional car horns announce the busy morning traffic. The vision is quickly gone, and Coach Glenn turns from her spot on the balcony, enters her office, and prepares for a full day's work.

Inside McKenzie Lawson Athletic Center, the women's intercollegiate athletic staff members are seated at the conference table: Joan Cronan, Donna Thomas, Angie Boyd Keck, Jenny Moshak, Kathy Harston, Dara Worrell, Jimmy Delaney, Todd Dooley, and Debby Jennings. Someone knocks on the door. Joan looks around the table and asks, "Are we ready?" Everyone nods. Joan says, "Bring in the coaches. It's time to begin another Tennessee Lady Volunteer season."

It's time to begin another Tennessee Lady Volunteer season.

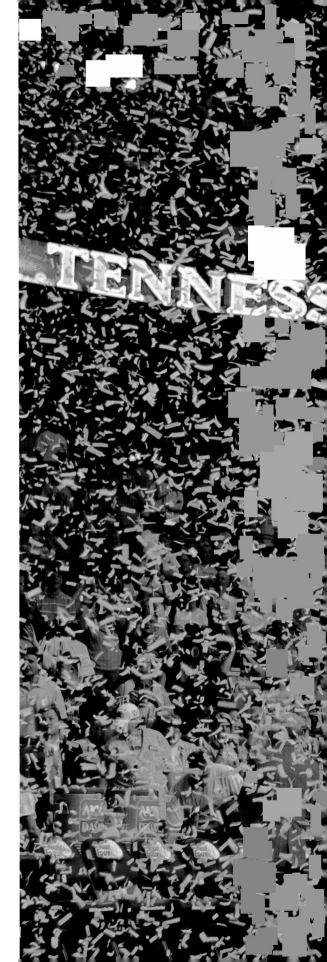

APPENDICES

Appendix 1

Task Force on Inter-collegiate Athletics for Women Recommendation Summary

Author's Note: The Task Force submitted its report to Chancellor Jack Reese on April 1, 1976. The files in the Special Collections Library at the University of Tennessee include this summary of recommendations. Additional pages and attachments referenced in the summary have not been located.

I-1. It is recommended that the following principles be considered basic to the intercollegiate athletics program for women and that the development of the program be measured against these:

1) The opportunity to participate in intercollegiate athletics is a desirable part of the student's total educational experience.

2) Esteemed values sought and achieved through men's athletic programs can also be sought and achieved through programs for women.

3) Intercollegiate athletics should be consistent with the educational commitments of this institution. If campus choices in athletics have not always been so compatible, this fact should not alter the determination that they now should be.

Majority Recommendation

I-2.A. It is recommended that women's athletics should adhere to the organization shown in Figure 1 (p.10). This identifies the program as a division in the School of Health, Physical Education and Recreation. A full-time head should be employed as soon as possible to direct the program, and the necessary clerical assistance should be secured. The head of the program should report to the Director of HPER and the Vice Chancellor for Student Affairs.

Minority Recommendation

I-2.B. It is recommended that women's athletics should adhere to the organization shown in Figure 2 (p. 11). The program for women would be a separate department within the Department of Intercollegiate Athletics. A full-time athletic director, reporting to the Director of Intercollegiate Athletics, should be appointed to direct the program as soon as possible.

I-3. It is recommended that the head of women's intercollegiate athletics be responsible for:

a) Promotion of intercollegiate athletics within the campus, state, region and nation.

b) Recruitment and selection of personnel for the program (e.g., coaches).

c) Development and implementation with appropriate University personnel of an overall plan for funding women's athletics.

d) Identification and solicitation of potential contributors.

e) Coordination with other athletic programs and related activities on campus.

f) Preparation and administration of the budget.

g) Implementation of institutional and other regulations relevant to the program.

h) Service as the institution's primary voice for women's athletics and its representative to state, regional and national bodies which govern women's intercollegiate athletics.

i) Evaluation of the program and associated personnel.

I-4. It is recommended that the advisory responsibilities of the Athletics Board be expanded to include women's athletics. Also, the head of women's athletics should be made an ex-officio member of the Board and its Executive Committee. A standing subcommittee of the Board should be appointed to advise the Head and the Board about matters germane to women's athletics.

I-5. It is recommended that the Sports Information Office in the Athletics Department provide the services needed by the women's intercollegiate program. Additional personnel required to fulfill this task should become a part of the Office and work under the direction of the Director of Sports Information.

I-6. It is recommended that coaching arrangements provide a combination of part-time and full-time assignments as need dictates, with no assignment being less than one-sixth time.

I-7. It is recommended that any combination of coaching and teaching be considered a temporary measure and be continued only until the women's athletics program is financially able to function without this kind of support.

I-8. In recognition of the statements above, it is recommended that neither academic rank nor tenure be awarded on the basis of coaching. An instructor-coach, however, should have the same consideration for rank and tenure on the basis of teaching and scholarly work as any other faculty member.

I-9. It is recommended that the 1976–77 intercollegiate program for women include teams in basketball, field hockey, gymnastics, tennis, track and field, swimming and volleyball.

I-10. It is recommended that those sports having the greatest potential for public and student interest and which are supported by existing high school programs and opportunities for intercollegiate competition be emphasized and the remaining sports be viewed as developmental.

I-11. The TFIAW recommends that scheduling of facilities shared by men's and women's athletic teams be assigned to the Assistant Director of Student Activities and that facilities be scheduled in conjunction with the men's and women's athletic directors.

I-12. It is recommended that plans for the development of a training room for women in the HPER Building be continued with provision of equipment comparable to the men's facility. The training room should be made available to women athletes as soon as possible.

I-13. It is recommended that the new varsity tennis courts be shared by men's and women's teams.

I-14. It is recommended that 10 to 14 full scholarships (preferably 14) be awarded in 1976; and that this number be increased during the following two years as follows: 22 in 1977 and 32 in 1978, to comply with Title IX requirements and to develop a sound, full-scale program.

I-15. It is recommended that the women's athletic director and the coaches develop the recruiting program. All procedures should be consistent with AIAW or other governing bodies' requirements.

I-16. It is recommended that affiliation with both AIAW and NCAA be continued.

I-17. It is recommended that UTK delegates to the two groups use their influence to continue the current collaborative effort to achieve the fullest possible agreement concerning national championships and the nature of national affiliation.

I-18. It is recommended that to meet minimally the needs of the program, the budget for FY-77 be $126,000; for FY-78, $173,400; and for FY-79, $214,500. Expenditures for each of these years are shown in the attached Table II (p. 21).

Appendix 2

End of Season Team Standings by Sport

Compiled as of spring 2008. Complete records of individual and team performances for each year are available in the University of Tennessee Women's Athletic Department Media Guides. An asterisk (*) indicates incomplete records.

Basketball				
Year	Final Season AP Ranking	Teams Played in Tournament (ranking)	Tournament Record	Finish
1977	5th (28–5)	#2 Immaculata, #1 Delta St., #20 Kansas St., #17 Mich. St.	3–1	3rd AIAW
1978	1st (27–4)	#8 Valdosta St., #6 Maryland	0–2	4th Southeast Region
1979	3rd (30–9)	#6 UCLA, #2 La. Tech, #19 Fordham, #7 Rutgers	3–1	3rd AIAW
1980	2nd (33–5)	#1 ODU, #4 So. Carolina, #6 Maryland, #13 Kansas State	3–1	2nd AIAW; SEC Tournament Champs; Regular Season Champs
1981	2nd (25–6)	#1 La. Tech, #3 ODU, #8 Maryland, #15 Ill. St.	3–1	2nd AIAW
1982	4th (22–10)	#1 La. Tech, #6 So. Cal, #17 Memphis St., Jackson St.	3–1	3rd NCAA
1983	10th (25–8)	#8 Georgia, #13 Ole Miss, South Carolina St.	2–1	2nd Mideast Region
1984	15th (23–10)	#5 So. Cal, #9 Cheyney, #3 Georgia, #12 Ala., MTSU	4–1	2nd NCAA
1985	13th (22–10)	#6 Ole Miss, UVA	1–1	3rd Mideast Region; SEC Tournament Champs; Regular Season Champs
1986	15th (24–10)	#3 So. Cal, #9 LSU, #2 Georgia, #14 Iowa	3–1	3rd NCAA
1987	7th (28–6)	#3 La. Tech, #4 Long Beach St., #2 Auburn, #11 UVA, Tenn. Tech	5–0	NCAA Champs
1988	1st (31–3)	#5 La. Tech, #10 UVA, #14 James Madison, Wake Forest	3–1	3rd NCAA; SEC Tournament Champions
1989	1st (35–2)	#2 Auburn, #5 Maryland, #7 Long Beach St., UVA, #18 LaSalle	5–0	NCAA Champs; SEC Tournament Champs
1990	4th (27–6)	#12 UVA, Clemson, ODU	2–1	2nd East Region; Regular Season Champs
1991	4th (30–5)	#2 UVA, #11 Stanford, #6 Auburn, #10 W. Ky., S.W. Mo. St.	5–0	NCAA Champs
1992	2nd (28–3)	#15 W. Ky., Rutgers	1–1	3rd Mideast Region; SEC Tournament Champs
1993	2nd (28–3)	#4 Iowa, #18 UNC, Northwestern	2–1	2nd Mideast Region; Regular Season Champs
1994	1st (30–2)	#6 La. Tech, North Carolina A&T, Clemson	2–1	3rd Mideast Region; SEC Tournament Champs; Regular Season Champs
1995	3rd (34–3)	#1 UConn, #12 Ga., #5 Tex. Tech, #8 W. Ky., Fla. Int., Fla. A&M	5–1	2nd NCAA; Regular Season Champs

Basketball (continued)

Year	Final Season AP Ranking	Teams Played in Tournament (ranking)	Tournament Record	Finish
1996	1st (32–4)	#5 Ga., #2 UConn, #11 UVA, #20 Kansas, Ohio St., Radford	6–0	NCAA Champs; SEC Tournament Champs; Regular Season Champs
1997	10th (29–10)	#2 ODU, #15 N. Dame, #1 UConn, #18 Colo., Ore., Grambling	6–0	NCAA Champs
1998	1st (39–0)	#4 La. Tech, Ark., #7 UNC, Rutgers, #15 W. Ky., Liberty	6–0	NCAA Champs; SEC Tournament Champs; Regular Season Champs
1999	2nd (31–3)	#10 Duke, #13 Va. Tech, Boston College, Appalachian St.	3–1	2nd East Region; SEC Tournament Champs; Regular Season Champs
2000	2nd (33–4)	#1 UConn, #8 Rutgers, #11 Tex. Tech, #19 UVA, #21 Ariz., Furman	5–1	2nd NCAA; SEC Tournament Champs; Regular Season Champs
2001	3rd (31–3)	#12 Xavier, St. Mary's College, Austin Peay	2–1	3rd Mideast Region; Regular Season Champs
2002	6th (29–5)	#1 UConn, #4 Vandy, Brigham Young, Notre Dame, Georgia St.	4–1	3rd NCAA; Regular Season Champs
2003	4th (33–5)	#1 UConn, #2 Duke, #11 Villanova, #15 Penn State, UVA, Alabama St.	5–1	2nd NCAA; Regular Season Champs
2004	2nd (31–4)	#6 UConn, #19 LSU, #10 Stanford, #15 Baylor, #25 DePaul, Colgate	5–1	2nd NCAA; Regular Season Champs
2005	3rd (30–5)	#7 Michigan St., #9 Rutgers, #14 Tex. Tech, Purdue, W. Carolina	4–1	3rd NCAA; SEC Tournament Champs
2006	6th (31–5)	#1 North Carolina, #9 Rutgers, George Washington, Army	3–1	2nd Cleveland Region; SEC Tournament Champs
2007	3rd (34–3)	#15 Rutgers, #2 North Carolina, Mississippi, Marist, Pittsburgh, Drake	6–0	NCAA Champs; Regular Season Champs
2008	1st (36–2)	Oral Roberts, Purdue, #15 Notre Dame, #8 Texas A&M, #6 LSU	5–0	NCAA Champs; SEC Tournament Champs

Overall Record, 1902–1975: 62 Seasons, 1040 Wins, 237 Losses

Cross Country

Year	National	District/Region	SEC
1974	—	—	—
1975	—	—	—
1976	—	—	—
1977	8th	1st (tie)	—
1978	—	3rd	—
1979	14th	3rd	—
1980	6th	3rd	—
1981	—	4th	—
1982	12th	3rd	—
1983	4th	1st	1st
1984	—	8th	3rd
1985	—	8th	3rd
1986	—	—	6th
1987	—	9th	4th
1988	—	11th	4th
1989	6th	4th	2nd
1990	12th	4th	1st
1991	—	8th	7th
1992	—	9th	5th
1993	—	10th	5th
1994	—	27th	8th
1995	—	—	9th
1996	—	24th	9th
1997	—	9th	6th
1998	31st	3rd	3rd
1999	—	9th	9th
2000	—	—	8th
2001	—	6th	2nd
2002	28th (tie)	1st	3rd
2003	24th	1st	1st
2004	21st	1st	1st
2005	28th	1st	1st
2006	28th	3rd	3rd
2007	—	4th	2nd
2008	—	4th	2nd

Golf

Year	NCAA	Region	SEC
1992–93	——	8th	3rd
1993–94	——	5th	4th
1994–95	——	8th	5th
1995–96	——	9th	5th
1996–97	6th	2nd	6th
1997–98	——	12th	4th
1998–99	——	13th (tie)	2nd
1999–2000	5th	4th	3rd
2000–01	——	11th	6th
2001–02	——	10th	3rd
2002–03	——	18th	3rd
2003–04	11th	7th	4th
2004–05	6th (tie)	1st (tie)	6th (tie)
2005–06	13th (tie)	1st	2nd
2006–07	17th (tie)	7th	3rd
2007–08	——	16th	8th

Rowing

Year	Race	Overall Team Results
1995–96	George Washington Invitational	8th (tie)
1996–97	Chattanooga Head Race	Champions
	Head of the Tennessee	2nd
	Head of the Chattahoochee	3rd
	Tennessee Cup	Champions
	Lexus Invitational	Champions
	Florida Crew Classic	Champions
	George Washington Invitational	5th
	Lexus Cup/Central Region Championships	5th
	NCAA Championships	9th (Varsity 4+)
1997–98	Chattanooga Head Race	2nd
	Head of the Tennessee	2nd
	Head of the Chattahoochee	2nd
	Tennessee Cup	2nd
	Lexus Invitational	3rd
	George Washington Invitational	7th (tie)
	Southern Intercollegiate Rowing Association Championships	Champions
	Lexus Cup/Central Regional Championships	6th
1998–99	Michigan State & Clemson	3rd
	George Washington Invitational	12th
	Southern Intercollegiate Rowing Association Championships	9th
	Lexus Central Sprints	7th (tie)
1999–2000	Chattanooga Head Race	2nd
	Clemson Invitational	13th (tie)
	Lexus Central Sprints	12th (tie)
2000–01	Head of the Tennessee	5th
	Head of the Chattahoochee	7th (tie)
	Southern Intercollegiate Rowing Association Championships	3rd
	Lexus South/Central Sprints	11th
2001–02	Chattanooga Head Race	Champions
	Head of the Charles	1st (Club 8+)
	Head of the Tennessee	4th
	Head of the Chattahoochee	5th
	Lexus Central/Southern Sprints	12th (tie)

Rowing (continued)

Year	Race	Overall Team Results
2002–03	Chattanooga Head Race	Champions
	Head of the Charles	1st (Club 8+)
	Head of the Tennessee	4th
	Head of the Chattahoochee	5th
	Lexus Central/Southern Sprints	6th
	NCAA Championships	16th (Varsity 8+)
2003–04	Chattanooga Head Race	Champions
	Lexus Central/South Sprints	6th (tie)
	NCAA Championships	10th (Varsity 8+)
2004–05	Chattanooga Head Race	Champions
	Aramark Central/South Sprints	5th
	NCAA Championships	8th (Varsity 8+)
2005–06	Chattanooga Head Race	Champions
	Head of the Tennessee	Champions
	Head of the Charles	1st (Championship 8+)
	Head of the Hooch	1st (Championship 8+)
	Louisville	Champions
	Princeton, George Washington University, University of Massachusetts	1st (Second Varsity 8+), 2nd (Varsity 8+ and Varsity 4+)
	Aramark Central/South Sprints	Champions
	NCAA Championships	14th (Varsity 8+), 5th (Second Varsity 8+), 6th (Petite Final—Varsity 4+), 2nd (Grand Final—Second Varsity/Open 4+)
2006–07	SIRA Championships	1st (Petite Final—Novice 8+)
	Aramark Central/South Sprints	3rd
	NCAA Championships	Full-team selection, 2nd (Petite Final—Second 8+), 3rd (Petite Final—First 8+), 3rd (Petite Final—Varsity 4+), 9th (overall team final standing)
2007–08	Aramark Central/South Sprints	8th
	NCAA Championships	Full team selection, 4th (C Final— First Varsity 8+), 5th (Grand Final—Second Varsity 8+), 5th (Petite Final—Varsity 4+), 11th (Overall team final standing)

Soccer

Year	Overall Record	SEC Record	SEC East Division	Postseason Ranking
1996	6–13–1	3–5	5th	SEC Tournament
1997	11–8	2–6	5th	
1998	12–8	5–3	4th	SEC Tournament
1999	8–11–1	5–4	6th	SEC Tournament
2000	12–8	7–2	2nd	SEC Tournament
2001	11–6–1	7–2	2nd (tie)	SEC Tournament, NCAA First Round
2002	18–6–1	6–2–1	Champions	SEC Tournament Champions, NCAA Sweet 16
2003	17–5–2	7–1–1	Regular-Season Champions	SEC Tournament Champions, NCAA Sweet 16
2004	17–5–2	10–1	Regular-Season Champions	SEC Tournament Finalist, NCAA Sweet 16
2005	15–6–2	10–1	Regular-Season Champions	SEC Tournament Champions, NCAA Second Round
2006	12–7–4	6–3–2	2nd (tie)	SEC Tournament Semifinalist, NCAA Sweet 16
2007	15–5–2	8–2–1	3rd	SEC Tournament Quarter-finalist, NCAA Sweet 16

Swimming and Diving

Year	SEC	National
1971–72	——	——
1972–73	——	——
1973–74	——	did not place
1974–75	——	did not place
1975–76	——	——
1976–77	——	did not place
1977–78	——	27th
1978–79	——	did not place
1979–80	——	did not place
1980–81	6th	26th
1981–82	4th	10th
1982–83	4th	19th
1983–84	5th	11th
1984–85	5th	33rd
1985–86	6th	39th
1986–87	5th	14th
1987–88	2nd	11th
1988–89	2nd	4th
1989–90	2nd	18th
1990–91	3rd	17th
1991–92	4th	18th
1992–93	6th	19th
1993–94	6th	14th
1994–95	3rd	12th
1995–96	3rd	9th
1996–97	3rd	11th
1997–98	5th	19th
1998–99	5th	18th
1999–2000	4th	28th
2000–01	5th	20th
2001–02	7th	22nd
2002–03	5th	18th
2003–04	4th	28th
2004–05	7th (tie)	24th (tie)
2005–06	5th	12th
2006–07	5th	10th
2007–08	4th	8th

Softball

Year	Overall Record	SEC Record	Postseason
1996	54–14	——	——
1997	45–22	20–7	2nd in Eastern Division, SEC Tournament
1998	37–31	13–15	3rd in Eastern Division. SEC Tournament
1999	44–27	17–11	Eastern Division Co–Champions, SEC Tournament, NCAA Regional No. 3
2000	29–34	5–22	5th in Eastern Division
2001	24–35	9–20	5th in Eastern Division
2002	35–25–18–17	4th in Eastern Division	——
2003	45–25	14–15	4th in Eastern Division, SEC Tournament
2004	55–16	20–8	Eastern Division Champions, SEC Tournament, NCAA Regional No. 6
2005	67–15	20–8	2nd in Eastern Division, SEC Tournament, Women's College World Series
2006	50–9	23–4	SEC Tournament Champions, Women's College World Series
2007	63–8	23–4	SEC Tournament Champions, Women's College World Series
2008	50–16	14–12	2nd in Eastern Division, SEC Tournament, NCAA Regional No. 13

Tennis

Year	Overall	SEC	Postseason Finish	ITA Ranking
1976–77	7–4*	——	State–2nd	——
1977–78	14–13*	——	State–1st	——
1978–79	14–3	——	State–1st, Region–4th	——
1979–80	16–4	——	SEC–3rd, State–2nd, Region–5th	——
1980–81	19–7	——	SEC–2nd, State–1st, Region–4th	——
1981–82	25–7	8–4	SEC–4th	
1982–83	21–12	7–5	SEC–4th	——
1983–84	9–16	3–9	SEC–9th	——
1984–85	14–14	3–8	SEC–6th	——
1985–86	14–14	1–9	SEC–8th	——
1986–87	15–13	2–7	SEC–8th	——
1987–88	17–8	6–3	SEC–5th	22nd
1988–89	15–7	7–2	SEC–3rd, NCAA–17th (tie)	17th
1989–90	19–8	7–4	SEC–4th, NCAA –9th (tie)	12th
1990–91	17–14	5–6	SEC–5th, NCAA–17th (tie)	14th
1991–92	20–9	9–4	SEC–3rd, NCAA–9th (tie)	11th
1992–93	13–14	7–6	SEC–6th	21st
1993–94	6–16	3–9	SEC–9th	39th
1994–95	16–8	8–3	SEC–3rd, NCAA–17th (tie)	12th
1995–96	16–13	8–4	SEC–5th	17th
1996–97	20–10	9–4	SEC–4th, NCAA 13th (tie)	13th
1997–98	20–11	8–6	SEC–6th, NCAA–13th (tie)	15th
1998–99	18–8	6–7	SEC–7th, NCAA–9th (tie)	14th
1999–2000	20–12	9–5	SEC–5th, NCAA–9th (tie)	14th
2000–01	25–4	10–1	SEC–2nd, NCAA–9th (tie)	6th
2001–02	21–10	7–4	SEC–5th, NCAA–3rd (tie)	12th
2002–03	22–7	9–2	SEC–2nd, NCAA–9th (tie)	10th
2003–04	15–14	7–4	SEC–4th, NCAA–9th (tie)	19th
2004–05	15–9	7–4	SEC–4th, NCAA–17th (tie)	18th
2005–06	12–13	6–5	SEC–5th, NCAA–33rd	32nd
2006–07	14–11	6–5	SEC–5th, NCAA–33rd	23rd
2007–08	15–10	6–5	SEC–4th, NCAA–33rd	24th

Track and Field

Year	State Indoor	State Outdoor	AIAW Indoor	AIAW Region Outdoor	Outdoor AIAW
1972	1st	1st	10th	no competition	10th
1973	1st	1st	10th	no competition	10th
1974	no competition	no competition	no competition	no competition	did not score
1975	no competition	no competition	no competition	no competition	did not score
1976	no competition	1st	no competition	no competition	did not score
1977	no competition	1st	no competition	no competition	4th
1978	no competition	1st	no competition	no competition	13th
1979	no competition	1st	no competition	no competition	3rd
1980	no competition	1st	no competition	no competition	4th
1981	no competition	1st SEC	2nd	no competition	1st
1982	no competition	1st SEC	2nd	no competition	2nd NCAA

Year	SEC Indoor	SEC Outdoor	NCAA Indoor	NCAA Region Outdoor	Outdoor NCAA
1983	no competition	1st	2nd	no competition	4th
1984	1st SEC	1st	2nd	no competition	2nd
1985	3rd	2nd	6th	——	7th
1986	3rd	3rd	2nd	——	4th
1987	4th	4th	2nd	——	4th
1988	3rd	3rd	10th	——	21st
1989	2nd	3rd	32nd (tie)	——	37th
1990	3rd	3rd	9th (tie)	——	6th
1991	3rd	3rd	6th (tie)	——	5th
1992	4th	5th	13th (tie)	——	9th (tie)
1993	5th	5th	did not score	——	18th
1994	4th	3rd	11th	——	5th

Track and Field (continued)

Year	SEC Indoor	SEC Outdoor	NCAA Indoor	NCAA Region Outdoor	Outdoor NCAA
1995	4th	3rd	18th	——	9th
1996	7th	9th	did not score	——	49th (tie)
1997	7th (tie)	7th	did not score	——	18th (tie)
1998	6th	7th	31st (tie)	——	15th (tie)
1999	5th	6th	32nd (tie)	——	20th (tie)
2000	8th	6th	did not score	——	did not score
2001	10th	9th	58th (tie)	——	60th
2002	7th	6th	42nd (tie)	——	39th (tie)
2003	9th	7th	23rd (tie)	7th	22nd (tie)
2004	2nd	6th	4th	2nd	7th (tie)
2005	1st	3rd	1st	1st	4th
2006	3rd (tie)	5th	18th (tie)	3rd	18th
2007	1st	4th	3rd	4th	27th (tie)
2008	2nd	4th	8th (tie)	2nd	13th

Volleyball

Year	Overall	SEC	Postseason
1973	38–6	——	State 1st; Region 2nd; AIAW 15th
1974	8–14*	——	State 8th
1975	17–8–6	——	State 2nd
1976	22–13–4*	——	State 2nd
1977	7–11–3*	——	State 1st; Region 4th
1978	20–14–3	——	State 2nd
1979	34–11	——	State 1st; SEC 2nd; Region 5th
1980	40–17	——	State 2nd; SEC 2nd; Region 2nd
1981	34–22	——	SEC 1st; NCAA 17th
1982	31–7	——	SEC 1st; NCAA 9th
1983	31–10	3–2	SEC 2nd; NCAA 9th
1984	35–11	5–1	SEC 1st; NCAA 9th
1985	12–24	3–3	SEC 4th
1986	23–13	2–4	SEC 5th
1987	18–18	4–3	SEC 3rd
1988	23–12	5–2	SEC 2nd
1989	13–15	5–3	SEC 4th
1990	12–17	4–4	SEC 3rd (tie)
1991	12–17	4–10	SEC 8th
1992	13–14	8–6	SEC 5th
1993	18–13	7–7	SEC 5th; NCAA 17th
1994	10–21	2–12	SEC 11th
1995	7–25	0–14	SEC East 5th
1996	17–16	6–8	SEC East 4th
1997	15–19	5–9	SEC East 4th
1998	19–10	7–7	SEC East 4th
1999	19–13	8–6	SEC East 2nd
2000	23–10	9–5	SEC East 3rd; NCAA 33rd
2001	16–11	7–7	SEC East 3rd
2002	20–11	8–8	SEC East 4th
2003	22–9	10–6	SEC East 2nd
2004	32–3	15–1	SEC East 1st; NCAA 9th
2005	25–9	13–3	SEC East 2nd; NCAA 3rd
2006	19–12	10–10	SEC East 3rd; NCAA First Round
2007	11–18	6–14	SEC East 5th

Appendix 3

Lady Volunteer All-America Honor Roll and Lady Volunteer Hall of Fame

Compiled from all available sources as of spring 2008

Basketball

Kodak All-America

Cindy Brogdon, 1976, 1978, 1979
Tamika Catchings, 1998, 1999, 2000, 2001
Daedra Charles, 1990, 1991
Sheila Collins, 1985
Shyra Ely, 2004
Bridgette Gordon, 1988, 1989
Tanya Haave, 1983
Lisa Harrison, 1993
Dena Head, 1992
Chamique Holdsclaw, 1996, 1997, 1998, 1999
Kara Lawson, 2003
Nikki McCray, 1994, 1995
Cindy Noble, 1981
Mary Ostrowski, 1982
Candace Parker, 2006, 2007, 2008
Semeka Randall, 1999, 2000
Jill Rankin, 1978, 1979, 1980
Patricia Roberts, 1977
Holly Warlick, 1980

Naismith Player of the Century (1900s)

Chamique Holdsclaw, 2000

Naismith Player of the Year

Chamique Holdsclaw, 1998, 1999
Tamika Catchings, 2000
Candace Parker, 2008

Naismith All-America Team

Tamika Catchings, 1999, 2000
Daedra Charles, 1991
Bridgette Gordon, 1988, 1989
Lisa Harrison, 1993
Dena Head, 1992
Chamique Holdsclaw, 1997, 1998, 1999
Michelle Marciniak, 1996
Nikki McCray, 1994, 1995
Candace Parker, 2007, 2008

Associated Press Player of the Year

Chamique Holdsclaw, 1998, 1999
Tamika Catchings, 2000
Candace Parker, 2008

Associated Press All-America Team

Tamika Catchings, 1999, 2000, 2001 (Second Team)
Shyra Ely, 2004 (Third Team)
Chamique Holdsclaw, 1997, 1998, 1999
Gwen Jackson, 2001 (Honorable Mention), 2003 (Honorable Mention)
Kellie Jollie, 1999, (Honorable Mention)
Kara Lawson, 2001 (Honorable Mention), 2002 (Third Team), 2003 (Second Team)
Candace Parker, 2006 (Second Team), 2007 (First Team)
Semeka Randall, 1999 (Second Team), 2000, 2001 (Honorable Mention)
Michelle Snow, 2001 (Honorable Mention), 2002 (Honorable Mention)
Shannon Bobbitt (Honorable Mention), 2008
Candace Parker, 2008

ESPY Awards Female Athlete of the Year

Chamique Holdsclaw, 1999
Candace Parker, 2008

ESPY Awards Women's Basketball Player of the Year

Chamique Holdsclaw, 1998, 1999
Tamika Catchings, 2001

ESPY Awards Underarmour Undeniable Performance Award

2007 Team

Honda-Broderick Cup Athlete of the Year

Chamique Holdsclaw, 1998
Candace Parker, 2008

Honda Cup Winner

Bridgette Gordon, 1989
Chamique Holdsclaw, 1997, 1998
Candace Parker, 2007, 2008

Kodak All-America Team

Shanna Zolman, 2006 (First Team)

NCAA Woman of the Year (Finalist)

Kara Lawson 2003

Sporting News Player of the Year

Chamique Holdsclaw, 1998, 1999

Sporting News All-America Team

Tamika Catchings, 1999, 2000
Chamique Holdsclaw, 1998, 1999
Semeka Randall, 1999 (Second Team)

Sports Illustrated Player of the Year

Chamique Holdsclaw 1998, 1999

Sports Illustrated All-America Team

Tamika Catchings, 1999, 2000
Chamique Holdsclaw, 1998, 1999

Sullivan Award

Chamique Holdsclaw, 1999

USA Basketball Player of the Year

Chamique Holdsclaw, 1997

USA Basketball Writers of America Player of the Year

Chamique Holdsclaw, 1998
Tamika Catchings, 2000
Candace Parker, 2007, 2008

USA Basketball Writers of America Rookie of the Year

Tamika Catchings, 1998

Francis Pomroy Naismith Award

Kara Lawson, 2003

WBCA Player of the Year

Chamique Holdsclaw, 1998, 1999
Tamika Catchings, 2000

Wade Trophy Winner

Daedra Charles, 1991
Candace Parker, 2007

John R. Wooden Player of the Year

Candace Parker, 2008

John R. Wooden All-America Team

Candace Parker, 2008

SEC Female Athlete of the Year

Candace Parker, 2008

SEC Freshman of the Year

Angie Bjorklund, 2008

Woody Hayes Award

Kara Lawson, 2004

ESPY Awards Best Coach-Manager

Pat Summitt, 2008

Naismith Coach of the Century (1900s)

Pat Summitt, 2000

Associated Press Coach of the Year

Pat Summitt, 1998

Naismith Coach of the Year

Pat Summitt, 1987, 1989, 1994, 1998, 2004

WBCA-Converse Coach of the Year

Pat Summitt, 1983, 1995, 1998

John and Nellie Wooden Coach of the Year

Pat Summitt, 1998

USA Basketball Writers of America Coach of the Year

Pat Summitt, 1998

2007 Best Leaders, U.S. News & World Report

Pat Summitt

ESPY Awards Co-Team of the Decade (1990s)

Jody Adams, 1989–93
Niya Butts, 1996–2000
Nikki Caldwell, 1990–94
Amanda Canon, 1998–2002
Tamara Carver, 1990–91
Kelli Casteel, 1988–92
Tamika Catchings, 1997–2001
Daedra Charles, 1988–91
Regina Clark, 1988–92
Kristen "Ace" Clement, 1997–2001
Abby Conklin, 1993–97
Latina Davis, 1992–96
Rochone Dilligard, 1991–94
Sarah Edwards, 1998–2001
Tonya Edwards, 1986–90
Kyra Elzy, 1996–2001
Peggy Evans, 1990–93
Teresa Geter, 1997–99

Misty Greene, 1995–98
Lisa Harrison, 1989–93
Debbie Hawhee, 1988–92
Dena Head, 1988–92
Chamique Holdsclaw, 1995–99
Marlene Jeter, 1990–92
Dana Johnson, 1991–95
Tiffani Johnson, 1994–97
Kellie Jolly, 1995–99
Brynae Laxton, 1995–98
Michelle Marciniak, 1993–96
Nikki McCray, 1991–95
Carla McGhee, 1986–90
Laurie Milligan, 1994–98
Pearl Moore, 1987–90
Semeka Randall, 1997–2001
Debbie Scott, 1988–90
Kim Smallwood, 1995–96
Melissa Smith, 1989–90
Tanika Smith, 1993–95
Michelle Snow, 1998–2002
Lashonda Stephens, 1996–2000
Pashen Thompson, 1993–97
Vonda Ward, 1991–95
Tiffany Woosley, 1991–95

Kodak 25th Anniversary Team

Chamique Holdsclaw, 1999

NCAA Team of the Decade (1980s)

Bridgette Gordon

NCAA 25th Anniversary Team (2006)

Chamique Holdsclaw
Bridgette Gordon
Pat Summitt (coach)

NCAA Tournament Most Outstanding Player

Tonya Edwards, 1987
Bridgette Gordon, 1989
Chamique Holdsclaw, 1997, 1998
Michelle Marciniak, 1996
Candace Parker, 2007, 2008

NCAA All-Final Four Team

Nicky Anosike, 2007
Shannon Bobbitt, 2007
Tamika Catchings, 1998, 2000
Daedra Charles, 1991
Tonya Edwards, 1987

Sheila Frost, 1989
Bridgette Gordon, 1987, 1989
Dena Head, 1991
Chamique Holdsclaw, 1996, 1997, 1998
Gwen Jackson, 2003
Tiffani Johnson, 1996
Kellie Jolly, 1997, 1998
Kara Lawson, 2003
Michelle Marciniak, 1996
Nikki McCray, 1995
Mary Ostrowski, 1984
Candace Parker, 2007, 2008
Shanna Zolman, 2004

Cross Country

AIAW All-America

Kathy Bryant, 1977, 1980
Linda Portasik, 1980
Brenda Webb, 1977, 1978

NCAA All-America

Valerie Bertrand, 1989
Kathy Bryant, 1981, 1982
Sharon Dickie, 2000
Jasmin Jones, 1989
Liz Natale, 1983
Alison Quelch, 1983
Brenda Webb, 1977, 1987
Patty Wiegand, 1989

Golf

NGCA All-America

Erin Kurczewski, 1998 (Honorable Mention)
Katharina Larsson, 1994 (Honorable Mention)
Abby Pearson, 1993 (Second Team)
Violeta Retamoza, 2003 (Second Team), 2005
Jessica Shepley, 2004 (Honorable Mention)
Nicole Smith, 2007 (Honorable Mention)
Marci Turner, 2006 (Second Team), 2007
    (Honorable Mention)
Young-A Yang, 1999 (Honorable Mention), 2000
    (Honorable Mention), 2001, 2002 (Second Team)

Rowing

US Rowing All-America

Amy Delashmitt 1997 (First Team)

CRCA Pocock All-America

Kaitlin Bargreen, 2003 (First Team),
    2004 (Second Team)
Chelsea Pemberton, 2003 (Second Team),
    2004 (First Team), 2005 (Second Team)
Andrea Bagwell, 2005 (Second Team)
Erin-Monique Shelton, 2006 (Second Team,
    2007 (First Team)

Soccer

NSCAA All-America

Ali Christoph, 2005 (First Team),
    2006 (Second Team)
Keeley Dowling, 2002 (Second Team),
    2003 (First Team), 2004 (First Team)

Soccer Buzz All-America

Ali Christoph, 2005 (Third Team),
    2006 (Third Team)
Keeley Dowling, 2002 (First Team),
    2003 (First Team), 2004 (First Team)
Sue Flamini, 2001 (Honorable Mention)
Kayla Lockaby, 2004 (Honorable Mention)

SoccerTimes.com All-America

Ali Christoph, 2005 (Second Team)
Keeley Dowling, 2003 (Second Team)

collegesoccer.com All-America

Keeley Dowling, 2001 (Honorable Mention)

Top Drawer Soccer National Team of the Season

Ali Christoph, 2005 (First Team), 2006 (First Team)
Genna Gorman, 2005 (Fourth Team)
Jenny Jeffers, 2005 (Second Team),
    2006 (Second Team)
Kylee Rossi, 2006 (Second Team)

Softball

NFCA All America Team

Monica Abbott, 2004, 2005, 2006, 2007
Tonya Callahan, 2007 (Second Team), 2008
India Chiles, 2007
Kristi Durant, 2005, 2006
Sarah Fekete, 2005, 2006
Lindsay Schutzler, 2005, 2006, 2007 (Second Team)

USA Softball National Collegiate Player of the Year

Monica Abbott, 2007

Women's Sports Foundation's Sportswoman of the Year in Team Sports Category

Monica Abbott, 2007

Swimming and Diving

All America

(1) Swimming

Janie Armington
Julie Barker
Stephanie Brinser
Liz Brown
Heather Burgess
J.B. Burrell
Catherine Byrne
Mari Carlson
Elizabeth Christy
Kate Chronic
Patty Clark
Tiffany Clay
Kathy Coffin
Brigid Corr
Heather Coulson
Julie Darby
Kari Ann Davis
Nicole deMan
Tori DeSilvia
Tara Doyle
Karla Driesler
Barb Ehring
Sandy Ferrin
Jacque Fessel
Jil Fletcher
Deidre Gildea
Michelle Gobrecht
Wendy Gwaltney
Pam Hanson
Jennifer Hesp
Libby Hill
Kathy Hoffman
Missy Hoy
Tracy Ignatosky
Raquel James
Karen Koleber
Page Kunst
Stephanie Livers
Sam Maccherola

Christine Magnuson
Kim Marsden
Carly Mathes
Jenny McGrath
Julie Millis
Jamie Minnich
Leslie Mix
Fabiola Molina
Teresa Moodie
Sarah Nichols
Tillie Patterson
Sarah Payette
Kari Peterson
Emily Plummer
Janet Risser
Yvette Robling
Peg Saalfeld
Jaime Sanger
Laura Sawyer
Teresa Schneider
Teresa Sestak
Monica Shannahan
Christie Shefchunas
Jill Sprecher
Julia Stowers
Abbi Terveer
Marti Tickle
Megan Tomes
Sarah Weis
Andrea Wentzel
Cheryl White
Susie Wright

(2) Diving

Jane Anthony
Tracy Bonner
Dawn Burton
Lizzy Flynt
Lauryn McCalley
Kathy Pesek
Kylee Wells
Jane Woodard

NCAA Championship Title, 100y Butterfly

Christine Magnuson, 2008

Tennis

All-America Singles

Vilmarie Castellvi, 2002, 2003

Michelle DePalmer, 1981

Tammy Encina, 2003

Margie Lepsi, 1995

Manisha Malhotra, 1997

Stacey Martin, 1989

Alison Ojeda, 2001

All-America Doubles

Vilmarie Castellvi, 2003

Shannon Kagawa, 1992

Paula Kelly, 1980, 1981, 1982

Peta Kelly, 1980, 1981, 1982

Margie Lepsi, 1996, 1997, 1998

Manisha Malhotra, 1996, 1997, 1998

Melissa Schaub, 2003

Mandy Wilson, 1992

Track and Field

All America

Marvena Almond, 1994, 1996

Sharrieffa Barksdale, 1981, 1982, 1983, 1984

Robin Benjamin, 1985, 1986, 1987

Kameisha Bennett, 2002, 2004

Princess Bennett, 1987, 1988

Valerie Bertrand, 1988, 1989, 1990

Mary Bolden, 1984

Kelia Bolton, 1983

Michelle Bookman, 1992, 1994, 1995

Janelle Briggs, 1997

Kathy Bryant, 1981, 1982, NCAA Champion

Anissa Campbell, 1996, 1997

Tracy Carrington, 1999

Courtney Champion, 2005, 2006

Myrtle Chester, 19881, 1982, 1984

Joetta Clark, 1981, 1982, 1983, 1984,
    NCAA Champion

Tara Coleman, 1988

Nicole Cook, 2002, 2003, 2004, 2005,
    NCAA Champion

Karol Davidson, 1984

Dedra Davis, 1993, 1994, NCAA Champion

Chantal Desrosiers, 1982

Sharon Dickie, 2001, 2003

Maureen Ferris, 1999

Stephanie Fields, 1992, 1994, 1995

Veronica Findley, 1983, 1984

Cheryl Finley, 1995

Benita Fitzgerald, 1980, 1981, 1982, 1983,
    NCAA Champion

Antoinette Gorham, 2002, 2004, 2005

Felicia Guilford, 2005

Jane Haist, 1977, 1978, AIAW Champion

Patricia Hall, 2005, 2006

Vonda Hammons, 1988

Kathi Harris, 1985

Alisa Harvey, 1984, 1985, 1986, 1987,
    NCAA Champion

Rose Hauch, 1979, 1980, 1981, 1982,
    AIAW Champion

Leslie Henley, 1998

Paula Hines, 1981

Vickie Hudson, 1992, 1994, 1995

Terry Hull, 1969, 1970, NGWS Champion

Lindsay Hyatt, 2004, NCAA Champion

Alicia Johnson, 1990, 1991

Jasmin Jones, 1988, 1989, 1990, 1991

Saidah Jones, 1997

Lynn Lashley, 1977

Tonya Lee, 1989, 1990, 1991, 1992

Pat Leroy, 1992, 1993

LaTonya Loche, 2005

Lesly Love, 1997, 1999

Tianna Madison, 2004, 2005, NCAA Champion

LaVonna Martin
1985, 1986, 1987, 1988, NCAA Champion

Karen McDonald, 1984

Carla McLaughlin, 1986, 1987

Denita Miller, 2001

Tisha Milligan, 1991

Shawn Moore, 1987, 1988, 1991

Liz Natale, 1983

Brooke Novak, 2004, 2005, NCAA Champion

Ilrey Oliver, 1983, 1984, 1985, 1986, 1987,
    NCAA Champion

Monica Olkowski, 1991

Toyin Olupona, 2004, 2005

Andrea Pappas, 2000

Pam Passera, 1984

Linda Portasik, 1981, 1982

Tisha Prather, 1990, 1992, 1993

Alana Preston, 1992, 1993, 1994, 1995

Alison Quelch, 1984

Cathy Rattray, 1981, 1982, 1983, 1984,
    NCAA Champion

Michelle Reasor, 1995

Vanessa Robinson, 1980

Tyangela Sanders, 1999

Menka Scott, 1989

Lisa Sherrill, 1981

Diane Slinden, 2001

Sandy Smith, 1980

Heather Sumpter, 1996, 1997

Kim Townes, 1993

Leslie Treherne, 2004, 2006

Dee Dee Trotter, 2002, 2003, 2004,
    NCAA Champion

Cleo Tyson, 2005, 2006

Patricia Walsh, 1982, 1983, 1984

Delisa Walton, 1980, 1981, 1982, 1983,
    NCAA Champion

Sue Walton, 1992, 1994, 1995

Brenda Webb, 1977, 1979, AIAW Champion

Kelli White, 1996, 1997, 1998, 1999

Patty Wiegand, 1988, 1989, 1990, 1991,
    NCAA Champion

Gina Wilbanks, 1988

Erica Witter, 1996, 1997, 1999

Jane Woodhead, 1987

USTCA National Indoor Coach of the Year

J. J. Clark, 2005

Volleyball

All-America

Kristen Andre, 2004 (AVCA All-America Honorable
    Mention), 2005 (Vball Magazine First-Team All-
    America, AVCA Second-Team All-America)

Sarah Blum, 2006 (AVCA All-America,
    Honorable Mention)

April Chapple, 1984 (Asics Tiger All-America,
    USVBA All-America, AVCA Second-Team
    All-America)

Julie Knytych, 2004 (AVCA Third-Team
    All-America), 2005 (AVCA All-America
    Honorable Mention)

Amy Morris, 2004 (AVCA All-America Honorable
    Mention), 2005 (Vball Magazine Third-Team
    All-America)

Michelle Piantadosi, 2004 (AVCA All-America
    Honorable Mention)

Beverly Robinson, 1982 (AVCA All-America
    First Team)

Yuliya Stoyanova, 2005 (AVCA All-America
    Honorable Mention), 2006 (AVCA All-America
    Honorable Mention)

National Coach of the Year

Rob Patrick, 2004 (CVU.com, 2005 Vball Magazine)

Lady Volunteer Hall of Fame

Ed Boling, 2001 (University of Tennessee Administration)

Lady Volunteer Hall of Fame (cont.)

Tracy Bonner, 2006 (Diving)

Angie Boyd (Keck), 2005 (Golf)

Cindy Brogdon, , 2003 (Basketball)

Liz Brown (Jarvis), 2003 (Swimming)

Catherine Byrne (Maloney), 2002 (Swimming)

April Chapple, 2003 (Volleyball)

Daedra Charles (Furlow), 2001 (Basketball)

Joetta Clark (Diggs), 2001 (Track and Field)

Shelia Collins, 2007 (Basketball)

Terry Crawford, 2002 (Track and Field Coach)

Nicole deMan (Dewes), 2007 (Swimming)

Karla Driesler (McQuain), 2006 (Swimming)

Tonya Edwards, 2006 (Basketball)

Benita Fitzgerald (Mosley), 2001 (Track and Field)

Gordon, Bridgette, 2001 (Basketball)

Tanya Haave, 2005 (Basketball/Volleyball)

Alisa Harvey, 2006 (Track and Field)

Lea Henry (Manning), 2005 (Basketball)

Tracy Ignatosky (Long), 2001 (Swimming)

Bridget Jackson (Chaira), 2007 (Softball)

Joe Johnson, 2004 (University of Tennessee Administration)

Jasmin Jones (Keller), 2004 (Track and Field)

Missy Kane (Bemiller), 2005 (Track and Field)

Paula Kelly, 2001 (Tennis)

Peta Kelly (Slade), 2001 (Tennis)

Bonnie Kenny, 2006 (Volleyball)

Robin Maine (Bugg), 2004 (Volleyball)

LaVonna Martin (Floreal), 2002 (Track and Field)

Nikki McCray (Pinson), 2004 (Basketball)

Carla McGhee, 2007 (Basketball)

Jenny McGrath (Weaver), 2004 (Swimming)

Cindy Noble (Hauserman), 2002 (Basketball)

Mary Ostrowski, 2006 (Basketball)

Cathy Rattray (Williams), 2003 (Track and Field)

Gloria Ray, 2001 (University of Tennessee Administration)

Trish Roberts, 2003 (Basketball)

Beverly Robinson (Buffini), 2001 (Volleyball)

Dianne Shoemaker (DeNecochea), 2007 (Volleyball)

Holly Warlick, 2002 (Basketball)

Helen Watson, 2007 (University of Tennessee Administration)

Patty Wiegand (Pitcher), 2002 (Track and Field)

Appendix 4

All-Time Roster of Lady Volunteers by Sport

Compiled from all available sources as of fall 2007

Basketball

Name	Hometown	Years
Jody Adams	Cleveland, TN	1989–93
Billye Anderton		1969–70
Mary Anderton		1926
Nicky Anosike	Staten Island, NY	2004–08
—— Argera		1971
Alberta Auguste	Marrero, LA	2006–08
Mary or Pauline Aycock		1922
Evelyn Baird		1924–26
Suzanne Barbre	Morristown, TN	1974–78
Carol Barfield		1971
Vicki Baugh	Sacramento, CA	2007–
Harriet Bauman		1904
Lucille Bean		1926
Angie Bjorklund	Spokane Valley, WA	2007–
Annis or Sara Blair		1922
Mary Virginia Blanton		1926
Shannon Bobbitt	New York, NY	2006–08
Cindy Boggs	Ducktown, TN	1974–75
Nell Bond		1924
Fonda Bondurant	South Fulton, TN	1975–77
Melinda Borthick		1972–74
Sherry Bostic	LaFollette, TN	1984–86
Nancy Bowman	Lenoir City, TN	1972–75
Gina Bozeman	Sylvester, GA	1981
Diane Brady	Calhoun, TN	1973–75
Barbara Brimi		1965–68
Cindy Brogdon	Buford, GA	1977–79
Marjorie Bryant		1922–23
Kathleen Burdick		1922
Niya Butts	Americus, GA	1996–2000

Name	Hometown	Years
Tasha Butts	Milledgeville, GA	2000–04
Catherine Cable		1926
Kelley Cain	Atlanta, GA	2007–
Linda Caldwell		1969–70
Nikki Caldwell	Oak Ridge, TN	1990–94
Abby Canon	Shelbyville, TN	2004–05
Amanda Canon	Shelbyville, TN	1998–2002
Sonya Cannon	Maryville, TN	1981–85
Ethel Capps		1926
Adelaine Carleton		1926
Hattie Carothers		1922
Sandy Carter		1974
Tamara Carver	Cosby, TN	1990–91
Kelli Casteel	Maryville, TN	1988–92
Tamika Catchings	Duncanville, TX	1997–2001
Lesia Cecil	Helenwood, TN	1985–86
Daedra Charles	Detroit, MI	1988–91
Becky Clark	Memphis, TN	1979–80
Regina Clark	Saginaw, MI	1988–92
Kristen Clement	Broomall, PA	1997–01
Susan Clower	Kingston, TN	1978–82
Susie Cole		1970
Lynne Collins	Blacksburg, VA	1980–84
Shelia Collins	Colbert, GA	1981–85
Abby Conklin	Charlestown, IN	1993–97
Ruby Conley		1924–25
Pam Cook	Duluth, GA	1982–83
Mary Cooke		1925
Elizabeth Cooley		1905
Mary Cooper		1906
Marie Copley		1972
—— Crestla		1926
Mabel Crow		1925
Dona Crow		1971
Elizabeth Curry	New Virginia, IA	2006–07
Bev Curtis	Acworth, GA	1979
Marjorie Dahnke		1926
Myrtle Damon		1907
Mary Daniel		1910

Name	Hometown	Years
Verdi D'Ardell		1922
Latina Davis	Winchester, TN	1992–96
LaToya Davis	Forsyth, GA	2000–04
Marjorie Davis		1907–08, 1910
Susie Davis	Hohenwald, TN	1976–79
Carolyn Davis Baxter		1963 or 1965
Fannie DeGolia		1903–04
Freda DeLozier		1975
Rochone Dilligard	Lebanon, TN	1991–94
Gail Dobson	Greeneville, TN	1971–75
Lillian Dodd		1905
Sybil Dosty	Tucson, AZ	2004–05
Mary Dozier		1926
Jackie Dunbar		1974
Barbara Dunn		1972–73
Kris Durham	Dunellen, NJ	1987–89
Sarah Edwards	Sevierville, TN	1998–2001
Tonya Edwards	Flint, MI	1986–90
Catherine Elkins		1925
Mary Ellis		1926
Cindy Ely	Canton, GA	1977–81
Shyra Ely	Indianapolis, IN	2001–05
Kyra Elzy	LaGrange, KY	1996–2001
Peggy Evans	Detroit, MI	1990–93
Sherri Fancher	Knoxville, TN	1976–79
Elizabeth Ferris		1924–25
Tye'sha Fluker	Pasadena, CA	2002–05
Susan Foulds	Annandale, VA	1979–81
—— Fox		1924
Claudia Frazier		1908–09
Valerie Freeman	Milledgeville, GA	1983–85
Ruthie Fritz		1969–70
Sheila Frost	Pulaski, TN	1985–89
Aimee Fuller		1974
Alex Fuller	Shelbyville, TN	2004–
Amy Gamble	Glendale, WV	1983–84
Marci Garner	Maryville, TN	1974–76
Jeanie Garth		1920
Teresa Geter	Columbia, SC	1997–99

Name	Hometown	Years
Mabel Gildersleeve		1904, 1906–07
Carol Goodwin		1963
Bridgette Gordon	DeLand, FL	1985–89
Liza Graves	Knoxville, TN	1975–78
Patricia Graves		1971
Lynne Greek	Donelson, TN	1969
Brenda Green		1963–66
Kathie Greene	New Market, TN	1975–76
Misty Greene	Decatur, TN	1995–98
Gloria Gregory		1963–66
Debbie Groover	Canton, GA	1977–81
Sue Groves		1974
Aubrey Guastalli	Westwood, MA	2004–05
Tanya Haave	Evergreen, CO	1980–84
Jennifer Hall		1969
Leanne Hance	Morristown, TN	1977–78
Nelle Hape		1920
Florine Harbert		1924–25
Mary Hardin		1909
Jerilynn Harper	Jefferson City, TN	1978–79
Anne Harris		1925
Lisa Harrison	Louisville, KY	1989–93
Pat Hatmaker	Knoxville, TN	1980–84
Debbie Hawhee	Greeneville, TN	1988–92
Margaret Hazelwood		1924–25
Dena Head	Canton, MI	1988–92
Lea Henry	Damascus, GA	1979–83
Mary Dell Hibler		1969–70
Gayle Hickey		1970–71
Agnes Hicks		1925–26
Jane Hill		1969
Maude Hite		1904–05, 1907
Terry Hobbs		1973
Maria Hohne		1974
Chamique Holdsclaw	Astoria, NY	1995–99
Grace Hood		1905–08
Trixie Hopson		1923

Name	Hometown	Years
Alexis Hornbuckle	Charleston, WV	2004–08
Karla Horton	Kershaw, SC	1984–87
Mary House		1920
Fannie Huling		1924–25
Brittany Jackson	Cleveland, TN	2001–05
Gwen Jackson	Eufaula, AL	1999–03
Jan Jardet		1969–72
Jackie Jarrell		1970
Gladys Jeter		1920
Marlene Jeter	Carlisle, SC	1990–92
Dana Johnson	Baltimore, MD	1991–95
Tiffani Johnson	Charlotte, NC	1994–97
Mary Johnson		1920
Michelle Johnson	Shelbyville, TN	1993, 1995
Kellie Jolly	Sparta, TN	1995–99
Florence Kehr		1910
Marguerite Kehr		1909–10
Maude Keller		1903
Janice Koehler	Nashville, TN	1974–76
Louise Lacy		1926
Tammy Larkey	Gray, TN	1981–83
Kara Lawson	Alexandria, VA	1999–03
Brynae Laxton	Oneida, TN	1995–98
Ann Lee		1969
Kyran Lenahan		1973–74
Cheryl Littlejohn	Gastonia, NC	1983–87
Inez Lovelace		1924–25
Alberta Lowe		1920
Jessica Lyman		1910
Evelyn Mabry		1926
Michelle Marciniak	Macungie, PA	1993–96
Pam Marr	Winter Park, FL	1982–86
Dawn Marsh	Alcoa, TN	1984–88

Name	Hometown	Years	Name	Hometown	Years	Name	Hometown	Years
Jennilee McCracken		1922–25	Diane Payne		1971	Shelley Sexton	Lake City, TN	1983–87
Melissa McCray	Johnson City, TN	1985–89	Jane Pemberton	Deer Lodge, TN	1975–76	Mary Moore Shanton		1926
Nikki McCray	Collierville, TN	1991–95	Lynn Pemberton		1972–73	Sydney Smallbone	Granger, IN	2007–
Courtney McDaniel	Bristol, TN	2000–04	Alice Perkins		1907–08	Louise Smalley		1923
April McDivitt	Connersville, IN	1999–2002	Margaret Perkins		1905–06	Kim Smallwood	Richmond, TX	1995–96
Carla McGhee	Peoria, IL	1986–90	Patty Petrone		1973	Jane Smartt		1965–68
Lisa McGill	Gatlinburg, TN	1976–79	Parry Pierce		1969	Maud Walker Smith		1924
Blanch McIntire		1903	Linda Piety		1970	Melissa Smith	Schofield, WI	1989–90
Cait McMahan	Maryville, TN	2006–	Shalon Pillow	Addyston, OH	1998–2002	Tanika Smith	Knoxville, TN	1993–95
Leta McNabb		1910	Essie Polk		1905–06	Michelle Snow	Pensacola, FL	1998–2002
Bertha Rose Miller		1906	Anne Pope		1922–23	Kristie Snyder	Knoxville, TN	1983–84
Grace Miller		1907–09	Lou Ann Powell		1969–70	Sidney Spencer	Hoover, AL	2003–07
Laurie Milligan	Tigard, OR	1994–98	Lelia Prestley		1926	Kathy Spinks	Forest Hills, KY	1984–88
Lucille Minton		1926	Diane Pruett		1971	Margaret Stark		1920
Zandra Montgomery	Cleveland, TN	1977–79	Burline Pullin		1972	LaShonda Stephens	Woodstock, GA	1996–2000
Nicci Moats	Daleville, VA	2006–07	Semeka Randall	Cleveland, OH	1997–2001	Anna Stokely		1923
Loree Moore	Lakewood, CA	2001–05	Jill Rankin	Phillips, TX	1979–80	Christine Stoltzfus		1909
Pearl Moore	Harriman, TN	1987–90	Linda Ray	Norris, TN	1981–85	Mildred Stradley		1923–26
Lucy Morgan		1920–22	Dominique Redding	Clearwater, FL	2003–07	Sue Thomas	Maryville, TN	1974–77
Lois Moriarty		1923	Colleen Rhea		1926	—— Thompson		1969
Jenny Morrill		1904	Genevieve Rice		1907–08	Pashen Thompson	Philadelphia, MS	1993–97
Tasheika Morris	Huntsville, AL	1999–2000	Emily Roberts	Sharon, TN	1976–77	Laura Thornburgh		1903–04
Karen Morton	Lake City, TN	1982–83	Patricia Roberts	Monroe, GA	1976–77	Mina Todd	Murray, KY	1980–81
Lindsey Moss	Alpharetta, GA	2005	Ashley Robinson	Grand Prairie, TX	2000–04	Nannie Todd		1906
Sabrina Mott	Brentwood, TN	1986–87	Katherine Rockwell		1920	Paula Towns	Fort Valley, GA	1980–84
Michelle Muñoz	Mason, OH	2001–02	Winona Roehl		1905	Gay Townson	Loudon, TN	1986–87
Gretchen Nelson		1909–10	Ann Scarbrough		1971	Mary Treadwell		1903
Margaret Nickerson		1910	Sue Schultze		1973–74	Jennifer Tuggle	Etowah, TN	1984–88
Cindy Noble	Clarksburg, OH	1978–81	Debbie Scott	Gallatin, TN	1988–90	Catherine Upchurch		1926
Kathy O'Neil	Newport, TN	1976–80	Gloria Scott	Cleveland, TN	1972–74	Agnes Vanneman		1920
Mary Ostrowski	Parkersburg, WV	1980–84	Virginia Scott		1920	Daisy Wade		1906
Candace Parker	Naperville, IL	2004–08	Joy Scruggs	Cleveland, TN	1971–75	Eve Waldrop		1971
Debbie Paschall		1972–73	Jan Seay	Albany, GA	1977–78	Sadie Ward		1904

Name	Hometown	Years
Vonda Ward	Northfield, OH	1991–95
Holly Warlick	Knoxville, TN	1976–80
Sarah Watkins		1923–25
Jackie Watson	Crossville, TN	1974–77
Edith Wayland		1907
Lisa Webb	Milledgeville, GA	1983–88
Helen Weller		1924
Anna Weyland		1906
Becky White		1926
Sa'de Wiley-Gatewood	Pomona, CA	2004–05
Frances Williams		1924–26
Jane Williams		1903–04
Katherine Williams		1903
Marion Wingate		1923
Margie Wyatt		1971
Tiffany Woosley	Shelbyville, TN	1991–95
Elizabeth Young		1926
Venessa Yow	Birmingham, AL	1972
Shanna Zolman	Syracuse, IN	2002–05

Cross Country

Name	Hometown	Years
Missy Alston	Nashville, TN	1974–76
Erin Anderson	Kent, OH	2000–02
Leah Anderson	Chattanooga, TN	1996–97
Jackie Areson	Delray Beach, FL	2006–
Amber Ayub	Knoxville, TN	1999–2002
Christy Baird	Knoxville, TN	1999–2003
Amy Bartosik	Kingsport, TN	1996–99
Susan Baxter	Seymour, CT	1981–83
Rolanda Bell	Laurelton, NY	2005–
Kameisha Bennett	Dayton, OH	2000–03
Monique Berarducci	Knoxville, TN	2001

Name	Hometown	Years
Lori Bertelkamp	Knoxville, TN	1977
Valerie Bertrand	Coram, NY	1986–89
Deedie Bise	Knoxville, TN	1974
Sarah Bowman	Warrenton, VA	2005–
Miriam Boyd	Port Huron, MI	1979–81
Jennifer Brewer	Lincoln Park, MI	1993–95
Janelle Briggs	Stone Mountain, GA	1997
Alyssa Bryant	Andersonville, TN	2006–
Kathy Bryant	Delaware, OH	1980–84
Megan Cauble	Knoxville, TN	2002–05
Gena Clare	Fairfax, VA	1985–86
Joetta Clark	South Orange, NJ	1981–82
Allison Clary	Columbia, SC	1996
Shannon Cline	Columbus, OH	1979
Jane Cobb	Ronceverte, WV	1978
Lynne Collazo	Ridgewood, NJ	1989–92
Rebecca Collins	Loveland, OH	1999–02
Nicole Cook	Petersburg, VA	2001–04
Cathy Corpeny	Kansas City, MO	1981–84
Christy Cupp	Lake City, TN	1989
Tanya Dawson	Memphis, TN	1992
Shari Demarest	Washington, IN	1975
Dorothy Denko	Krakow, Poland	1997–98
Sharon Dickie	Grand Blanc, MI	1998–2002
Janet Easterday	Oak Ridge, TN	1986–87
Lynn Emery	Wichita, KS	1976–78
Ann Farrar	Oak Ridge, TN	1975
Maureen Ferris	Cleveland, OH	1994–98
Sara Fieweger	Hope, ME	1993
Pam Fillmore	Knoxville, TN	1983–84
Edra Finley	Mobile, AL	2005
Shara Flacy	Ardmore, TN	1974–75
Katie Flaute	Dayton, OH	2002–06

Name	Hometown	Years
Rose–Anne Galligan	County Kildare, Ireland	2006
Amanda Gillam	Finksburg, MD	1992–94
Jennifer Gordon	Burke, VA	2001
Antoinette Gorham	Glenarden, MD	2003–04
Sharon Gough	Pittsburgh, PA	1976
Katherine Green	Alpharetta, GA	1997–98
Felicia Guliford	Gallup, NM	2002–06
Jill Hall	Knoxville, TN	1975
Vonda Hammons	Jefferson City, MO	1985–88
Alisa Harvey	Fairfax, VA	1983–86
Laura Haynes	Knoxville, TN	1993–96
Sue Anne Heins	Knoxville, TN	1985
Laura Heiser	Knoxville, TN	1995
Melissa Hiller	Nashville, TN	1994–97
Eileen Hornberger	Laureldale, PA	1980–82
Beth Huff	Janesville, WI	1982
Lindsay Hyatt	Auburn, CA	2003
Alicia Johnson	Carrollton, TX	1989–91
Jasmin Jones	Hackensack, NJ	1987–90
Cathy Kirchner	Wilmington, DE	1977–78
Amy Kirkland	Knoxville, TN	1975
Page Kunst	Cincinnati, OH	1992
Lynn Lashley	Raleigh, NC	1976–79
Tonya Lee	Mount Holly, NJ	1991
Sigrid Lokrhiem	Oak Ridge, TN	1995
Pam Lyons	Memphis, TN	1997
Heidi Magill-Dahl	Orem, UT	2007–08
Katrice Malcom	Decatur, GA	1993–96
Meghan Mantlo	Nashville, TN	1996–99
Beth Marlow	Memphis, TN	1994–97
Carly Matthews	Winston–Salem, NC	2003–05
Elizabeth McCalley	Knoxville, TN	2001–04
Ellen McCallister	Bristol, TN	1979–81

Name	Hometown	Years
Kimarra McDonald	Lumberton, NJ	2005–
Donna McLain	York, PA	1980–84
Shawn Moore	Philadelphia, PA	1989
Robin Mortel	Brooklyn, NY	2004–05
Teal Mowery	Rochester, NY	1991–92
Sharon Mustin	Oak Ridge, TN	1981
Tiffany Myers	Germantown, TN	1990
Liz Natale	Newton, MA	1982–83
Brooke Novak	Kaukauna, WI	2001–04
Cindy O'Bryant	Chattanooga, TN	1990–93
Monica Olkowski	Marlton, NJ	1990–91
Monica O'Reilly	Abbeyleix, Ireland	1982–85
LeAnn Parker	Kingsport, TN	1985
Kelly Parrish	Ocala, FL	2006
Kathy Perez	Knoxville, TN	1984
Kristen Permakoff	Knoxville, TN	1989–90
Linda Portasik	Alexandria, VA	1979–82
Angie Pothier	Vancouver, WA	1998–99
Alison Quelch	MacQuarie Fields, Australia	1983–84
Amy Ranker	Liberal, KS	2001
Michelle Reasor	Fort Worth, TX	1993–94
Amy Reeves	West Point, GA	1994
Lisa Richardson	Nürnberg, Germany	1988–91
Kristen Ritter	Frederick, MD	1996–98
Brittany Sheffey	Bellport, NY	2007–
Betty Shell	Kettering, OH	1976–77
Sally Sligar	Louisville, KY	1975–76
Staci Snider	Saratoga Springs, NY	1991
Joanne Soldano	Oak Ridge, TN	1978–79
Leah Soro	Knoxville, TN	2005–
Jessica Southers	Ashland, KY	2000–03
Dina Spagnoli	Arlington, VA	1990–91
Krista Stewart	Drexel Hill, PA	1993–94

Name	Hometown	Years
Brenda Stone	Newport, TN	1974–75
Tere Stouffer	Auburn Hills, MI	1986–87
Michelle Strothers	Williamsport, PA	1988–91
Marianne Sturr	Dayton, OH	1976
Mindy Sullivan	Lubbock, TX	2002–05
Celeste Susnis	Wheatfield, IN	1990–93
Lauren Taylor	Morristown, TN	1997
Sally Thomas	North Indialantic, FL	1979
Megan Thompson	Florissant, MO	1990–93
Barb Tieperman	Arkansas City, KS	1976–78
Leslie Treherne	Chesapeake, VA	2003–06
Katie Van Horn	Glendora, NJ	2006–
Lynn Waldrop	Alto, GA	1974
Caitlin Ward	Gibsonia, PA	2005
Mindy Watkins	Canastota, NY	1996–99
Renn Watkins	Wake Forest, NC	2000
Brenda Webb	Kettering, OH	1977–78
Jill Weber	Celenia, OH	1984–85
Bridget White	Birmingham, AL	1985–86
Laurel White	Rocky Mount, NC	1996
Patty Wiegand	Canastota, NY	1987–90
Gina Wilbanks	Springfield, MO	1985–88
Scottie Wilkerson	Hermitage, TN	1983
Charlotte Williams	Knoxville, TN	1974–75
Michelle Winterer	Lake St. Louis, MO	1985–86
Phoebe Wright	Signal Mountain, TN	2006–
Roberta Wright	Greeneville, TN	1978
Rachel Zamata	Henderson, TN	2003–05
Sharon Zook	Boca Raton, FL	1974

Golf

Name	Hometown	Years
Teesha Ash	Chattanooga, TN	2003–05

Name	Hometown	Years
Stacey Bergman	Fort Dodge, IA	1998–2000
Angie Boyd	White Pine, TN	1992–94
Ginny Brown	Austin, TX	2006–
Sarah Bonner Shanks	Kingsport, TN	2004–05
Diana Cantú	Monterrey, Mexico	2006–
Holly Cantwell	Morristown, TN	2003–06
Nicole Cavalcanti	Pittsford, NY	1999–2000
Caroline Cole	Mansfield, TX	1998–2001
Susan Conger	Oviedo, FL	1992–94
Jennifer Davis	Seymour, TN	2004–07
Mary Jan Fernandez	Henderson, NV	2001–04
Leah Hagedorn	Fort Oglethorpe, GA	2006–08
Heather Humphreys	Knoxville, TN	2002–03
Rachel Ingram	Benton, TN	2006–08
Golda Johansson	Lund, Sweden	2002–06
Shelley Kinder–Anderson	Clarksville, TN	1992–95
Ryan Kirk	Hixson, TN	2001–03
Erin Kurczewski	Merritt Island, FL	1994–98
Susan Lanier	Pulaski, TN	1998–99
Katharina Larsson	Skoghall, Sweden	1992–94
Jessica Lindbergh	Ahus, Sweden	1996–99
Amy Livsey	Corpus Christi, TX	1993–97
Heather March	Roswell, GA	1998–99
Angela Oh	Maple Shade, NJ	2006–08
Wendi Patterson	Atlanta, GA	1994–95
Abby Pearson	Florence, SC	1992–94
Tai Perry	Unionville, PA	2000–04
Christie Reed	Coral Spring, FL	2004–05
Violeta Retamoza	Aguascalient-esm, Mexico	2002—06
Alyson Richards	Knoxville, TN	1995–96
Tina Schneeberger	WR–Neustadt, Austria	1998–2001
Jessica Shepley	Oakville, Ontario	2001–05

Name	Hometown	Years
Emily Sills	Knoxville, TN	2007–
Erin Simmons	The Woodlands, TX	1999–2001
Nicole Smith	Riverside, CA	2005–
Sofi Stromgren	Harestad, Sweden	1992–96
Rachel Thompson	Ripley, TN	1994–98
Marci Turner	Tompkinsville, KY	2004–08
Malin Tveit	Romelanda, Sweden	1996–97
Anna Umemura	Honolulu, HI	1997–2001
Rebecca Watson	Edinburgh, Scotland	2007–
Skyli Yamada	Sandy, UT	1994–98
Young–A Yang	Tae–Gu City, South Korea	1998–2001
Rosanna Zernatto	Treffen, Austria	1999–2000

Rowing

Name	Hometown	Years
Jaclyn Adams	Midlothian, VA	2003–04
Claire Allain	Franklin, LA	1998
Marissa Allen	Hendersonville, TN	2002–05
Ashley Anders	Kingsport, TN	2003–04
Ashley Andrews	Martinez, GA	1997–2000
Catherine Angel	Knoxville, TN	2001
Erin Artz	Woodbridge, VA	2001–04
Lindsey Ashton	Collierville, TN	2001
Jessica Ayers	Alpharetta, GA	2004–08
Andrea Bagwell	Hendersonville, TN	2002–05
Kaitlin Bargreen	Lake Stevens, WA	2002–05
Sarah Becker	San Diego, CA	2005–06
Sally BeVille	Signal Mountain, TN	2000–03
Brandi Bohleber	Morristown, TN	1999–2000
Nicole Bold	Jackson, MS	2001–04
Christy Boner	Mt. Juliet, TN	2005
Carla Box	Nashville, TN	1996–97
Leslie Boyle	Longwood, FL	1999–2000

Name	Hometown	Years
Jennifer Bradley	Fairfax, VA	1999–2002
Dani Bregar	Wichita, KS	2005–07
Brittany Brewer	Indianapolis, IN	1999–2000
Renee Brittle	Dublin, VA	2004–08
Lizzie Brown	Cincinnati, OH	2001–04
Kate Brownlee	North Gower, Ontario	2005–
Carla Brownlee	Bristol, TN	1996
Libuse Bruncvikova	Litomerice, Czech Republic	2007–
Ryan Bush	Chattanooga, TN	2004
Ashley Butturini	Oak Ridge, TN	2004–05
Jocelyn Campbell	Memphis, TN	2005–
Melina Cawthon	Chester County, TN	2001
Caitlyn Cleary	Knoxville, TN	2004
Abby Coe	Knoxville, TN	1999
Genevieve Collins	Dallas, TX	2004–08
Julie Coltrin	Collegedale, TN	1996
Jenny Cone	Greenville, SC	1996–97
Jennifer Conowall	Greensboro, NC	1997–98
Kelly Cooper	Hixson, TN	1997
McKenzie Craig	Pittsburgh, PA	2002–05
Rochelle Crim	Memphis, TN	1997
Stephanie Davis	Martin, TN	2003–06
Amy Delashmit	Maryville, TN	1996–97
Melissa DiCerbo	Hixson, TN	2002–05
Cara DiPierro	Shrewberry, MA	1998
Tharin Dobbs	Mt. Juliet, TN	2005–06
Nina Dobratz	Portland, OR	2004–08
Rachel Dooley	Marysville, WA	2007–
Mary Dreusike	Huntington Station, NY	2007–
Rachel Dutkosky	Cordova, TN	2005–07
Mackenzie Earle	Clinton, TN	2001
Lindsay Ehrlich	San Diego, CA	2005–07
Ashley Evans	Oak Ridge, TN	1997

Name	Hometown	Years
Sarah Fair	Pittsburgh, PA	1999
Barrett Farmer	Arlington, VA	1999
Brittany Farmer	Arlington, VA	2000
Natalie Fecher	Knoxville, TN	2001
Evangeline Ferrell	Woodbury, TN	1996–97
Ariana Fitzgerald	Alexandria, VA	2003
Katie Flanagan	Roswell, GA	1999
Dana Forbes	Cincinnati, OH	2002–05
Kelly Ford	Glen Gardner, NJ	1996–99
Elizabeth Freeman	Altamonte Springs, FL	2002–03
Kristen Galloway	Knoxville, TN	2003–06
Krista Gearing	Fenwick, Ontario	2004–08
Jennifer Gerlach	Richmond, VA	2004–05
Elizabeth Gibney	Knoxville, TN	1997–98
Hilary Gilmore	Nashville, TN	2002–03
Jaclyn Gonzales	Brentwood, TN	2005–06
Teresa Good	North Augusta, Ontario	2005
Hillary Graber	Bettendorf, IA	2003
Erin Gray	Wuerzburg, Germany	2007–
Johanna Greenberg	Hamilton, Ontario	2007–
Abbey Griffin	Franklin, TN	1998–01
Lindsey Groves	Winter Park, FL	2003
Mary Gruzalski	Oak Ridge, TN	2001–03
Giulia Guerrero	Clarksville, TN	2004–07
Katie Hall	Soddy Daisy, TN	1996–97
Marie Hanscom	Dumfries, GA	1998–2001
Pam Harder	Mayette, NJ	2005–07
Heather Hardt	Collierville, TN	1998
Sarah Harper	Roswell, GA	1996–97
Grace Harrington	Memphis, TN	1999–2002
Suni Hartsfield	Maryville, TN	1997
Raegan Haser	Germantown, TN	1997
Allyson Heard	Chattanooga, TN	2004–06

Name	Hometown	Years	Name	Hometown	Years	Name	Hometown	Years
Claire Hennesy	Mt. Juliet, TN	2001–02	Joyce Kranzke	Murfreesboro, TN	1999–2001	Joni Mullinix	Mt. Juliet, TN	2005–06
Roberta Hern	Knoxville, TN	1999–2000	Kelly Kravitz	Olympia, WA	2002–03	Jennifer Murchie	Maryville, TN	1996–98
Lindy Herzog	Longview, WA	1999–2000	Lauren Kueck	Oak Ridge, TN	1998–2001	Sara Neill	Oak Ridge, TN	1999–2000
Rachel Hickman	Collierville, TN	2005–06	Mary Beth Lewis	Andersonville, TN	2001–03	Sidney Newman	Halls, TN	2007–08
Michelle Higdon	Columbia, TN	2001–02	Heather Lewis	Chattanooga, TN	2000	Claire Newton	Orlando, FL	2001–03
Heather Hill	Knoxville, TN	2003–06	Kristen Logan	Knoxville, TN	1999–2001	Sarah Norsworthy	Cleveland, TN	1998–99
Renee Hines	Nashville, TN	2005–07	Kay Logan	Knoxville, TN	2000–03	Molly Oellerich	Arlington, VA	2003–06
Liza Hinton	Knoxville, TN	1998	Alexis Lombard	Knoxville, TN	1998–2000	Katie Payne	Parksville, British Columbia	2003–06
Kelly Hitzing	Jacksonville, FL	1997	Adrienne Long	Cleveland, TN	2004–05	Chelsea Pemberton	Jacksonville, FL	2002–05
Danielle Hmielewski	Cookeville, TN	2005–07	Sarah Long	Norris, TN	2001–02	Jennifer Pietrowski	Cheektowaga, NY	1996
Jamie Hoffman	Sarasota, FL	1999–2001	Davida Lopez	Dayton, OH	2001–02	Nicola Rasnick	Bluff City, TN	1996
Kelly Hohenbrink	Oak Ridge, TN	1997	Jewel Ludwigsen	Brentwood, TN	2007–08	Megan Reinhart	Milford, OH	1997–2000
Holly Holmes	Springfield, TN	2003–04	Lindsay MacLeod	Elkton, VA	1998	Heather Resig	Knoxville, TN	1997–2000
Kimberly Hoogenboom	Rochester Hills, MI	1996–97	Pam Mandrell	Maryville, TN	1997–98	Janece Rittenberry	Houston, TX	1996–97
Tammy Horton	Rockledge, FL	1998–2001	Olivia Marnell	Cincinnati, OH	2004–05	Katie Ross	Saratoga Springs, NY	2007–
Kelly Hoskins	Bristol, VA	2004	Heather Marshall	Hixson, TN	2002	Crystal Ruble	Asheville, NC	1998
Kelly Hotaling	Central Bridge, NY	2001–02	Lauren Matteis	Boca Raton, FL	1998	Lindsay Sagar	Dublin, OH	2001–02
Taylor Howe	Goodlettsville, TN	2004–06	Rachel Mayberry	Woodbridge, VA	2003–06	Diane Samu	Knoxville, TN	2003–04
Caroline Howell	Davenport, IA	2005–	Tina Mazzolini	Cleveland, TN	1997–2000	Alecia Scates	Knoxville, TN	1998–99
Elizabeth Humberd	Clarksville, TN	2001–02	Amy McCormick	Knoxville, TN	2003–05	Gretchen Schule	Arlington, VA	1999
Brittany Hunley	Knoxville, TN	2004–07	Amy McIntosh	Cleveland, TN	2001–04	Beth Schwartz	Columbia, TN	2002–06
Stephanie Hunley	Knoxville, TN	2007–	Caroline McKittrick	Oak Ridge, TN	1999	Rachel Scott	Hendersonville, TN	1996
Sarah Hutcheson	Orlando, FL	2003–06	Shannon McMahon	Altamonte Springs, FL	1999–2002	Jody Scott	Oak Ridge, TN	1996–98
Kelly Irwin	O'Fallon, IL	1998–99	Christi Mertens	Hilton Head, SC	1998	Brittany Sehring	Alpharetta, GA	2007–
Amanda Jackson	Maryville, TN	1999	Keri Meslar	Chantilly, VA	2001	Ellen Semran	Glen Ellyn, IL	1998
Kara Jenkins	Loudon, TN	1997–99	Laura Miller	Columbus, MS	2007–	Erin–Monique Shelton	Wellington, New Zealand	2005–
Kristen Johnson	Germantown, TN	1996–97	Leslie Mix	Issaquah, WA	1998	Alex Shiskov	Mississauga, Ontario	2005–08
Ruth Ann Johnson	Johnson City, TN	2007–	Marisa Mohan	San Diego, CA	2004–08	Jessica Shreder	Atlanta, GA	2003–04
Lindsay Jones	Evans, GA	2003–04	Rachel Montgomery	Knoxville, TN	1996	Margaret Shriver	Kiethville, LA	1996–99
Mary Jones	Huntsville, AL	2004–08	Kacey Montgomery	Apopka, FL	2000–03	Roshauna Singh	Vienna, VA	2007–
Kate Kelsey	Clarksville, TN	2000–01	Michele Moore	Hixson, TN	1997–2000	Nicole Small	Alpharetta, GA	1999–2000
Katie King	Knoxville, TN	1996	Erin Moore	St. Louis, MO	2000–01	Leah Smelser	Macon, GA	2004–07
Kelly Kraiss	Orlando, FL	2000–03	Sage Morgan	Hixson, TN	1998	Traci Smith	Hixson, TN	1996–98

Name	Hometown	Years
Ashley Smith	Lexington, NC	2000–01
Kate Snider	Ramona, CA	2007–08
Nilou Soltanian	Knoxville, TN	2005–06
Dana Southard	Oak Ridge, TN	1997
Shelly Stanton	Johnson City, TN	1999–2000
Virginia Stokes	Germantown, TN	1996
Sara Stout	Columbia, TN	2000
Bre Sweet	Lafayette, NJ	1999–2000
Jennifer Tagg	Nashville, TN	1997
Angela Taylor	Germantown, TN	1996–97
Whitney Tehan	Edmond, OK	2003
Laura Thompson	Memphis, TN	1997–2000
Deanna Thonnard	Oak Ridge, TN	1997
Kelly Todd	Oak Ridge, TN	2005–06
Melissa Toms	Annapolis, MD	2007–
Abby Tucker	Knoxville, TN	2001–02
Erika Twedt	Prairie Farm, WI	2000–01
Jovanna Vick	Pleasant View, TN	2002–05
Katie von Peters	Chattanooga, TN	2003–06
Tori VonderAhe	Cincinnati, OH	2001
Ruth Waldrop	Florissant, MO	2007–
Kim Walsh	Eads, TN	1998–2000
Ashley Warbington	Nashville, TN	1997
Dawn Ware	Spring City, TN	1999–2000
Kendra Warren	Franklin, TN	2004–08
Marissa Weaver	Roswell, GA	1999–2000
Carol Weigand	Dalton, GA	2002
Lauren Wells	London, Ontario	2002–06
Eileen Welsh	Northfield, NJ	2004
Christine Werve	Germantown, TN	1998–99
Lelia Wheatley	Nashville, TN	1996–97
Ashley Williams	Chattanooga, TN	2005–06
Steppie Williams	Collierville, TN	2003–06

Name	Hometown	Years
Amber Williams	Sevierville, TN	2000–01
Katie Zajac	Bybee, TN	2001
Debby Zmistowski	Palm Beach Gardens, FL	1999–2000

Soccer

Name	Hometown	Years
Jackie Acevedo	Austin, TX	2005
Melissa Amado	Surrey, British Columbia	2003–06
Molly Baird	Raleigh, NC	2006–
Natalie Balash	Plano, TX	1996–98
Amy Ballew	Springfield, VA	2005
Tori Beeler	Knoxville, TN	1997–2000
Kelley Bell	Farragut, TN	1997
Miriam Bennett	Sparta, NJ	2002–03
Kelly Berrall	Roswell, GA	1997–2000
Kathy Blakemore	Kingsport, TN	1996
Mia Boyd	Kingwood, TX	2005–06
Shannon Braly	Glen Ellyn, IL	2000
Nikki Bratta	Knoxville, TN	2000–03
Lindsay Brauer	Ormond Beach, FL	2004
Chrissy Brooker	Atlanta, GA	2000
Molly Buns	West Chester, OH	2005
Allison Campbell	Livonia, MI	1998–99
Meghan Chismark	Collierville, TN	1999
Ali Christoph	Columbus, OH	2003–06
Cameron Conway	Knoxville, TN	1999, 2001–02
Mimi Couns	Farragut, TN	2001–04
Melissa Covington	Nashville, TN	1996–98
Casey Crawford	Mandeville, LA	2005
Alex Crimmins	Cary, NC	2005
Lindsay Criss	Knoxville, TN	2000
Marisha Crowe	Cordova, TN	2002–03
Grace Cuenin	Midlothian, VA	2007
Ashley Dawes	Waukesha, WI	2001–04

Name	Hometown	Years
Ellen Dean	Memphis, TN	1998–02
Molly Delk	Cookeville, TN	2007–
Anna Dempsey	Germantown, TN	1996–97
Kristen Doukakis	Highlands Ranch, CO	2003–06
Lauren Duncan	Atlanta, GA	2001
Keeley Dowling	Carmel, IN	2001–04
Julie Edwards	Glenmoore, PA	2007–
Tanya Emerson	Capistrano Beach, CA	2007–
Jordan Falcusan	Plymouth, MI	2006–07
Sue Flamini	Cranford, NJ	2001–04
Anna Fisher	Franklin, TN	2007–
Kim Hull Flower	Mound, TX	1996–2000
Anne Glees	Rockford, IL	1997
Genna Gorman	Lakewood, CO	2004–05
Erica Griffin	Memphis, TN	2004–07
Jessica Griffith	Chattanooga, TN	2002
Ali Halverson	Belleair, FL	2007–
Heather Handel	Germantown, TN	1996–99
Jodie Hanlon	Troy, NY	1996–97
Bethany Himel	Germantown, TN	1996–97
Sharon Holmes	Oak Ridge, TN	1999–01
Michelle Imgram	Clifton, VA	2005–
Sarah Jackyra	Cary, NC	2006–
Jenny Jeffers	Lake Zurich, IL	2003–06
Jaimel Johnson	Kettering, OH	2005–
Kassie Kees	Brentwood, TN	1996–98
Sharon Kelly	Brantford, Ontario	1996–98
Holly Kimble	Livonia, MI	1996–97
Sarah Kitchin	Crofton, MD	2005–
Keree Koeppel	Scottsdale, AZ	1996
Erica LaShomb	Greeneville, TN	2000–03
Jen Laughridge	Wilson, NC	1998–2002
Kayla Lockaby	Hamilton, OH	2001–04
Stacey Longino	Ann Arbor, MI	1996–99

Name	Hometown	Years
Stephanie Lovely	Edmond, OK	2003
Alyssa Lyon	New Orleans, LA	1998
Melissa Majcher	Pittsburgh, PA	1996–99
Véronique Maranda	Saint–Lambert, Quebec	2005–06
Debbie Markovich	Addison, IL	1996–97
Jen Marrett	Binghamton, NY	1999
Kristin McGrath	Durango, CO	2001–04
Kendyl Michner	Germantown, TN	1997–99
Tara Minnax	Tampa, FL	1998–2002
Marie–Eve Nault	Trois-Rivieres, Quebec	2000–03
Rachael Newkirk	Roswell, GA	1997–2000
Ashley Owens	Murrieta, CA	2007–
Kim Patrick	Pleasanton, CA	2001–02
Lyndsey Patterson	Puyallup, WA	2001–04
Marchele Patterson	Puyallup, WA	2003
Vanessa Phillips-Bosshart	Vernon, CT	2002-05
Hayley Prendergast	Hingham, MA	2004–07
Connie Pullum	Farragut, TN	2000–01
Whitney Rayburn	Nashville, TN	1996–98
Emily Redberg	Brooklyn Park, MN	2003–07
Heather Redecker	Ft. Lauderdale, FL	1996–99
Melissa Rose	San Diego, CA	2006
Kylee Rossi	Pennington, NJ	2005–
Kim Sgarlata	Memphis, TN	1998–2001
Sarah Shivley	Tampa, FL	1996–99
Kyrstin Smith	Acworth, GA	2007–
Laura Lauter Smith	Farragut, TN	1997–2000
Brooke Sweeney	Tampa, FL	1996–99
Melissa Speros	Lancaster, PA	2007–
Cori Stevens	Greensboro, NC	2001–02
Devon Swaim	Levittown, PA	2006–
Brooke Sweeney	Tampa, FL	1996–99
Carie Swibas	Lakewood, CO	2000–03
Tracy Swibas	Lakewood, CO	2000–03

Name	Hometown	Years
Shayna Teutsch	Albuquerque, NM	1997–2000
Lisa Tipton	Knoxville, TN	1997–2000
Kelsey Troutman	Tucker, GA	2007–
Sarah Van Sickle	Knoxville, TN	2005–
Marcelle Van Yahres	Charlottesville, VA	2000–01
Leslie Vineyard	St. Louis, MO	2005–
Alissa VonderHaar	Bolingbrook, IL	2007–
Amanda Watts	Duluth, GA	2004
Lindsey Wiest	Toms River, NJ	2001–03
Rhian Wilkinson	Baie d'Urfe, Quebec	2000–03
Talia Wright	Chattanooga, TN	2002–05
Kirby Zwickel	Indianapolis, IN	2003–04

Softball

Name	Hometown	Years
Monica Abbott	Salinas, CA	2004–07
Christy Anch	Ashburn, VA	2003–04
Kim Anders	Erwin, TN	2003–04
Danielle Arriaga	Miami, FL	2003–04
Sarah Ayres	Roseville, CA	1997–99
Tiffany Baker	East Ridge, TN	2007
Kristen Bass	Chattanooga, TN	2003
Jackie Beavers	Warren, OH	1996–2000
Kortney Bell	Castaic, CA	2005–06
Brittany Bessho	Marietta, GA	2004–05
Crystal Bobo	Nolensville, TN	2002
Nicole Borg	Millbrae, CA	2001–02
Whitney Bradshaw	Powell, TN	2002
Angela Brewer	East Ridge, TN	2003–04
Natalie Brock	Nashville, TN	2005–06
Alicia Brown	Clinton, TN	2006
Tonya Callahan	Holden, MO	2005–08
Nadia Cameron	Fairfield, CA	1999–2000
Katherine Card	Soddy Daisy, TN	2003–06

Name	Hometown	Years
India Chiles	Louisville, KY	2004–07
Ashley Cline	Gallatin, TN	2004–05
Alexia Clay	Rochester, IN	2007
Shannon Doepking	Acton, CA	2005–08
Kristi Durant	Placentia, CA	2003–06
Leigh Ann Ellis	Barboursville, WV	2001–02
Holly Ellison	Bryan, TX	2000
Sarah Fekete	Maryville, TN	2003–06
Mandie Fishback	Banks, OR	2003–04
Kelli Fitzgerald	Lakewood, CA	1996–99
Annie Fletcher	San Diego, CA	2000–01
Candice Fode	San Marcos, CA	1996–97
Allison Fulmer	Maryville, TN	2007–
Kelli Glass	Jensen Beach, FL	1998–99
Kelly Grieve	Asheville, NC	2008–
Jennifer Griffin	Whittier, CA	2006–07
Lillian Hammond	Chattanooga, TN	2006–08
Kristen Hays	Phoenix, AZ	2003
Liane Horiuchi	Wahiawa, HI	2006–07
Tiffany Huff	Saugus, CA	2007–
Ellisha Humphrey	Knoxville, TN	2001–04
Stephanie Humphrey	Knoxville, TN	2000–03
Jennifer Hutson	Greenbrier, TN	1996
Bridget Jackson	Glendale, AZ	1996–97
Stacey Jennings	Aurora, CO	2003–05
Nicole Johnson	Knoxville, TN	2001
Nicole Kajitani	San Bernardino, CA	2006–
Janette Koshell	Granite Bay, CA	2000–01
Jennifer Lapicki	Oldwick, NJ	2008–
Hannah Low	Miwuk, CA	2001–02
Anita Manuma	Ewa Beach, HI	2007–
Lauren Mattox	Charlotte, NC	2003–04
Rachael Mink	Corryton, TN	2001

Name	Hometown	Years
Chandra Mogan	Fontana, CA	2008–
Maura Mollet	Yukon, OK	1998–2001
Marissa Monroe	Sweetwater, TN	2004
Heather Moore	Bethany, OK	1996–97
Nicole Murray	Carmichael, CA	2000–02
Kenyail Norris	Grand Prairie, TX	1996–99
LaDonna Oliver	Dayton, TN	2005
Jennifer Ortiz	San Diego, CA	1996
April Phillips	Charlotte, NC	1997–2000
Danielle Pieroni	Madison, TN	2006–
Leslie Poole	Rootstown, OH	2000
Kenora Posey	Los Angeles, CA	2005–08
Melissa Radley	Woodrising, Australia	2000–01
Jodi Ramirez	Sacramento, CA	1997–98
Tracy Reidhead	Taylor, AZ	1996–97
Amber Rhinehart	Citrus Heights, CA	2001–04
Megan Rhodes	Nashville, TN	2005–08
Carissa Roustan	Temecula, CA	2001–02
Cherrae Rushton	Sacramento, CA	1998
Caitlin Ryan	Knoxville, TN	2005–08
Kim Sanders	Placentia, CA	2003
Nicole Schaeffer	Yorktown, VA	2001–02
Lindsay Schutzler	Monterey, CA	2004–07
Nikki Sexton	Knoxville, TN	2001–02
Andie Sherman	Penryn, CA	2001–02
Jennifer Springs	Jasper, TN	2000
Kelsey Stander	Paradise Valley, AZ	2008–
Jenny Steele	Soddy Daisy, TN	1996–99
Carrie Swinford	Carrollton, OH	1996–99
Blaine Teasley	Tucson, AZ	2002–03
Maria Torres	Parana, Argentina	1999–2002
Sarah Vaughn	Lenoir City, TN	2006
Amanda Venable	Rio Linda, CA	1999–2000

Name	Hometown	Years
Buffy Walker	Carlsbad, NM	1996–99
Ashton Ward	Charlotte, NC	2008–
Lisa Warren	Escondido, CA	1998–99
Chemil Washington	Vancouver, WA	2003
Erinn Webb	Hemet, CA	2007–
Natalee Weissinger	Madison, TN	2007–
Katie Williams	Bartlett, TN	2000
Adrianna Wilson	Cypress, CA	1999–2002
Jessica Wilson	Brentwood, TN	2003
Kara Wingate	Reisterstown, MD	1999
Lisa Wyatt	Cincinnati, OH	1996–97

Swimming and Diving

Swimming

Name	Hometown	Years
Luciana Abe	São Paulo, Brazil	1996–98
Aleksa Akerfelds	Bronxville, NY	2007–
Veronique Alderson	West Point, NY	1982–83
Melissa Allen	Augusta, GA	1973–75
Marcella Amar	Rio de Janiero, Brazil	1994–97
Catherine Andrews	Jacksonville, FL	1979–80
Janie Armington	Indianapolis, IN	1982–83
Raellen Arnold	Sevierville, TN	2000–03
Jen Arnold	San Rafael, CA	1993–96
Katherine Ashley	Belle Meade, NJ	1990–91
Tatiana Athayde	Rio de Janiero, Brazil	2002–05
Claire August	Duluth, GA	1996–97
Jenny Banner	Knoxville, TN	1977–79
Julie Barker	Palm Springs, FL	1981–84
Beth Barr	Pensacola, FL	1989–90
Alex Barsanti	Hummelstown, PA	2007–
Noelle Bassi	Franklin Lakes, NJ	2002–03
Amy Baxter	Huntsville, AL	1984–88

Name	Hometown	Years
Deborah Baxter	Knoxville, TN	1985–86
Missy Bell	Springfield, VA	1997–2001
Sarah Bervoets	Nashville, TN	1984–86
Kim Blair	Knoxville, TN	1985–88
Jessica Blevins	Bluefield, WV	2001–05
Kara Boland	Lafayette Hill, PA	2002–05
Brooke Boncher	West Newbury, MA	2006–08
Susan Borman	Wichita Falls, TX	1982–83
Melissa Brackett	Chattanooga, TN	1972–74
Nicole Brannock	Ellicott City, MD	1999–2003
Graciela Breece-Rodriguez	Boulder, CO	2002–05
Brenda Breese	Sylvania, OH	1975–76
Stephanie Brinser	Richmond, VA	1988–92
Lindsey Brock	Roswell, GA	1999–2002
Betsy Brockman	Batavia, OH	2002–06
Eeiron Brown	Kingsport, TN	1995–97
Liz Brown	Richmond, VA	1980–84
Heather Burgess	Midlothian, VA	1984–88
J. B. Burrell	Lansing, MI	1981–83
Christy Bussard	Knoxville, TN	1974–76
Catherine Byrne	Detroit, MI	1988–92
Misty Cain	Marietta, GA	2003–07
Carol Calloway	Maryville, TN	1976–78
Laura Campbell		1974–75
Laura Capps	Knoxville, TN	1974–75
Mari Carlson	Huntsville, AL	1986–88
Michele Cary	Prince George, VA	1981–83
Elizabeth Christy	Indianapolis, IN	2003–07
Kate Chronic	Boulder, CO	1983–84
Meg Cifers	Knoxville, TN	1974–75
Patty Clark	North Palm Beach, FL	1981–84
Tiffany Clay	Mason, OH	2003–07
Paige Clemmens	Prospect, KY	1973–74

Name	Hometown	Years	Name	Hometown	Years	Name	Hometown	Years
Kristin Clodfelter	Corpus Christi, TX	1989–91	Shelley Eaton	Terrace Park, OH	1996–97	Susan Hamre	Birmingham, AL	1971–72
Libby Cochran	Maryville, TN	1975–80	Barb Ehring	Levittown, PA	1976–78	Laura Hancock	Spanish Fort, AL	1998–2002
Betsy Cofer	Reston, VA	1978–79	Amy Elfman	Doylestown, PA	1991–92	Pam Hanson	La Crosse, WI	1997–2001
Kathy Coffin	Colonial Heights, VA	1982–84	Azurdee Engel	Decatur, GA	1997–2001	Lynn Hardiman	Tampa, FL	1972–76
Keely Cone	Greenfield, IN	1986–87	Susan Erasmus	Westville, South Africa	1983–87	Sallye Hartman	Gates, TN	2004–06
Cary Conley	Healdsburg, CA	1996–99	Alison Evangelista	Medford Lakes, NJ	1984–87	Karen Hartwig	Verona, NJ	1978–79
Mary Conlin	Knoxville, TN	1972–75	Morgan Farrell	Pensacola, FL	2007–	Rebecca Hartzell	Sellersville, PA	1996–97
Valerie Conte	Bensenville, IL	1998–2002	Laura Fehrman	St. Charles, IL	2004–08	Keira Heath	Greenwich, CT	2006–07
Liz Cooper	Bloomfield Hills, MI	1985–87	Tanya Felton	Leesburg, FL	1997–2001	Lynn Heestand	Oak Ridge, TN	1975–76
Kathy Corcoran	Cincinnati, OH	1983–86	Valerie Fenter	Spring, TX	2001–02	Jenny Heffernan	Greeneville, TN	1998–2001
Brigid Corr	Great Neck, NY	1988–89	Sandy Ferrin	Sunnyvale, CA	1978–82	Jennifer Hesp	San Antonio, TX	1987–91
Heather Coulson	Richmond, VA	1987–91	Jacque Fessel	Cincinnati, OH	2002–06	Jennifer Hettich	Louisville, KY	2000–01
Dinah Cox	Knoxville, TN	1978–79	Kelly Finley	Holland, PA	2005–06	Libby Hill	Sunnyvale, CA	1980–84
Susan Craig	Donelson, TN	1978–79	Jill Fletcher	Knoxville, TN	1977–80	Kathy Hoffman	Beavercreek, OH	1988–92
Jane Cross	Oak Ridge, TN	1978–79	Nancy Fosnaught	Cookeville, TN	1983–85	Carrie Hollman	Fort Myers, FL	1979–81
Bryttany Curran	Cary, NC	2006–	Valerie Franse	Knoxville, TN	1979–81	Julie House	Nashville, TN	1978–81
Lisa Czarniecki	Cincinnati, OH	1982–83	Amber Fuller	Yakima, WA	2000–01	Kerry Howland	Wheaton, IL	1973–76
Amy Danchik	Plano, TX	2000–02	Susan Furkin	Columbia, IL	1999–2000	Missy Hoy	Somerset, MA	1987–91
Julie Darby	Franklin, TN	1987–91	Katie Gehring	Punta Gorda, FL	2005–	Leah Hughes	Knoxville, TN	1984–86
Bambi Davis	Chattanooga, TN	1975–77	Dierdre Gildea	Cocoa Beach, FL	1985–89	Tracy Ignatosky	Reading, PA	1986–89
Kari Ann Davis	Antioch, CA	1993–97	Sandy Glafenhein	Fort Lauderdale, FL	1976–80	Clarie Jackson	Murfreesboro, TN	1978–81
Liane Deere	Nashville, TN	1980–82	Ellie Glover	Asheville, NC	1974–75	Raquel James	Port of Spain, Trinidad	1989–93
Karen Delk	Willingboro, NJ	1979–81	Michelle Gobrecht	Elizabethtown, PA	1992–96	Dianne Johnson	Maryville, TN	1977–78
Nicole deMan	Walnut Creek, CA	1992–96	Wendy Goldman	Kingsport, TN	1984–85	Julie Johnson	Columbia, MO	1982–83
Tori DeSilvia	Syracuse, NY	1995–98	Angie Graham	Fort Myers, FL	1992–93	Kerste Johnson	Houston, TX	1971–72
Sandy Dibble	Greeneville, TN	1980–81	Jenny Grathwohl	Cincinnati, OH	1988–92	Peggy Johnson		1974–75
Caroline Dill	Greenville, SC	1981–82	Mollie Graves	Knoxville, TN	1974–75	Bianca Jones	Palm Beach, Australia	1999–2002
Mary Doyle	South Orange, NJ	1977–78	Diane Green	Sunnyvale, CA	1981–82	Maureen Jones	Sarasota, FL	1981–83
Tara Doyle	Brentwood, TN	1981–82	Nancy Gribben	Weston, Ontario	1990–94	Maria Jugan	Knoxville, TN	2005–
Karla Driesler	Bartow, FL	1983–87	Wendy Gwaltney	Richmond, VA	1985–87	Kathy Kearney	Hendersonville, TN	1983–84
Annabel Droussiotis	Limassoi, Cyprus	1984–88	Bethany Hall	Knoxville, TN	1999–2001	Meghan Keefer	Fort Wayne, IN	2003–04
Michelle Duvall	Broken Arrow, OK	1992–94	Doreen Haller	Fort Myers, FL	1978–81	Kathy Keirstead	Bristol, TN	1980–82
Sally Dzikowski	Partin, NJ	1973–74	Liz Hamann	Antioch, TN	1978–80	Laura Kersey	Boca Raton, FL	1986–90

Name	Hometown	Years
Michele King	York, PA	2006–
Anne Kitzrow	Kingsport, TN	1975–77
Ashley Knapik	Baltimore, MD	2006–07
Karen Koleber	Washington, MI	1984–88
Janice Krauser	Fort Lauderdale, FL	1971–72
Kristen Krenitsky	Rochester, NY	1992–94
Becky Krone	Dover, PA	1990–92
Page Kunst	Cincinnati, OH	1988–92
Jeanne Landry	Lafayette, TN	1971–72
Michelle Lane	Dunwoody, GA	1988–92
Betsy Lange	Hinsdale, IL	2005–
Linda Lee	Oak Ridge, TN	1977–78
Gina Leekley	Wilmette, IL	1978–80
Robin Lewis	Huntingdon, CT	1990–92
Stephanie Livers	Elizabethtown, KY	1992–96
Danielle Lundy	Austell, GA	2002–04
Julia Lutz	Lilburn, GA	2003–06
Angie Lynch	Granger, IN	1992–96
Melanie Maassen	Los Alamos, NM	1999–2001
Sam Maccherola	Mount Airy, MD	2005–07
Christine Magnuson	Tinley Park, IL	2004–08
Jennifer Mancini	Raleigh, NC	1995–98
Kim Marsden	Kinnelon, NJ	1987–89
Therese Marsh	Sydney, Australia	1983–84
Susan Marshall	Dalton, PA	1982–84
Paula Marsiglia	Sáo Paulo, Brazil	1996–98
Dana Martin	Brentwood, TN	1977–79
Tonya Mashburn	Durham, NC	1990–92
Emily Massey	Knoxville, TN	1976–77
Carly Mathes	Kettering, OH	2005–
Sarah McCall	Knoxville, TN	2005–
Trish McCollum	Knoxville, TN	1992–93
Susan McFarland	Milan, TN	1977–78

Name	Hometown	Years
Lisa McGill	Gatlinburg, TN	1977–78
Kristin McGrath	Durango, CO	2003–05
Jenny McGrath	Knoxville, TN	1988–92
Erin McGriff	Fort Myers, FL	1994–98
Katie Melka	Marietta, GA	2000–03
Julie Millis	Ormond Beach, FL	1992–96
Jamie Minnich	Ashland, OH	1993–95
Elaina Mitek	Marietta, GA	1991–93
Leslie Mix	Issaquah, WA	1993–98
Fabiola Molina	São José dos Campos, Brazil	1994–98
Teresa Moodie	Harare, Zimbabwe	1998–2000
Carol Moore	Memphis, TN	1972–74
Marti Moravcikova	Prague, Czech Republic	2007–
Jenny Mund	Knoxville, TN	1974–77
Courtney Naparlo	Williamsburg, VA	2000–03
Brittany Nauta	Tampa, FL	2005–
Karla Neal	Murfreesboro, TN	2006–07
Marcia Nemeck	Knoxville, TN	1975–76
Sarah Nichols	Camarillo, CA	1995–99
Suzy Norcliffe	Jacksonville, FL	1998–2001
Nancy Nutter	Henderson, TN	1979–80
Wendy Oakes	Chattanooga, TN	1990–91
Allison O'Dell	Knoxville, TN	1976–78
Kaitlyn Orstein	Pittsburgh, PA	2004–05
Julie Paque	Shorewood, WI	1976–78
Julie Parkes	Belfast, Northern Ireland	1983–84
Cindy Parkinson	Knoxville, TN	1982–83
Jennifer Parsons	Brentwood, TN	1994–96
Tillie Patterson	Knoxville, TN	1983, 1987
Sarah Payette	Sebastopol, CA	1995–99
Kari Peterson	Dhahran, Saudi Arabia	1998–2000
Elizabeth Philp	Adelaide, Australia	1998–2002

Name	Hometown	Years
Cortney Piper	Gross Pointe Woods, MI	1998–2002
Emily Plummer	Concord, CA	1994–98
Caroline Poling	Columbia, TN	2005–06
Mary Kirk Pollard	Charlotte, NC	2005–07
Nancy Purvis	Brentwood, TN	1994–96
Ashley Quinn	Knoxville, TN	2005–
Jackie Ramser	Houston, TX	1975–76
Christi Reed	Lillian, AL	1989–90
Sharon Regas	Knoxville, TN	1974–76
Sarah Ridgway	St. Croix, Virgin Islands	2003–05
Janet Risser	Austin, TX	1981–84
Amy Roberts	Boxboro, MA	2002–03
Cynthia Roberts	Blacksburg, VA	1980–81
Yvette Robling	Muncie, IN	1992–93
Sara Rodenburg	Lansing, IL	1993–94
Kathy Rorn	Oak Ridge, TN	1972–73
Kristy Rorn	Oak Ridge, TN	1974–75
Linda Rule	Copperhill, TN	1974–78
Peg Saalfeld	Richmond, KY	1981–82
Jamie Saffer	Roswell, GA	2006–
Laura Sawyer	Cleveland, TN	1983–84
Teresa Schneider	Ellicott City, MD	1985–86
Allison Sells	Seymour, TN	1979–80
Anne Serina	Atlanta, GA	1994–96
Teresa Sestak	Binghamton, NY	1985–88
Karen Seykora		1973–74
Monica Shannahan	San Diego, CA	1998–2002
Kelly Shea	Oakland, CA	1996–97
Kelly Shedden	Franklin, PA	1996–98
Christie Shefchunas	Franklin, PA	1993–97
Karen Sherman	South Charleston, WV	1987–88
Linda Sherwin	Kingsport, TN	1975–76
Tina Silbersack	Cincinnati, OH	1992–96

Name	Hometown	Years
Ann Skaggs	Columbus, OH	1972–73
Mallory Slaughter	Huntsville, AL	1988–90
Lexie Smith		1972–73
Megan Smith	Bend, OR	1994
Karen Soard	Oak Ridge, TN	1971–72
Kristin Souppa	Naperville, IL	2001–03
Michelle Spears	Maryville, TN	1982–83
Jill Sprecher	Cincinnati, OH	1995–99
Beverly Stancell	Knoxville, TN	1987–88
Natalie Stevens	Concord, TN	1979–80
Julia Stowers	Knoxville, TN	2001–05
Ashley Sudduth	Greenville, SC	1992–96
Laura Temple		1974–75
Taryn Ternent	Edenvale, South Africa	2002–04
Allison Terry	San Diego, CA	1992–93
Abbi Terveer	Lima, OH	2002–06
Bonnie Thor	Knoxville, TN	1974–76
Karen Thor	Knoxville, TN	1977–79
Marti Tickle	Johnson City, TN	1976–80
Laura Tomes	Cincinnati, OH	2006–
Megan Tomes	Cincinnati, OH	2003–07
Diane Townsend	Cleveland, TN	1981–83
Livia Trevisan	Londrinia, Brazil	2001–02
Sarah Turner	Cincinnati, OH	1992–96
Lisa Vandersluis	Oak Ridge, TN	1981–82
Danyelle Vincent	Greenbrae, CA	2004–08
Randi Vogel	Maineville, OH	2002–04
Dianna Vogel	Denville, NJ	1987–90
Beth Wallace	Holland, PA	1976–78
Tricia Watson	Crossville, TN	1973–74
Tricia Weaner	Gettysburg, PA	2007–
Marcelle Webber	Durban, South Africa	1984–86
Rachael Weightman	Longwood, FL	1990–91

Name	Hometown	Years
Sarah Weis	Sylvania, OH	1988–92
Mary Nan Welch	Concord, TN	1975–76
Andrea Wentzel	Dover, PA	1988–92
Erikka Westman	Brentwood, TN	1999–2000
GeeGee Wharton	Wenatchee, WA	1986–87
Cheryl White	Elilicott City, MD	1993–96
Katy White	Allen, TX	1997–2000
Linda White	Vienna, WV	1978–79
Carol Wiegand	Shorewood, IL	1982–84
Kim Wild	Knoxville, TN	1979–80
Amanda Wilding	Williamsburg, VA	1995–97
Daena Wilds	Versailles, KY	1980–81
Christy Williams	Maryville, TN	1979–81
Sue Wilson	Knoxville, TN	1975–77
Sarah Wingfield	Fort Pierce, FL	1999–2003
Nancy Winkler	Stony Brook, NY	1987–88
Cathy Wojcik	Old Hickory, TN	1978–81
Susan Wright	Knoxville, TN	1977–80
Elizabeth Wueste	Norcross, GA	2001–05
Ashley Yeager	Mechanicsburg, PA	2003–07
Debbie Yonke	Spring City, TN	1986–87
Marianna York	Yuba City, CA	1992–94
Franca Zaretzky	Brooklyn, NY	1987–88
Kate Zenda	Marblehead, MA	1988–92

Diving

Name	Hometown	Years
Dawn Andreas	Austin, TX	1993–94
Jane Anthony	Peachtree City, GA	1983–87
Alicia Ball	Knoxville, TN	1995–99
Sara Benton	Knoxville, TN	1973–76
Stacy Binyon	Southlake, TX	1999–2003
Tracy Bonner	Houston, TX	1992–97
Debbie Brandenburg	Cincinnati, OH	1979–80

Name	Hometown	Years
Sandy Britton	Germantown, TN	1974–77
Dawn Burton	Long Beach, CA	1994–97
Heather Chapman	Indianapolis, IN	2002–03
Dianne Demontbreun	Gallatin, TN	1977–78
Maria Dietz	Minnetonka, MN	1986–90
Marci Eppler	Lutherville, MD	1978–79
Traci Felty	Bristol, TN	1980–81
Martha Flowers	Knoxville, TN	1976–78
Lizzy Flynt	Auburn, AL	1998–2001
Linda Fritz	Madison, CT	1978–79
Brittany Fulmer	Maryville, TN	2003–07
Heidi Gilbert	Houston, TX	1988–92
Angela Harms	Aloha, OR	1999–2000
Lauren LeRoy	Oshkosh, WI	2004–08
Sue Lichtenberger	Cleveland, TN	1973–74
Vicky Linnell	Prospect, South Australia	2005–08
Mary Long	Lexington, SC	1978–80
Lee Mahan	Decatur, GA	1973–76
Liz Mauldin	Huntsville, AL	1985–86
Lauryn McCalley	Moultrie, GA	2001–05
Staley McCartney	Knoxville, TN	2005–
Allison Menger	Wimberley, TX	1990–94
Gailya Miazza	Simsbury, CT	1978–79
Summer Miller	McKinney, TX	1994–96
Bethany Minser	Maryville, TN	1998–2000
Laine Owen	Norman, OK	1991–92
Kathy Pesek	Houston, TX	1995–99
Jill Pierce	Knoxville, TN	2007–
Mary Reker	Chattanooga, TN	1984–85
Karla Richardson	Oak Ridge, TN	1981
Susan Rosenvinge	Oak Ridge, TN	1980–84
Jaime Sanger	Plymouth, MN	1999–2003
Cheri Sears	Atlanta, GA	1994–98

Name	Hometown	Years
Lara Shostle	Louisville, KY	1987–88
Ashley Showalter	Knoxville, TN	2002–03
Natalie Shropshire	Miami, FL	1973–74
Michele Tenut	Hendersonville, TN	1987–88
Patti Turpin	Bristol, TN	1978–79
Laura Vallas	New Orleans, LA	1978–80
Kylee Wells	Russiaville, IN	2000–04
Barbara White	Crossville, TN	1978–80
Jane Woodard	Cape Town, South Africa	1997–2000

Tennis

Name	Hometown	Years
Ally Abisch	Miami Beach, FL	1983–87
Felicia Abrams	North Miami Beach, FL	1982–84
Rosalía Alda	Round Rock, TX	2007–
Wendy Anderson	Lexington, KY	1988–92
Sally Appelbaum	Miami Beach, FL	1980–84
Elizabeth Arnold	Nashville, TN	1984–86
Kristin Bachochin	Libertyville, IL	1993–96
Delaine Barkley	Knoxville, TN	1981–83
Amy Bartlett	Powder Springs, GA	1999
Pam Baughman	Alameda, CA	1982–84
Shari Brimmer	Green Bay, WI	1984–88
Vilmarie Castellvi	Guaynabo, PR	1999–2003
Tracy Chappell	Cookeville, TN	1983–87
Sabrina Cherichella	Lake Hopatcong, NJ	1985–89
Patti Cioffi	Knoxville, TN	1982–84
Ann Marie Circle	Kennesaw, GA	1987–88
Heather Clark	Indianapolis, IN	1987–88
Crystal Cleveland	Delray Beach, FL	1999–2003
Erin Cohn	Dallas, TX	2001–04
Brooke Cordell	Soddy Daisy, TN	2000–02
Mary Louise Coughlin	Knoxville, TN	1984–86

Name	Hometown	Years
Michelle DePalmer	Knoxville, TN	1980–84
Mary Ann Dickerson	Morristown, TN	1985–87
Whitney Dill	Knoxville, TN	1996–98
Janet DiNocla	Vienna, WV	1978–79
Deanne Dunkle	Centerville, OH	1985–89
Dee Eldridge	Knoxville, TN	1986–87
Tammy Encina	Miami Beach, FL	2002–04
Elizabeth Evans	Nashville, TN	1977–78
Linda Evers	Nashville, TN	1976–80
Claudia Farace	Baltimore, MD	2001–04
Jaime Ferman	North Miami Beach, FL	1986–88
Emily Fisher	Stockton, Australia	1991–95
Beth Ford		1976–77
Heidi Frensz	Milwaukee, WI	1979–83
Kim Gates	Grandville, MI	2000–02
Kim Glassman	Jackson, TN	1995–96
Cathy Greene		1976–77
Blakeley Griffith	Middleburg, VA	2003
Brittany Haley	Nashville, TN	1989–90
Catherine Hall	Boone, NC	1997–2001
Kellie Hancock		1976–77
Angela Harr	Bristol, TN	1976–78
Stephanie Harris	Chattanooga, TN	2005–06
Kelli Heaton	Aiken, SC	1996–98
Gesa Hein	Poering, Germany	1993–94
Majen Immink	Kent, UK	2001–04
Sally Isbell	Knoxville, TN	1976–78
Anna Ivan	Palo Alto, CA	1987–88
Kathy Johnson	Clarksville, TN	1986–88
Jennifer Jones	Memphis, TN	1980–82
Victoria Jones	Tyne & Wear, UK	2003–07
Paula Juels	North Little Rock, AR	1990–94
Shannon Kagawa	Hilo, HI	1991–93

Name	Hometown	Years
Paula Kelly	Brisbane, Australia	1978–82
Peta Kelly	Brisbane, Australia	1978–82
Celestine Kelly	Brisbane, Australia	1981–85
Megan Kerr	Lexington, KY	2002
Terri Kirk	Raleigh, NC	1977–81
Breanna Kray	Surrey, British Columbia	2001–04
Angy Kreis	Louisville, TN	1984–87
Carter Lackey	McLean, VA	1992–93
Mary Jo Landry	Bradenton, FL	1986–87
Laura Lawliss	Atlanta, GA	1976–79
Tse Lan Lee	Knoxville, TN	1989–93
Margie Lepsi	Willow Springs, IL	1994–98
Erin Lowrey	San Diego, CA	1994–98
Sabita Maharaj	Gainesville, FL	2002–05
Tu Mai	Tampa, FL	1993–95
Manisha Malhotra	Bombay, India	1994–98
Bryce Marable	Darien, IL	2004–06
Stacey Martin	Largo, MD	1988–89
Dawn Martin	St. Clair Shores, MI	1989–91
Caitriona McCarthy	Dublin, Ireland	1993–95
Heather McEvoy	Memphis, TN	1992–96
Michelle McMillen	East Palestine, OH	1989–93
Jennifer Meredith	Marietta, GA	2007–
Beth Mitchell	Crossville, TN	1982–83
Daron Moore	North Hollywood, CA	2004–05
Debbie Moringiello	North Brunswick, NJ	1989–93
Melina Morrow	Montgomery, AL	2002–04
Annette Musick	Erwin, TN	1982–84
Chris Nagel	West Bloomfield, MI	1984–88
Dana Noel	Bloomington, MN	1999–01
Lee Nunnally		1978–79
Allison Ojeda	San Antonio, TX	1998–02

Name	Hometown	Years
Melanie Olsen		1976–79
Samantha Orlin	Miami, FL	2005–
Wendy Ouwendijk	Somis, CA	1988–89
Meiling Parks	Abilene, TX	1998–2000
Mariette Pieters	Morristown, TN	1985–87
Hayley Prendergast	Hingham, MA	2006
Sara Pritchard	Bradenton, FL	1995
Candy Reid	Surrey, England	1996–2000
Farah Reynolds	Englewood, TN	1981–83
Ashley Robards	Henderson, KY	2001–05
Megan Russell	Wichita, KS	1997–98
Melissa Schaub	Lexington, OH	2002–06
Ghizela Schutte	Cape Town, South Africa	2005–08
Vinny Seiverling	Hershey, PA	1997–99
Becky Simmons	Knoxville, TN	1989–90
Maria Sorbello	Mackay, Australia	2007–
Debbie Southern	Winston–Salem, NC	1977–81
Pam Southern	Memphis, TN	1981–82
Carrie Spinner	Boca Raton, FL	1995–96
Karen Stewart	Brisbane, Australia	1979–81
Becky Tolson		1976–77
Connor Vogel	Germantown, TN	2006–08
Ann Waggoner	Huntsville, AL	1987–89
Caitlin Whoriskey	Boca Raton, FL	2006–
Mandy Wilson	Thornton, Ontario	1988–92
Agnes Wiski	Flushing, NY	1998–2002
Emily Woodside	Clinton, SC	1995–99
Beth Yeager	Nashville, TN	1978–80
Melissa Zimpfer	Dayton, OH	1992–95
Zsófia Zubor	Nyiregyhaza, Hungary	2006–08

Track and Field

Name	Hometown	Years
Phyllis Alexander		1973–76
Nia Ali	Philadelphia, PA	2007
Vata Allen		1980
K. C. Allen	Huntingtown, MD	2000
Debbie Alley		1978–79
Marvena Almond	Knoxville, TN	1993–97
Missy Alston	Nashville, TN	1974–77
Abbe Ames		1974–76
Vanessa Anderson		1976
Leah Anderson	Chattanooga, TN	1997
Erin Anderson	Kent, OH	2001–03
Sasha Anderson	Nashville, TN	2007
Jessica Andrews	Rockford, TN	2002–05
Alice Anum		1972
Jackie Areson	Delray Beach, FL	2007–
Jorie Armstrong	Memphis, TN	1991
Zjakhaania Askew	Alexandria, VA	1995–96
Kelly Austin		1980
Amber Ayub	Knoxville, TN	2000–03
Christy Baird	Knoxville, TN	2000–03
Sharrieffa Barksdale	Harriman, TN	1981–84
Tyler Barnes	Ewing, NJ	2007–
Pam Barnett	Walkersville, MD	1991
Amy Bartosik	Kingsport, TN	1997–2000
Teresa Baugh		1978
Susan Baxter	Seymour, CT	1982–83
Sonya Bell	Charlotte, NC	2001–02
Rolanda Bell	Laurelton, NY	2006–
Tori Bellon		1974
Robin Benjamin	Capitol Heights, MD	1985–88
Clara Bennett		1972–73
Princess Bennett	Cleveland, OH	1987–88

Name	Hometown	Years
Kameisha Bennett	Dayton, OH	2000–04
Monique Berarducci	Knoxville, TN	2002
Mandy Bergey	Hillsboro, OR	2000–02
Krista Berryman		1979
Lori Bertelkamp	Knoxville, TN	1978–79
Valerie Bertrand	Coram, NY	1987–90
Shea Bible	Houston, TX	1990–93
Christina Billings	Madison, WI	2001–03
Jessica Bishop	Corbin, KY	2002
Bridgitte Bittner		1978–79
Paulette Blalock	Long Beach, CA	1986
Laura Blank		1978
Cathy Bodkin	Hendersonville, TN	1986–88
Lauren Bogaty		1998
Mary Bolden		1984
Frenke Bolt	Zutphen, Holland	1999–2000
Kelia Bolton	San Jose, CA	1983–84
Michelle Bookman	Missouri City, TX	1991–95
Sarah Bowman	Warrenton, VA	2006–
Miriam Boyd	Port Huron, MI	1980–81
Pat Brake		1975
Jennifer Brewer	Lincoln Park, MI	1994–95
Janelle Briggs	Stone Mountain, GA	1996–99
Keena Brooks	Temple Hills, MD	2001
Ariel Brooks	Miami, FL	2005–07
Shemea Broom	Abilene, TX	1993
Ginny Browning	Kingsport, TN	2007–
Kathy Bryant	Delaware, OH	1980–83, 1985
Alyssa Bryant	Andersonville, TN	2007–
Janet Buhrow		1976–78
Megan Burch	Manchester, TN	1994–97
Claudia Burton	Oak Ridge, TN	2005–07
Leigh Ann Burton	Atlanta, GA	2007–

Name	Hometown	Years
Tiara Butler		2003
Anissa Campbell	Ironton, OH	1995–98
Karen Carbin	Louisville, KY	1985–88
Tracy Carrington	Fort Worth, TX	1998–99
Debbie Carter		1975
Megan Cauble	Knoxville, TN	2003–05
Courtney Champion	Lawrenceville, GA	2005–08
Myrtle Chester	Laurel, MD	1981–84
Gena Clare	Fairfax, VA	1986–88
Carrie Clark		1973
Joetta Clark	South Orange, NJ	1981–84
Allison Clary	Columbia, SC	1997
Shannon Cline		1980
Alma Cobb		1980
Jane Cobb		1979–80
Diane Coffey		1978–79
Marsha Cole		1974
Rebecca Cole	Knoxville, TN	2007–08
Tara Coleman		1988
Lynne Collazo	Ridgewood, NJ	1990–94
Rebecca Collins	Loveland, OH	2000–03
Regina Colson		1975
Nicole Cook	Petersburg, VA	2002–05
Cathy Corpeny	Kansas City, MO	1981–84
Samantha Coulson	Roswell, GA	2000–02
Sarah Coury		2000
Jane Cox		1973
Cassandra Crawford		1976
Christy Cupp	Lake City, TN	1990
Debbie Cutler		1975–76
Sara Dalton	Kettering, OH	1999
Brittany Daniels	Tracy, CA	2007–
Karol Davidson		1984

Name	Hometown	Years
Dedra Davis	Nassau, Bahamas	1993–94
Tanya Dawson	Memphis, TN	1993
Shari Demarest		1975–77
Dorothy Denko	Krakow, Poland	1997–98
Chantal Desrosiers	Repentigny, Quebec	1982–84
Shanna Dickenson	Cincinnati, OH	2005–08
Sharon Dickie	Grand Blanc, MI	1999, 2001–03
Sally DiScenza		1975–76
Rashida Dodson	Indianapolis, IN	2000–01
Sally Dumas		1972
Barbara Dunn		1972
Allison Dupree	Syracuse, NY	1988–89
Janet Easterday	Oak Ridge, TN	1987
Kathy Echols		1975–76
Lindsay Eck	Beloit, KS	2001–02
Michelle Elfervig	Germantown, TN	1995–98
Christie Elwin	Adelaide, Australia	2000–03
Lynne Emery		1977–80
Alicia Essex	Purcellville, VA	2006–08
Ann Farrar		1974
Maureen Ferris	Cleveland, OH	1995–99
Stephanie Fields	Temple, TX	1991–95
Sara Fieweger	Hope, ME	1994
Pam Fillmore	Knoxville, TN	1984–85
Veronica Findley	Kingston, Jamaica	1983–84
Cheryl Finley	Lawton, OK	1994–95
Edra Finley	Mobile, AL	2004–06
Benita Fitzgerald	Dale City, VA	1980–83
Shara Flacy		1975–76
Katie Flaute	Dayton, OH	2003–06
Kelly Flowers	Westerville, OH	2001–03
Kim Fontenot	El Torro, CA	1993
Talayna Fortunato	Johnson City, TN	2000

Name	Hometown	Years
Rukiya Foster	New Brunswick, NJ	1994
Melissa Foster		1978–80
Debbie Freedenbourg		1975
Rose–Anne Galligan	County Kildare, Ireland	2007
Alice Gardner		1975
Christy Gearhiser	Chattanooga, TN	1985
Beth Gehring	Chardon, OH	1997–2000
Amanda Gillam	Baltimore, MD	1993–95
Desi Gillespie	Knoxville, TN	1983–84
Kathy Goldstein		1977–79
Jennifer Gordon	Burke, VA	2002
Antoinette Gorham	Glenarden, MD	2002–05
Sharon Gough		1977–78
Serena Gray	Memphis, TN	2000
Katherine Green	Alpharetta, GA	1998
Gretchen Grimaud		1977
Janea Grimes	Newport, TN	2007–08
Felicia Guliford	Gallup, NM	2003–06
Jane Haist	Canada	1977–79
Jill Hall		1976
Patricia Hall	St. Ann, Jamaica	2005–07
Vonda Hammons	Jefferson City, MO	1986–89
Chardae Hancock	Denver, CO	2007–
Cary Hardy	Birmingham, AL	2000
Quintessa Harps	Griffin, GA	1996–98
Kathi Harris	West Bloomfield, MI	1983, 1985
Alisa Harvey	Alexandria, VA	1984–87
Annie Hatmaker		1976
Rose Hauch	Chesterville, Ontario	1979–82
Marilyn Haynes		1974
Laura Haynes	Knoxville, TN	1994–97
Aoife Hearne	Waterford, Ireland	2001–02
Hertz Heidi		1977–78

Name	Hometown	Years
Leslie Henley	Manchester, TN	1994–98
Jane Herron		1972
Jenny Hill		1974–75
Melissa Hiller	Nashville, TN	1995–97
Paula Hines	Capitol Heights, MD	1981
Karen Hodgkinon	Blytheville, AR	1987–88
Tracy Hopkins		1983–84
Eileen Hornberger	Laureldale, PA	1981–83
Vickie Hudson	Temple, TX	1992–95
Beth Huff	Janesville, WI	1981–82
Terry Hull	Greeneville, TN	1969–70
Lita Hurtson		1974
Lindsay Hyatt	Auburn, CA	2004
Mallery Ivy	Omaha, NE	1989–92
Mahuli Jakubek		1979
Pavi'Elle James	Miami, FL	2007
Gloria Johnson		1974
Alicia Johnson	Carrolton, TX	1990–92
Natalie Johnson	Silver Spring, MD	1998–2000
Donna Joiner		1972
Brenda Joiner		1974
Angie Jones		1983–84
Brittany Jones	Pompano Beach, FL	2007–
Jasmin Jones	Hackensack, NJ	1988–91
Saidah Jones	Stone Mountain, GA	1994–98
Holly Kane	Knoxville, TN	2007–
Kathy Kearfott		1979
Judy Penton Keener		1972–73
Marcia Keeton	Trotwood, OH	1989
Chris Kimball	Skaneateles, NY	1981
Javita Kirby	Tampa, FL	1993–94
Cathy Kirchner	Wilmington, DE	1978–81
Sharon Kirk		1975–76

Name	Hometown	Years
Marquita Knight	Buffalo, NY	1997–2000
Kelly Kobia	Oviedo, FL	1993
Janice Koehler		1974
Emily Krainik		1976–77
Donna Lake		1979–80
Lynn Lashley		1977–80
Celriece Law	Denver, CO	2005–
Lynne Layne	New Rochelle, NY	2007–
Jana Lee		1976
Audrey Lee	Osteen, FL	1993
Tonya Lee	Mt. Holly, NJ	1989–92
Pat Leroy	Dallas, TX	1990–93
Jennifer Lewellen	Kernersville, NC	2007–
Susan Lichtenberger		1976–77
LaTonya Loche	Bastrop, LA	2005–08
Lesly Love	Knoxville, TN	1997–2000
Pam Lyons	Memphis, TN	1998
Heidi Magill–Dahl	Orem, UT	2007–08
Anne MacKinnon	Wharton, NJ	1983
Tianna Madison	Elyria, OH	2004–06
Katrice Malcom	Decatur, GA	1994–97
Michelle Manery	Houston, TX	1990–91
Susan Manning	Scaly Mountain, NC	1978–81
Meghan Mantlo	Nashville, TN	1997–2000
Beth Marlow	Memphis, TN	1995–97
Karla Marshall	Detroit, MI	2002
LaVonna Martin	Dayton, OH	1985–88
Carly Matthews	Winston–Salem, NC	2004–07
Elizabeth McCalley	Knoxville, TN	2002–05
Ellen McCallister	Bristol, TN	1980–83
Kathy McCann		1977–78
Molly McCaughey	Galena, OH	1983
Vanessa McClinic		1976

Name	Hometown	Years
Karen McDonald	Sioux Falls, SD	1984–85
Kimarra McDonald	Lumberton, NJ	2006–
Lindsey McFarland	Austin, TX	2002–05
Amara McKell	Nashville, TN	2005–08
Donna McLain	York, PA	1981–83
Carla McLaughlin	Durham, NC	1986–88
JoAnne McLeod		1978–79
Kim McMillan		1977
Lauren McNeil	Easton, PA	2002–03
Ann McPherson	Harrison, TN	1981
Ramona Melvin		1980
Denita Miller	Liberal, KS	2001–03
Tisha Milligan	Bridgeville, DE	1990–91
Zakiah Modeste	Mt. Vernon, NY	1996–97
Kayla Montgomery	Fresno, CA	1995–96
Lissa Moore		1977
Shawn, Moore	Philadelphia, PA	1987–88, 1990
Leslie Morris		1977–78
Jabeanna Morris	Snellville, GA	1997–98
Robin Mortel	Brooklyn, NY	2005–08
Teal Mowery	Rochester NY	1992–93
Laura Mozingo	Clinton, TN	1983–86
Jena' Murphy	Memphis, TN	2007–
Sharon Mustin	Oak Ridge, TN	1981–82
Tina Myers		1978
Brittany Napoli	Howell, NJ	2007–
Liz Natale	Newton, MA	1984
Tracy Nelson	Plainfield, NJ	1982–85
Brooke Novak	Kaukauna, WI	2002–06
Cindy O'Bryant	Chattanooga, TN	1990–93
Katie O'Connell	Collierville, TN	2007–
Carolyn O'Hara	Conyers, GA	2003–04

Name	Hometown	Years
Ilrey Oliver	St. Thomas, Jamaica	1983–87
Monica Olkowski	Marlton, NJ	1991–92
Toyin Olupona	Orilla, Ontario	2002–05
Monica O'Reilly	Laoise, Ireland	1983–87
Marsha Outlaw		1976
Tammy Owens		1978–79
Andrea Pappas	San Jose, CA	1999–2000
Kelly Parrish	Ocala, FL	2007
Pam Passera	McMurray, PA	1981–84
Carrie Pendley		2000
Kristen Permakoff	Knoxville, TN	1990
Althea Peterson		1978–79
Pam Pettus		1976–79
Linda Portasik	Alexandria, VA	1980–83
Angie Pothier	Vancouver, WA	1999–2000
Tisha Prather	Atlanta, GA	1990–93
Alana Preston	West Palm Beach, FL	1992–95
Angela Pruitt		2003
Burline Pullin		1974–76
Alison Quelch	New South Wales, Australia	1983–85
Virginia Quellmalz	Mt. Clemens, MI	1992–93
Amy Ranker	Liberal, KS	2001–02
Cathy Rattray	Kingston, Jamaica	1981–84
Michelle Reasor	Fort Worth, TX	1994–95
Jamie Rebella	Merrill, WI	2002–04
Amy Reeves	West Point, GA	1995
Jessica Reust	Knoxville, TN	2003–05
Deidre Reynolds	Roswell, GA	2000
Kendra Rhyne	Andersonville, TN	2002–05
Ashley Rice		2004
Lana Rice	Oakland, CA	1986–87
Lisa Richardson	Nurnberg, Germany	1989–92
Barb Rieperman		1977–80

Name	Hometown	Years
Erin Rinear	Lacey, WA	1996–98, 2000
Kristen Ritter	Frederick, MD	1997–2000
LaTish Roach	Memphis, TN	2000
Rita Robinson	Louisville, KY	1985
Vanessa Robinson		1985
Elisa Roby		1976–79
Taylor Rotella	Knoxville, TN	2007–
Missy Rutherford		1978–80
Jan Sadler	Nashville, TN	1986
Tyangela Sanders	Knoxville, TN	1999
Menka Scott	Decatur, GA	1985, 1987–89
Rachel Secrest	Hixson, TN	2006–07
Samantha Sedgwick	Westport, CT	2007–
Stacey Seifert	Knoxville, TN	1995–97
Lois Sewell		1974–76
Millicent Shabazz	Radford, VA	1990
Lynn Sheffield		1975–77
Brittany Sheffey	Bellport, NY	2007–
Betty Shell		1977–78
Iman Shelton		1997
Lisa Sherrill	Durham, NC	1980–81
Phyllis Silcock		1975–77
Shannon Simmons	Knoxville, TN	1995
Sally Sligar		1976–77
Diane Slinden	Menomonie, WI	1999–2002
Kim Smallwood	Richmond, TX	1996–97
Sandy Smith		1980
Kelly Smith	San Diego, CA	1996–97
Staci Snider	Saratoga Springs, NY	1992
Joanne Soldano		1977–80
Leah Soro	Knoxville, TN	2006–
Jessica Southers	Ashland, KY	2001–04
Dina Spagnoli	Arlington, VA	1991

Name	Hometown	Years
Krista Stewart	Drexel Hill, PA	1993–94
Brenda Stone		1974–76
Tere Stouffer	Auburn Hills, MI	1986–87
Donna Stoyas		1973
Michelle Strothers	Williamsport, PA	1989–92
Mary Ann Sturr		1977
Mindy Sullivan	Lubbock, TX	2003–06
Heather Sumpter	Pasadena, CA	1996–97, 1999–2000
Celeste Susnis	Wheatfield, IN	1991–94
Katrina Swanson		1984
Leah Swift		1976
Jeneba Tarmoh	San Jose, CA	2007–08
Carol Taylor		1974
Janine Tessarzik	Altamont, NY	2000–03
Sally Thomas		1980
Stephanie Thomas	Dale City, VA	1982–84
April Thomas	Albany, GA	2005–07
Kim Thompson		1976–77
Brenda Thompson		1977–78
Megan Thompson	Florissant, MO	1991–94
Susan Thornton	Nashville, TN	1977–80
Erica Tittsworth	Racine, WI	2000–01
Penny Towers		1980
Kim Townes	Highland Springs, VA	1993–96
Leslie Treherne	Chesapeake, VA	2004–07
Dee Dee Trotter	Decatur, GA	2002–04
Cleo Tyson	Huntsville, TX	2005–08
Tamara Van Duyn	Port Jefferson Station, NY	1997
Katie Van Horn	Glendora, NJ	2006–
Erika van Reenen	Norcross, GA	2001
Sara Vigil	Tucson, AZ	2004
Jeanne Villegas	Carmel, NY	1986–88
Rhoda Visser	McMurray, PA	1985

Name	Hometown	Years
Jenny Vonderfecht	Jonesborough, TN	2000
Eve Waldrop		1972
Lynn Waldrop		1974
Shelley Walker	Corryton, TN	1994–96
Jackie Wallace	Williamsburg, VA	1982–85
Patricia Walsh	Waterford, Ireland	1982–85
Delisa Walton	Detroit, MI	1980–83
Sue Walton	Columbus, GA	1992–95
Laura Ward		1974–76
Caitlin Ward	Gibsonia, PA	2003–06
Holly Warlick	Knoxville, TN	1977
Renn Watkins	Wake Forest, NC	2001
Mindy Watkins	Canastota, NY	1997–2000
Lori Weaver	Afton, TN	1982–85
Brenda Webb		1977–79
Jill Weber	Celina, OH	1985–86
Tania Wells	Memphis, TN	1981
Amanda Wentland	Grand Blanc, MI	1999
Bridget White	Birmingham, AL	1986
Kim White	Memphis, TN	2007–
Laurel White	Rocky Mount, NC	1997
Kelli White	Oakland, CA	1996–99
Patty Wiegand	Canastota, NY	1988–91
Gina Wilbanks	Four Oaks, NC	1986–89
Charlotte Williams		1975–76
Val Williams		1975–77
Frederica Winley	Queens, NY	1985–89
Michelle Winterer	Lake St. Louis, MO	1986–87
Erica Witter	Hamilton, Ontario	1996–99
Jane Woodhead	Lewiston, ME	1987–90
Meredith Woods		2000
Roberta Wright		1978–79

Name	Hometown	Years
Catherine Wright	Knoxville, TN	2003–06
Phoebe Wright	Signal Mountain, TN	2006–
Venessa Yow	Birmingham, AL	1972–74
Zsa Zsa Yow	Birmingham, AL	1974–77
Rachel Zamata	Henderson, TN	2003–06
Sharon Zook		1972–75

Volleyball

Name	Hometown	Years
Kristen Andre	Kelseyville, CA	2002–05
Megan Arner	Sonoma, CA	2000–01
Abby Bayona	Redondo Beach, CA	1985
Jena Berg	Bristol, WI	2006–08
Mandy Bergey	Hillsboro, OR	1998–99
Robin Bise	Knoxville, TN	1975–78
Niki Bishop	Richland, MI	1990–93
Abbey Blazer	Wilmington, NC	1995–96
Sarah Blum	Tulsa, OK	2003–06
Beverly Bond	Knoxville, TN	1978–79
Alfreda Booker	Miami, FL	1979–80
Diane Borgerding	Cincinnati, OH	1982–85
Krista Brenner	Valley Springs, CA	2006–
Erika Brez	Washington, MO	1998–99
Tamala Brightman	Cordova, TN	1990–93
Mindy Britten	Kennedy, MN	1996–97
Cheri Brooks	Toronto, Ontario	1977
Amy Buchanan	Phoenix, AZ	1992–94
Cynthia Buggs	Compton, CA	2003–04
Brenda Cantwell	Anchorage, AL	1981–83
Laurie Caraher	Chicago, IL	1984–87
Caley Carter	Great Bend, KS	2001
April Chapple	Inglewood, CA	1981–84
Betsy Chavez	Playa del Rey, CA	1981–83

Name	Hometown	Years
Carol Cheade	Rio de Janeiro, Brazil	2006–
Teri Childress	Knoxville, TN	1976–79
Meg Chislett	Knoxville, TN	1975–77
Milan Clarke	Santa Monica, CA	2005–
Lauren Clayton	Knoxville, TN	1996–99
Kristen Clements	Manhattan, IL	1999–2000
Cindy Clowers	Knoxville, TN	1975, 1977
Mary Clare Coghlan	Northridge, CA	2001
Alex Compeau	Oxford, MI	2000–02
Trinia Cuseo	Forestville, CA	2000–01
Wendy Dilworth-Pitcher	Birmingham, AL	1990–93
Kristy Dobson	Jonesboro, AR	1988–91
Mary Doyle	South Orange, NJ	1977–79
Deb Dyer	Manassas, VA	1967–68
Karen Dyer	Knoxville, TN	1988–91
Stephanie Ehlers	Mountain View, CA	1985–88
Jennifer Elliott	Kyle, TX	1999–2000
Lori Emberton	Dearborn Heights, MI	1978
Janet England	Knoxville, TN	1975–78
Kelsey Fautsch	Chisago Lakes, MN	2005–07
Martha Flowers	Knoxville, TN	1977–79
Mindy Flynn	Louisville, KY	2005–
Nikki Fowler	Dallas, TX	2007–
Dianne Frerker	Belleville, IL	1988
Jasmine Fullove	Ft. Wayne, IN	2002–05
Beverly Garner	East Ridge, TN	1980–82
Whitney Gifford	Dallastown, PA	2001–04
Marie Gillcrist	Vienna, Austria	1978–81
Kerry Ginter	Portage, MI	1994–97
Chloe Goldman	Monterey, CA	2007–
Mary Gossett	Oxon Hill, MD	1981–84
Tanya Haave	Evergreen, CO	1980, 1984
Kim Hackler	Norris, TN	1980–83

Name	Hometown	Years
Pam Hackler	Norris, TN	1980–81
Denise Hagler	Ft. Wayne, IN	1989
Tiffany Hamilton	Mesa, AZ	1992–93
Kelly Hanlon	Aurora, CO	1995–97
Heather Harrington	Pasadena, TX	2002–05
Mary Heinecke	Irvine, CA	1995–98
Janelle Hester	Davenport, IA	1999–02
Leah Hinkey	Glenwood Springs, CO	2006–
Courtney Huettemann	LaSalle, IL	1994–97
Nikki Huffman	Omaha, NE	2001
Lisa Huntley	Deerfield Beach, FL	1979–80
Christine Hynes	Jefferson, GA	1983–84
Mahuliena Jakubek	Sudbury, Ontario	1978–79
Christina Jestila	Phoenix, AZ	1996–98
Joselyn Johnson	Muncie, IN	2004–08
Wendy Jones	Muncie, IN	1986–89
Bonnie Kenny	Meriden, CT	1980–83
Lynn Klus	Crown Point, IN	1988–90
Stephanie Knight	Gilbert, AZ	1998–2000
Julie Knytych	LaGrange Park, IL	2002–05
Melissa Kowalski	Knoxville, TN	1997–99
Megan LaBernz	Kingwood, TX	1993
Laurén LaFlamme	Byron, CA	2004–
Erica Lear	Columbus, IN	1998–01
Kris Ledbetter	San Bernardino, CA	1984–85
Lisa Lee	Franklin, TN	1978–79
Cissi Lennartsson	Gislaved, Sweden	1993–94
Lynn Lovingier	Mission Viejo, CA	1995–98
Jaye Loyd	Stockton, CA	2006–
Robin ME	Dennison, TX	1980–83
Barb Mannix	Cincinnati, OH	1986
Kylie Marshall	Puyallup, WA	2006–
Pam McMahan	Knoxville, TN	1981–82

Name	Hometown	Years
Lezli McPhail	Richardson, TX	1980–81
Kelly Meador	Springfield, TN	1992
Jenny Meeks	Chattanooga, TN	1994–96
Morgan Miltner	Dover, FL	2002–03
LeeAnn Mitchell	Memphis, TN	1979–80
Donna Monaco	LaGrange Park, IL	1984–86
Molly Mooney	Muncie, IN	1991–94
Terri Moore	Silver Lake, KS	1978
Amy Morris	Michigan City, IN	2003–05
Jamie Mossburg	Knoxville, TN	2000
Nancy Mueller	St. Libory, IL	1988–91
Ingrid Mueller	Buffalo, NY	1979
Ann Mullins	Nashville, TN	2003–04
Jamie Myers	Maryville, TN	1985–89
Kristan Nastulski	Milwaukee, WI	1988–91
Mary Natwick	Morristown, TN	1976–79
Chelsea Noble	Vandalia, OH	2005–07
Kenyail Norris	Grand Prairie, TX	1995
Kim Obiala	Orland Park, IL	1995–98
Melissa Olmsted	Elburn, IL	1982–83
Laura Paul	Ballwin, MO	1999–2000
Pam Paule	Freeburg, IL	1988
Andrea Peterson	Los Angeles, CA	1998–2001
Michelle Piantadosi	Boca Raton, FL	2001–04
Farren Powe	Mobile, AL	2006–
Lauren Proctor	Mansfield, OH	1998–99
Jackie Ramsdale	Kingsport, TN	2005
Amy Rauch	Mishawaka, IN	1989–90
Beverly Robinson	Decatur, GA	1982–83
Jennifer Rudy	Broadview, IL	2002–03
Annie Sadowski	Wheaton, IL	2003–06
Stephanie Scheper	Edgewood, KY	1983–85
Holly Schetzsle	Pataskala, OH	2001

Name	Hometown	Years
Jodee Scott	Anchorage, AK	1995–96
Kelli Scott	Peoria, AZ	1999–2002
Dianne Shoemaker	Brooklyn, MI	1985–88
Janet Simonitsch	Independence, MO	1984–85
Maureen Skalitzky	Oak Lawn, IL	1986
Jennifer Smith	El Cerrito, CA	1992
Kathy St. Clair	Kingsport, TN	1974–77
Anna Stakkestad	Göteborg, Sweden	1993
Lisa Stegman	Colorado Springs, CO	1985–88
Lisa Stewart	Farrell, PA	1983
Yuliya Stoyanova	Sofia, Bulgaria	2004–08
Allison Stricklin	Huntington Beach, CA	1994–95, 1997
Michelle Taylor	Moulton, AL	1978–80
Sonja Thomas	Cleveland, OH	1991–94
Connie Thomas	Kalamazoo, MI	1989
Michelle Thomas	Baldwinsville, NY	1996
Vonda Ward	Northfield, OH	1994
Christy Warren	Salem, OR	1995–98
Tiffany Washington	Kalamazoo, MI	1990–93
Shannon Weatherby	Marietta, GA	1986
Laura Wessberg	Uppsala, Sweden	1984
Rachel Westfield	Nashville, TN	1996
Kathy Williams	Knoxville, TN	1974–77
April Williams	Gap, PA	1981
Ariana Wilson	Cincinnati, OH	1997–2001
Annetten Young–Gillcrist	Lakewood, CO	1987–90
Brittany Zahn	Charlotte, NC	2003–04
Erin Zammett	Huntington, NY	1996
Beth Zarestky	Oak Ridge, TN	1997

Appendix 5

Lady Volunteer Olympians

Compiled from all available sources as of fall 2007. Unless otherwise noted, the player or coach listed represented the United States.

Basketball

Cindy Brogdon, 1976 Montreal Games, silver medal

Tamika Catchings, 2004 Athens Games, gold medal; 2008 Beijing Games

Daedra Charles, 1992 Barcelona Games, bronze medal

Nancy Darsch (UT assistant coach), assistant coach of gold medal–winning US teams at 1984 Los Angeles Games and 1996 Atlanta Games

Bridgette Gordon, 1988 Seoul Games, gold medal

Lea Henry, 1984 Los Angeles Games, gold medal

Chamique Holdsclaw, 2000 Sydney Games, gold medal

Kara Lawson, 2008 Beijing Games

Nikki McCray, gold medal at 1996 Atlanta Games and 2000 Sydney games

Carla McGhee, 1996 Atlanta Games, gold medal

Cindy Noble, 1980 Moscow Games (boycott); gold medal at1984 Los Angeles games

Candace Parker, 2008 Beijing Games

Jill Rankin, 1980 Moscow Games (boycott)

Patricia Roberts, 1976 Montreal games, silver

Patricia Head Summitt (UT coach), silver medal as US team member, 1976 Montreal Games; assistant coach, 1980 Moscow Games (boycott); head coach of gold medal–winning US team, 1984 Los Angeles Games

Holly Warlick, 1980 Moscow Games (boycott)

Softball

Monica Abbott, 2008 Beijing Games

Swimming

Christine Magnuson, 2008 Beijing Games, 100m fly

Fabiola Molina (representing Brazil), 2000 Sydney Games, 100-meter butterfly, 100-meter backstroke

Theresa Moodie (representing Zimbabwe), 1996 Atlanta Games, 100-meter freestyle

Julia Stowers, 2000 Sydney Games, 4x200 meter freestyle relay, Gold Medal.

Track and Field

Alice Anum (representing Ghana), 1964 Tokyo Games, 100 meter; 1968 Mexico City Games, 100 meter

Sharrieffa Barksdale, 1984 Los Angeles Games, 400-meter hurdle

Andy Bloom (UT assistant coach), 2000 Sydney Games, shot put, 4th place

J. J. Clark (UT coach), assistant coach, 2008 Beijing Games

Joetta Clark, 1988 Seoul Games, 800 meter; 1992 Barcelona Games, 800 meter, 7th place; 1996 Atlanta Games, 800 meter; 2000 Sydney Games, 800 meter

Terry Crawford (UT coach), head coach, 1988 Seoul Games

Dorothy Doolittle (UT coach), assistant coach, 1992 Barcelona Games

Veronica Findley (representing Jamaica), 1984 Los Angeles Games, 400-meter relay, 8th place

Benita Fitzgerald, 1980 Moscow Games (boycott), 100-meter hurdle; 1984 Los Angeles Games, 100-meter hurdle, gold medal

Jane Haist (representing Canada), 1976 Montreal Games, discus

Missy Alston Kane (Bemiller), 1984 Los Angeles Games, 1500 meter

LaVonna Martin, 1988 Seoul Games, 100-meter hurdle; 1992 Barcelona Games, 100-meter hurdle, slver medal

Ilrey Oliver (representing Jamaica), 1984 Los Angeles Games, 400 meter and 1600-meter hurdle, 5th-place finish in latter event

Cathy Rattray (representing Jamaica), 1980 Moscow Games, 1600-meter hurdle; 1984 Los Angeles Games, 400 meter and 1600-meter relay, 5th-place finish in latter event; 1988 Seoul Games, 400 meter and 1600-meter relay, 5th-place finish in latter event; 1992 Barcelona Games, 1600-meter relay, 5th place

Dee Dee Trotter, 2004 Athens Games, 400 meter, 5th place, and 1600-meter relay, gold medal; 2008 Beijing Games

Patricia Walsh (representing Ireland), 1984 Los Angeles Games, discus, 9th place

Delisa Walton, 1988 Seoul Games, 800 meter, 5th place

Erica Witter (representing Canada), 2000 Sydney Games, 400-meter relay

Volleyball

Beverly Robinson, 1988 Seoul Games

Brogdon

Catchings

Charles

Darsch

Gordon

Henry

Holdsclaw

Lawson

McCray

McGhee

Noble

Parker

Rankin

Roberts

Summitt

Warlick

Abbott

Magnuson

Molina

Moodie

Stowers

Barksdale

Bloom

Clark

Clark

Crawford

Doolittle

Findley

Fitzgerald

Haist

Kane Bemiller

Martin

Oliver

Rattray

Trotter

Walsh

Walton

Witter

Robinson

Appendix 6

Head Coaches by Sport and Years

Compiled as of spring 2008. Complete records of individual coaches are available in The University of Tennessee Women's Athletic Department Media Guides.

Basketball

Year	Name
1903	Katherine Williams
1904	Jenny Morrill
1905	L. T. Bellmont
1906	Essie Polk
1907	T. S. Myers
1908	W. C. Burnley
1909	Andrew Weisenberg
1909–10	Howard Sandburg
1920	Mary Douglas Ayres
1922–23	Mabel Miller
1924	Fay Morgan
1925–26	Ann Huddle
1960–68	Nancy Lay
1969–70	Joan Cronan
1971–74	Margaret Hutson
1974–Present	Pat Summitt

Cross Country

Year	Name
1974–83	Terry Crawford
1984–87	Gary Schwartz
1988–91	Missy Kane
1992–94	Ann Bertucci
1995	Dorothy Doolittle
1996–99	Brenda Webb
2000–01	Rodney Rothhoff
2002–Present	J. J. Clark

Field Hockey

Dropped from Program in 1977

Year	Name
1970–72	Nancy Lay
1973–75	Jean Lewis
1976	Barbara Mullinix

Golf

Year	Name
1992–95	Linda Franz–Cook
1995–2000	Lori Brock
2000 (interim coach)	Judi Pavon
2000–Present	Judi Pavon

Gymnastics

Dropped from program in 1977

Year	Name
1972–76	Donna Donnelly

Rowing

Year	Name
1995–97	Susannah Iacovino
1997–Present	Lisa Glenn

Soccer

Year	Name
1996–99	Charlie MacCabe
2000–Present	Angela Kelly

Softball

Year	Name
1996–2001	Jim Beitia
2002–Present	Ralph and Karen Weekly

Swimming and Diving

Swimming

Year	Name
1971–72	Frank Bryant
1972–73	Allan Spreen
1973–74	Ida Ezell
1974–75	Janie Tyler
1975–76	Janie Tyler
1976–77	Janie Tyler
1977–78	Joe Gentry
1978–79	Joe Gentry
1979–80	Joe Gentry

Swimming and Diving (cont.)

Year	Name
1980–81	Terry Carlisle
1981–82	Terry Carlisle
1982–84	Terry Carlisle
1984–85	Terry Carlisle
1985–86 (began season)	Terry Carlisle
1985–86 (completed season)	Bonnie Dix & Chip Hastings
1986–87	Dave Roach
1987–88	Dave Roach
1988–90	Dave Roach
1990–93	Pete Raykovich
1993–2005	Dan Colella
2005–Present	Matt Kredich

Diving

Year	Name
1971–72	Allan Spreen
1972–73	Allan Spreen
1973–74	Allan Spreen
1974–75	Allan Spreen
1975–76	Not available
1976–77	Brad Laughner
1977–78	Not available
1978–79	Vicky Bringle
1979–80	Kent Cousineau
1980–81	Kent Cousineau
1981–82	Steve Rudder
1982–84	John Goddard
1984–85	Jim Whalen
1985–86 (began season)	Beth Anne Beck
1985–86 (completed season)	Dan Laak
1986–87	Dan Laak

Swimming and Diving (cont.)

Year	Name
1987–88	Craig Ford
1988–90	Jim Kennedy
1990–93	Dave Parrington
1993–2005	Dave Parrington
2005–Present	Dave Parrington

Tennis

Year	Name
1963–67	Nancy Lay and Jo Hobson
1968–69	Joyce Tabor
1970	Sue Donel
1971–72	Donna Cleland
1973–74	Gloria Ray
1974–75	Sandra Standing
1976–78	Mary Jane Ramsey
1978–81	Mary Ellis Richardson
1981–83	Frank Ackley
1983–87	Elizabeth Henderson
1987–97	Mike Patrick
1997–Present	Mike Patrick and Sonia Hahn–Patrick

Track and Field

Year	Name
1972–73	Nancy Stubbs
1974–84	Terry Crawford
1985–88	Gary Schwartz
1989–97	Dorothy Doolittle
1998–2002	Myrtle Ferguson
2003–Present	J. J. Clark

Volleyball

Year	Name
1958	Jean Wells
1959–64	Nancy Lay
1965–72	Jo Hobson
1973–74	Kaye Hart
1975	Diane Hale
1976	Jody Lambert
1977–78	Bud Fields
1979–86	Bob Bertucci
1987–90	Sandy Lynn
1991–96	Julie Hermann
1997–Present	Rob Patrick

SELECTED BIBLIOGRAPHY

Archival Documents

Begalla, Martha E. "Final Task Force on Intercollegiate Athletics for Women Report." April 1, 1976. Special Collections Library, University of Tennessee, Knoxville.

Johnston, A. Montgomery, to Earl Ramer. Letter. September 26, 1972. Earl Ramer Papers. Special Collections Library, University of Tennessee, Knoxville.

"History of the Lady Vol Boost-Her Club." February 2001. Women's Intercollegiate Athletics Department, University of Tennessee, Knoxville.

"Resolution Adopted by the 69th NCAA Convention, January 8, 1975." Official NCAA document. Earl Ramer Papers. Special Collections Library, University of Tennessee, Knoxville.

Watson, Helen, to Walter Herndon. Letter. October 26, 1972. Earl Ramer Papers. Special Collections Library, University of Tennessee, Knoxville.

Articles in Newspapers and Periodicals

Adams, Ike. "Women's Athletics Lacks UT Support." *UT Daily Beacon,* January 28, 1974.

Boling, Ed. "Positive Image Through Athletics." *UT Daily Beacon,* May 9, 1974.

"DGWS National Intercollegiate Athletic Championships for Women." *Journal of Health–Physical Education–Recreation.* February 1968.

Ebersole-Boukouzis, Dee. "Basketball Fever!" *Studio 2B* (Girl Scouts of the USA publication). Collection 11–13 (2002): 35.

Elder, Sara Lynn. "Team Funded by Doughnuts." *UT Daily Beacon,* March 5, 1973.

"A Fair Shake for Women's Sports: The Fight Goes On." *UT Daily Beacon,* July 9, 1976.

"Furrow Gives to Women's Athletics." *UT Daily Beacon*, May 30, 1974.

Hawes, Kay. "Women's Sports Enter NCAA Arena." *NCAA News,* December 6, 1999.

Jennings, Debby. "Lady Volunteer Coaches Predict 'Exciting and Interesting' Seasons." *UT Daily Beacon,* October 5, 1976.

McDonald, Bob. "Girls' Basketball Big Hit; Play Carolina Saturday." *UT Daily Beacon,* February 7, 1969.

"Money Woes Cripple Women's Athletics." *UT Daily Beacon*, September 18, 1972.

"New Director Selected for Women's Athletics." *UT Daily Beacon,* August 3, 1976.

Parkinson, Mitch. "Money Called the Problem." *UT Daily Beacon,* July 13, 1976.

———. "Poll Reveals Student Attitudes on Women's Athletics." *UT Daily Beacon,* July 20, 1976.

———. "A Revolution in Women's Athletics." *UT Daily Beacon,* July 9, 1976.

———. "Women's Athletic Director Raring to Go." *UT Daily Beacon,* August 6, 1976.

———. "Woodruff, Ramer: Women's Athletic Program Headed in Right Direction." *UT Daily Beacon,* July 16, 1976

Schriver, Robert. "Women's Sports." *UT Daily Beacon,* August 16, 1974.

"UT Co-Eds Seek to Better Their Statues in Sports." *Knoxville News Sentinel,* February 9, 1972.

Books

Klein, Milton M. *Volunteer Moments: Vignettes of the History of The University of Tennessee 1794–1994.* Knoxville, TN: Office of the University Historian, 1966.

Lay, Nancy E. *The Summitt Season.* Champaign, IL: Leisure Press, 1989.

Summitt, Pat. *Raise the Roof.* New York: Broadway Books, 1998.

———. *Reach for the Summitt.* New York: Broadway Books, 1998.

Interviews by Author

Abbott, Monica. Tape recording. June 9, 2007. Knoxville, TN.

Arnone, Joe. October 17, 2006. Knoxville, TN.

Andrews, Rosalind. February 6, 2006. Knoxville, TN

Bailey, Sarah Fekete. Tape recording. April 25, 2007. Knoxville, TN.

Barksdale, Sharrieffa. Telephone interview, tape recording. March 8, 2007.

Bayh, Birch. Telephone interview, tape recording. January 25, 2007.

Begalla, Martha Eagleton. 16 November 2006.

Bemiller, Missy Kane. Tape recording. February 22, 2007. Knoxville, TN.

Blum, Sarah. Tape recording. April 16, 2007. Knoxville, TN.

Boling, Edward J. June 15, 2006. Knoxville, TN.

Brogdon, Cindy. Telephone interview, tape recording. May 23, 2007.

Brooks, Tara. Tape recording. September 11, 2007. Knoxville TN.

Bryant, Kathy. Telephone interview, tape recording. March 8, 2007. Knoxville, TN.

Buffini, Beverly Robinson. Telephone interview, tape recording. March 19, 2007.

Carter, Marc and Susie. October 16, 2006. Knoxville TN.

Catchings, Tamika. E-mail interview. March 7, 2007.

Charles-Furlow, Daedra. Tape recording. February 9, 2007. Auburn, AL.

Chery, Buffy Walker. Telephone interview, tape recording. April 12, 2007.

Clark, J. J. January 16, 2007. Knoxville, TN.

Crawford, Terry. Telephone interview, tape recording. February 26, 2007.

Crews, Vilmarie Castellvi. Telephone interview, tape recording. March 7, 2007.

Curry, Elizabeth. Tape recording. September 12, 2007. Knoxville, TN.

Cronan, Joan. Tape recording. May 18, 2007. Knoxville, TN

Davidson, Linda. Tape recording. June 29, 2006. Knoxville, TN.

Dearstone, Mickey. July 25, 2006. Knoxville, TN.

Deathridge, Gloria. Tape recording. November 14, 2006. Knoxville, TN.

Delaney, Jimmy. Tape recording. November 29, 2006. Knoxville, TN.

Diggs, Joetta Clark. Telephone interview, tape recording. April 16, 2007.

Donehew, Danielle. August 14, 2007. Knoxville, TN.

Dowling, Keeley. Tape recording. July 19, 2006 and January 23, 2007. Knoxville, TN.

Dykes, Archie. Telephone interview. April 12, 2007.

Edwards, Tonya. Telephone interview, tape recording. May 17, 2007.

Fain, Craig. Telephone interview, tape recording. March 30, 2007.

Fain, Lynne Greek. Tape recording. March 21, 2007. Knoxville, TN.

Flamini, Sue. Tape recording. April 18, 2007. Knoxville, TN.

Floreal, LaVonna Martin. Telephone interview, tape recording. February 20, 2007.

Floyd, Delisa Walton. E-mail inverview. April 11, 2007.

Furrow, Ann Baker. March 26, 2007. Knoxville, TN.

Glenn, Lisa. August 23, 2006. Knoxville, TN.

Gordon, Bridgette. Telephone interview, tape recording. April 11, 2007.

Grubb, Jen Laughridge. July 19, 2006. Knoxville, TN.

Haave, Tanya. Telephone interview, tape recording. March 19, 2007.

Hahn-Patrick, Sonia. January 11, 2007. Knoxville, TN.

Handy, Deb Dyer. Tape recording. April 9, 2007. Knoxville, TN.

Harvey, Alisa. Telephone interview, tape recording. February 21, 2007.

Hauch, Rosemarie. Telephone interview, tape recording. April 17, 2007.

Headecker, Tracy Bonner. Telephone interview, tape recording. March 19, 2007.

Hinch, Tonya. E-mail interview. June 22, 2007.

Holdsclaw, Chamique. E-mail interview. March 7, 2007.

Houser, Grace Harrington. Telephone interview, tape recording. March 17, 2007.

Howland, Kerry. May 24, 2007. Knoxville, TN.

Jarvis, Liz Brown. Tape recording. February 15, 2007. Knoxville, TN.

Jennings, Debby. August 8, 2006. Knoxville, TN.

Johnson, Joseph E. June 14, 2006. Knoxville, TN.

Keck, Angela Boyd. September 5, 2006. Knoxville, TN.

Keller, Jasmin Jones. Tape recording. March 19, 2007. Knoxville, TN.

Kelly, Angela. Tape recording. July 19, 2006. Knoxville, TN.

Kelly, Paula. E-mail interview. May 2, 2007.

Kredich, Matt. August 22, 2006. Knoxville, TN.

Larsson, Katharina. E-mail interview. June 3, 2007.

Lawson, Kara. Telephone interview, tape recording. April 17, 2007.

Lord, Sharon. Tape recording. January 17, 2007. Knoxville, TN.

Madison, Tianna. Telephone interview, tape recording. February 20, 2007.

Mahony, Crystal Cleveland. E-mail interview. May 1, 2007.

Maloney, Catherine Anne. Tape recording. March 3, 2007. Duluth, GA,

Martin, Kristen. September 5, 2006, and 30 March 2007. Knoxville, TN.

Mason, Heather. October 27, 2006. Knoxville, TN.

McInnis, Malcolm. December 6, 2006. Knoxville, TN.

Montgomery, Kacey. E-mail interview. August 20, 2007.

Moore, Billie. Telephone interview. January 11, 2008.

Morgan, Rebecca. Tape recording. April 18, 2007. Knoxville, TN

Moshak, Jenny. Tape recording, July 6, 2006, and April 5, 2007. Knoxville, TN.

Mosley, Benita Fitzgerald. Telephone interview, tape recording. March 29, 2007.

Ostrowski, Mary. Tape recording. February 14, 2007. Knoxville, TN.

Parker, Candace. Tape recording. April 23, 2007. Knoxville, TN.

Parrington, Dave. January 10, 2007. Knoxville, TN.

Passera, Pam. Telephone interview. April 13, 2007.

Patrick, Mike. Tape recording. July 25, 2006. Knoxville, TN.

Patrick, Robert. August 21, 2006. Knoxville, TN.

Pavon, Judith. Tape recording. August 15, 2006. Knoxville, TN.

Pearson, Abby. Telephone interview. May 28, 2007.

Pitcher, Patty Wiegand. Tape recording. May 6, 2007. Knoxville, TN.

Randles, Alberta. June 18, 2007. Knoxville, TN.

Ray, Gloria. June 27, 2006. Knoxville, TN.

Rice, Brian. Tape recording. February 21, 2007. Knoxville, TN.

Scheurer, Philip A. July 21, 2006. Knoxville, TN.

Slade, Peta Kelly. E-mail interview. May 2, 2007.

Smith, Laura Lauter. February 17, 2007. Morristown, TN.

Sowers, Linda Franz. Telephone interview. May 18, 2007.

Spencer, Sidney. E-mail interview. April 30, 2007.

Sprouse, Ann Lee. Telephone interview. January 14, 2008.

Summitt, Pat. Tape recording. May 11, 2007. Knoxville, TN.

Sutton, Suzy. July 31, 2007. Knoxville, TN.

Thomas, Donna. September 18, 2006. Knoxville, TN.

Thornton, Susan. Tape recording. May 5, 2007. Cookeville, TN.

Trimble, Donna. Telephone interview. June 10, 2007. Knoxville, TN.

Trotter, Dee Dee. February 13, 2007. Knoxville, TN.

Warlick, Holly. Tape recording. January 31, 2007. Knoxville, TN

Weaver. Jenny McGrath. Telephone interview, tape recording. March 28, 2007.

Weekly, Karen. January 23, 2007. Knoxville, TN.

Weekly, Ralph. January 23, 2007. Knoxville, TN.

Williams, Cathy Rattray. Telephone interview, tape recording. March 14, 2007.

Wood, Denise. Tape recording. March 29, 2007. Knoxville, TN.

Worrell, Dara. Tape recording. April 23, 2007. Knoxville, TN.

Wynn, Katie. June 18, 2007. Knoxville, TN.

Wyrick, Pat. February 11, 2007. Knoxville, TN.

Yang, Young-A. February 7, 2007. Knoxville, TN.

Young, Zsa Zsa Yow. November 6, 2006. Knoxville, TN.

Media Guides

Women's Intercollegiate Athletics Department, University of Tennessee. *Basketball: Lady Volunteers Tennessee Media Guide, 2006–07.*

———. *Cross Country: Lady Volunteers Tennessee Media Guide, 2006–07.*

———. *Golf: Lady Volunteers Tennessee Media Guide, 2006–07.*

———. *Rowing: Lady Volunteers Tennessee Media Guide, 2006–07.*

———. *Soccer: Lady Volunteers Tennessee Media Guide, 2006–07.*

———. *Softball: Lady Volunteers Tennessee Media Guide, 2006–07.*

———. *Swimming and Diving: Lady Volunteers Tennessee Media Guide, 2006–07.*

———. *Tennis: Lady Volunteers Tennessee Media Guide, 2006–07.*

———. *Track and Field: Lady Volunteers Tennessee Media Guide, 2006–07.*

———. *Volleyball: Lady Volunteers Tennessee Media Guide, 2006–07.*

Online Sources

"Catch the Stars: The Official Foundation of Tamika Catchings." *Catchin24.com.* Tamika Catchings Web site. http://www.catchin24.com/foundation/.

"Chamique Holdsclaw." *USA Basketball* Web site. http://www.usabasketball.com/bioswomen/chamique_holdsclaw_bio.html.

"Title IX Legislative Chronology" (adapted from the University of Iowa's "History of Title IX Legislation, Regulation and Policy Interpretation"). *Women's Sports Foundation* Web Site. http://www.womenssportsfoundation.org./cgi-bin/iowa/issues/history/article.html?record=875.

Theses

Auerbach, Patrick Evan. "AIAW Large College/Division I Basketball's Impact on *Women's* Intercollegiate Athletics, 1971–1982." Master of Science Thesis. Human Performance and Sport Studies, University of Tennessee, 1994.

Hobson, Jo Frankie. "A Study to Determine the Feasibility of Establishing Standards for an Intercollegiate Athletic Program for Women in Tennessee." Master of Science Thesis. Physical Education, University of Tennessee, 1966.

Hornbuckle, Adam R. "Women's Sports and Physical Education at The University of Tennessee: 1899–1939." Master of Arts Thesis. History, University of Tennessee, 1983.

Kloiber, Eric John. "True Volunteers: Women's Intercollegiate Athletics at the University of Tennessee, 1903 to 1976." Master of Science Thesis. Human Performance and Sport Studies, University of Tennessee, 1994.

In the Footsteps of Champions was designed and typeset on a Macintosh OSX 10.4.11 computer system using InDesign CS3 software. The body text is set in 10/15 Sabon and display type is set in Rockwell and Trade Gothic. This book was designed and typeset by Chad Pelton and manufactured by Everbest Printing Company Limited.